EMPLOYMENT LAW PRACTICE SERIES

General Editor: PROFESSOR JOHN McMULLEN

National Head of Employment Law, Pinsents
Professor of Labour Law, University of Leeds

THE LAW OF INDUSTRIAL ACTION AND TRADE UNION RECOGNITION

EMPLOYMENT LAW PRACTICE SERIES

General Editor: Professor John McMullen
National Head of Employment Law, Pinsents
Professor of Labour Law, University of Leeds

The series aims to publish books that examine important aspects of UK and EC employment law in an analytical manner yet with practical application. They are intended to be of use to both practitioners and academics alike.

The Law of Industrial Action and Trade Union Recognition

JOHN BOWERS QC
MICHAEL DUGGAN
and
DAVID READE

Foreword by
Mr Justice Burton

President of the Employment Appeal Tribunal and
Chairman of the Central Arbitration Committee

OXFORD
UNIVERSITY PRESS

OXFORD
UNIVERSITY PRESS

Great Clarendon Street, Oxford OX2 6DP

Oxford University Press is a department of the University of Oxford.
It furthers the University's objective of excellence in research, scholarship,
and education by publishing worldwide in

Oxford New York

Auckland Bangkok Buenos Aires Cape Town Chennai
Dar es Salaam Delhi Hong Kong Istanbul Karachi Kolkata
Kuala Lumpur Madrid Melbourne Mexico City Mumbai Nairobi
São Paulo Shanghai Taipei Tokyo Toronto

Oxford is a registered trade mark of Oxford University Press
in the UK and in certain other countries

Published in the United States
by Oxford University Press Inc., New York

British Library Cataloguing in Publication Data

Data available

Library of Congress Cataloging in Publication Data

Data available

ISBN 0–19–926965–3

1 3 5 7 9 10 8 6 4 2

Typeset in Garamond by
Cambrian Typesetters, Frimley, Surrey

Printed in Great Britain
on acid-free paper by
Biddles Ltd., King's Lynn

GENERAL EDITOR'S PREFACE

The law relating to trade union recognition and industrial action is complex and fast changing. Much of British labour law is affected severely by changes in Government. But collective labour law is realigned on these occasions perhaps more than most areas. A study of the law in this area involves a review of the legal regulation of the power imbalance inherent in the employment relationship. Speaking of its importance and of the relative weaponry of strike and lockout, Sir Otto Kahn Freund stated: 'there can be no equilibrium in industrial relations without a freedom to strike' (*Labour and the Law* 2nd edn, p 226). Where, as another labour law scholar puts it, the importance of legal study of the subject comes in, is this: 'Agreement on the importance of this freedom, however, leaves open the question of how far it is or should be protected or limited by law . . .' (Lord Wedderburn, *Labour and the Law* 3rd edn, p 512). Nonetheless, despite its key importance, the subject is less well covered in ordinary text books and many practitioners lose sight of the area once they have finished their degree studies in labour law. We believe that this text therefore fills an important gap for the employment lawyer.

The aim of the authors' work is to provide a comprehensive analysis of the law on industrial action and trade union recognition. It deals with the principles of economic torts, the relevance of common law defences, and the trade dispute immunity (which is, as authors state, a 'shuttlecock' between the Judiciary and Parliament). The authors equip the reader with a thorough grounding of first principles in this area. They highlight the complexity of the rules introduced by the Thatcher Government concerning ballots; and examine less common forms of industrial action such as sit-ins and lock-outs. Employment lawyers need to understand both the collective and the individual dimension of industrial action and this book duly covers the effect of strikes on the individual employment contract, unfair dismissal rules and social benefits.

It is timely that the authors have also covered the new law on statutory trade union recognition, a regime which is destined to survive the Government's review in 2003 of the Employment Relations Act 1999. The authors also bring to bear their first hand experience of the rules relating to applications under the Act for trade union recognition and highlight the emerging 'case law' of the Central Arbitration Committee.

The aim of this series is to provide analysis of the law combining intellectual rigour with practical relevance. In this I believe the authors have admirably succeeded.

Professor John McMullen
Leeds
December 2003

FOREWORD

What was in 1987 the very first book on the *The Modern Law of Strikes* has now evolved into *The Law of Industrial Action and Trade Union Recognition* and has become a staple requirement for all those in the employment field. As we all aim to improve and enhance industrial relations, and ever more mechanisms are created to achieve conciliation and partnership between the two sides of industry, it is still essential to understand, evaluate and provide for the alternative: while as for trade union recognition, this has once again taken *central* stage, and this book contains so far as I know the first detailed consideration of the actual operation of the new statutory scheme by reference to the cases reported on the CAC's website, and it is a masterly analysis. The extraordinary industry of John Bowers QC, Michael Duggan and David Reade, and their extensive knowledge of the subject combine to ensure that this book is not only immensely readable but a vital tool for unions and employers, arbitrators and conciliators, lawyers and judges alike.

Mr Justice Burton
President of the Employment Appeal Tribunal and
Chairman of the Central Arbitration Committee

PREFACE

We have all enjoyed writing this book. Two of us worked on the original work *The Modern Law of Strikes* in 1987 since when much has changed. We have been joined by David Reade and have now included the law on trade union recognition which is a fascinating area under the jurisdiction of Sir Michael Burton as Chair. We thank him for his gracious Foreword to this book.

Labour law is very dynamic. In order to prove the point, on the very date when we were writing the Preface (2 December 2003) the Government published the Employment Relations Bill. This Bill seeks to implement some of the changes which had been recommended as a consequence of the Review of the Employment Relations Act 1999. The recommendations of that review are considered in the main body of the work. A copy of the Bill can be found at www.publications.parliament.uk/pa/pabills.htm. It is not practical to make the consequent revisions to the text and in any event the Bill may undergo amendment during the course of its progress through Parliament. We thus can only highlight the areas which the Bill addresses so far as they impact upon this book using the clause numbers in the present version of the Bill.

Trade Union Recognition

There will be:

- the power for the CAC to shorten the period over which the parties are to seek to agree the appropriate bargaining unit (cl.2);
- an obligation upon an employer to provide information to the Union following the acceptance of an application by the CAC (cl.3);
- amendment of the provisions on determination of the appropriate bargaining unit by the CAC, to make clear that the employer's view on any other bargaining unit it considers appropriate should be taken into account (cl.4);
- provision for the appointment of a suitably qualified independent person

to allow communication between the union and the workers after the acceptance of an application for recognition (cl.5);

- power for the CAC to extend the notification period, under para 24, over which the parties may notify it that they do not want a ballot to be conducted (cl.6);
- provision for postal votes for absent workers where a workplace ballot has been ordered (cl.7);
- clarification that existing recognition agreements only block applications if they include all of the following: pay, hours and holidays (cl.8);
- amendments to the notice provisions for an employer wishing to terminate negotiating arrangements (cl.9);
- a right of appeal against the demand for the costs of the conduct of a ballot (cl.10);
- revision to the Secretary of State's power to amend the schedule (cl.11);
- a power for the Secretary of State to make orders to enable the CAC to require the provision of information about workers to enable communication (cl.12);
- a power for the Secretary of State to make orders to deal with the amalgamation of unions or changes in the identity of employers (cl.13);
- a power to enable the CAC to require an employer to provide information about union membership and employment in a bargaining unit (cl.14);
- a definition of pay so as to exclude pension issues (cl.15); and
- a power for ACAS to require the provision of information from the parties where it is seeking to bring about a settlement of a recognition dispute (cl.16).

Industrial Action

There are:

- new provisions about the information to be provided about the employees to be balloted for industrial action (cl.17);
- new provisions about the information to be provided about the employees in a notice of industrial action (cl.20); and
- amendments relating to the provisions protecting employees from dismissal during protected industrial action (cl.21).

We are grateful to our publishers, OUP, not least for accommodating our several late changes which have meant that the book is up to date as of

2 December 2003. We also thank all of our colleagues at Littleton Chambers. The book is dedicated to the memory of Lord Gladwin of Clee, who started his career as a union representative on Grimsby Docks and became a distinguished leader of the GMB, and a member both of the House of Lords and the Employment Appeal Tribunal.

John Bowers
Michael Duggan
David Reade

Littleton Chambers
3 Kings Bench Walk
Temple
London EC4

CONTENTS—SUMMARY

TABLE OF CONTENTS

TABLE OF CASES

TABLES OF LEGISLATION

Secondary Legislation

International Instruments

1

INTRODUCTION

The freedom of employees to combine and to withdraw their labour is their fundamental safeguard against the inherent imbalance of power between the employer and the individual employee. This freedom has to be accepted as a hallmark of a free society.

(Green Paper, *Trade Union Immunities*, Cmnd 8218, 1981)

The right of trade unions to induce workers to support industrial action by withdrawing their labour is 'a right which was first conferred by Parliament in 1906, which has been enjoyed by trade unions ever since and which is recognized as encompassing a fundamental human right': Millett LJ in *LU v NUR* [1996] ICR 170

Strikes are usually considered to be an indication of a breakdown in properly ordered collective bargaining, in the same way as wars are seen as an aberration and defeat for international law. Some however see them as a necessary irritant which may draw attention to underlying difficulties which may otherwise simmer away. They certainly draw publicity towards matters which otherwise would go unknown to the general public.   **1.01**

A. The Last Twenty Years

There has been much litigation surrounding strikes and other industrial   **1.02**

1

action in the last 20 years and it is not difficult to trace the reasons for this to the reforms made by the Employment Act 1982 and the Trade Union Act 1984, two of the five major statutes passed by the Thatcher Conservative Government. The former rendered trade unions liable in tort, thus providing the employer with a claimworthy defendant, and making the claiming of damages a real possibility. The 1984 statute required the unions to hold ballots. Moreover, the ballot must be carried out under certain narrowly worded criteria; indeed taking this Act and the accompanying Code of Practice together there are 34 restrictions and requirements in respect to strike ballots. As far as the unions were concerned, this was part of a major anti-union drive by the Thatcher Government to reduce their powers and influence, and also to destroy their bank balances. The key themes from the Government's point of view was to give the unions back to their members by providing for union democracy in ballots and to give more time for negotiations to take place because of the need for the unions to give so many days' notice of a ballot and then industrial action taking place. The unions would retort that if this were the true reason it is odd that the beneficiary of a failure by the union to comply is not a union member who has not been given a vote (although a right for him to complain was added later) but the employer, who remains the most frequent source of applications to court.

The lawyer has thus become an essential member of the industrial relations team, although his role is not quite as 'up front' as his American counterpart. He or she is, however, likely to be involved in many aspects of an industrial relations strategy, from drafting a collective agreement to advising on the possibility of mass dismissals to seeking injunctions.

1.03   The Blair Government has only tinkered at the margins with this Thatcherite settlement on industrial action. The Employment Relations Act 1999 did change the law on unfair dismissal of strikers and there was some tidying up of the balloting provisions. At the time of writing, there is in progress a Government review of the impact of the Employment Relations Act 1999, but present indications are that there will be not much change to the current law. There is thus a closer consensus between the parties' hierarchies (although not necessarily the activists) on the central issues than ever before. The only likely change from a Conservative Government if elected would be a re-examination of restrictions on strikes in essential services. However, previous successive governments have reviewed that possibility and found it not the right time to act.

Although the newspaper and mining industries have traditionally provided **1.04** the focus for most litigation, there are few areas which are substantially unionized which have not been witnessed some employers seeking remedies in the courts. The major industrial conflagrations of the 1980s saw much new law made, or existing but unused doctrines rediscovered by the courts. The Stockport 'Messenger' dispute, the miners' dispute and the 'Wapping' dispute stand out as the major *causes célèbres*. In the miners' strike of 1984–5 receivers were appointed for the first time to run a trade union's affairs, and interim declarations of unlawfulness were granted. It was, however, notice-able that the most important actions were brought not by the employer, but by disaffected union members who wanted to work through the currency of the major dispute. They did not use the new legislation mentioned above but founded their actions largely on the common law contract of trade union membership between member and union. The National Coal Board itself sought and gained only one injunction to restrain picketing (in Nottinghamshire) and then did nothing to enforce it even though it was widely ignored by the miners. The primary legal interventions were by (apparently well-funded and co-ordinated) groups of working miners, enforcing their contracts of membership with the National Union of Mineworkers. The common law was indeed alive and well and apparently kicking at the unions. In the Wapping dispute, the several injunctions gained by News International Ltd and its various associated companies were based primarily on the absence of ballots as required by the 1984 Act.

The criminal law also played a central role in those major disputes. There **1.05** were no less than 10,372 criminal charges brought during the miners' strike (*The Times*, 20 March 1985), although many people charged were subse-quently acquitted in the courts. Week after week pickets were also arrested on the Wapping picket line. Since then, however, strikes have rarely been accom-panied by violence.

B. The Change in Temperature

Notwithstanding that the Blair Government has not intervened much in **1.06** industrial relations law, there has been a perceptible change in the industrial legal temperature, and a shift in the balance against the employer. We suggest that there are two primary influences for this and one influence from which unions might have expected more than it has delivered so far. The first is that the remedy of dismissal has diminished to vanishing point because of the reforms made in 1999. Dismissal has always been a primary remedy for the employer, and often the threat of dismissal was enough without following through on it. Since 1971, in broad terms, the employer could dismiss the striking workforce with impunity if all were dismissed and none was re-engaged within three months of dismissals. In 1999 the Employment Relations Act stated, in general terms (see p 187 ff for details), that a dismissal within the first eight weeks of participation in industrial action was automatically unfair. This has changed significantly the economics of dismissal in such circumstances, to a point where employers will rarely consider dismissal even to be an option for them. Although definitive information is naturally hard to come by, it is understood that there has only been one case in which the employees have been dismissed in an official strike since then (involving Fluid Dynamics Ltd). Thus the strategy adopted by the employers in the Wapping print dispute of dismissing a whole workforce would no longer be possible. It remains possible to dismiss without incurring any possibility of unfair dismissal claims only if the action is unofficial action, which is extremely rare.

1.07 The second factor is the general approach of the judges to their role in strike injunction cases. This is particularly important because so few cases go to a full trial so that the whole issue is determined on the balance of convenience and the judges' exercise of discretion. Traditionally the judges were hostile to strikes and did not mind who knew it: Lord Diplock for example said that the trade dispute immunities (which the unions regard as the bulwark of their freedom to strike at all) were 'intrinsically repugnant to anyone who has spent his life in the practice of law'. The miners' strike saw much new law being created to assist the non-striking miners, and a very hostile climate from the judiciary. In his masterly study, *Labour and the Law* (Sweet and Maxwell, 1972, p 1) Professor Kahn Freund said that:

> the common law knows nothing of a balance of collective forces . . . This and not only the personal background of the judiciary explains the inescapable fact that the contribution which the courts have made to the orderly development of collective labour relations has been infinitesimal . . . A series of lectures on labour law is not the best place to extol the virtues of the common law.

The modern judge is much more circumspect and does not find the notion of collective action an anathema as did judges some decades ago. It is difficult to imagine judges today searching through the interstices of eighteenth century law reports to detect a new tort of intimidation to outflank the trade dispute immunity defined by Parliament as occurred in *Rookes v Barnard* [1964] AC 1129. This tort had been described in the Court of Appeal itself in the same case as 'obscure unfamiliar and peculiar'. Two recent industrial dispute cases (both of which are discussed in detail later) would, in our view, have been decided differently by an older generation of judges. These cases are *P v NAS/UWT* [2003] IRLR 309 where a very liberal approach was taken to the meaning of terms and conditions in the trade dispute formula and *Burgess v Stevedoring Services Ltd* [2003] IRLR 810 which diverges from the approach taken by Lord Denning in *Secretary of State for Employment v ASLEF (No. 2)* [1972] 2 QB 455 in relation to action lawful in itself which may be taken wilfully to disrupt the undertaking that the same is in breach of contract.

One area where the unions might have expected more however is the impact of human rights law. Article 11 of the European Convention on Human Rights (given direct effect in English law by the Human Rights Act 1998) states that everyone has a right to freedom of association, including the right to form and join trade unions for the protection of one's interests. Restrictions on that right, if they are to be lawful, must be prescribed by law, and be necessary in a democratic society in the interests of inter alia the protection of the rights and freedoms of others (Art 11(2)). The restriction must be proportionate to the interest pursued. Contracting states are given a margin of appreciation to determine what measures are necessary and proportionate. The Strasbourg court has been consistently hostile to a right to strike in cases such as *Schmidt and Dahlström v Sweden* 6/2/76 Series A no. 21; *Gustafsson v Sweden* (1996) 28 EHRR 409; *Schettini v Italy* Application no. 29529/95 9 Nov 2000, *Unison v UK* [2002] IRLR 497 and *Federation of Offshore Workers' Trade Unions v Norway* (App 38190/97, 27/6/02) (see para 16.06 below). **1.08**

C. Complexity

The law on strikes and picketing is now exceedingly complex, an overlay of common law and statutory interventions and the subject of conflicting political pressures. As a Canadian commentator put it, we have witnessed 'a see-saw vendetta between the legislature and the courts' (A. W. R. Carothers, *Collective Bargaining Law in Canada*, p 57). The law of tort, on which the superstructure is based, has not been systematized, while proper advice on the immunities still requires a complete grasp of the history since the Trade Disputes Act 1906. Lord Diplock gave voice to the problems this might cause for the layman in **1.09**

Merkur Island Shipping Corp. v Laughton [1983] ICR 490, 510C, which itself was decided before yet another major layer was added in 1984.

> . . . what the law is, particularly in the field of industrial relations, ought to be plain. It should be expressed in terms that can be easily understood by those who have to apply it even at shop floor level . . . Absence of clarity is destructive of the rule of law; it is unfair to those who wish to preserve the rule of law.

Both political parties have shied away from any codification in the area.

D. What the Parties Want From the Law

1.10   It is worth examining what the employer wants from the law. It is clearly not the role of the courts to weigh up the merits or otherwise of the parties' contentions. The employer may, however, wish to use legal action in general and injunction relief in particular, in order to 'bring the strike to a head' or to aim to shift the focus of the dispute to a national level in the expectation (which may not always be borne out) that the national union officials may be more amenable to settlement than those on the shop floor. An injunction may give the employer a major tactical advantage at an early stage in the dispute. He will, however, have to be very careful how he follows up such a victory— an application for committal for contempt must be treated with great circumspection even in the most bitter dispute since it risks making 'martyrs' of those so committed, as occurred in the 1970s with the 'Pentonville Five' dockers. Moreover, the employer has to weigh the fact that starting litigation means that he may in due course have to reveal details about the inner workings of his business which he would prefer to keep secret from the unions.

The unions probably want nothing more from the law than that it should leave them and their members alone. The only time the union is likely to initiate litigation in a dispute is in claims for unfair dismissal. Unlike injunctions which may be sought in hours, these applications are unlikely to be heard for three or four months, and in a major dispute with many applicants the delay may be much greater.

E. The Changing Nature of Strike Activity

1.11   1,323,300 working days were lost in 2003 in the UK from 146 stoppages of work. This was more than twice the total in 2001 and was the highest annual total since 1990. The actual number of stoppages has fallen sharply from the 1980s when the average annual number was 1,129 to 273 as the average for the 1990s. Two disputes in 2002 accounted for 60 per cent of the total days lost (National Statistics Feature, Labour Disputes in 2002 by Joanne Monger). Over the last few years there has been a reduction in the days lost in the private as opposed to the public sector; the CBI analysis of data suggests that 90 per cent of days lost occurred in the public or recently privatized sector. Other recent trends may be discerned:

- Some 50 per cent of disputes concern pay; 25 per cent working conditions; 15 per cent other issues. Surprisingly few concern recognition of trade unions and this may be seen as a testimony to the success of the statutory recognition procedures in taking the heat out of this as an issue for collective dispute.
- There have been new forms of organization of industrial action through the internet, and informal action groups; this may increase (especially the organizing of spontaneous picketing) but in most cases groups will need the experience and resources of a union behind them to render industrial action capable of being effective.
- The timeframe of some disputes has been extended, most notoriously the national fire strike which stumbled on between May 2002 and March 2003.
- There are now very few 'all out strikes' which are expected to last weeks or months; rather, strikes are discontinuous with the union selecting certain dates well in advance.
- The number of 'wildcat' unofficial strikes has much diminished, although there were important walkouts by ground staff at Heathrow Airport in July 2003 and the Royal Mail workers in October 2003 to remind us of bygone days when this was a major problem throughout British industry.

F. Recognition

One of the most persistent causes of strikes over the years has been the request for trade union recognition. The law has intervened to provide a peaceful route to the settlement of such claims. This is now contained in the Trade Union and Labour Relations (Consolidation) Act 1992 following the Labour Government's reforms of the Employment Relations Act 1999. Para 4.16 of the Labour Government's Paper, *Fairness at Work* (Cm 95, 1998) put

1.12

forward the benefit of a statutory scheme as occurring 'without the disputes which have resulted from recognition claims under the current law. A statutory procedure offers a means of settling disputes without industrial action'. There were earlier experiments with the Industrial Relations Act 1971 and the Employment Protection Act 1975 which were not very happy. Many lessons from those times have been learnt in the new system which is complex but seeks to keep the courts away by way of judicial review. Although applications to the Central Arbitration Committee (CAC) under these provisions have been many fewer than originally predicted, it has stimulated growth in a number of voluntary agreements so that 84 of Britain's top companies do recognize trade unions in some form. It is too early to judge the success of the present legislation as compared to its predecessors, but the CAC is an institution respected by all sides.

2

INDUSTRIAL ACTION AND THE INDIVIDUAL CONTRACT OF EMPLOYMENT

A. The Basic Principles

Employers will rarely want to sue their employees directly for striking in **2.01** breach of their contracts of employment, both in the interests of good industrial relations and because of the low level of damages they are likely to be awarded (see Chapter 14 for a full discussion). A more attractive remedy lies against the striking employees' union in tort, following the Employment Act 1982.

The illegality of action within the contract of employment is, however, vital in providing the necessary element of unlawfulness for torts such as intimidation, inducing breach of contract and conspiracy. We will consider the distinction between a strike and other industrial action, such as a work to rule, overtime ban, or working with enthusiasm, in Chapters 6 and 9.

The basic principle of the common law is that a strike which is not preceded **2.02** by notice terminating the strikers' respective contracts of employment is unlawful and a repudiatory breach of contract (cf. para 2.05). There is no distinction in this respect between official and unofficial strikes, nor between unconstitutional and constitutional action (that is, where the union has fulfilled all the procedures laid down in a collective agreement before a strike).

In modern conditions strikers only rarely give due notice of termination of their own employment, since the object of the action will be not to sever relations altogether with the employer, but rather to press for different terms, so that the relationship may continue on those revised conditions. In *Rookes v Barnard* [1963] 1 QB 623, Donavan LJ said:

> The strikers do not want to give up their jobs; they simply want to be paid more for it or to secure some other advantage in connection with it. The employer does not want to lose his workforce; he simply wants to resist the claim. Not till the strike has lasted some time, and no settlement is in sight, does one usually read that the employers have given notice that unless the men return to work their contracts will be terminated and they will be dismissed.

B. The Strike as a Fundamental Breach of Contract

Where no strike notice is given

2.03   Where there is no notice of strike action, the courts have no hesitation in treating strike action as a breach of contract. This is because, as Phillips J put it in *Simmons v Hoover Ltd* [1977] ICR 61, 76, there is:

> . . . a settled, confirmed and continued intention on the part of the employee not to do any of the work which under his contract he had been engaged to do, which was the whole purpose of the contract. Judged by the usual standards such conduct by the employee appears to us to be repudiatory of the contract of employment.

A repudiation entitles the other party to the contract to accept the contract as at an end, should he so wish. The concept of repudiation in the context of industrial action other than strike action is considered in Chapter 6.

The EAT hedged their bets in the *Simmons* case only to the degree that 'We should not be taken to be saying that all strikes are necessarily repudiatory although usually they will be'. The example they gave of what may not be repudiatory conduct was where the strike was 'in opposition to demands by an employer in breach of contract', in which case employees might be merely accepting his repudiation. Much would turn on the way in which the union's strike call was expressed. Moreover, management has a wide prerogative to change works rules, and there is no reported case in which a strike has been held not to be a breach of contract by the employees (see also *Bowes & Partners v Press* [1894] 1 QB 202). Further, the principle has been extended to one-day protest strikes.

Where strike notice is given

Lord Denning MR's remarks in *Stratford (J.T.) and Son v Lindley* [1965] AC 269 still hold good from the legal point of view and in reality: 'The strike notice is nothing more nor less than a notice that the men will not come to work. In short, they will break their contract'. The contract will remain alive for so long as the employer chooses not to exercise his right to accept the employees' fundamental breach as terminating the contract (*Rookes v Barnard* [1964] 2 AC 1129, 1204 *per* Lord Devlin).   **2.04**

In *Solihull Metropolitan Borough v National Union of Teachers* [1985] IRLR 211, the union argued that by stipulating that the NUT representative should give the head teacher notice of commencement of their actions against providing cover for the teachers (for full facts see para 5.54), it was giving sufficient notice at law. This argument, however, was not accepted by the court. Rather, Warner J held that this was merely notice of *collective* action, not by or on behalf of any individual teacher. Moreover, the head teacher would be uncertain whether a teacher was a member of the union or not and whether they would obey the union's call or not.

At one time it was thought that the strikers in effect dismissed themselves and that the act of striking automatically brought the contract to an end, but this concept of 'constructive resignation' is probably unsound in the light of the criticism of the automatic theory of termination of the contract of employment in *London Transport Executive v Clarke* [1981] IRLR 166.

C. Alternative Legal Analyses

Any other legal analysis is subject to difficulties, but we will examine those which have been put forward.

Suspension of contract

In *Morgan v Fry* [1968] 2 QB 710, Lord Denning MR made a determined   **2.05**

11

effort to substitute suspension of contract for breach as the true analysis of a strike. He held that there was an implied term that each party to the contract accepted its suspension by strike action if due notice was given. This was 'an implication to be read into the contract by modern law as to trade disputes. If a strike takes place, the contract of employment is not terminated. It is suspended during the strike; and revives again when the strike is over.' The *Donovan Report* (the *Royal Commission on Trade Unions and Employers' Associations* Cmnd 3623, 1968), at paragraph 944, rejected the general principle of suspension on the grounds of 'considerable technical difficulty', citing problems over unofficial, unconstitutional strikes and other forms of industrial action. The concept is also difficult to apply in the position of a strike which is never in fact settled, and it is unclear whether the doctrine would apply to a ban on overtime in breach of contract or a 'go-slow'. Moreover, it is open to the objection that there can be no implied term which would contradict an express term, and the obligation to work is an express term at the very heart of the contract of employment.

The union terminating on behalf of its members

2.06 The idea that the union, by going on strike, is in fact giving notice on behalf of its members of termination of individual contracts of employment is also fraught with difficulties. In general the union does not necessarily act as the agent of individual workers. The only exception is where the members specifically authorize the union to act as their agent, which is rare. Each employee is in any event likely to have different notice periods, so that if the union did purport to terminate, it would have to be careful to give different periods for each employee (see *Ideal Casements v Shamsi* [1972] ICR 408, *Solihull v NUT* (above)). There are now greater problems than at the time when the idea was formulated, in that the union's action in effectively handing in the members' resignations would deprive each one of their claim of unfair dismissal or redundancy, unless it could be said that the union was reacting to a fundamental breach of contract by the employer. This would put a premium on careful phrasing of any strike notice by the union in a highly charged atmosphere. A notice of insufficient length would in any event be a breach of contract (*Denaby and Cadeby Main Collieries v Yorkshire Miners' Association* [1906] AC 384).

Termination of existing terms with offer of new terms

In *Morgan's case* (above), Davies LJ saw a strike as a notice to terminate the present contractual terms coupled with an offer to work on new terms. **2.07**

D. Strike-free Agreements

Britain's industrial relations image used to be tarnished in the 1950s and 1960s by its reputation as a strike-prone country; indeed, strikes were known as the 'British disease'. This view was never in fact wholly fair or accurate but gained wide currency in political and financial circles; the United Kingdom came about half-way down the league table of countries who lost the most working days through strikes. Nevertheless, this reputation, not helped by the 'winter of discontent' in 1978/79, fuelled worries amongst many employers, notably Japanese and US high-technology industries, who wished to invest in Britain. The rise of the new technology industries saw the rise of 'strike-free agreements', which were entered into in particular by the Electrical, Electronic, Telecommunication and Plumbing Union and the Amalgamated Union of Engineering Workers. **2.08**

The agreement is normally presented as a package in which a no-strike clause is linked with agreements on flexible working, worker participation in decisions, single status for all staff and, to the chagrin of other unions, a single union agreement. The strike, as a bargaining lever, was normally replaced by 'pendulum arbitration', in which an arbitrator chooses between the employer's and the union's offer, with no mid-way compromise solution. The logic was that this would stimulate realistic negotiating strategies.

Such agreements have varied in coverage; nearly all, however, contain a clause ruling out strikes while negotiation or arbitration is in progress. Those that proffer pendulum arbitration as a solution usually provide that the decision of the arbitrator will be final.

It is doubtful whether strike-free deals could ever have become the norm and political expediency limited the acceptability of such agreements to a few trade unions. Moreover, agreements were concentrated in expanding, new technology industries where disputes have focussed primarily on pay rises. Given the political movement in the Amalgamated Engineering and Electrical Union (AEEU) (into which the EEPTU merged) towards the left, it is unlikely that any further strike-free agreements will be entered into.

2.09 The general principle is that a collective bargain is presumed not to be intended to be legally enforceable. This common law position was established in *Ford Motor Co v AEU* [1969] 2 QB 302, and is now embodied in the Trade Union and Labour Relations (Consolidation) Act 1992, s 179, by which such a bargain is unenforceable at law unless 'the agreement is (a) in writing and (b) contains a provision which (however expressed) states that the parties intend that the agreement shall be a legally enforceable contract' (*National Coal Board v National Union of Mineworkers* [1986] IRLR 439).

2.10 There are further hurdles if the collective bargain contains provisions which inhibit the taking of industrial action, or have the effect of doing so. This may only be incorporated in the individual contract of employment if the following stringent conditions are satisfied (Trade Union and Labour Relations (Consolidation) Act 1992, s 180):

(1) The collective agreement is in writing.
(2) It contains an express statement that the clause is incorporated into the individual contract of employment.
(3) It is reasonably accessible at the workplace and available during working hours.
(4) Each trade union party to the agreement is independent.
(5) The individual contract expressly or impliedly incorporates such a term.

2.11 Only a few strike-free agreements are declared to be legally enforceable. The advantages for the employer in having such an agreement enforceable in the courts are twofold, namely that: the damages recoverable for breach of contract may be greater than those available in tort; and the employer may be able to define widely the actions on the part of the union members which will render the union liable.

3

LIABILITY FOR STRIKES: THE ECONOMIC TORTS

A. Introduction

3.01 Although Parliament has intervened over many decades to regulate the conduct of strikes by statutory provision, the so-called economic torts continue to play a central role in proscribing industrial action on the part of trade unions or their members. The statutory provisions have been built up around the framework of these common law torts by providing immunity from tortious liability for certain acts in contemplation or furtherance of a trade dispute, which immunity can be withdrawn in certain specified situations (see Chapters 4 and 5).

3.02 The court must ask four questions (*Merkur Island Shipping Corp. v Laughton* [1983] IRLR 218, *Dimbleby & Sons Ltd v National Union of Journalists* [1984] 1 WLR 427):

(1) Whether the claimant has a cause of action at common law.

(2) Whether the defendant is acting in contemplation or furtherance of a trade dispute between claimant and defendant. If so, the Trade Union and Labour Relations (Consolidation) Act 1992, s 219 (previously the Trade Union and Labour Relations Act 1974, s 13, as amended) gives immunity from action in tort where the defendant:
   (a) induces a person to break a contract;
   (b) threatens that a contract will be broken or its performance interfered with or that he will induce a person to break a contract or interfere with its performance;
   (c) agrees with others to procure the doing of any such act.

(3) If the action is in contemplation or furtherance of a trade dispute but is not taken against the primary employer in dispute, to have immunity the action must fall within the narrow area of secondary action which is now contained in TULR(C)A, s 224. The action will not be protected where one of the facts relied upon for the purpose of establishing liability is that there has been secondary action which is not lawful picketing.

The Employment Act 1980, s 17(3) had contained *three* exceptions in the case of secondary action, namely when:
   (a) the principal purpose was directly to prevent or disrupt the supply during the dispute of goods or services under a subsisting contract between the employer in dispute and the secondary employer and the action taken was likely to achieve that purpose (the first customer, first supplier exception); or

(b) the principal purpose was directly to prevent or disrupt the supply of 'goods or services under a subsisting contract between an associated employer of the primary employer and another person and the goods or services are in substitution for goods and services which would, but for the dispute, have fallen to be provided by the primary employer and the secondary action is against the associated employer or his contractor'; or

(c) the action was taken by lawful pickets (that is, those picketing at their own place of work) or a trade union official attending with his members.

The Thatcher Government considered that exceptions (a) and (b) were no longer justified when it looked at industrial action in *Removing Barriers to Employment* (Cm 655, 1989) though it considered (c) was still necessary to protect picketing which was itself lawful under TULR(C)A, s 220. For further consideration of s 220 see Chapter 8.

(4) In order to retain immunity from certain torts there must be an affirmative ballot amongst those likely to be engaged in the action. See Chapter 5.

This chapter will consider the general industrial torts. It will be seen that, despite the torts forming the bedrock of liability of unions involved with industrial disputes, their genesis lies in different judicial attitudes of the late nineteenth/early twentieth century and the exact scope of the torts remains controversial and bitterly disputed. **3.04**

B. The Classic Fact Situations

There are two classic fact situations which form the normal sequence of events in industrial disputes. **3.05**

Direct action

The first situation involves direct action. It applies where the trade union, its members or officials: **3.06**

(1) persuade or procure the employer's workers or a third party (customers or suppliers) to breach their employment or commercial contracts with the employer; or alternatively

(2) directly interfere with such contracts by using unlawful means. The interference itself need not amount to a breach on the part of the employees or a third party. The third party will normally be a supplier or otherwise in a commercial contract with the employer.

The first fact situation may be shown as follows:

1. Union persuades or procures	⟹	Workers to breach contract of employment	⟹	With employer
		OR		
2. Union persuades or procures	⟹	Third party	⟹	With employer
		OR		
3. Union itself interferes by unlawful means	⟹	With workers contracts of employment of third or party contracts	⟹	With employer

Indirect action

3.07 The second situation, which may be called indirect action, occurs when a union, its members or officials persuade or procure the employees of the third party to take industrial action (e.g. by blacking the target's goods), in consequence of which the third party's contract with the target is breached or otherwise interfered with. The action is thus one step removed from the target; the third party may even be a primary target with the ultimate target of the action a secondary target. In other words, the third party is the victim of direct action, the ultimate object, that is, the target is the victim of indirect action.

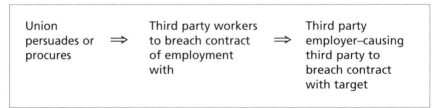

Union persuades or procures	⟹	Third party workers to breach contract of employment with	⟹	Third party employer–causing third party to breach contract with target

The constituents of the torts vary depending upon the element of unlawful- **3.08**
ness involved. Unlawful means may reside in the breach of contract between
the third party employees and the third party or a breach of the commercial
contract between the third party and the target. It is apparent from the
authorities that the boundaries of unlawfulness in this respect are not closed.
There is still, however, considerable dispute as to the extent of liability where
it is alleged that contracts have been interfered with, as opposed to breached.

The torts can be divided into the following classification, although it should **3.09**
be noted that nomenclature varies considerably both in the cases and in academic treatises, and the categories are by no means watertight (and indeed it
is not certain that all are torts at all!).

(1) Direct inducement of breach of contract.
(2) Direct procurement of breach of contract.
(3) Indirect procurement of breach of contract.
(4) Interference with business.
(5) Interference with contract.
(6) Intimidation.
(7) Duress.
(8) Conspiracy.

C. Direct Inducement of Breach of Contract

Direct inducement of breach of contract occurs in the context of strikes or **3.10**
other industrial action when the defendant, with the intention of bringing
about such a result, persuades an employee or third party to breach his
employment or commercial contract with the claimant thereby causing the
claimant loss, the defendant not having any justification for such persuasion
and being unable to rely upon the statutory immunity.

The strike leader will almost always induce the breach by the strikers of their **3.11**
contracts of employment and by reason thereof the employer's commercial
contracts of supply or delivery will be breached. It is enough that the union
has persuaded the employee to breach his contract of employment with the
employer.

The tort of direct inducement was first recognized in the seminal case of **3.12**
Lumley v Gye (1853) 2 E & B 216, where it was culled from the action for

19

enticement of a servant. The antique facts were that the defendant theatre owner persuaded an opera singer to sing for the delectation of his patrons at Her Majesty's Theatre, thus inducing her to break an exclusive engagement for three months, about which he knew full well, at the claimant's rival Queen's Theatre. The unlawful action consisted of the breach of the singer's contract of employment and the defendant was liable even though he did not use unlawful means to bring about the breach.

3.13　Lord Watson in *Allen v Flood* [1898] AC 1, stated the principle as:

> He who **wilfully induces another** to do an **unlawful act** which, but for his persuasion would or might never have been committed is rightly held to be responsible for the wrong which he has procured . . . he will incur liability if he knowingly and for his own ends induces that other person to commit an actionable wrong. (Authors' own emphasis.)

3.14　In *Temperton v Russell* [1893] 1 QB 715, it was held that the tort went beyond inducement of breach of the contract of employment, so that if by striking the employees broke their employers' contracts of supply or delivery, the strike organizers might be responsible for the inducement of breach of that supply contract. Thus, the breach may be of the contract of employment or of the commercial contract.

3.15　The tort may be committed through agents (*Daily Mirror Newspapers v Gardner* [1968] 2 QB 762, *Stratford (J.T.) and Son Ltd v Lindley* [1965] AC 269, *South Wales Miners Federation v Glamorgan Coal Co.* [1905] AC 239).

3.16　Although the tort is indirect in that the acts of persuasion are not directed at the claimant, it is direct in that the defendants persuade someone who is a party to the contract breached and the defendants must intend to cause loss to the *claimant* (cf. *Thomson (D.C.) & Co. v Deakin* [1952] Ch 646, *Merkur Island Shipping Corp. v Laughton* [1983] 2 AC 570, *Falconer v ASLEF and NUR* [1986] IRLR 331; and see 'knowledge and intent' under indirect procurement at pp 24–26). It is submitted that the case of *Torquay Hotel Co. Ltd v Cousins* [1969] 2 Ch 106 is in this sense a case of direct inducement, although a finding of liability at all was controversial because of the existence of an exclusion clause. The owner of the claimant company criticized the action of the Transport and General Workers Union in an inter-union dispute in the Torquay area. Powerless to take action against the hotel, the union organizers contacted members of the union who drove for Esso Ltd, which supplied the hotel with fuel, to instruct them to cease supplying the hotel. In fact it appears that Esso decided not to deliver when informed that the strike was official. The breach was therefore directly induced rather than procured, since the union intended to procure a breach by Esso, which would have been a party to the contract breached and the defendants intended to cause loss to the claimant through such breach.

However, the conclusion that there had been a breach was controversial because Esso were protected by a clause excluding their liability, in the following terms:

> Neither party shall be liable for any failure to fulfil any term of this agreement, if fulfilment is delayed, hindered or prevented by any circumstance whatever which is not in their immediate control, including, but without limiting the generality of the foregoing, strikes, lockouts, labour disputes of any kind, partial or general stoppages of labour, refusals to perform any kind of work (whether any of the foregoing relate to the parties' own workmen or others) . . . In the event of any of the foregoing circumstances arising, Esso shall be at liberty to withhold, reduce or suspend deliveries hereunder to such extent as Esso in their absolute discretion may think fit and shall in no case be bound to purchase or arrange for deliveries from any other suppliers.

The majority of the Court of Appeal decided that the clause was 'an exception from liability for non-performance rather than an exception from an obligation to perform' (*per* Russell LJ at 143). It assumed a failure to fulfil a term of the contract and excluded liability for damages for that breach in stated circumstances. Winn LJ thought that the clause only gave immunity from a claim in damages and did not prevent the right to treat the contract as repudiated by a continuing breach (see also Interference at p 42).

There is Canadian authority that the existence of a picket line is an induce-**3.17**
ment of breach of contract (*Hersees of Woodstock v Goldstein* (1963) 38 DLR 2d 449). Further, the inducer will be liable even though the person induced is perfectly willing to breach the contract (*British Motor Trades Association v Salvadori* [1949] Ch 556).

The inducer may be liable for breaches other than breach of contract (as to **3.18**
which see section below) although the tort will not be made out unless the act that has been induced is unlawful. In *Patrick Stevedores Operations Pty Limited v International Transport Workers Federation* [1998] 2 Lloyd's Rep 523, the ITF (in London) was alleged to have induced, or to have threatened to induce, disruptive acts in the dockyards of Japan, the USA and Europe in furtherance of a trade dispute in Australia. It was held by Thomas J that no

interlocutory (now interim) injunction would be granted because, amongst other matters, it had not been shown that the alleged acts would be unlawful in the places where they were to be done. Thomas J stated:

> It seems to me essential that Patrick provide evidence that blacking of the type that is taken in ports in other countries is at least in breach of the employees' contract, if not unlawful. I do not think it can necessarily be assumed that it is even in breach of contract. I suggested that a sufficient picture would emerge by examination of the law of Australia's major trading partners, Japan, the USA and one or two countries in continental Europe.

> I consider that clear evidence would be required in the particular circumstances of this application. This court is being asked to use its injunctive powers on an interlocutory basis in connection with an industrial and political dispute in another sovereign state by requiring the ITF in this jurisdiction and throughout the world not to induce its affiliates to take industrial action which Patrick accept can be lawful in other sovereign states. It may well be that such action in relation to this political and industrial dispute in Australia might be entirely in accordance with the law as well as the social and political views prevalent in that state, though contrary to the law currently applicable in Australia and the policies being pursued by the Federal Government of Australia.

> Before exercising such powers in this unprecedented situation, the court would need to have before it material that explains the precise basis on which such lawful action in one sovereign state is unlawful for the purposes of the tort of intimidation or inducing breach of contract in Australia, if that is the governing law or, by the law of England and Wales, if that is the governing law. Such evidence is not before the court.

3.19 The judge did not consider that such evidence had been shown and refused the application. The difference between direct and indirect inducement was considered in *Middlebrook Mushrooms Ltd v TGWU & Ors* [1993] ICR 612. The employer employed about 300 members of the TGWU. After a disagreement about cost cutting, employees took industrial action and 89 employees were dismissed. The TGWU carried out a propaganda exercise by distributing leaflets outside supermarkets which stocked the employer's mushrooms, urging customers not to buy the mushrooms. As the supermarkets had a number of sources of supply the customers could only show their support by not buying mushrooms at all from the supermarkets that were targeted. The employer sought an interim injunction against the union as it was concerned that the supermarkets would not stock their mushrooms at all. The Court of Appeal discharged the injunction that had been granted at first instance. There was no direct inducement or interference and it was necessary to show that the persuasion or inducement had been directed at one of the parties to the commercial contract before the tort could be made out. The TGWU had merely sought to exert influence on customers who were free to make up their own minds. This was indirect inducement or interference which required unlawful means to be tortious. Hoffmann LJ described the difference between direct and indirect inducement:

> The essential difference between direct inducement as in *Lumley v Guy* and indirect inducement as in *D C Thomson v Deakin* is one of causation. If the person immediately responsible for bringing the pressure or inducement to bear was the defendant or someone for whose acts he was legally responsible, the inducement is direct. If it was a third party, responding to the defendant's inducement or persuasion but exercising his own choice in the matter and not being a person for whom the defendant is legally responsible, the inducement is indirect.

Since the inducement was indirect it was necessary to show unlawful means, which the union had not employed.

D. Direct Procurement of Breach of Contract

The constituent elements of this tort are similar to those of direct inducement except that the unlawfulness stems *also* from the unlawful means by which the defendant procures the breach (see also at para 3.40 ff for a consideration of the use of unlawful means). **3.20**

The breach is 'procured' so that the party in breach has not been persuaded by inducement to commit the breach but has had no choice in the matter. For example, removing essential tools or kidnapping an employee could amount to procurement. These examples were given in *Thomson (D.C.) & Co v Deakin* [1952] Ch 646. In *Torquay Hotel Co. Ltd v Cousins* [1969] 2 Ch 106, Lord Denning gave an example of administering a noxious potion to a singer to prevent her going onstage. The difference between procurement and inducement is that with inducement the person induced has the choice of breaking his contract (and external pressure is no excuse), whilst with procurement the person does not exercise a choice but is compelled to breach his contract. The procurement must be committed by unlawful means and this requirement keeps the tort within reasonable bounds. **3.21**

3.22 It has been argued that the third party may not be in breach since he had no choice about the situation which arose and a plea of frustration may be pleaded.

E. Indirect Procurement of Breach of Contract

3.23 The common situation in which this tort arises is where union organizers call out on strike employees of a third party in breach of their contracts of employment, thereby procuring a breach of contract between the third party and the ultimate target. This was a typical dispute scenario in the 1970s although it has diminished in recent years not least because of legislative restrictions on secondary action and other methods being used (see, eg, the *Middlebrook Mushroom* case).

3.24 Unlawful means must be used against the third party in this situation before tortious liability can arise. Such unlawful means are usually found in the breach of the strikers' contracts of employment. In *Torquay Hotel Co. Ltd v Cousins* (above), Lord Denning agreed with Morris LJ's comment in *Thomson (D.C.) & Co. v Deakin* (above) at page 702, that there is a 'distinction between "direct persuasion to break a contract" which is unlawful in itself and the "intentional bringing about of a breach by indirect methods involving wrongdoing"'. The Master of the Rolls stated that: 'This distinction should be maintained, else we should take away the right to strike altogether'. This distinction was maintained in *Middlebrook Mushrooms Ltd v TGWU & Ors* [1993] ICR 612; see pages 27, 34.

3.25 It is necessary to consider:

(1) The common fact situation of the tort; and
(2) The constituent elements of the tort and defences, namely:
  (a) knowledge of contract and intent to bring about breach;
  (b) inducing or procuring the breach;
  (c) breach of contract or other duty;
  (d) causal connection;
  (e) use of unlawful means;
  (f) loss to the claimant;
  (g) statutory immunity; and
  (h) justification.

(1) The common fact situation

The clearest example is *Stratford (J.T.) and Son v Lindley* [1965] AC 269. The **3.26** claimant was the chairman of companies A and B. A owned Thames motor barges while B hired them out to companies which employed their own crews. Forty-five employees of A were members of the Transport and General Workers Union, while three belonged to its smaller rival, the Watermens' Union. Both organizations sought negotiating rights in respect of the employees of A. When the TGWU made a breakthrough around the negotiating table, the WU sought to achieve the same end by industrial muscle. Recognizing that such muscle was very flabby in A, they put pressure on B by calling on members in companies to which B's barges were hired, not to return them to moorings when their contracts ended. The breaches of the hire agreements were achieved indirectly, but the claimant gained an injunction to restrain such action, since the union had induced the hirers' employees to act in breach of their contracts in order to procure, and with the aim of procuring, a breach of contract between their respective employers and B on which the unions sought to exert pressure.

In *Thomson v Deakin* (at 697) Jenkins LJ offered a general statement of the **3.27** requirements for the tort, which was approved by the House of Lords in *Merkur Island Shipping Corp. v Laughton* [1983] 2 AC 570 and adopted in *Falconer v ASLEF and NUR* [1986] IRLR 331 (see also *Shipping Company Uniform Inc v International Transport Workers' Federation* [1985] IRLR 71). Jenkins LJ stated that it must be shown:

> . . . first that the person charged with actionable interference *knew* of the existence of the contract *and intended* to procure its breach; secondly, that the person so charged did *definitely and unequivocally* persuade, induce or procure the employees to breach their contracts of employment with the intent mentioned; thirdly, that the employees so persuaded, induced or procured did in fact *break* their contracts of employment and fourthly that the breach of the contract forming the alleged subject of interference ensued as a *necessary consequence* of the breach of the employees concerned of their contracts of employment. (Authors' italics.)

Each of these elements must also exist in the direct inducement or direct procurement torts, although their nature may vary slightly. In *Merkur Island Shipping Corp. v Laughton*, O'Connor LJ saw no difference in principle between persuading a man to break his contract with another, preventing him by physical restraint from performing it, making his performance of it impossible by taking away his tools or machinery, and making his performance of it impossible by depriving him, in breach of their contracts of services, of his employees.

3.28 In the *Thomson* case, however, there was no liability for indirect procurement of breach of the main contract between suppliers and publishers since the employees of the suppliers did not break their contracts of employment. This analysis by Jenkins LJ forms the basis for further discussion of the constituents of the economic torts. (For the facts of *Thomson v Deakin* see causal connection at p 33).

3.29 In order that a claimant may successfully sue, the tort must have been committed without justification recognized by law and the statutory immunities must not apply.

(2) The constituent elements

(a) Knowledge of contract and intent to bring about breach

3.30 The economic torts are generally based on intention and knowledge. These requirements place limitations on the parties injured by the defendant's actions and thus on those who may bring an action, preventing what would otherwise be enormous chains of liability. In general, the defendant should foresee the possibility of a breach of contract and desire the result. The old cases demanded the stringent standard that the defendant must have actual knowledge of the contract breached and some cognizance of its terms. (*Thomson v Deakin* (above), *Long v Smithson* [1918] 88 LJ KB 223, *Smithies v National Association of Operative Plasterers* [1909] 1 KB 310). Over time it has been shown that while ignorance may be bliss it will not always excuse liability. In *Cunard SS Co. Ltd v Stacey* [1955] 2 Lloyd's Rep 247, strike organizers ought to have known that, on calling their strike, union members would thereby break their contracts as seamen. They could not just turn a blind eye.

3.31 In *Emerald Construction Co. Ltd v Lowthian* [1966] 1 WLR 691, Higgs and Hill were the main contractors for a building and entered into a subcontract with the claimants to supply labour. The union disapproved of such labour-only subcontractors and sought to persuade Higgs and Hill to terminate the contract with the claimant. The evidence of the union officials who called the strike was that the union intended only that the contract should be lawfully terminated. The particular contract in issue required a long period of notice for lawful termination. The court held that the union was reckless as to the terms of the labour-only contract, and that their lack of actual knowledge of its terms, especially of the length of notice required to be given, could not absolve it from liability. Lord Denning MR thought that: 'even if [the defendants] did not know of the actual terms of the contract, but had the means of knowledge which they deliberately disregarded that would be enough'. After the issue of proceedings, the claimant showed to the union defendants a copy of the material contracts and still they did not desist from their action. Diplock LJ considered that the defendant was liable if he 'intended to have the contract ended by breach if it could not lawfully be ended'. The difficult notion of motive appears to be the uppermost consideration. A similar view was taken by Slade J in *Greig v Insole* [1978] 3 All ER 449, 488. He stated that: 'It is not necessary for the claimant to show that the defendant knew of the precise terms of the relevant contract; it will suffice for the claimant to prove that the defendant knew of the existence of the contract, provided that he can prove also that the defendant intended to procure a breach of it'.

In *British Industrial Plastics Ltd v Ferguson* [1940] 1 All ER 479 it was held **3.32** that an honest but mistaken belief that an inducement would not lead to a breach of contract could absolve the defendant from liability where the defendant had taken steps to satisfy himself that no element of unlawfulness would be involved. However, a defendant may be fixed with constructive knowledge (that is, the knowledge which he ought to have) in certain cases. In the *Merkur Island* case, Sir John Donaldson MR said that 'the defendants must in my judgment be deemed to have known of the almost certain existence of contracts of carriage' (see also *McMahon (James) v Dunn and Dolan* [1964] 99 ILTR 45, *Falconer v ASLEF and NUR* [1986] IRLR 331). The trend seems to be towards imposing liability although the defendant's knowledge of the existence of contracts is sketchy, although the courts in recent years appear to have adopted a more restrictive approach (cf. the requirement in interference of contract cases at para 3.74). However, the union will only be deemed to have knowledge of the existence of a commercial contract where it is clearly appropriate in the circumstances. In *Middlebrook Mushrooms Ltd v TGWU & Ors* [1993] ICR 612 the Court of Appeal was not prepared to find that the union had knowledge of the commercial contract between the employer and the supermarket, for the supply of mushrooms. Neill LJ stated:

there is no evidence of the existence or terms of any contracts between the employers and the supermarkets . . . It is clear that in many cases a third party may be deemed to know of the almost certain existence of a contract and indeed of some of its likely terms. The *Merkur Island* [1983] IRLR 218 case (which involved a charter party) and the *Union Traffic* [1989] IRLR 127 case (which involved a road haulage company) are clear examples. But in this case we are dealing with a commodity with a very short shelf life and where conditions of over-supply exist. It may be, and one can only speculate, that there are no long-term contracts, or even short-term contracts, in existence and that the employers make their supplies on terms which provide for very short periods of notice or even no notice at all . . . in certain circumstances the existence of a contract can be inferred. In the present case, however, I do not consider that the employers have established even a shadowy case that the appellants know of the existence or terms of contracts between the employers and supermarkets with which the appellants intend to interfere.

3.33 The case may be contrasted with *Union Traffic Ltd v Transport & General Workers Union* [1989] IRLR 127 where a transport haulage depot had been closed down by picketing at short notice. Although there was no evidence of the contractual terms upon which the hauliers operated, Bingham LJ said, at p 129, 18: 'It would, in my judgment, be very surprising indeed if a road haulage depot or container depot could be closed down completely at very short notice without causing the owner to break or fail to perform any existing contract.'

3.34 In *TimePlan Education Group Ltd v National Union of Teachers* [1997] IRLR 45, the NUT wrote to a New Zealand teaching union, NZEI, explaining that they were in dispute with the claimants, who were advertising in NZEI's magazine for agency teaching staff to work in the UK, about the terms on which teachers were supplied. As a result, NZEI cancelled further advertising. It was alleged that the NUT had unlawfully interfered with the continuing contract between NZEI and the agency for the publication of the advertisements. The Court of Appeal held that there was no justification for finding constructive knowledge of a continuing advertising contract, or any intention to induce breach of a contract of which the union was unaware. Therefore, the union committed no tort. It was stated that:

> The NUT did not know of a continuing contract and could not properly be taken to have intended that it should be breached . . . Mr Goudie went so far as to suggest that the NUT's behavior was reckless, and that this went to both knowledge and intention. To establish recklessness, it must be shown that the NUT was indifferent as to whether there was a contract or not, and, if there

was, as to whether that contract was broken. The evidence goes nowhere near justifying such a conclusion.

It should be noted, however, that where the defendant knows of the terms of the contract but has a mistaken belief about the legal results this may be enough for there to be liability (*Solihull Metropolitan Borough v National Union of Teachers* [1985] IRLR 211).

3.35 Where it is possible for the act to be performed lawfully, in the absence of specific evidence that the defendant intended to bring about a breach, that is, that it was intended the third party would take the unlawful route, the defendant should not be liable (*Patrick Stevedores Operations Pty Ltd v International Transport Workers Federation* [1998] 2 Lloyd's Rep 523). In *Boxfoldia v National Graphical Association (1982)* [1988] IRLR 383; ICR 752, a notice to strike was given in terms that were ambiguous. It was held that the notice did not have to be interpreted as an intended breach where it could be interpreted as a notice to lawfully terminate contracts. However, on the facts, the notice did not give or purport to give contractual notice of termination of the employment contracts of the members employed by the claimants called out on strike; the union induced their members to break their contracts of employment.

(b) Inducing or procuring the breach of contract

3.36 It is necessary that the words or actions used did in fact: (a) amount to an inducement or procurement; and (b) that there is a causal connection between the procurement or inducement and the breach of contract.

3.37 The line between inducement (which establishes liability) and the giving of advice (which does not) is a difficult one to draw. If the union organizer merely announces to his members that the employer is going to halve their pay from the end of the month and they immediately strike in protest, the organizer is not liable for the tort. In *Thomson (D.C.) & Co. v Deakin* [1952] Ch 646, there was no inducement since the defendants merely stated the facts as they saw them, and 'Bowaters [the claimants' suppliers], for reasons which I doubt not were prudent, took the line that they would not order any man either to load or to drive paper for the claimant.' (Lord Evershed MR at 685). Their Lordships thought that the passing of information could not be an inducement for these purposes.

3.38 In the *Torquay Hotel* case, however, Winn LJ was not so sure the distinction could be maintained: 'A man who writes to his mother-in-law telling her that the central heating in his house is broken may thereby induce her to cancel an intended visit.'

The facts in the case were that a union official had approached Alternative Fuels and had stated that there would be 'repercussions' if they supplied more oil. This was sufficient to amount to inducement. Lord Pearce in *Stratford (J. T.) and Son v Lindley* [1965] AC 269, 333, thought that: 'The fact that an inducement . . . is couched as an irresistible embargo rather than in terms of seduction does not make it any the less an inducement.'

3.39 An inducement must contain some element of pressure, persuasion or procuration. Advice intended to have persuasive effect can suffice (see also *Allen v Flood* [1898] AC 1). In *Camellia Tanker SA v International Transport Workers' Federation* [1976] ICR 274, however, the defendants, in informing their members of negotiations with the claimant over pay, did not induce them to break their contracts. Moreover, the breach of the commercial contract of the claimant was not the necessary result of the unions' activities (see also *Square Grip Reinforcement Co. Ltd v MacDonald* 1968 SLT 65, 72, *White v Riley* [1921] 1 Ch 1). The fact that the third party co-operates in the wrongdoing does not prevent there being an inducement: *British Motor Trades Association v Salvadori* [1949] Ch 556. In *Law Debenture Trust Corpn PLC v Ural Oil Corpn Ltd* [1995] 1 All ER 157, [1994] 3 WLR 1221 the Court of Appeal held that the tort was made out where the defendant actively co-operates with the third party in a course of action which the defendant knows is inconsistent with the contract between the third party and claimant. So the question for the court to consider appears to be whether the defendant has merely informed employees of relevant circumstances or has gone one stage further and has induced a breach of contract by attempting to persuade the party in breach to take a certain stance.

(c) Breach of contract or other duty

3.40 A breach of contract is a fundamental requirement for these torts. This excludes from liability certain situations which some would argue should be actionable, in circumstances where there is no breach but the employer has been presented with an ultimatum using industrial pressure. In *Allen v Flood* [1898] AC 1, the defendant boilermakers informed management that they would 'knock off work if the claimant shipwrights were not dismissed'. This was not unlawful since the boilermakers were free to leave without breaking their contracts because they were engaged by the day (see Lord Diplock in *Hadmor Productions Ltd v Hamilton* [1983] 1 AC 191). The defendants do not, however, avoid liability merely because they do believe that the functions they are inducing their members not to carry out are not contractually binding. Warner J rejected a submission to this effect in *Solihull Metropolitan Borough v National Union of Teachers* [1985] IRLR 211.

There must be a breach of an existing contract for the tort to be committed. **3.41** There is apparently 'no tort of wrongfully inducing a person not to enter a contract', according to Megarry J in *Midland Cold Storage Ltd v Steer* [1972] Ch 630. He thought that 'unless hedged about with many restrictions such a tort would have an extremely wide ambit that would be likely to work as much injustice as justice'. In some cases, however, 'a regular course of dealing may have hardened into an implied contractual relationship, so there is in fact an inducement to breach that relationship rather than merely pressure not to enter into a new contract' (cf. *dicta* of Lord Denning in *Torquay Hotel Co. Ltd v Cousins* [1969] 2 Ch 106, 139). It should be noted that Megarry J's view was given tentatively on an interim motion and that liability for failure to enter a contract may now arise if the ground for refusal is failure to recognize or consult trade unions under TULR(C)A, s 222.

It should be noted that TULR(C)A 1992, s 245 provides that, for the **3.42** purpose of the economic torts, any person who holds office or employment under the Crown shall be deemed to have a contract of employment with the Crown. This removes the vexed question of the status of certain civil servants who may otherwise only be regarded as holding an independent office under the Crown. In relation to the prison service, by the Criminal Justice and Public Order Act 1994, s 127, a person who organizes industrial action may commit a special statutory tort.

Breach of an equitable duty will suffice for liability. In *Prudential Assurance* **3.43** *Co. v Lorenz* (1971) 11 KIR 78, trade union members who refused to submit insurance premiums which they had collected in the course of their employment 'were enjoined from this course of action since it induced breach of the equitable duty they owed to their principal' (see also *Boulting v Association of Cinematograph, Television and Allied Technicians* [1963] 2 QB 606; *Royal London Mutual Insurance Society Ltd v Williamson* (1921) 37 TLR 742). The House of Lords in *Universe Tankships Inc of Monrovia v International Transport Workers Federation* [1982] IRLR 200; ICR 262 was not prepared to extend the doctrine to cover a claim in quasi contract for the repayment of monies allegedly paid under duress.

3.44   It was stated in *Meade v London Borough of Haringey* [1979] ICR 494 that an injunction may have been granted in a case where it was alleged that there was a breach of statutory duty, although the dispute had been settled by the time the case had reached the Court of Appeal. School caretakers went on strike with the effect of closing the schools and parents sought an injunction based upon breach of statutory duty by the council to provide schooling. It is submitted that the observations in the case are incorrect since there was no actionable breach of statute so that there was no breach which gave a right to the claimants to sue the third party (the council). (See *Lonrho Ltd v Shell Petroleum Co Ltd (No 2)* [1982] AC 173.) Since no action for damages lay by the parents against the school there was no right to bring a claim and in *E (a minor) v Dorset County Council* [1994] 4 All ER 640; 3 WLR 853 and *X (a minor) v Bedfordshire County Council*; *E (a minor) v Dorset County Council* [1995] 3 All ER 353 the proposition in the *Meade* case was considered to be unsound. The orthodox, and it is submitted the correct, approach that there can be no claim unless the breach of statutory duty is actionable was confirmed and adopted in *Barretts & Baird (Wholesale) Ltd v Institution of Professional Civil Servants* [1987] IRLR 3 and *Associated British Ports v Transport and General Workers Union* [1989] IRLR 191, affirmed by HL at [1989] ICR 557.

3.45   The constituents of the tort are not made out by an inducement to unfairly dismiss an employee (*Wilson v Housing Corporation* [1997] IRLR 346). It is necessary for there to be an actionable wrong in the courts of common law as opposed to a specialist tribunal. Furthermore, the court so decided because Parliament has set up the right to claim unfair dismissal by the machinery of statute and a party should not be able to circumvent the statutory requirements by being able to bring a tortious claim.

3.46   Where the industrial action is taking place overseas, issues of conflicts of laws may arise. Whether or not there has been the commission of a tortious act will usually be based upon the law of the place where the act is carried out. (Private International Law (Miscellaneous Provisions) Act 1995, s 11). For these purposes it will be the place where the act is carried out and not the place where the inducement takes place that is relevant (*Metall und Rohstoff AG v Donaldson Lufkin & Jenrette Inc* [1990] 1 QB 391). Where the applicable law is English law it will still not be tortious to persuade a person to do an act which is *lawful* in the jurisdiction where the act is carried out. In *Patrick Stevedores Operations Pty Ltd v International Transport Workers Federation* [1998] Lloyd's Rep 523, the ITF, which was based in London, was alleged to have induced or threatened to induce disruptive acts in the dock-yards of Japan, the USA and Europe in furtherance of a trade dispute taking place in Australia. Thomas J held that, although the Federation had encouraged affiliate members to do all that they could to boycott the company's ships, there was no evidence that the action taken would give rise to a breach of the employment contracts under the laws of the ports in which the actions were taking place.

(d) Causal connection

There must be a chain of causation between the inducement or procurement **3.47** and loss caused by the inducement or procurement. This proposition is illus-trated by *Thomson (D.C.) & Co. v Deakin* [1952] Ch 646. The claimant was a printing company whose policy was strictly to refuse employment to trade unionists. Employees had to sign a written undertaking that they would not join any union. However, NATSOPA had 75 secret members at the company's plant. They called these members out on strike and asked other unions to disrupt the company's activities in any way possible. Members of the Transport and General Workers Union employed by Bowaters informed their employers that they might not be prepared to deliver paper to Thomsons, and others who were loaders refused to load it. These threats remained only threats because Bowaters of their own accord decided not to supply paper. Bowaters wrote to the claimant that: 'We are prevented from performing our contract by the action of trade unions which has put a stop to any of your papers being loaded at and delivered from . . .'. It could not be proved that deliveries had in fact been prevented by the union's threats. Lord Evershed MR said (at 686): 'The links in the chain which connect the defendants with the claimants are . . . very insubstantial'. Although there was thus a breach of the commercial contract between Thomsons and Bowaters, the employees were never in breach of their own contracts of employment, since they were never called upon to make their threats real. In *Stratford (J.T.) and Son v Lindley* [1965] AC 269 Lord Pearce said (at 333F):

> In a case where the defendant does not communicate any direct pressure of persuasion to the contract breaker but merely procures indirectly the breach I am inclined to agree with the *dictum* of Jenkins LJ [1952] Ch 697 that it must

be shown that breach of the contract forming the alleged subject of interference ensued as a necessary consequence of the breaches by the employees concerned of their contracts of employment.

3.48 Where inducement is employed as opposed to procurement, the person induced has some choice whether he will breach his contract. The inducement may be overwhelming, verging even on the borders of compulsion. Nevertheless, the law expects the party induced to remain strong and not to buckle under the threats of the threatening party. If he does, he has no comeback against them. There is little authority on this point, but Upjohn LJ did say in *Boulting v ACTT* [1963] 2 QB 606, 640 that: 'If A procures B to breach his contract with C . . . B has no right at law to restrain A from attempting to suborn him from his duty to C. He must resist A's efforts by strength of will.' It is, however, necessary to show that the defendant continues to cause the breach (*Long v Smithson* (1918) 88 LJKB 223).

(e) The use of unlawful means

3.49 Whilst unlawful means are unnecessary for direct inducement, in cases of procurement they will form an essential constituent of the torts. The usual form of unlawful means will be breaches of the contracts of employment or commercial contracts.

3.50 Not every breach of a penal statute will constitute unlawful means. 'A mere prohibition on members of the public generally from doing what it would otherwise be lawful for them to do is not enough.' Thus in *Lonrho Ltd v Shell Petroleum Ltd (No.2)* [1981] 2 All ER 456, where this doctrine was enunciated, the claimant had no cause of action for an 'innominate tort . . . of causing foreseeable loss by an unlawful act' (at 462). Lord Denning MR nevertheless held in *Associated Newspapers Group Ltd v Wade* [1979] ICR 664, 690, that if the union 'uses its industrial strength to invade the freedom of the press', that would constitute unlawful means. The authority of this proposition is open to doubt. (See in detail Interference at para 3.60 ff).

The issue arose again in *Barrett & Baird (Wholesale) Ltd v Institution of Professional Civil Servants* [1987] IRLR 3. The Meat and Livestock Commission employed 630 fatstock officers at private sector abattoirs throughout the country. They carried out the certification procedures necessary to obtain subsidies and export meat under the common agricultural policy. They were called out on a one-day lightning strike by their union, the IPCS, in support of a pay claim. The claimant owned an abattoir whose business was affected, and they claimed that the union was interfering with their business by unlawful means, that is, the inducement or procurement of a breach, by the Intervention Board for Agricultural Products or MLC, of their duties under the Agriculture Act 1967 and the European Communities Act 1972. Henry J thought that it was eminently arguable that a duty was owed to the claimant but it was not to provide them with a strike-free system. There was nothing to suggest that the industrial action would bring the certification system to a grinding halt.

His Lordship also rejected the contention that the unlawful means could arise from the actual breach by a fatstock officer of his contract of employment with the MLC. This would mean that an employee could not obey his union's strike call without leaving himself personally open to a claim by a third party whose business happened to be affected by the striker. It had to be shown that the striker's predominant purpose was injury to the claimant rather than furtherance of his own self-interest. This could not be established here since the action was being taken for more pay.

What constitutes unlawful means would in the end appear to be a question of fact and degree in each case although there must clearly be an actionable wrong in order for unlawful means to be used (and see the cases at (c) above).

(f) Loss to the claimant

It is in the nature of these torts that the claimant must show he has suffered **3.51** economic loss. Where an injunction is sought to prevent the loss occurring the claimant must show he is in imminent danger of suffering substantial harm. If there is no loss, actual or apprehended, there is no cause of action, whether for damages or an injunction (*Sefton v Tophams Ltd (No.2)* [1965] Ch 1140).

(g) The statutory immunity

Where industrial action comes within the terms of the 'golden formula' (see **3.52** Chapter 4), by TULR(C)A 1992, s 219 (previously the Trade Union and Labour Relations Act 1974, s 13(1)), immunity exists for acts which would otherwise be actionable as inducement to, breach of, or interference with contract. However, it appears that with procurement, if the cause of action is based upon the unlawful means used, then the s 219(1) immunity may not apply because in effect the claimant is not simply alleging inducement or procurement of breach of contract but also commission of another tort (eg intimidation) (*Merkur Island Shipping Corp. v Laughton* [1983] IRLR 218).

3.53 Moreover, if the unlawful act which is induced or procured amounts to more than a breach of contract the immunity may be lost. In *Meade v London Borough of Haringey* [1979] 2 All ER 1016 it was recognized that a breach of statutory duty may suffice (although see above for the argument in later cases, which was accepted, that the breach of statutory duty must be actionable in itself) whilst in *Prudential Assurance Co. v Lorenz* (1971) 11 KIR 78 there was a breach of fiduciary duty; in both cases the immunity was lost. In *News Group Newspapers v SOGAT 82 and others* [1986] IRLR 337, 350, Stuart-Smith J thought that there would be no immunity where the torts of nuisance or intimidation were committed even though it was these torts which caused the breach or interference with the contract. This analysis gives effect to the word 'only' in s 219(1) (see Chapter 4). The unlawful act must be actionable and, in this respect, the *Meade* case is incorrect in so far as it held that a mere breach of statutory duty that is not actionable may found a claim.

(h) Justification

3.54 In many cases the statutory immunity will not apply because the facts do not come within the terms of the golden formula. Since, at least with the tort of direct inducement, liability may arise although the defendant has not acted unlawfully, it will be a defence if he can show that he had just cause or excuse for what he did. Although it has been said that it will not be possible to rely on the justification defence where unlawful means are used by the defendant (*Read v Friendly Society of Co operative Stonemasons of England, Ireland and Wales* [1902] 2 KB 732; see also *Smithies v National Association of Operative Plasterers* [1909] 1 KB 310). It has been argued that this is too forthright a statement as 'there might be a case where the defendant could justify his action as being the lesser of two evils' (*Harvey on Industrial Relations and Employment Law,* Butterworths at N.14.2358).

3.55 Different views have been expressed as to the scope of the justification defence, although these have tended to be based upon the perceived ambit of liability after *Allen v Flood* [1898] AC 1.

In *Glamorgan Coal Co. v South Wales Miners' Federation* [1903] 2 KB 545, Romer LJ stated:

I respectfully agree with what Bowen LJ said in the *Mogul* case (at [1889] 2 QBD 618) when considering the difficulty that might arise whether there was sufficient justification or not. The good sense of the tribunal which had to decide would have to analyse the circumstances and to discover on which side of the line each case fell. I will only add that in analysing or considering the circumstances I think that regard might be had to the nature of the contract broken; the position of the parties to the contract; the grounds for the breach; the means employed to procure the breach; the relation of the persons; procuring the breach to the person who breaks the contract, and, also, I think the object of the person procuring the breach.

Brimelow v Casson [1924] 1 Ch 302 appears to be the only case so far decided on the issue of justification and adopts the same wide approach as Romer LJ. Chorus girls who appeared in the King Wu Tut review were paid such meagre wages that they were forced to resort to prostitution to eke out a living. The union called a strike. Russell J held that it was justified in inducing the girls to breach their contracts, stating that: 'If justification does not exist here, I can hardly conceive the case where it would be present.' However, *Brimelow v Casson* was doubted by Simonds J in *Camden Nominees Ltd v Forcey* [1940] 1 Ch 352, who thought that the justification defence must be limited to a case where the defendant has a legally recognizable duty to act (but cf. *Posluns v Toronto Stock Exchange and Gardiner* (1964) 46 DLR (2d) 210).

It would appear that the pursuit of bona fide trade union objectives may in some circumstances act as justification (*Crofter Handwoven Harris Tweed Co. v Veitch* [1942] AC 435). However, in *TimePlan Education Group Ltd v National Union of Teachers* [1997] IRLR 457 it was argued that there was a defence of justification where the claimant agency persistently undercut national rates of pay for teachers. There was no breach on the facts but the Court of Appeal stated that the defence of justification would have failed if there had been a breach. Gibson LJ stated that, although the union was interested, he could not 'see even the beginning of an argument that this would have justified the knowing and intentional breach of an advertising contract. The NUT had no moral or other duty to interfere other than its member's (*sic.*) interests.'   **3.56**

Certain duties may provide an absolute defence; it will be a defence, for example, for the defendant to show that he was complying with a statutory duty (*Black v Admiralty Commissioners* [1924] KB 661).   **3.57**

3.58   The extent to which moral duties may suffice is questionable (*Greig v Insole* [1978] 3 All ER 449, 492). In the *Greig* case, Slade J commented:

> counsel for the defendants emphasised the impersonal and disinterested motives of the ICC in doing what it did and referred me to the decision of Gale J in the Ontario Court in Posluns v Toronto Stock Exchange and Gardiner. In my judgment, however, the motives of this nature do not, as such, give rise to a defence of justification either generally under English law or on the particular facts of this case.

This was confirmed in the commercial case of *Pancommerce SA v Veecheema BV* [1983] 2 Lloyd's Rep 304.

3.59   The bona fide exercise of a legal right may provide justification as in *Granby Marketing Services Ltd v Interlego AG* (1984) 1 RPC 209 where the defendant asserted a legal right in good faith which had the effect of the third party breaching its contract with the claimant. In *The Nadezhda Krupskaya* [1997] 2 Lloyd's Rep 35, Rix J was of the view that a contractually valid exercise of the right of withdrawal or the acceptance of a repudiation under a head charter would not be tortious even if it was done with the intention of destroying the sub-charter (although there was a breach on the facts). Where the defendant has a right which is equal or superior to that of the claimant the defendant will be justified in exercising the right to taking steps which have the same consequence (see *Edwin Hill & Partners v First National Finance Corpn plc* [1988] 3 All ER 801).

F. Interference with Contract

3.60   The watershed case of *Allen v Flood* [1898] AC 1 (where there was no allegation of conspiracy) appeared to make settled law that interference with a contract without breach did not become unlawful merely by reason of the fact that the interference was carried out maliciously. Indeed, Lords Watson, Hershel, MacNaghten, Davey and Jones thought that interference could not be the basis for a cause of action. Nevertheless, three years later, in *Quinn v Leathem* [1901] AC 495, a differently constituted House of Lords felt able to say that there was a tort of *conspiracy* to commit an unlawful act where the act comprised interference with the claimant's contract. The case would have opened up a wide potential liability for unions if it had created a general tort of interference with contract, but the decision might be limited to the tort of conspiracy (*Ware and De Freville Ltd v Motor Trade Association* [1921] 3 KB 40).

A wide divergence of judicial views on the true analysis of interference can **3.61** be detected in *Stratford (J. T.) and Son v Lindley* [1965] AC 269. Lord Reid doubted 'whether a breach of contract was necessary to constitute a tort', but Lord Donovan considered that this argument was 'as novel and surprising as I think that the members of this House who decided *Crofter Handwoven Harris Tweed Co. v Veitch* would have done'. Statute had since 1906 given an immunity from action for interference with contracts, which appeared to recognize the existence of liability. In *Rookes v Barnard* [1964] 2 AC 1129 Lord Reid, however, thought that it was in order to enact something 'necessary to achieve their object if the law should go one way but unnecessary if it went the other way'.

Lord Denning MR maintained a sustained campaign to make the tort of **3.62** interference one of the bedrocks of liability in industrial disputes and there were some dicta in cases which provided support for this in that others had been prepared to relax the requirement of a *breach* of contract before tortious liability could arise. In *Thomson (D.C.) & Co. v Deakin* [1952] AC 646, Jenkins LJ said that: 'The breach of contract complained of must be brought about by some act of a third party (whether alone or in concert with the contract breaker) which is in itself unlawful, but that act need not necessarily take the form of persuasion or procurement or inducement of the contract breaker.'

Although the judgments in *Rookes v Barnard* (above) dealt centrally with **3.63** the tort of intimidation, Lord Devlin offered the view that:

> If one man, albeit by unlawful means, interferes with another's right to earn his living or dispose of his labour as he wills and does so maliciously, that is, with intent to injure without justification, he is, if there is such a tort, liable in just the same way as he would undoubtedly be liable if he were acting in combination with others.

The issue arose directly in *Torquay Hotel Co. Ltd v Cousins* [1969] 2 Ch 106, **3.64** because of the exclusion clause in the agreement between the claimant and fuel suppliers, Esso, that Esso would not be liable in contract for failure to supply fuel if that failure arose from an industrial dispute (see para 4.49). The union argued, relying on the exclusion clause, that its blacking did not induce a breach of contract and thus gave rise to no liability. Russell LJ narrowly interpreted the exclusion clause as 'an exception from liability for non-performance', holding therefore that there had in fact been a breach of contract. Winn LJ suggested that if the contract could be performed in mode

A or mode B, it would be tortious to prevent performance in mode A even if it could still be performed in mode B. The reasoning has been criticized by Elias and Ewing who described it as a 'dubious expedient' (1982 CLJ 321). Lord Denning MR adopted the more robust approach that: 'If one person without just cause or excuse deliberately interferes with the credit or business of another and does so by unlawful means, that is by an act which he is not at liberty to commit, then he is acting unlawfully.'

He so understood the basis of *Stratford v Lindley* and *Rookes v Barnard* and defined the requirements of the tort in the following terms:

> First, there must be interference in the execution of a contract. The interference is not confined to procurement of a breach of contract. It extends to a case where a third person prevents or hinders one party from performing his contract, even though it be not a breach. Second, the interference must be deliberate. The person must know of the contract, or, at any rate, turn a blind eye to it and intend to interfere with it: see *Emerald Construction Co. Ltd v Lowthian* [1966] 1 WLR 691. Third, the interference must be direct. Indirect interference will not do.

(See also *Acrow (Automation) Ltd v Rex Chainbelt Inc.* [1971] 1 WLR 1676 at 1682, *Ex p Island Records* [1978] 3 All ER 824, 830.)

3.65 In *Associated Newspapers Group Ltd v Wade* [1979] 1 WLR 697, Lord Denning MR widened the principle by suggesting that interference with the freedom of the press was so contrary to public policy as to amount to unlawful means. The blacking by the National Graphical Association of advertisements in a local newspaper with which it was in dispute was held to constitute unlawful means, partly because it prevented some public authorities and local councils from complying with their statutory duties to publish formal notices of proposed actions. This was notwithstanding that neither party could enjoin the unlawfulness by independent causes of action. An act contrary to the Restrictive Practices Act 1956 has also been held obiter to suffice (*Daily Mirror Newspapers Ltd v Gardner* [1968] 2 QB 762).

3.66 The existence of the two torts (of interference with contract and interference with business) was affirmed by the House of Lords in *Hadmor Productions Ltd v Hamilton* [1983] 1 AC 191 and *Merkur Island Shipping Corp. v Laughton* [1983] 2 AC 570. It is necessary to consider them separately.

G. Interference with Business

It is a tort for a trade union or its members to interfere with the trade, busi-   **3.67**
ness or employment of another by using unlawful means, thereby causing
loss to the other. Secondary action is almost certain to involve commission of
this tort. In *Hadmor Productions Ltd v Hamilton* (above) the claimant alleged
that ACTT officials threatened to persuade union members to refuse to
transmit television programmes produced by it and that this was interference
with the claimant's business by unlawful means. Thames TV had acquired a
licence to transmit the programmes but was not contractually bound to do
so. The claimant could, however, complain that its commercial *expectation*
that the programmes would be broadcast was interfered with, since that
expectation was 'shattered' by the blacking. Lord Denning MR said in the
Court of Appeal that 'we now have a separate and distinct tort of interference
with the business of another by unlawful means'.

For liability to be made out, it is necessary for the claimant to show that the   **3.68**
defendant has harmed him intentionally and without just cause or excuse
and has used unlawful means to achieve this end. It is not a tort merely to
intentionally, unjustifiably or spitefully harm another's business but it is to
unlawfully so harm the business so that interference with business *without
unlawful means will not be tortious.* The unlawful conduct is at the heart of
the action. This is done indirectly where the defendant commits acts which
are unlawful against a third party with intent to harm the claimant or
commits a tort against the claimant through the third party with intent to
harm the claimant.

There is an issue whether it is sufficient for the claimant to show that he has   **3.69**
been damaged in his business generally or whether it is necessary to show
more specific loss. In *Lonrho plc v Fayed* [1990] 2 QB 479 there was an issue
as to whether the defendant had interfered by unlawful means by perpetrat-
ing a fraud on the Secretary of State. Lonrho and the Fayed brothers were in
competition to take over the Harrods store. Lonrho was unable to progress
its bid when it was referred by the Secretary of State to the Monopolies and
Mergers Commission. The Fayed bid was accepted and Lonrho asserted that
the Fayeds had avoided a reference to the Commission by making fraudulent
representations to the Secretary of State, and that they deliberately interfered
with Lonrho's business by such unlawful means. The Fayeds asserted that
there was no cause of action based upon a lost opportunity to make a

takeover bid as this was not a sufficient interest. On an interim application, Pill J agreed but the Court of Appeal held that the point in issue must go to trial. The House of Lords were not asked to rule on this issue. The constituents of the tort will be considered in the next sections.

H. Interference with Trade or Business

3.70 In *Merkur Island Shipping Corp. v Laughton* [1983] AC 570 Lord Diplock stated that 'interfering with trade or business by unlawful means is a genus of torts of which procuring breach is a species'. The point is important since the breadth of the trade dispute immunity turns on it; this is discussed in greater detail in Chapter 4. The facts in the *Merkur* case followed the familiar pattern in shipping cases. The International Transport Workers' Federation organized blacking of the claimant's Liberian registered ship after a crew member complained about low wages. When the ship sought to leave the port of Liverpool, tugmen and lock-keepers refused to assist its free passage. The House of Lords agreed with Parker J that the tort of interfering by unlawful means with the performance of a contract was made out. The unlawful means consisted of procuring the tugmen and lockmen to break their contracts of employment by refusing to carry out operations on the part of the tugmen and the port authorities that were necessary *to* enable the ship to leave the dock. The contractual duty under the charter was to 'prosecute voyages with the utmost dispatch'. The claimant could not rely on the tort of procurement since there was a *force majeure* clause that *inter alia* stated 'in the event of loss of time due to boycott of the vessel in any port or place by shore labour or others . . . payment of hire shall cease for time thereby lost'. Lord Diplock distinguished for these purposes between the primary obligations of the parties to perform under the contract, and their secondary obligations, to pay damages for breach, and said (at 608B): 'All prevention of due performance of a primary obligation under a contract was intended to be included in the definition of interference, because the secondary obligation was excluded by some *force majeure* clause.'

The union was therefore liable despite the clause.

3.71 The tort of interference with contract was further extended in *Falconer v ASLEF and NUR* [1986] IRLR 331 (for further details, see Chapter 7). Judge

Henham held that the unions were liable for preventing the return to Sheffield of a British Rail passenger, adopting the statement of the law by Jenkins LJ in respect of indirect procurement of breach of contract in *Thomson (D.C.) & Co. v Deakin* [1952] Ch 646, already cited in p 25. The union could not rely on the exclusion clause between the claimant and British Rail because they had caused a breach of British Rail's primary obligation under its contract with the claimant. (See further The Citizen's Charter at Chapter 7.)

There must have been some disruption or deviation from the performance of the commercial contract. Where the interference is indirect the means of interference must be unlawful. In *Middlebrook Mushrooms Ltd v TGWU* [1993] IRLR 232 the Court of Appeal distinguished between direct and indirect interference as follows: direct interference occurs when the defendant seeks directly to influence one of the parties to the contract but where the pressure is brought to bear on a stranger to the contract (such as the shoppers) the case is one of indirect interference so that unlawful means are needed. **3.72**

It is necessary to consider: **3.73**

(1) knowledge of business or contract;
(2) unlawful means;
(3) intent to harm the claimant;
(4) loss to the claimant;
(5) justification.

(1) Knowledge of business or contract

In the *Merkur* case Lord Diplock thought that 'the more indirect the action of the defendants, the more difficult may it be to prove their knowledge of an intention to interfere with the performance of the principal contract'. He dealt with the issue of knowledge of the contract interfered with on the basis that there 'can hardly be anyone better informed than ITF as to the terms of the sorts of contracts under which ships are employed'. In *Falconer v ASLEF and NUR* (above) the judge held that the claimant was one of an identifiable group of people in a contractual relationship with British Rail and the fact that his actual name and description were not known to the defendants did not prevent his claim. The claimant was one of an identifiable class and could claim as such. **3.74**

3.75   The tort was made out in *News Group Newspapers Ltd v SOGAT 82 and others* [1986] IRLR 337, since all those on the trade union side knew that there was a distribution contract between News International and TNT Road Freight. It was the intention of the defendants to obstruct by nuisance or intimidation the departure of TNT's lorries, and there was evidence that TNT's lorries were substantially delayed on occasions when the marching, rallies and demonstrations gave rise to nuisance and intimidation.

(2) Unlawful means

3.76   The defendant must use unlawful means to cause the interference with business or contract. This is usually taken to mean a civil wrong (but cf. *Daily Mirror Newspapers v Gardner* [1968] 2 QB 762). There is no right of action where the unlawful means involve breach of a statutory duty save where the legislation was passed for the benefit of a particular class of individuals, and where the legislation created a public right and a particular member of the public suffered direct and substantial damage other than and different from that which was common to the rest of the public. This was not the case in *Lonrho Ltd v Shell Petroleum Ltd (No. 2)* [1982] AC 173, where the claimant claimed that the unlawfulness resided in a breach of the Rhodesian Sanctions Order. Lord Diplock rejected the proposition (at 187) that: 'whenever a lawful business carried on by one individual in fact suffers damage as a result of a contravention by another individual of any statutory provision the former has a civil right of action against the latter for such damage'.

3.77   In principle, any tort ought to be sufficient if it is done with the intent to harm the claimant. (See *GWK Ltd v Dunlop Rubber Co Ltd* (1926) 42 TLR 376 where the tort of trespass was indirectly committed when Dunlop substituted its own tyres for that of Allied tyres on a show car belonging to GWK.)

3.78   Where the third party does not suffer loss there will have been no completed tort but the loss may instead be suffered by the claimant as in *National Phonograph Co Ltd v Edison Bell Co Ltd* [1908] 1 Ch 335. The tort of deceit was perpetrated on a third party wholesaler, who had covenanted not to sell to the defendant, in order to obtain the claimant's gramophones and the defendant was thereby liable for interfering with the claimant's business by unlawful means. Although it was at one time asserted that a wider definition of 'unlawful' may be applied; namely that unlawful means an act that the defendant is not at liberty to commit, a wrong by the defendant rather than to the third party, notably by Lord Denning in *Torquay Hotel v Cousins*, this potential expansion of liability was rejected in *Lonrho Ltd v Shell Petroleum Co Ltd (No. 2)* above. (See also *Michaels v Taylor Woodrow Developments Ltd* [2000] 4 All ER 645, 661 and *Stocznia Gdanska SA v Latvian Shipping Co Latreefer Inc* [2001] 1 Lloyd's Rep 537.)

Where the defendant breaks its contract with the third party in order to harm **3.79** the claimant's business the House of Lords held in *Rookes v Barnard* [1964] AC 1129 that a claimant could not complain of a breach of contract with a third party and it was the threat that made out the tort of intimidation. Since motive or purpose is irrelevant, it is the threat that makes the breach tortious so that a mere breach of contract is not sufficient without more. However, in *Barretts & Baird (Wholesale) Ltd v Institution of Professional Civil Servants* [1987] IRLR 3 and *Stocznia Gdanska SA v Latvian Shipping Co Latreefer Inc* [2001] 1 Lloyd's Rep 537 a breach of contract was accepted as being sufficient.

(3) Intent to harm the claimant

It is necessary to show: **3.80**

(1) that it was the defendant's purpose to harm the claimant; and
(2) that there was a causal connection between the harm suffered by the claimant and the defendant's act.

In *Dimbleby & Sons Ltd v National Union of Journalists* [1984] IRLR 67 CA; **3.81** [1984] IRLR 160 HL, the union declared that the printers TBF were blacked and instructed its members not to produce copy for newspapers printed by them. That induced breaches of contract by the claimant's employees and interfered with the printers' business. Dimbleby still managed to continue to produce their newspapers and have them printed by TBF. They nevertheless obtained an injunction on the ground of interference, even though it was argued that the journalists had not caused an interference because Dimbleby had in fact performed the contract (see also *Thomson (D.C.) & Co. v Deakin* [1952] Ch 646, 697, 699). The defendant did, however, clearly intend to injure the claimant. The claimant had to rely on such a tort since an inducement claim would have fallen within the trade dispute immunity (see also *Thomas v National Union of Mineworkers (South Wales Area)* [1985] IRLR 136). A further difficulty with the *Dimbleby* case is that the acts were in fact aimed at the printers rather than Dimbleby.

3.82 The requirement of intent to harm the claimant was stressed in *Barretts &*
Baird (Wholesale) Ltd v Institution of Professional Civil Servants [1987] IRLR
3. Henry J decided that in the case of a lightning strike by fatstock officers
(see p 34 for the facts) there was no cause of action since:

> . . . the industrial action being taken here is perfectly straightforward industrial
> action taken for improved pay . . . it is a national strike. There is no is evidence
> of any independent, let alone predominant, desire to injure the claimants at
> whose premises they work . . . There is no evidence to suggest that the fatstock
> officers would not have struck if their industrial action had not injured the
> claimant.

(See also *Van Camp Chocolates Ltd v Aulesebrooks Ltd* [1984] 1 NZLR 354.)

3.83 In *Falconer v ASLEF and NUR* [1986] IRLR 331 a county court judge awarded
damages to an intending passenger. Harvey at Chapter N, para 14.2413 points
out the *Dimbleby* case misled the judge into awarding damages as the union
members were simply striking for better terms for themselves and the union
did not act with a view to harming Mr Falconer or disrupting his contract.

3.84 Although it is necessary to show that the defendant's purpose in harming the
third party was to inflict loss upon the claimant this does not have to be the
predominant purpose. It is sufficient if it is one of the purposes (see *Lonrho*
plc v Fayed [1990] 2 QB 479).

(4) Loss to the claimant

3.85 It is of course necessary for the claimant to show that he has suffered loss. A
tradesman may recover for normal business losses (*Exchange Telegraph Co. v*
Gregory & Co. [1896] 1 QB 147) whilst a workman may in some circumstances recover loss of earnings where his contract has been interfered with
(*Edwards v SOGAT* [1971] Ch 354.) The damages must, however, be referable to the act so that the loss caused by the act must be particularized
(*Lonrho plc v Fayed (No. 5)* [1994] 1 All ER 188).

(5) Justification and statutory immunity

3.86 Since unlawful means are required for this tort it will be a rare situation
where a justification defence will succeed (see *Read v Friendly Society of*
Operative Stonemasons of England, Ireland and Wales [1902] 2 KB 732). The
issue has not been discussed in the recent cases. A full discussion of the statutory immunity is at pages 69 to 100.

I. Intimidation

The tort of intimidation is of ancient pedigree, although it has only recently been invoked in industrial disputes. We will consider in turn its history, the necessary threats, the person threatened and the statutory immunity.   **3.87**

History

In 1620 a defendant threatened to maim anyone who did business with the claimant. The claimant was able to recover damages in respect of loss suffered because potential customers had been scared away (*Garret v Taylor* (1620) Cro Jac 567). In 1793 the master of a slave-trading ship (A) in the Cameroons fired at a canoe which was about to carry on business with another vessel (B) and the natives, in panic, ceased to trade with B as a result of the volley. On an action by the owners of the vessel B, the Court of Common Pleas decided that the master of A was liable in damages for intimidation. The claimant had lost financially as a result of the threat of violence and should receive damages (*Tarleton v McGawley* (1793) 1 Peake 270). From these seeds the tort of intimidation has grown and was a little-known remedy for threats of violence until the House of Lords revolutionized its use in *Rookes v Barnard* [1964] 2 AC 1129 to comprise a threat of a breach of contract.   **3.88**

Pearson LJ had described the tort in the Court of Appeal as 'obscure, unfamiliar and peculiar' ([1963] 1 QB 623, 695). The manner in which the House of Lords developed the tort set alarm bells ringing throughout the trade union movement, since it then fell outside the immunities of the golden formula.

The defendants, including a branch chairman, a shop steward and a full-time union official, Silverthorne, were officials of the Association of Engineering and Shipbuilding Draughtsmen. All but Silverthorne were employed by BOAC. They threatened to call their members out on strike if non-unionists were not removed by management within three days to ensure that their informal closed shop was maintained. The tort of inducement of breach of contract could not be utilized since the employee was lawfully dismissed with notice and no one had to carry out the threat, so that no contracts of employment were in fact breached. The House of Lords was, however, satisfied that the tort of intimidation had been committed and awarded exemplary damages. The threat to act in breach of contract was unlawful. Counsel had, somewhat surprisingly, conceded that a no-strike clause of a collective agreement had been incorporated into the contracts of individual employees. Lord Devlin stated (at 1209): 'I find nothing to differentiate a threat of breach of contract from a threat of physical violence or any other illegal threat. All that matters is that, metaphorically speaking, a club has been used. It does not matter to the claimant what the club is made of—whether it is a physical club or an economic club or tortious club or an otherwise illegal club.'

Lord Reid (at 1169) thought that 'threatening a breach of contract may be a much more coercive weapon than threatening a tort, particularly when the threat is directed against a company'. The House of Lords rejected the argument by the defendants that this allowed by a sidewind a person not a party to a contract to sue on it. Liability was imposed for an unlawful threat against BOAC which indirectly but intentionally caused loss to the claimant. There are many difficulties with the case which have to be worked out in the authorities. It is, for example, difficult to see on what basis Silverthorne was liable when he was a full-time union official and not an employee of BOAC and thus could not have threatened a breach of contract. The unlawful act that was said to be involved is also rather unclear, for if the union members had gone on strike they would not have been liable, being within the golden formula. The action of the union members in going on strike would have been unlawful, even if non-actionable (cf. TULR(C)A 1974, s 219(3)). The decision therefore possibly portends a greater liability for threats than carrying out the action (see also Lord Diplock in *Hadmor Productions Ltd v Hamilton* [1983] AC 191, 229). In *News Group Newspapers Ltd v SOGAT 82 and others* [1986] IRLR 337, Stuart-Smith J stated that the tort of intimidation is not complete unless the person threatened succumbs to the threat and damage is suffered. Injunctive relief can, however, be granted to restrain threats. The learned judge formulated the tort as follows (at 347):

> The tort of intimidation is committed when 'A' delivers a threat to 'B' that he will commit an act or use means unlawful against 'B', as a result of which 'B' does or refrains from doing some act which he is entitled to do, thereby causing damage either to himself or 'C'. The tort of intimidation is one of intention and the Claimant, whether it be 'B' or 'C' must be a person whom 'A' intends to injure.

Threats

3.89 Central to the tort is the requirement of a threat. In *Hodges v Webb* [1920] Ch 70, 89, the court defined a threat as 'an intimation by one to another that unless the latter does or does not do something, the former will do something which the latter does not like'. As with inducement, the difficulty is in drawing the line and distinguishing threats from warnings or advice (see also *Camellia Tanker SA v International Transport Workers' Federation* [1976] ICR 214, 284).

It would not have been sufficient in *Rookes v Barnard* (above) if there had merely been communication 'informing BOAC that the men would strike if the terms were not accepted' (see also *Huntley v Thornton* [1957] 1 WLR 321, 344). In *Crofter Handwoven Harris Tweed Co. v Veitch* [1942] 1 AC 435, however, Lord Wright said that: 'There is nothing unlawful in giving a warning or intimation that if the person addressed pursues a certain course of conduct, others may act in a manner which he will not like and will be prejudicial to his interests, as long as nothing unlawful is threatened or done'. **3.90**

The claimant must prove that the threats were intended to coerce and to have the effect of harming him. In *News Group Newspapers Ltd v SOGAT 82 and others* [1986] IRLR 337 (at 106), it was said that swearing and shouting would not in themselves necessarily amount to threats but words such as 'Scab, we'll get you' amounted to threats of violence. The judge was also influenced by the surrounding circumstances of such threats, namely 'employees being followed, molested, assaulted and subjected to criminal damage to their cars and houses; the taking of photographs of employees, noting of car numbers and "rolls of dishonour" of "scabs"'. **3.91**

The person threatened

The tort may be committed indirectly, as in *Rookes v Barnard,* or directly. Unlawful threats may be actionable by the person threatened. There is some authority for the proposition that the person who submits to a threat may claim the loss resulting therefrom—so-called two-party intimidation (*D. C. Builders v Rees* [1966] 2 QB 617, 625). However, where the threat is resisted it will only be if it is carried out that a claim is likely, otherwise no loss results. For example, if a union organizer tells the employer that if he does not concede higher wages, he will paralyse the company's operations, and the employer does not give such an increase, yet the union leader finds his fierce words are not backed up by the membership, there is no cause of action. As we have seen, the tort is not complete unless the person threatened succumbs to the threat and damage is suffered (the *News Group Newspapers Ltd* case (above), 107). **3.92**

Immunity

3.93 The development of the tort threatened to envelop all strike activity in a cloak of liability. The 1964 Labour Government therefore, in its Trades Disputes Act 1965, soon extended the trade dispute immunity to this tort where a person was acting in contemplation or furtherance of a trade dispute. TULR(C)A 1992, s 219(1)(b) now provides the current form of that immunity where the action 'consists in threatening that a contract (whether one to which he is a party or not) will be broken or its performance interfered with or that he will induce another person to break a contract or interfere with its performance'.

3.94 The provision was widened in 1976 to cover threatened breaches of commercial contracts, but there is no protection against intimidation which is unlawful secondary action, nor where it arises by way of picketing save as is lawful under TULR(C)A 1992, s 220.

J. Duress

3.95 It is possible that the tort of intimidation may come to be subsumed under 'the developing law of economic duress', as Lord Diplock described it in *Universe Tankships Inc. of Monrovia v International Transport Workers' Federation* [1982] ICR 262. It is doubtful whether duress is truly an economic tort. For the moment intimidation and duress must be considered separately. The leading case was another skirmish in the long war between the International Transport Workers' Federation and shipowners who sailed under flags of convenience. The Universe Sentinal owed by the claimant was blacked on its berthing at Milford Haven. To release the ship the claimant acceded to all of the defendant's demands including the payment of $80,000 to the ITF of which $71,720 was an estimate of wages due to the crew as a backdated wage settlement and $6,480 was earmarked for the ITF's welfare fund, which provided port facilities for foreign sailors. As soon as the ship was freed the claimant demanded the return of the contribution on the grounds that it was paid on a void purpose. The ITF held the money on resulting trust and it was paid under a contract which was vitiated by duress. Lord Scarman stated that economic pressure amounted to duress if the object had no choice but to submit to the pressure and the pressure exerted was illegitimate (at [1983] AC 385): 'The remedy to which *economic* duress gives rise is not an action for damages but an action for restitution of property or money exacted under such duress and the avoidance of any contract that has been induced by it.'

If, however, the pressure was applied in contemplation or furtherance of a trade dispute the pressure would be legitimate since it would be wrong for the courts to impose liability by way of restitution which could not be imposed in tort. TULR(C)A 1992, s 219 affords: **3.96**

> . . . an indication which your Lordships should respect of where public policy requires that the line should be drawn between what kind of commercial pressure upon an employer in the field of industrial relations ought to be treated as legitimised despite the fact that the will of the employer is thereby coerced and what kind of commercial pressure in that field does not amount to economic duress.

The result is somewhat limited since counsel for the defendant conceded that the pressure did amount to economic duress. Lord Scarman nevertheless commented that: 'Duress can, of course, exist even if the threat is one of lawful action; whether it does so depends on the nature of the demand.' ([1982] ICR, 289). (See also outside the industrial field *Pao On v Lau Yiu Long* [1980] ICR, 614, *Barton v Armstrong* [1976] AC 104.) **3.97**

The *Universe Tankships* case was followed in relation to a strike in *B & S Design v Victor Green Publications Ltd* [1984] ICR 419. In September 1978 the claimants agreed to erect stands for the defendants at Olympia for an international fire, security and safety exhibition. The employees of a subsidiary company of the claimants, which was providing some of the materials, refused to work at Olympia without increased severance payments in respect of redundancies which had already been announced. This meant that the price to the defendants would rise by £9,000 and, faced with the prospect of a strike if they did not agree, the defendants agreed to pay the £9,000 demanded. In fact they deducted £4,500 when the money was due, and when sued for it claimed back the £4,500 actually paid on the grounds that it was paid under duress. Eveleigh LJ quoted with approval (at 423F) the judgment of Lord Diplock in the *Universe Tankships* case ([1982] ICR at 272–3) that: **3.98**

> The rationale is that his [the defendant's] apparent consent was induced by pressure exerted upon him by that other party which the law does not regard as legitimate, with the consequence that the consent is treated in law as revocable unless approbated either expressly or by implication after the illegitimate

pressure has ceased to operate on his mind. It is a rationale similar to that which underlies the avoidability of contracts entered into and the recovery of money exacted under colour of office, or under undue influence or in consequence of threats of physical duress.

The money was found to be paid under duress and the defendants were entitled to recover the money. There was duress since: '. . . it was implicit in negotiations between the parties that the claimants were putting the defendants into a corner and it was quite apparent to the defendants, by reason of the claimants' conduct, that unless they handed over the £4,500 the claimants would walk off the job' (Griffiths LJ at 426C).

K. Conspiracy

3.99 Since industrial action is by its nature collective, involving as it does workers acting in combination, it is self-evident why the law of conspiracy has long had a leading role to play in this area. It was only a few years after the abolition of the criminality of trade unions as conspiracies by the Conspiracy and Protection of Property Act 1875, that the courts developed a tort of conspiracy with similar components.

Willes J described the tort in *Mulcahy v R* (1868) LR 3 HL 306, 317 as consisting of 'the agreement of two or more to do an unlawful act, or to do a lawful act by unlawful means'. In *Kuwait Oil Tankers v Al Bader* [2000] 2 All ER Comm 271, it was stated that conspiracy consists of the suffering of loss or damage 'as a result of unlawful action taken pursuant to a combination or agreement between the defendant and another person or persons to injure him by unlawful means, whether or not it is the predominant intention of the defendant to do so'.

3.100 A conspiracy to commit a crime or a tort is clearly included within this class, but it is uncertain whether conspiracy to breach a contract is also included (*Rookes v Barnard* [1964] 2 AC 1129, 1210 *per* Lord Devlin). While there must be an agreement of some kind, action in pursuit of the compact need only be taken by one conspirator. The second part of the definition, the tort known as unlawful means conspiracy, has occasioned the most difficulty, since it may render unlawful acts done by two or more people which would have been lawful when performed by an individual. Parliament has therefore considered it necessary to create an immunity in respect of this tort, though as with the other torts the immunity can be lost in certain circumstances.

The tort of conspiracy may exist in two forms. Conspiracy to injure consists   **3.101**
of the combination of two or more to harm the claimant where the predominant purpose of the defendants is to inflict harm on the claimant as opposed to furthering their own legitimate purpose. Conspiracy to use unlawful means consists in the combination of two or more to harm the claimant by the use of conduct that is inherently unlawful, whatever the purpose of the combination. The Court of Appeal decided that it was always necessary to show that the defendants acted with the predominant purpose of harming the claimant in *Metall und Rohstoff AG v Donaldson Lufkin & Jenrette Inc* [1990] 1 QB 391 and, if this approach had been allowed to stand, unlawful means conspiracy would thereby have been abolished as a separate tort. However, the House of Lords restored the position in *Lonrho plc v Fayed* [1991] 3 All ER 303 where it was held that intent must be distinguished from purpose so that if the defendants intentionally used unlawful means to harm the claimant the tort was committed whatever their motive, but if the defendants intentionally inflicted harm by means lawful in themselves the tort was committed if they acted with the predominant motive or purpose of inflicting harm. There are thus two species of the same tort.

The leading case is *Quinn v Leathem* [1901] AC 495, although debate still   **3.102**
rages about the significance and the distinction between it and *Allen v Flood* [1898] AC 1. In the *Quinn* case officials of the appellant union asked the respondent to dismiss a non-unionist and on his refusal to do so told him that an important customer would be warned to cease dealing with him under threat of a strike at his workplace if he denied the request. A jury found that the union's motive was to injure the respondent rather than to promote the interests of the union. On appeal, five members of the House of Lords decided that this was actionable as a tortious conspiracy notwithstanding that the defendants had not committed any otherwise unlawful act in inducing the customer not to trade with the claimant.

The apparent conflict between *Quinn v Leathem* and *Allen v Flood* has   **3.103**
already been mentioned. In the *Allen* case (which lacked the element of combination) the defendant union official threatened to call out on strike boilermakers employed by the claimant unless the shipwrights then employed by the same employer were dismissed. This mere interference with

employment was not tortious and just the addition of an element of spite or malice did not change the position, since conduct not otherwise tortious did not become so because it was done with the deliberate intention to cause economic harm to others.

3.104 The cases have been reconciled on the basis that the *Quinn* case involved conspiracy, to which different considerations apply (see *Ware and De Freville Ltd v Motor Trade Association* [1921] 3 KB 40). The constituents of the tort of conspiracy not involving unlawful means were delineated by the House of Lords in *Mogul Steamship Co. v McGregor, Cow & Co.* [1892] AC 25, as follows:

(1) combination of two persons;
(2) intentionally causing loss; with
(3) the predominant purpose to injure rather than to further a legitimate interest.

(1) Combination

There must be an actual agreement between the parties and not merely coincidental acts on their part. One party can, however, be liable in conspiracy although he himself could not carry out the unlawful act (*Rookes v Barnard* (above) where the union official could not break his contract as he was not employed by BOAC but he could be liable in conspiracy).

(2) Intentionally causing loss

Intent to injure the claimant is a necessary element in conspiracy. In *Lonrho Ltd v Shell Petroleum Co. Ltd (No. 2)* [1982] AC 173 the House of Lords assumed that the defendants were acting to further their business interests. Sanctions were imposed by the United Kingdom Government against Rhodesia when it unilaterally declared independence. The defendants combined to supply oil to Southern Rhodesia in breach of the Southern Rhodesia (Petroleum) Order. The claimant alleged that this conspiracy had caused him loss since it had extended the sanctions period against Rhodesia thus preventing the claimant from supplying oil via its pipeline. Lord Diplock stated that he was against extending the scope of the civil tort of conspiracy beyond acts done in execution of an agreement entered into by two or more persons for the purpose not of protecting their own interests but of injuring the interests of the claimant.

The claimant must show some loss in order to have a cause of action.

(3) The predominant purpose to injure rather than further a legitimate interest

As with most other economic torts, a justification defence may be asserted for conspiracy. Traders often attempt to create a monopoly and this has received the blessing of the common law (see *Sorrell v Smith* [1925] AC 700). In the *Mogul Steamship* case, it was said that 'otherwise most commercial men would be at risk of legal liability in their legitimate trading practices and competition will be dead'. Yet *Quinn v Leathem* appeared to decide that different rules pertain to trade unions. However, in *Crofter Handwoven Harris Tweed Co. v Veitch* [1942] AC 435, the House of Lords held that trade union objectives can be a legitimate justification. The Transport and General Workers Union combined with Stornaway dockers to prevent yarn imports from the Scottish mainland in order to achieve a closed shop. The House of Lords thought that this was justified since the predominant motive was the promotion of the combiners' legitimate interest in that they wished to secure the elimination of price competition which was holding down wages at the largest spinning mill where their members were employed. Lord Wright said that: 'The true contrast is between the case where the object is the legitimate benefit of the combiners and the case where the object is deliberate damage without any such just cause.'

Courts have held the following combinations legitimate: **3.105**

(1) attempts to force an employer into refusing to employ trade unionists (*Thomson (D.C.) & Co. v Deakin* [1952] Ch 646);
(2) a campaign against a colour bar (*Scala Ballroom (Wolverhampton) Ltd v Ratcliffe* [1958] 3 All ER 220);
(3) the enforcement of a closed shop (*Reynolds v Shipping Federation Ltd* [1924] 1 Ch 28).

However, no justification existed in *Huntley v Thornton* [1957] 1 All ER 234, where members of a district union committee expelled the claimant, a fellow member, because of a personal grudge and a desire for vengeance.

In the case of a conspiracy to use unlawful means the defendants must   **3.106** combine to do some act which is itself unlawful in order to harm the claimant; intent to harm the claimant is necessary though purpose is irrelevant (*Lonrho plc v Fayed* [1992] 1 AC 448; [1991] 3 All ER 303).

The conspiracy will not be actionable unless actual loss has been caused to the claimant (see *Lonrho plc v Fayed (No. 5)* [1994] 1 All ER 188).

3.107 Lastly we must consider statutory immunity. By TULR(C)A 1992, s 219(2) a combination to do any act in contemplation or furtherance of a trade dispute is not actionable in tort if the act is one which, if done by one person alone, would not be actionable. The immunity will apply, then, to conspiracy to do an unlawful act by lawful means but, as we have seen, not to the 'unlawful means' form of conspiracy.

L. Suing a Trade Union

Historical development

3.108 Unions were originally considered to be protected from suit because they were merely unincorporated associations. The vital decision to the contrary in *Taff Vale Ry. Co. v Amalgamated Society of Railway Servants* [1901] AC 426 revolutionized the legal position and gave impetus to the progress of the then infant Labour Party. The Liberal Government reversed the position by the Trade Disputes Act 1906, s 4, so that unions could not be sued at all. This remained the position until the Industrial Relations Act 1971, when unions were appropriate defendants in claims of unfair industrial practices. Section 14 of the Trade Union and Labour Relations Act 1974 turned the clock back to 1906, so that trade unions had immunity from suit save that unions could now be sued for breach of duty resulting only in personal injury and in respect of property.

3.109 Section 15 of the Employment Act 1982 was probably the single most important feature of the legislation of the Thatcher Government since it opened the door to mulcting unions in damages where industrial action has been authorized or endorsed and not thereafter repudiated by the union hierarchy. The rationale expressed in the Green Paper, *Trade Union Immunities* (Cmnd 8218, 1981) for this reform (para 112) was that: 'If trade unions were made financially responsible . . . they could be expected in their own interest to exert greater internal discipline over their officials and members, particularly in respect of unofficial action.' Unions may now be sued like any other person or company even though the union is not an incorporated association (see *Electrical, Electronic, Telecommunication and Plumbing Union v Times Newspapers Ltd* [1980] 3 WLR 98). The only major difference between the position of other defendants and a trade union is that the amount to be recovered is limited (see para 14.03).

Union branches

There is more doubt over the amenability of a trade union branch to suit.   **3.110**
This arose directly in *News Group Newspapers Ltd v SOGAT 82 and others*
[1986] IRLR 337, since the claimants sued three London branches of
SOGAT which it claimed were organizing picketing at the Wapping,
Bouverie Street, and Grays Inn Road premises of News International. The
London Clerical Branch of SOGAT appeared to have argued in the sequestration case of *News Group Newspapers Ltd v SOGAT 82* [1986] IRLR 227
that it was *not* a trade union. The claimants thus sought to sue the three
branches by way of suing the branch secretary as representing the branch and
relying on the Rules of the Supreme Court, Order 15, r 12 (now CPR 19),
on representative actions that: 'Where numerous persons have the same
interest in any proceedings . . . the proceedings may be begun, and, unless
the Court otherwise orders, continued, by or against any one or more of
them as representing all or as representing all except one or more of them'.

Stuart-Smith J did not consider that this was a proper approach to suing a
branch of SOGAT. The members of the branches would have different
defences as only a small proportion of the branch involved in picketing and
demonstrating outside the Wapping Factory of News International plc and
thus could not have the same interest in the proceedings (see, eg, *London
Association for Protection of Trade v Greenlands Ltd* [1916] 2 AC 15, *Roche v
Sherrington* [1982] 1 WLR 599, *United Kingdom Nirex Ltd v Barton, The
Times* 14 October 1986, cf. *Michaels (M.) (Furriers) Ltd v Askew* (1983) 127
SJ 597, CA, see para 11.59). On the other hand, the branches fell within the
definition of trade union in TULRA 1974, s 28(1) (now the Trade Union
and Labour Relations (Consolidation) Act 1992, s 1) and were thus themselves capable of suing and being sued in their own right. The definition was
an organization consisting 'wholly or mainly of workers of one or more
descriptions and is an organization whose principal purposes include the
regulation of relations between workers of that description . . . and employers or employers' associations'.

Stuart-Smith J relied as authority for this approach on the case of *British
Association of Advisers and Lecturers in Physical Education v National Union of
Teachers* [1986] IRLR 497. There the Court of Appeal held that although an
association, because of its size and constitution, could not carry out all the
functions of a bigger trade union, this did not mean that it did not fall within

the statutory definition. The association did not have to demonstrate any particular capacity or effectiveness or frequency of intervention in its role of regulating the relations between its members and their employers. The case concerned an attempt to strike out the claimant as a party to the litigation since it was an unincorporated association and could not sue in its own name. This plea succeeded before Sir Neil Lawson, but his decision was overturned on appeal.

Thus, in *News Group Newspapers Ltd v SOGAT 82 and others* [1986] IRLR 337, the representative claims against the union branches were all struck out. The consequence is that in another case, the branch funds might be separately sequestrated if branch officers acted in breach of a court order. Moreover, the branch would have to hold a ballot under the Trade Union and Labour Relations (Consolidation) Act 1992 just as any other trade union if it is to have immunity in tort. It should, however, be noted that the same result would not necessarily be reached in relation to other trade union branches where the constitutional structure is quite different from that of SOGAT.

Vicarious liability

3.111　Even when a union itself has been amenable to suit, the liability of a union for the acts of its shop stewards and other officials has been a vexed issue in industrial dispute cases, especially because unions have frequently claimed that they are not supporting action whilst giving 'nod and wink' support. It is necessary to consider the position at common law before reviewing the statutory code for the economic torts laid down in the 1992 Act. Questions of liability or motions for contempt will be considered last.

Common law

3.112　There was very little discussion of the liability of a trade union for its members before the Industrial Relations Act 1971, but development of principle was necessitated by the considerable amount of litigation against trade unions under that statute. The leading case at common law (that is, not under the current statutory codification) is *Heaton's Transport (St. Helen's) Ltd v Transport and General Workers' Union* [1973] AC 15. A committee of shop stewards at Liverpool mounted a campaign against container traffic and, in particular, blacked lorries of the employers. Two of the companies blacked complained under the Industrial Relations Act 1971 of unfair industrial practices by the union. A similar application was made in regard to action at Hull docks. The union did not appear in court until it had been fined £5,000 and £50,000 for disobedience to injunctions. It then argued that the union was not liable for its shop stewards' actions either on the unfair industrial practices for which it was found liable, or in contempt of the restraining orders made.

The House of Lords decided that in accordance with the rules and practice of the union, the shop stewards had implied authority to act in the interests of the members they represented and, in particular, to defend and improve their rates of pay and working conditions, which they might do by negotiation or by industrial action at the relevant place of work. They were not, however, authorized to do any act outside union rules or policy. In this regard, it made no difference whether the stewards were treated as employees or agents of the union. Their Lordships held that the union could, however, repudiate the action of its shop stewards. Lord Wilberforce said:

> To be effective in law a withdrawal or curtailment of any existing actual authority of an agent must be communicated by the principal to the agent in terms which the agent would necessarily understand forbidding him to do that which he had previously been authorised to do on the principal's behalf.

The evidence did not show that this had been done. It is, however, somewhat difficult to detect an overall principle in this case, and, in particular, whether the possibility of repudiation exists outside the special area of contempt proceedings.

The issue soon came again before the House of Lords in *General Aviation Services (UK) v Transport and General Workers' Union* [1985] ICR 615, which was decided in 1974. An unofficial shopstewards' liaison committee organized blacking at London Airport of ground handling services provided by a private company. Their action was contrary to union policy, as various national officials had explained to them. The House of Lords decided on these facts that the union had not given express or implied authority for this course of action and so was not liable. Lord Wilberforce considered that a legalistic analysis fitted to identifying responsibility in a limited company was not appropriate to the situation of trade unions. Rather, the question must be determined on the basis of custom and practice, with attention being paid to all the evidence.

3.113

Clearly, the union is not liable for its members for all of their acts as

3.114

members. That would open the floodgates of liability. This was expressed in *United Kingdom Association of Professional Engineers and Newell v Amalgamated Union of Engineering Workers* [1972] ICR 151, where the court went on to say that: 'equally, no member is personally responsible for the action of a union just because he is a member . . . a trade union can only act through its officials and it is responsible for their actions so long as they are acting within the apparent scope of their authority'.

3.115 In *Thomas v National Union of Mineworkers (South Wales Area)* [1985] IRLR 136, the South Wales Area of the NUM was held responsible through its constituent lodges for colliery gate mass picketing, since the officers of lodges played a significant part in organizing the pickets even though the attendance on particular occasions was spontaneous. There was, moreover, no evidence that lodge officials had ever discouraged such attendance. The ordinary principles of common law vicarious liability set out in the *Heaton's Transport* case applied, since the torts committed were not the economic torts covered by the Employment Act 1982. The lodges were acting on behalf of the South Wales union for the purpose of enabling the union to pursue its object of advancing the interests of its members. The national union was not, however, liable, since it had no control over the South Wales picketing.

3.116 The issue was also vital in *News Group Newspapers Ltd v SOGAT 82 and others* [1986] IRLR 337 (for the facts, see para 8.24), where the union defendants strongly denied that they were liable for pickets and demonstrations which had degenerated into violence and obstructions, since the leadership of the respective unions had at all times insisted that all actions should be peaceful. Again the statutory code was irrelevant, since the tort committed was a species of nuisance. The judge decided that they were not liable simply because they organized a march or picketing during the course of which tortious acts were committed by third parties, even though such acts could be foreseen by reason of the previous experience of mass pickets. Stuart-Smith J, however, applied the general nuisance principles enunciated in *Sedleigh-Denfield v O'Callaghan* [1940] AC 880, that a person 'continues' a nuisance, here obstruction of the highway, 'if with knowledge or presumed knowledge of its existence he fails to take any reasonable means to bring it to an end though with ample time to do so'. On the facts, the conduct of the pickets had been 'the same virtually day after day since the start of the dispute; it must be well known to those concerned in the defendant unions'. At Wapping, 'although it is not the invariable pattern, violence and nuisance have occurred with sufficient frequency, particularly on those occasions when a large number of people attend and there is no proper control, for it to amount to a detectable pattern'. The unions could, according to the judge, have exercised substantial control over their members, but had not done so. No one had, for example, been disciplined for breaches of union rules on the picket line. The burden is thus on the trade union to take every practicable step to ensure that the picketing is 'peaceful and lawful'. If, despite taking all such steps, a union is unable to prevent unlawfulness on the picket line, it may have to revoke any instructions it has given to its members to picket, or be faced with liability.

Pickets are frequently joined by sympathizers, who are not involved in the trade dispute at all. Those sympathizers may commit unlawful acts. If the incident is a one-off, albeit foreseeable, then the union will not be liable providing it maintains a policy of lawful, peaceful picketing. If, however, the activities occur again and again, the union may be liable on the basis of implied authorization of the acts or continuance thereof.   **3.117**

The statutory code

Section 20 of the Trade Union and Labour Relations (Consolidation) Act 1992 provides a statutory codification of the vicarious liability of trade unions for their officials but it applies only to liability for the torts of inducing breach of contract, intimidation and conspiracy.   **3.118**

The union will be liable only if the act is authorized from the beginning or endorsed at a later stage by: **3.119**

(1) The principal executive committee, however so called, provided that such committee was acting within the union rules.
(2) Any other person empowered by the rules to authorize such acts. In this context, the word 'rules' means the express rule book or any other written rule which is a term of the contract between the member and the union.
(3) The president or general secretary of the union, or its equivalent, whether or not either has or has not express power to so authorize action under the rules.
(4) Any committee of which an employed official regularly reports save where that official or committee is prevented by the union rules from authorizing or endorsing such action. This is in most cases likely to refer to a district or branch committee.

(5) An employed official of the union. 'Official' is defined in the Trade Union and Labour Relations (Consolidation) Act 1992, s 20(2)(c) as including workplace and union officers, so that the use of the word 'employed' makes clear that only the latter are included.

3.120 In *Express and Star Ltd v National Graphical Association (1982)* [1985] IRLR 455, [1986] IRLR 222 CA, which has subjected the section to the closest scrutiny, the Court of Appeal ultimately decided that the provision was not appropriate since the matter at issue was contempt, which was not a 'proceeding in tort'. The facts do, however, offer a textbook example of the issues which may arise.

In this case, NGA members were called out on strike at the Express and Star print works in a dispute over the introduction of new printing technology. Several companies which had dealings with the plaintiff were 'blacked'. The NGA at first threatened disciplinary action against any member who ignored its instructions but later sent a circular to all branches withdrawing instructions to strike. No ballot had been held and the plaintiff secured an injunction on this ground against the union. The employer then complained of four breaches of the injunction and the judge found that two cases were proved. The important feature of the case for present purposes lies in the way in which the judge dealt with the argument of the union that it did not authorize or endorse the action in breach of the order.

In the first incident, the evidence showed that the West Midlands branch secretary had accosted five typesetters employed by the company which printed weekly newspapers for the plaintiff, and persuaded three to break their contracts of employment by means of an offer to pay them £160 per week until the men found other jobs and the threat of loss of their union cards if they continued to work.

In the second incident, the judge held that a national officer and national council member had let it be known at a meeting of members in north Wales that the union wanted the blacking to continue and that there had been 'nods and winks' given to members that it should do so.

The union argued at first instance that what was then the Employment Act 1982, s 15 now TULR(C)A, s 20 did not apply, since by subsection 2 it concerned only 'proceedings in tort'. Skinner J decided that the contempt application was merely a step in the original tort proceedings.

On this definition, the branch secretary and two national officers were all employed officials who had authorized the breaches of the injunction, so that the union was prima facie liable for their actions. The union then claimed that they could not be 'responsible persons' since none of the acts complained of was authorized by the union's rules. The judge did not think that this was the correct test. Rather, the court should ask whether the employed officials *were prevented by* the rules from authorizing the acts in question, and there was in fact nothing to prevent them.

Demonstrating the complexity of the definition, the judge then had to consider whether the acts had been repudiated. He thought not, since the union had never accepted its responsibility for the acts done. In the case of the national officer who had attended the meeting in north Wales, the general secretary of the union had written to that national officer saying that if in support of the branch secretary he had infringed an order of the court, the general secretary repudiated any authorization or endorsement which might have been given. The judge could not, however, characterize this as a repudiation but rather as a conditional and rather half-hearted reprimand. A true repudiation must involve an open disavowal of the acts of the official concerned and must at the very least be communicated to the victims of the tort in question. Here, it had been communicated to the claimants only in an affidavit in the contempt proceedings. This could not be characterized 'as soon as reasonably practicable' after the authorization had come to the general secretary's knowledge within the language of the statute. Altogether, there were too many nods and winks from the union's head office for the action to have been wholly repudiated. The union was, in summary, 'paying lip service to the terms of the order but plainly breaking it'. The judge thought it was 'inconceivable that they would do that unless encouraged to do so from above'. **3.121**

The Court of Appeal did not agree that the then current EA 1982, s 15 applied to the case since contempt proceedings were not 'proceedings in tort . . . brought against [the] trade union . . . for the purposes of determining in those proceedings whether the union is liable in respect of the action in question . . .', which governed the applicability of the section. Where there are contempt proceedings for a wilful contumacious contempt of a court order, the sole question is whether the alleged contemnor has done the acts prohibited by the words of the court order. Their Lordships decided that on the facts, Skinner J had reached the correct conclusion. **3.122**

M. Intra-union Actions

Introduction

3.123 There have been a number of actions against the trade union hierarchy for calling strikes in breach of the unions' own rules. Such litigation came to the fore during the miners' strike of 1984–85, based on the common law principle that the union rule book constitutes a contract between the union and each member. In that strike member–union litigation had more impact than employer–union action. The central issues in such cases are:

(1) when strike action is official; and
(2) the extent to which one union may give another funds to support a dispute; and
(3) whether a union can indemnify pickets against fines.

When is strike action official: ultra vires activities

3.124 Union leaders must not breach the union rules in calling individual action. In *Clarke v Chadburn* [1984] IRLR 350 an injunction was granted to working miners to the effect that the call by the National Union of Mineworkers of a national strike without holding a ballot was in breach of r 43 of the union's rules. The judge held on an application for interim relief that the injustice which would be caused to the union if an injunction were granted was less than that which would be caused to the working miners if the order sought were not given. Without the order the claimants would be subject to all the daily unpleasantness of crossing picket lines which were stated to be 'official'. There was the risk of reproaches and insults and of disciplinary action, from which His Lordship thought it proper to protect the claimants, since the strike was not properly called pursuant to the union's own rule book.

3.125 *Taylor v National Union of Mineworkers (Derbyshire Area)* [1985] IRLR 99 was another action in the miners' strike saga of litigation. The claimants applied *ex parte* for an order restraining the Derbyshire union and its officers from using or procuring or permitting the use of the Derbyshire union funds in support of the strike. Some £1.7 million had allegedly been spent in its support as at the date of the action. An injunction was granted as sought, since the rules of the union expressly provided for allowances to be made to members but only on an official strike called in accordance with the union rules. It was thus held to be impossible to imply a power for the officers to make a precisely similar allowance to members on unofficial strike. Whatever was custom and practice in the union could not conflict with the express rules as properly interpreted.

The rule in *Foss v Harbottle* (1843) 2 Hare 461 (to the broad effect that an **3.126** action cannot be brought by shareholders in a company to pursue wrongs done to the company but only by the company itself) does not prevent an action against individual union officers where the allegation is made that funds have been applied in ultra vires activities. Such acts cannot be ratified by a majority of the membership. In *Taylor v NUM (Derbyshire Area)* (above), the judge decided that 'any member is entitled to insist that the funds of the body be used exclusively in furtherance of its objects, those objects to be inferred from its constitution' (para 15) (see also *Howden v Yorkshire Miners' Association* [1903] 1 KB 308, *Edwards v Halliwell* [1950] 2 All ER 1064).

Union officers who sanction payments to unofficial strikers where such **3.127** payments are in breach of union rules are liable to reimburse the union on the basis of the fiduciary duty which they each owe to the union. An application for summary judgment was, however, inappropriate in such an action in *Taylor v NUM (Derbyshire Area)* (above), since the majority of members could resolve to take no action to remedy the wrong done to the union. In reaching this decision, Vinelott J bore in mind that 85 per cent of the membership had obeyed the call to go on strike and there was no question that the payments had been made in conscious breach of the rules or for the personal private benefit of the union officials. He would thus not make the order sought also in the hope that 'the members will be able to work together in the future for their common benefit within the rules of the union'.

Support by one union for another in dispute

One union may also be restrained from going to the aid of another which is **3.128** pursuing an unlawful strike. In *Hopkins v National Union of Seamen* [1985] IRLR 157 the NUS decided to support the National Union of Mineworkers during the miners' strike. The claimant, a member of the NUS, sought to restrain the use of its funds for such purpose on the grounds, inter alia, that the strike was not a valid national stoppage under the rules of the NUM, and thus any payment in its support was ultra vires the NUS rules. Scott J did not consider that the distinction between an official and unofficial strike by another union's rule book provided a proper yardstick for deciding whether payments from NUS funds were in pursuance of the objects of the NUS. Therefore, that union might properly form the view that the alleviation of hardship and distress amongst the families of striking miners was something which would further the interests of its own rules in enhancing the possibility that more collieries would stay open than otherwise and that there would be more coal for transport around the coast. There was, however, no power to raise a weekly levy here, since this was in effect an increase of contributions required from members which could be done only by the biennial or special general meeting rather than by executive action. The funding was thus ultra vires, and in any event would be worthless since the NUM was in the hands of the sequestrators at the time.

Indemnifying pickets

3.129 Another controversial issue is the extent to which the union may indemnify picketing expenses and fines from union funds. This issue first surfaced in *Drake v Morgan* [1978] ICR 56. In pursuance of a journalists' strike, many National Union of Journalists members were charged with offences connected with picketing, and some were fined. The NUJ National Executive Committee passed a resolution that the union would indemnify members against the fines so imposed save for offences involving physical violence. Forbes J refused an application for an injunction to restrain the union on the basis that the resolution had been passed *after* the offences had been committed and therefore was not an indemnity accorded to members who might commit offences. The judge considered that different considerations might, however, arise if continued resolutions authorizing the expenditure of funds might lead to an expectation that a union would indemnify its members against the consequences of future offences.

3.130 A similar issue arose in the South Wales miners' picketing case, *Thomas v National Union of Mineworkers (South Wales Area)* [1985] IRLR 136 (see para 8.29). Scott J there decided that it would be ultra vires the rules of the union for its officers to embark upon and finance a form of picketing which would be bound to involve criminal acts. It was not unlawful, however, if the picketing was merely capable of involving criminal acts. The instant resolution that 'any subsequent fines would be paid by the union' was void, but if the union wished to relieve members arrested for picket line offences in individual cases, it could do so. The only essential criterion was that such a resolution was in the interests of the union and its membership as a whole.

Statutory action

As we have already seen, under the Trade Union and Labour Relations (Consolidation) Act 1992, s 62 an individual member of the union may seek to restrain his union acting without a ballot. There is an individual action where the members of the union including himself are likely to or have been induced to take part or continue to take part in industrial action without the support of a ballot. This may be the failure to carry out a ballot at all or to hold a ballot fully in accordance with the relevant provisions of TULR(C)A described in Chapter 5.

3.131

The court may on such an application 'make such order as it thinks appropriate for requiring the person by whom the act of inducement has been or is likely to be done to take steps to ensure that no or no further act is done by him to induce any person to take part or continue to take part in the industrial action and that no person engages in conduct after the making of the order in such industrial action' (s 62(3)). This may include the granting of an interim injunction (s 62(4)).

4

THE TRADE DISPUTE IMMUNITY

A. History

The trade dispute immunity, or 'golden formula' as it is commonly known, **4.01**
dates back to the Conspiracy and Protection of Property Act 1875, which
gave certain immunities from action in respect of picketing. However, it was
the Trade Disputes Act 1906, which followed on from the seminal decisions
in *Taff Vale Ry Co. v Amalgamated Society of Railway Servants* [1901] AC 426
and *Quinn v Leathem* [1901] AC 495, that extended immunity to strike
action. On the other hand, it restricted the *proper* range of subject-matter to
disputes 'connected with the employment or non-employment, terms of

employment or conditions of labour of any person'. The Industrial Relations Act 1971 introduced the new name of 'industrial dispute' but the concept was essentially the same. The Labour Government extended the scope of the immunity to take account of the wider interests of trade unions, and the extended range of topics for collective bargaining.

This reached its high point in the Trade Union and Labour Relations Act 1974, but the immunities were then seriously eroded by the Thatcher Government's Employment Acts 1980 and 1982. The 1982 Act provided that the *dispute* must relate *'wholly* or mainly' to the issues specified as *being* legitimate trade disputes whereas the earlier formulation had required that it be 'connected with' one or more of them.

The Trade Union Act 1984 further restricted immunity by providing that an official strike is only immune if a ballot has been held in full conformity with Part II of the statute.

It is vital that there should be immunity in order to implement a freedom to strike, which is necessary in a free society. In the Green Paper, *Trade Union Immunities* (Cmnd 8218, 1981) para 382, the Conservative Government explained that:

> . . . immunities are not simply legal provisions which could be abolished outright. Without some legal protection—however circumscribed—it would be impossible for trade unions or individuals to organize industrial action without risk of civil proceedings and the ultimate safeguard of a collective withdrawal of labour would be effectively nullified.

Nevertheless, the wording of the immunity for trade disputes has been one of the shuttlecocks of British politics. The judges' interpretation of the provisions has, according to A.W.R. Carothers, *Collective Bargaining Law in Canada*, p 57, exhibited 'a see-saw vendetta between the courts and the legislature'. The law is highly complex and the judges have been unwilling to develop a high degree of rationalism. There are many pitfalls for the trade unionist especially in relation to the several torts not clothed with immunity and awaiting development. Sir John Donaldson in *Merkur Island Shipping Corp. v Laughton* [1983] 2 AC 570, recognized the current chaotic position and considered that since this legislation affected the man on the shopfloor it should be expressed in clear and simple English, As Elias, Napier and Wallington put it (*Labour Law*, Butterworths, 1980, p 210):

> Any account of the law cannot ignore the fact that its present shape has been

the result of a game of cat and mouse, played between the courts and legislature for more than a century, in which Parliament has consistently tried to maximise and the courts almost as consistently to minimise the extent to which the taking of industrial action attracts legal sanctions.

The Blair Government has not changed the reforms that were put in place by the Conservative Governments so that, although there has been some 'tinkering' with other areas, especially ballots and dismissals during industrial action, the immunity remains essentially the same as that enacted by the 1982 Act.

The immunity is currently found in the Trade Union and Labour Relations **4.02** (Consolidation) Act 1992, s 219, as amended, which provides:

(1) An act done by a person in contemplation or furtherance or a trade dispute shall not be actionable in tort on the ground only—
   (a) that it induces another person to break a contract or interferes with its performance; or
   (b) that it consists in his threatening that a contract (whether one to which he is a party or not) will be broken or its performance interfered with, or that he will induce another person to break a contract or to interfere with its performance.
(2) An agreement or combination by two or more persons to do or procure the doing of an act in contemplation or furtherance of a trade dispute is not actionable in tort if the act is one which if done without any such agreement or combination would not be actionable in tort.
(3) Nothing in subsections (1) and (2) prevents an act done in the course of picketing from being actionable in tort unless it is done in the course of attendance declared lawful by section 220 (peaceful picketing).
(4) Subsections (1) and (2) have effect subject to sections 222 to 225 (action excluded from protection) and to sections 226 (requirements of ballot before action by trade union) and 234A (requirement of notice to employer of industrial action); and in those sections 'not protected' means excluded from the protection afforded by this section or, where the expression is used with reference to a particular person excluded from that protection as respects that person.

Person

A person who does an act in contemplation or furtherance of a trade **4.03** dispute is protected. It does not matter whether such a person is an officer of the union or not. The law draws no distinction between official and unofficial action in this respect, although the responsibility of the union for it differs.

The protected torts

4.04   The torts protected against are:

(1) Inducement of breach of contract (s 219(1)(a)). This will cover inducement to breach a contract of employment or a commercial contract.

(2) Interference with contract or inducement of such interference
(s 219(1)(a)).

(3) Intimidation (s 219(1)(b)). This will cover threats to induce a breach of
contract or to interfere with contract.

(4) Conspiracy (s 219(2)). Conspiracy to do an act in contemplation or
furtherance of a trade dispute is not actionable if the act would not be
actionable when done by an individual. Acts protected under s 219(1) will
not be rendered actionable if there is a conspiracy to commit such an act.

The direct and indirect forms of the torts will be covered. However, indirect
procurement or interference is likely to be secondary action and deprived of
protection by s 219(4) and 224(1) (see further on secondary action pp
96–100).

4.05   Before considering the scope of the immunity it is necessary to review
precisely the constituents of a 'trade dispute'. We will consider each of the
following in turn:

• the meaning of dispute;
• contemplation or furtherance of a dispute;
• the parties to the dispute;
• the meaning of trade dispute.

B. Meaning of Dispute

4.06   The concept of a 'dispute' in the statute is neither self-reflective nor self-
fulfilling. The union cannot argue that the strike itself *is* the dispute. Rather
the dispute must arise from some grievance or other and, in most cases
within the trade dispute formula, the grievance should be brought to the
attention of the employer who should have some prospect of redressing the
grievance. As Lord Weddurburn comments (op. cit. p 565): 'A union official
has never been permitted to prepare for and create his own dispute and then
contemplate or further it.'

BBC v Hearn [1977] IRLR 273 illustrates that trade unions should be care-   **4.07**
ful about the way in which they formulate their grievance in order for it to
be considered as a dispute. BBC technicians who were members of the
Association of Broadcasting Staffs refused to participate in transmitting the
F A Cup Final to South Africa because of its apartheid policy. The
Association argued that they were locked in dispute with the BBC about
whether there should be a condition in the terms of service that they should
not be compelled to transmit broadcasts to South Africa whilst it had offensive racial laws. Lord Denning MR, however, described the unions' action as
merely 'coercive interference unrelated to a trade dispute'. There had been no
previous suggestion by the union that such a term should be incorporated
into the employment contract of its members. If there had been, the immunity would have come into play. As the then Master of the Rolls said, the
Association would have had immunity if it had only said: 'We would like you
to consider putting a clause in the contract by which our members are not
bound to take part in any broadcast which may be viewed in South Africa'.

Lord Diplock has, however, confirmed in *NWL Ltd v Woods* [1979] 3 All ER   **4.08**
614, 633–4 that the *ratio* of the *Hearn* case will be strictly construed. Moreover,
in *Mercury Communications Ltd v Scott-Garner* [1983] 3 WLR 914, para 60)
May LJ said: 'Almost *ex hypothesi* there will always be at least one element of
coercive interference in any industrial dispute'. Lord Denning's description of
the conflict as 'coercive interference', therefore, should not be taken too liter-
ally lest it unduly reduces the definition of dispute and the scope of the immunity. It may not be followed in another case.

C. Contemplation or Furtherance of a Dispute

TULR(C)A 1992, s 219 extends to acts done in contemplation of a trade   **4.09**
dispute, that is, before the actual dispute has become a live issue between
employer and employee. In *Beetham v Trinidad Cement Ltd* [1960] AC 132,
Lord Denning MR considered that a dispute 'exists whenever a difference
exists, and a difference exists long before the parties have become locked in
combat. . . . It is sufficient that they should be sparring for an opening'. (See
also *Health Computing Ltd v Meek* [1981] ICR 24.)

The word 'contemplation' has caused some difficulty. Lord Loreburn in   **4.10**
Conway v Wade [1909] AC 506, 509 thought it meant that:

either a dispute is imminent and the act is done in expectation of and with a view to it, or that the dispute is already existing and the act is done in support of one side to it. There must be a dispute, however its subject-matter may be defined, and a mere personal quarrel or a grumbling or an agitation will not suffice. It must be something definite and of real substance.

4.11 In the same case, Lord Simon said that: 'To contemplate a trade dispute is to have before the mind some objective event or situation, but it does not mean a contemplation, meditation or resolve in regard to something as yet wholly within the mind of a subjective character.' In *Bent's Brewery Co. Ltd v Hogan* [1945] 2 All ER 570, the union sent a questionnaire to union members in which they were asked to reveal details of the income of the public houses in which they worked. The company regarded this information as confidential but this in itself did not mean that a dispute had come into existence. Although the results of the questionnaire were to be used in the submission of a pay claim, as yet it could only relate to the *possibility* of a dispute at some future time. The action of the union thus had no immunity within the terms of the golden formula (see also *Health Computing Ltd v Meek* [1980] IRLR 437; [1981] ICR 24).

4.12 Nor will there be any protection for acts carried out *after* the dispute has been concluded. In *Stewart v Amalgamated Union of Engineering Workers (Engineering Section)* [1973] ICR 128, following the settlement of a dispute, the trade union blacked the vehicles of the claimant haulage firm as a punishment for the claimant's stance during the strike. It was held that the union's action was not in furtherance of a trade dispute since the dispute was over when the blacking was imposed.

4.13 However, a trade dispute may exist where the employer concedes to the demands of the union, thereby making an escalation of industrial action by the union unnecessary. This rule can be found in TULR(C)A 1992, s 244(4) which provides:

> an act, threat or demand done or made by one person or organisation against another which, if resisted, would have led to a trade dispute with that other, shall be treated as being done or made in contemplation of a trade dispute with that other, notwithstanding that because that other submits to the act or threat or accedes to the demand no dispute arises.

This subsection reverses the decision of the Court of Appeal in *Cory Lighterage Ltd v Transport and General Workers' Union* [1973] ICR 339 where Buckley LJ said that: 'If someone threatens me with physical injury unless I hand over my wallet and I hand it over without demur no one could sensibly say there has been any dispute about my handing over the wallet'. It was stated in *London Borough of Newham v National and Local Government Officers' Association* [1993] IRLR 83 that a dispute continues as long as one side honestly and genuinely believes that there is still a dispute. However, the court in any event found that there was a 'real and live dispute' and it is difficult to see how the above case can be reconciled with the House of Lords decision in *Express Newspapers Ltd v McShane and Ashton* [1980] AC 672. The test of whether there is a 'dispute' is objective, not subjective as the *Newham* case appears to state. The test whether an act is 'in contemplation or furtherance' of a trade dispute is subjective, though, as Lord Wilberforce stated, there are objective and subjective elements:

> there is an objective element in 'furtherance' which the court must appraise. It should do so in the light of the evidence, giving due weight but not conclusive force to the genuine belief of those who initiate the action in question. On the facts of this case and on the evidence available, the action taken (viz of blacking the PA copy) was reasonably capable of furthering the trade dispute.

Whilst the test of whether there is a trade dispute is an objective one, the test **4.14** for the party claiming immunity to show that they are acting in contemplation of furtherance of a dispute is subjective. The party must honestly and genuinely think that they are helping one side in a trade dispute which concerns the matters listed in s 244. The House of Lords confirmed this approach in *Express Newspapers Ltd v McShane and Ashton* (*supra*). In *Duport Steels & Ors v Sirs & Ors* [1980] ICR 161 a strike was called over a pay dispute with the British Steel Corporation. This was a trade dispute. However, the union also called out members employed by the private sector steel companies with whom there was no dispute. It was held that this was an act taken with the genuine purpose of furthering the trade dispute with the British Steel Corporation as the union had an honest belief that the shortage of steel would put pressure on the Government to settle the public sector dispute. The facts would now come within the loss of immunity provisions relating to secondary action.

Where the party in question is supporting a dispute which comes within one **4.15** of the matters listed in s 244 the fact that the party may also have political motives will not prevent the actions being in contemplation or furtherance of a trade dispute. 'The presence of an improper motive is relevant only if it is so overriding that it negatives any genuine intention to promote or advance the dispute' (*Associated British Ports & Ors v TGWU* [1989] IRLR 291).

D. Parties to the Dispute

Introduction

4.16 The golden formula in previous formulations gave immunity to workers against actions in relation to disputes between workers and workers. Disputes over demarcation between jobs, recognition of unions for particular groups of workers and those relating to single unions were at various times also covered. The Employment Act 1982, however, returned to the philosophy of the Industrial Relations Act 1971 that the employer should not suffer losses by reason of action which is not his concern over differences not of his making. By the Employment Act 1982, s 18(2) the immunity was limited to relate to a dispute between workers and their own employer and this is now contained in TULR(C)A, s 244(1). An inter-union dispute is thus excluded but it may draw in the employer who may have an interest in maintaining inter-union harmony. On the other hand a trade dispute, by TULR(C)A 1974, s 219(1)(e), may relate wholly or mainly to 'the membership or non-membership of a trade union on the part of the worker'. Another limiting effect introduced by the Employment Act 1982, s 18(2) and now contained in s 244 is that a dispute with an employer other than one's own is not protected.

Definition of worker

4.17 The scope of the immunity would be substantially limited if a union were to be deprived of its protection because some of its members had lost their jobs in the course of the strike as dismissals themselves are often the catalyst for industrial action or its continuation. TULR(C)A 1992, s 244(5) therefore defines 'worker' to include a person whose employment was terminated in connection with the dispute or was itself one of the circumstances giving rise to the dispute. Subject to s 244(5) a dispute between workers and their employer means a dispute with those who are currently working so that prospective employment is excluded altogether (*University College London Hospital NHS Trust v UNISON* [1999] IRLR 31, considered further at page 84).

Crown employees are included as are National Health Service workers (TULR(C)A 1992, ss 273, 279). Members of the armed forces and police are excluded and they have no immunity from actions in tort at all (TULR(C)A

1992, s 280). The word 'worker' also includes a person who provides services other than to a professional client. This might include a painter or builder but not a lawyer or an accountant. (See discussion on trade union recognition at Chapter 18.)

The Criminal Justice and Public Order Act 1994, s 127 makes it unlawful for prison officers to go on strike. The Government announced in May 2003 that this provision is to be repealed following the success of a Voluntary Agreement signed by the Prison Officers' Association, the Prison Governers' Association and the Prison Service in 2001. The repeal is to be implemented by a Regulatory Reform Order and is likely to be effected in early 2004 (see *Home Office Press Release 13N/03* of 21 May 2003).

The identity of the employer

The courts have occasionally been prepared to lift the veil of incorporation **4.18** in trade disputes cases, where it is proper to do so, to prevent an employer artificially changing its identity in order to claim that the dispute was not with it. Lord Denning MR said in *Examite Ltd v Whittaker* [1977] IRLR 312 that: 'the words employers and workers in TULRA apply to employers whatever particular hat those employers may wear from time to time'. The facts of the case were that the Amalgamated Union of Engineering Workers went on strike at the business of Baldwin's Industrial Services, which was later in the dispute taken over by the claimant. The claimant failed in their argument that any dispute was not with them. In *The Marabu Porr* [1979] 2 Lloyd's Rep 331, the fact that shipowners arranged for a service company to employ and pay crew members did not prevent the owners being parties to a dispute with the International Transport Workers' Federation over the rates of pay of the crew.

However, the House of Lords would not lift the veil in *Dimbleby & Sons Ltd* **4.19** *v National Union of Journalists* [1984] IRLR 161, in relation to secondary action and this perhaps foreshadows a stricter approach by the courts.

Employers' associations and trade unions

Before its repeal in 1982, TULRA 1974, s 29(4) provided that the involve- **4.20** ment of an employers' association (such as the Engineering Employers' Federation) automatically meant that the constituent employers became parties to the dispute. Similarly, a dispute in which a trade union was involved was deemed to be a dispute with the workers which it represented. The effect of the subsection can be seen in *Camellia Tanker SA v International Transport Workers' Federation* [1976] ICR 274. The ship *Camellia* sailed under the Panamanian flag and was 'blacked' at Liverpool when its owners refused to comply with the demands of the ITF about pay. This qualified as a trade dispute notwithstanding that there was no evidence that the crew itself was dissatisfied with its lot before the ITF had intervened. Templeman J recognized that: 'Trade unions may wish to raise a dispute with an employer not only to protect labour aboard a vessel but also to protect unionists who form the crews of the other ships. . . . Trade unions are not in blinkers looking only at the men whom they managed to sign on the dotted line'.

4.21   Similarly, in *Universe Tankships Inc. of Monrovia v International Transport Workers' Federation* [1983] 1 AC 366, 386B, the court stated: 'These disputes would qualify as trade disputes under the definition in section 29 so long as they were connected with the terms and conditions of employment of the crew of the *Universe Sentinel*, however unwelcome to those members the intervention of the ITF in their affairs might be'.

4.22   A different principle would be applied today since the repeal of s 29(4) by EA 1982, s 18(5). The section was repealed because the Government believed it allowed trade unions to involve workers in a dispute willy nilly and gain the immunity.

4.23   The only reported case so far to raise directly the issue of the change of wording is *Mercury Communications Ltd v Scott-Garner* [1984] Ch 37. The union was challenged that the dispute was part of a general political campaign by the union. The latter's argument that its members were involved because of the threat to their jobs was unsuccessful.

4.24   A union has general authority to act for its members in respect of a strike so that specific authorisation is unnecessary (*Beetham v Trinidad Cement Ltd* [1960] AC 132) although the balloting provisions of the TULCRA 1992 must be complied with.

Disputes between employers

4.25   Disputes between employers are not protected by immunity, nor is a union if it offers support to one side in such a difference (*Larkin v Long* [1915] AC 814).

E. Trade Dispute

Definition

The list of matters which may qualify as a trade dispute is intended to sepa-   **4.26**
rate the sheep of industrial grievances, which it is considered legitimate for
trade unions to be involved with, from the goats of non-trade matters, such
as political and personal quarrels. TULR(C)A, s 244 (previously TULRA
1974, s 29(1) as amended by EA 1982, s 18) gives immunity from action in
the specified torts where there is:

> . . . a dispute between *workers and their employer*, which relates wholly or
> mainly to one of the following, that is to say—
> (a) terms and conditions of employment, or the physical conditions in which
>   any workers are required to work;
> (b) engagement or non-engagement, or termination or suspension of: employ-
>   ment or the duties of employment, of one or more workers;
> (c) allocation of work or the duties of employment as between workers or
>   groups of workers;
> (d) matters of discipline;
> (e) the membership or non-membership of a trade union on the part of a
>   worker;
> (f) facilities for officials of trade unions;
> (g) machinery for negotiation or consultation, and other procedures, relating
>   to any of the foregoing matters, including the recognition by employers or
>   employers' associations of the right of a trade union to represent workers
>   in any such negotiation or consultation or in the carrying out of such
>   procedures.

The subsection has given rise to a considerable amount of litigation and it is
necessary to consider its wording in detail.

Related wholly or mainly

Until 1982 a dispute had only to be 'connected with' one of the acceptable   **4.27**
subjects within TULRA 1974, s 29(1). The Employment Act 1982 amended
the 1974 Act so that the dispute must be 'related wholly or mainly' to one of
the subjects and this phrase is contained in s 244 of the 1992 Act. This is
among the most important of the reforms ushered in by the 1982 legislation,
since it significantly limited the scope of the immunity. The Green Paper on
Trade Union Immunities accepted that: 'In many disputes it is by no means
easy to separate the different events or decide which is predominant.'

4.28 The restriction as enacted sought to deal with the wide connotation given to 'connected with' in cases such as *NWL Ltd v Woods* [1979] 1 WLR 1294, where the House of Lords considered that there need only be a genuine *connection* between the dispute and the relevant subject-matter and that the industrial dispute issue need not be predominant in the minds of the strikers. Lord Scarman's requirement was merely that the connection be 'real and not ostensible'. Lord Diplock stated at p 1304:

> Even if the predominant object were to bring down the fabric of the present economic system by raising wages to unrealistic level . . . this would not . . . make it any less a dispute connected with terms and conditions of employment—and thus a trade dispute, if the actual demand that is resisted by the employer is—as to terms and conditions on which his workers are to be employed.

4.29 The significance of the 1982 reform arose centrally in *Mercury Communications Ltd v Scott-Garner* [1984] Ch 37, although the Court of Appeal gave little firm guidance on the matter for application in future cases. The union objected to the Government's privatization and liberalization of telecommunications. The claimant was one of the first licensed telecommunications operators besides British Telecom and stood to gain immediately from new Government policy. The claimant planned to establish a digital communications network partly using the BT network. The national executive of the Post Office Engineers Union instructed its members, the vast majority of whom were employed by BT, not to connect 'Project Mercury' to the BT system and this was followed by a 'day of action' in October 1982 and a series of selective strikes in October 1983. The catalyst for legal action came when BT ordered employees to interconnect the two systems and the union responded by instructing employees not to connect Mercury to the British Telecom system, blacking Mercury shareholders (including Cable and Wireless and BP) and BT services at Mercury's premises, and threatening to take industrial action against any customer of Mercury.

4.30 At first instance, Mervyn Davies J refused to grant an injunction to the employers on the ground that the union was likely to establish at trial that there was a dispute relating 'wholly or mainly' to 'termination of employment' within the scope of what is now TULR(C)A 1992, s 244(1)(b) since the privatization and liberalization policy might be attended by redundancies. His Lordship, surprisingly, saw no distinction between 'connected with' in the old legislation and 'relating wholly or mainly' in the new statute. The Court of Appeal thought that this was a misdirection and felt able to exercise their discretion afresh to grant the injunction. Their Lordships considered in detail the significance of the altered statutory language but reached rather different conclusions, which, although not crucially important on the facts of the case, are of considerable significance. All three concurred that the dispute was wholly or mainly about Government policy. Although the union honestly and fervently believed that their campaign was in the best interests of the jobs and conditions of service of employees in the industry, it did not follow that industrial action in the course of that campaign constituted a dispute 'wholly or mainly' about the threat of redundancy if the monopoly were not maintained. Sir John Donaldson thought that:

> In context the phrase 'wholly or mainly relates to' directs attention to what the dispute is about and, if it is about more than one matter, what it is mainly about. What it does *not* direct attention to is the reason why 'the parties are in dispute'. A contributory cause of the dispute and possibly the main cause is the belief that redundancy ('termination of employment' in the words of the section) is just around the corner, but the dispute is not about that nor, if it be preferred, relates wholly or mainly to pay . . .

He thought Parliament intended a relatively restricted meaning to be given to the phrase 'relates wholly or mainly to' and the most obvious way to find out what a particular dispute is about is to inquire what the men concerned said to management at the time. Here it was fatal that the union at no stage referred to the job security arrangements between the union and British Telecom which provided procedures for handling redundancies.

May LJ commended an 'ordinary common-sense approach analogous to that which is adopted when a court has before it a question of causation'. He saw the present action as springing from a 'political and ideological campaign seeking to maintain the concept of public monopoly against private competition'. He felt that he had to look forward to trial, using his experience in conducting litigation to assess the affidavits, and so doing he did not expect the union to succeed in its defence. For Dillon LJ it was 'the state of mind of the members which the court' has to consider in assessing whether there was a trade dispute. This had to be judged objectively; the say-so of the union's general secretary was insufficient (cf. *Express Newspapers Ltd v McShane and Ashton* [1980] AC 672). Moreover, it was necessary to consider not merely the occasion which caused the dispute to break *out* but also the reason *why* there was a dispute. The court 'must very often be entitled to infer that the members are by their action endorsing proclaimed objectives of the union and that, conversely, the union is by its public statements about the trade dispute speaking on behalf of its members'. Whether there is a trade dispute is a 'mixed question of fact and law but primarily fact'. Sir John Donaldson in the *Mercury* case conceded the possibility that there could be a 'satellite disagreement' which does not constitute a dispute between the parties to the disagreement. Counsel for the employers had argued that to come within the section there must be a primary disagreement capable of being resolved by negotiation and if resolved ending all matters in the dispute.

4.31 Where a dispute ostensibly falls within the subject-matter of a trade dispute the motives activating the parties to the dispute should not necessarily take the dispute outside the definition. In *Norbrook Laboratories Ltd v King* [1984] IRLR 200, the Northern Ireland Court of Appeal decided that motivation was quite irrelevant to the statutory issue. The case dealt with the state of the law before the introduction of the 'wholly or mainly' test but the principle laid down there would be followed today. The trial judge had decided that the first defendant had called a strike because the employers would not reinstate workers made redundant, but that he had no immunity because there was at trial uncontradicted evidence of his general hostility to the claimant. The appeal was upheld since evidence of hostility was irrelevant.

4.32 Lord Lowry considered that 'action prompted by a bad or sinister motive does not fail by reason of the motive to the action in the furtherance of a trade dispute. Sir Galahad's purity of heart is not required in order to obtain the protection of the statute.' To negate the defence it would be necessary to show that the defendants acted from pure malice. Evidence of hostility was relevant only if it was so far-reaching as to negate any genuine intention to promote or advance a dispute against the claimant (see also to the same effect, *Dallimore v Williams & Jesson* (1912) 29 TLR 67).

4.33 In *London Borough of Wandsworth v. National Association Of Schoolmasters/ Union of Women Teachers* [1993] IRLR 344 the court held that the union's instruction to its members to boycott tests and assessments associated with the national curriculum dispute was a trade dispute between the union and the Secretary of State for Education within the meaning of the definition in TULR(C)A 1992, s 244. The Court of Appeal found that the dispute mainly related to the terms and conditions of employment of the union's members. Consequently, the union had immunity from liability in tort for inducing breach of contract.

F. Legitimate Trade Disputes

We now consider some of the issues which may form the subject-matter of a trade dispute under s 244(1).

Terms and conditions of employment (s 244(1)(a))

This section relates to the terms and conditions of employment, or the phys-   **4.34**
ical conditions in which any workers are required to work. In *BBC v Hearn*
[1977] IRLR 273 Lord Denning and Roskill LJ accepted that the words
'terms and conditions' in TULR(C)A 1992, s 244(1)(a) were of wide import,
although they did not cover the facts of that case. Indeed the majority of
disputes are about terms and conditions of employment. These will include
'not only the contractual terms and conditions but those terms which are
understood and applied by the parties in practice, or habitually or by
common consent, without ever being incorporated into the contract'. In the
Hearn case employees blacked television broadcasts to South Africa. There
was no dispute as there had been no demand that it be a term and condition
that workers should not be obliged to broadcast to South Africa. Lord
Denning MR suggested that a claim by the union for a contractual clause to
the effect that members should not be required to take part in broadcasts
which were to be viewed in South Africa would be sufficient to link a dispute
to terms and conditions.

In *Universe Tankships Inc. of Monrovia v International Transport Workers'*   **4.35**
Federation [1983] 1 AC 366, 386, Lord Diplock, however, said that the
phrase was 'limited to terms which regulate the relationship between an
employee and his [employer]', and did not extend to the relationship with
third parties. Lord Scarman's version was slightly wider, taking in customary
benefits and reasonable expectations (at 402).

To qualify, there must, however, be a dispute about the current contract and   **4.36**
judges have occasionally commented that the claims of a union are so prepos-
terous as not to be conceivably genuine. One of the defendant union's arguments in *Dimbleby & Sons Ltd v National Union of Journalists* [1984] 1 WLR
427, 433, was that there was a dispute over terms and conditions in that
there had to be implied a term in the journalists' contracts entitling them to
refuse to comply with instructions given to them by the employers to provide
copy of the kind they were employed to obtain if the NUJ gave them an

instruction to the contrary. Lord Diplock stated that 'it passes beyond the bounds of credibility that any responsible newspaper proprietor would agree to such a term in the contracts of employment with his journalists'. There was only a minimal likelihood that this contention would succeed in providing a defence at the full hearing, since there was: '. . . no vestige of any claim by the NUJ itself or by the NUJ journalists that their current contracts of employment by Dimbleby—and it is only the current contracts that can be relevant to this case—contained a term entitling them to refuse to comply with instructions given to them by Dimbleby to provide copy.'

4.37   The phrase does not cover terms which regulate a relationship between the employer and some third party or a demand, say, that an employer contribute to a political party. This was made clear in *Universe Tankships Inc. of Monrovia v International Transport Workers' Federation* [1982] 2 All ER 67. The issue was whether the ITF could insist that the employer contribute to the Federation's welfare fund, and the court did not consider that this was conceivably related to terms and conditions of employment.

4.38   The dispute may be about terms and conditions though there is a political angle to it (*Westminster City Council v UNISON* [2001] EWCA Civ 443; [2001] IRLR 524). This case is considered in more detail under 'political disputes'.

4.39   However, the terms and conditions must relate to the employees' terms and conditions with their current employer. In *University College Hospital NHS Trust v UNISON* [1999] IRLR 31 there was strike action against an NHS Hospital Trust because the Trust refused to obtain a guarantee from a consortium, with whom they were contracting to run a new hospital, that employees who were transferred and all future employees would receive terms and conditions equivalent to those of trust employees who were not transferred for a period of up to 30 years. It was held that terms and conditions could not concern the terms and conditions of workers who would in future obtain employment with the new employers.

4.40   A similar approach was taken in *London Underground Ltd v National Union of Rail Maritime and Transport Workers* [2001] IRLR 229 where a guarantee was sought by the unions with regard to terms and conditions of employees where the London Underground intended to transfer the running of parts of the underground to private companies for a future period of 30 years, the duration that the private companies were to take over. Some 5,500 of 16,000 employees were likely to have been affected so that a substantial number of employees remained, for whom the union acted. It was held that this was not a trade dispute within s 244. The primary focus of assurances related to those who would be transferred so that it did not make any difference that some employees would remain.

The House of Lords considered whether a dispute about terms and condi- **4.41** tions included a dispute about how the terms and conditions are to be applied in *P v NAS/UST* [2003] UK HL 8, ICR 386. There was a term in teachers' contracts that they had to comply with the reasonable instructions of the head. The head gave directions that a disruptive pupil must be taught in classes but the union refused. It was argued that a dispute about the reasonableness of an employer's instruction was not a trade dispute. The House of Lords held that there was a trade dispute. Lord Bingham stated that:

> I would accordingly read the statutory definition as covering a genuine dispute between employees and their employer relating wholly or mainly to the job the employees are employed to do or the terms and conditions on which they are employed to do it. If this test is applied to the facts of the present case . . . it is plain that the dispute between the teaching staff and the governing body as their employers related directly to the job the teachers were required to do and were unwilling to do, which was to teach P.

Lord Hoffmann decided that the dispute was about the contractual obligation of the teachers to teach P and that this could be characterized as a dispute whether there was such a term and condition or over whether there should be such a contractual obligation. Further 'a dispute about what the workers are obligated to do or how the employer is obligated to remunerate them, at any level of generality or particularly, is about terms and conditions of employment'.

Termination of employment (s 244(1)(b))

This section relates to the engagement or non-engagement or termination or **4.42** suspension of employment or the duties of employment of one or more workers. The concept includes redundancies which are genuinely feared by a union although not necessarily imminent. In *Health Computing Ltd v Meek* [1980] IRLR 437, NALGO sought as a matter of policy to ensure that its members in the National Health Service did not cooperate with the claimant, a private company which sought to supply computer systems to the NHS.

Goulding J accepted the union's claim that the dispute was about potential redundancies. He thought that the apprehensions held by the union were sincere and that the dispute was objectively connected with termination of employment 'whether an impartial observer would regard such apprehension as firmly based or not' (see also *General Aviation Services (UK) v Transport and General Workers' Union* [1975] ICR 276).

4.43   The dispute may arise about redundancies because it is apprehended that greater competition with another company may cause the employers of the strikers to declare redundancies in due course. In *Crazy Prices (NI) Ltd v Hewitt* [1980] IRLR 396, the policy of the TGWU in Northern Ireland was to prevent the sale of sliced bread at a price more than three pence below the recommended retail prices. The claimant sold loaves imported from the Irish Republic at nine and a half pence below this sum. The defendant instructed members of the TGWU employed in Northern Ireland bakeries not to supply bread to the claimant. The Northern Ireland Court of Appeal decided that the dispute was concerned with employment in Northern Ireland bakeries, and said that: 'A dispute may be connected with such matters involving industrial relations even though the connection is not immediate or proximate'. It is, however, open to considerable speculation whether the same result would be reached after the amendments that were made by the Employment Act 1982, now in TULR(C)A 1992.

4.44   In *Hadmor Productions Ltd v Hamilton* [1983] 1 AC 191, the union relied on the fears of its members that if programmes produced by outside independent facility companies were transmitted by Thames TV, instead of programmes which Thames TV produced itself with its own employees, this might lead to redundancies. Lord Diplock saw this as a classic instance of a trade dispute arising out of a union's fears for job security at a period of high unemployment. It was not fatal to this argument that no redundancy notices had yet been issued at the time of the blacking.

Suspension in the section includes suspension with or without pay.

Allocation of work (s 244(1)(c))

4.45   By s 244(1)(c) there may be a dispute about allocation of work or the duties of employment between workers or groups of workers. Demarcation disputes were included within the definition of a trade dispute in the 1906 statute, but the Industrial Relations Act 1971 removed this immunity even though the Donovan Commission saw good reason to retain it (see *Cory Lighterage Ltd v Transport and General Workers' Union* [1973] ICR 339). Following the 1982 amendments to TULRA 1974, s 29 a dispute about the allocation of work or the duties of employment between workers or groups of workers may only refer to demarcation disputes between workers or groups employed by the *same* employer. Such a dispute may indeed easily bring in the employer as an active party (*Langston v Amalgamated Union of Engineering Workers* [1974] ICR 180). In *Dimbleby & Sons Ltd v National Union of Journalists* [1984] 1 All ER 751, the subsection provided no immunity in an argument about the allocation of work to TBF (Printers) Ltd (whose sister company had a long-standing dispute with the union) by Dimbleby & Sons, who published newspapers. Dimbleby's newspapers were normally printed by its associated printing company but the printing by this company had been prevented by a trade dispute and so Dimbleby entered into a contract with TBF Printers Ltd which was considered to be 'anti-union'. The union instructed journalists not to supply copy to Dimbleby which was going to be printed by TBF Printers. The House of Lords thought that s 244(1)(c) could only apply where there was a dispute about the allocation of work between workers and groups of workers and the *same employer*. This was not so here, as the associated company and TBF Printers Ltd were different employers.

The House of Lords in the *Hadmor* case thought that the dispute would have arguably fallen under this head and probably also under s 244(1)(g).

G. Unprotected Disputes

A number of disputes which are of common occurrence stand outside the definition in TULR(C)A 1992, s 224 and are thus unprotected by the trade dispute immunity. It is necessary to consider them in detail. **4.46**

Personal disputes

A dispute arising from pure malice or a clash of personalities cannot be a *trade* dispute (though cf. the question of motive). The *locus classicus* of this position is Lord Loreburn's dictum in *Conway v Wade* [1909] AC 506, 512 that: 'If some meddler sought to use the trade dispute as a cloak beneath which to interfere with impunity in other people's work or business, a jury would be entirely justified in saying that what he did was done in contemplation or **4.47** furtherance, not of a trade dispute, but of his own designs, sectarian, political or purely mischievous as the case might be.'

There must be more than 'a mere personal quarrel or a grumbling or an agitation. . . . It must be something definite and of real substance.'

4.48   A poisonous atmosphere was the background to a non-trade dispute in *Huntley v Thornton* [1957] 1 All ER 234. The claimant alienated his fellow workers when he refused to take part in a one-day strike. They refused to work with him and the union's Hartlepool District Committee sought to ensure that he would not get another job in the area by striking against any company which offered him one. Harman J considered that the union was acting in a personal vendetta and had no protection at law.

4.49   Similarly, in *Torquay Hotel Co. Ltd v Cousins* [1969] 2 Ch 106, the Court of Appeal decided that the blacking by the TGWU of the claimant's hotel was caused by a desire to suppress criticism of the union by the claimant's managing director, a Mr Chapman. His criticism related to the union's conduct in a strike over recognition at a different hotel. Russell LJ said (at 143B) that: 'Action against the other [hotels] is designed to lead to action by the others by way of recognition of the defendant as a negotiating body; industrial action, against the Imperial Hotel would have no such aim; it could only be, it seems to me, to punish Mr Chapman for the expression of views unpalatable to the union'.

4.50   The House of Lords, in *Stratford (J.T.) and Son v Lindley* [1965] AC 269 was of the opinion that the dispute was more about inter-union rivalry than terms and conditions of employment. Lord Pearce said (at 335) that: 'It would appear on the evidence so far given that the defendants were contemplating merely the advancement of their union's prestige in rivalry with another union'.

Political disputes

4.51   The trade dispute definition has never been so broad as to include political disputes. It was on this ground that the General Strike of 1926 was declared unlawful in the rather strange, and generally criticized, decision of Astbury J in *National Sailors' and Firemen's Union of GB and Ireland v Reed* [1926] 1 Ch 536. Reports that disgruntled groups of miners would seek to have the miners' strike of 1984–85 declared unlawful on this ground came to nothing. It may now be easier to declare a strike political and not covered by immunity by reason of the change in the proximity to industrial grievances, from 'connected with' to 'related wholly or mainly to' (see pp 69–71). It is not, however, always easy to draw the line between political and trade disputes, as Roskill LJ recognized in *Sherard v Amalgamated Union of Engineering Workers* [1973] IRLR 188 at para 20, where he thought it was easy for someone to put a strike in the former category when 'what that person really means is that the object of the strike is something of which, as an individual, he objectively disapproves'. Furthermore, since the Government is a major employer and crucially affects the employment prospects of many millions whom it does not directly employ it may be difficult to say when a dispute with the Government is about employment or politics (cf. *Mercury Communications Ltd v Scott-Garner* [1984] Ch 37). Nevertheless, in its capacity as employer, the Government is treated no differently from any other management. By TULRA 1974, s 224(2) a dispute between a Minister and workers may be a trade dispute even where he is not the employer if he must approve a settlement. It must be remembered that the motivation of the strikers is not the real issue but rather what the strike is about. As Lord Diplock said in *NWL Ltd v Woods* [1979] 1 WLR 1294 (before the changes ushered in by the Employment Act 1982): 'Even if the predominant object were to bring down the fabric of the present economic system by raising wages to unrealistic levels . . . this would not, in my view, make it any less a dispute connected with terms and conditions of employment and thus a trade dispute'.

The courts have held industrial action to be political where the object has been to protest against what was the Industrial Relations Bill (*Associated Newspapers Group v Flynn* (1970) 10 KIR 17); to protest against the Conservative Government's economic policies (*Beaverbrook Newspapers Ltd v Keys* [1978] IRLR 34); and to prevent mail deliveries to South Africa (*Gouriet v Union of Post Office Workers* [1978] AC 435).   **4.52**

The distinguishing feature of most political strikes is that the employer struck against can have no direct effect on the decisions protested against. On the other hand, in the *Sherard* case the Court of Appeal would not treat a one-day strike protesting against the Government's wage freeze policies as political because many union members were employed by the Government. Disputes will also be protected where employees are directly affected by Government policies, for example, on denationalization where redundancies may occur (*General Aviation Services (UK) v Transport and General Workers' Union* [1974] ICR 35).   **4.53**

4.54 Protests against Government policy are not covered. In *Associated British Ports plc v TGWU* [1989] IRLR 291 there were negotiations between the union and employers over a national agreement to replace the National Dock Labour Scheme, which the Government intended to repeal. When the negotiations broke down, the union called a major strike, supported by a ballot. It was argued that the dispute about the new agreement was between the union and the employers and the dockers were engaged in a non-trade dispute for political reasons, namely a dispute about the abolition of the dock scheme. This argument was rejected at first instance and it was not repeated on appeal.

4.55 It was held in *London Borough of Wandsworth v National Association of Schoolmasters* [1993] IRLR 344 that where there was a proposed boycott of assessment of pupils under the National Curriculum there was a trade dispute which related wholly or mainly to the terms and conditions of its members. The dispute was a trade dispute within the meaning of s 244 since it mainly related to the terms and conditions of employment of the union's members. The concern was about working time, namely it was in protest against the excessive workload and unreasonable imposition made upon teachers, as a consequence of national curriculum assessment and testing.

4.56 In *Westminster City Council v UNISON* [2001] EWCA Civ 443; IRLR 524 the union opposed the Council's policy of externalization, part of which was to contract out its Assessment and Advice Unit to a private company. The Council's employees would have been transferred to a private company under the Transfer of Undertakings (Protection of Employment) Regulations 1981. The union was of the view that the conditions would deteriorate and threatened strike action. The Court of Appeal held that the dispute was about whether the workers should be forced to change their employer and so was about terms and conditions. Pill LJ stated: 'I reject the suggestion that this was in substance a high-minded dispute about public policy and conflicts of interest masquerading as a dispute about terms of employment'.

See also *University College Hospital NHS Trust v UNISON* [1999] IRLR 3.

Overseas disputes

4.57 TULR(C)A 1992, s 244(3) includes a dispute even though the subject matter was beyond British shores. A trade dispute might exist even though it relates to matters outside Great Britain but only so long as the person or persons whose actions are said to be in contemplation or furtherance of the trade dispute are 'likely to be affected by the outcome of the dispute' in respect of one of the legitimate matters within s 244(1). The utility of this provision to the unions is designed to be and is likely to be quite minimal. For example, a boycott of the employer by reason of, say, his South African connections is unlikely to be a valid trade dispute (cf. *Gouriet v Union of Post Office Workers* (above)). Much action in support of overseas employees will be caught by the 'secondary action' provisions in any event.

Union recruitment strikes

Unease at the manner in which SLADE (Society of Lithographic Artists **4.58** Designers and Engravers) were seeking to compel union membership among graphic arts designers led the Conservative Government, as one of its first acts in 1979, to establish an inquiry by A. Leggatt QC. His report, *Certain Restrictive Union Recruitment Activities* appeared in 1980 (Cmnd 7706). As a first step to the implementation of the inquiry's recommendations, the Employment Act 1980, s 18 singled out certain strikes, aimed at ensuring that workers become union members, for proscription. The scope of the section was widened by the Employment Act 1982. Section 12 of the 1982 Act rendered it unlawful on the ground of a requirement of trade union membership to refuse to include any person on a list of approved suppliers of goods or services; to terminate a contract for the supply of goods and services; to exclude anyone from a list of persons from whom tenders are invited; to fail to permit a person to submit, tender or to otherwise determine not to enter into a contract with a person for the supply of goods and services.

The Employment Act 1988, s 10 further extended these provisions to *any* **4.59** action (indirect or direct) where the reason was that the employer was using non-union labour or refusing to discriminate (as defined) against non-union labour. These provisions are contained in TULR(C)A 1992, ss 222(1), (2), (4) and (5) which prevents attempts to maintain the closed shop by action even where such could not be legally maintained in any event. By s 222(1):

> An act is not protected if the reason, or one of the reasons, for which it is done is the fact or belief that a particular employer—
> (*a*) is employing, has employed or might employ a person who is not a member of a trade union, or
> (*b*) is failing, has failed or might fail to discriminate against such a person.

4.60   Section 222(3) further provides that an act was not protected if it constitutes, or is one of a number of acts which together constitute, an inducement or attempted inducement of a person—

> (*a*) to incorporate in a contract to which that person is a party, or a proposed contract to which he intended to be a party, a term or condition which is or would be void by virtue of section 144 (union membership requirement in contract for goods or services), or
>
> (*b*) to contravene section 145 (refusal to deal with person on grounds relating to union membership).

4.61   This withdrawal of the immunity is contained in s 225(2), which provides:

> An act is not protected if—
> (*a*) it interferes with the supply (whether or not under a contract) of goods or services, or can reasonably be expected to have that effect, and
> (*b*) one of the facts relied upon for the purposes of establishing liability is that a person has—
> > (i)   induced another to break a contract of employment or interfered or induced another to interfere with its performance, or
> > (ii) threatened that a contract of employment under which he or another is employed will be broken or its performance interfered with, or that he will induce another to break a contract of employment or to interfere with its performance, and
> (*c*) the reason, or one of the reasons, for doing the act is the fact or belief that the supplier (not being the employer under the contract of employment mentioned in paragraph (*b*)) does not, or might not—
> > (i)   recognize one or more trade unions for the purpose of negotiating on behalf of workers, or any class of worker, employed by him, or
> > (ii) negotiate or consult with, or with an official of, one or more trade unions.

4.62   The withdrawal of the immunity applies only to secondary and not to primary action. The issues were discussed in *Messenger Newspapers Group Ltd v National Graphical Association* [1984] IRLR 397. The claimant was a holding company which had a typesetting subsidiary, Fineward Ltd, in Stockport where an NGA closed shop operated so that only members of that union could be employed. The claimant expanded into the Bury area where a typesetting company, CAPS Ltd, was established and into the Warrington area where a company, Messenger Printing Ltd, was set up to print its newspapers. The employees at Bury and Warrington voted in a secret ballot against a closed shop agreement with the NGA. This led to an official dispute, in which six NGA members who were on strike at Fineward were dismissed.

The NGA persuaded members of the NUJ to refuse to submit copy to the Messenger Group and asked local advertisers not to use the Messenger Group papers, as well as unsuccessfully seeking to persuade suppliers to break contracts with the Group. Pickets were set up at the Bury and Warrington plants and this amounted to secondary picketing as against the claimant company. The court, *inter alia,* held that by the Employment Act 1982, ss 12 and 14, the picketing and other attempts to interfere with contracts with CAPS Ltd and Messenger Printing Ltd were in themselves unlawful: (a) as secondary action; and (b) because they were acts with the purpose to compel the claimant to accept the closed shop.

Employer/employer dispute

The definition of trade dispute does not include disputes between employ-   **4.63**
ers. In *Larkin v Long* [1915] AC 814 an employer's association tried to get the claimant to join and the union offered to call a strike against the claimant as it knew the claimant would have to improve terms and conditions of employment if the employer joined the association. The House of Lords held that the dispute remained one between the association and the employer and was not a trade dispute.

H. The Scope of the Immunity

The enacting provision of TULR(C)A 1992, s 244 must be considered in   **4.64**
some further detail in reviewing the scope of the trade dispute immunity. We have already examined the precise torts against which there may be an immunity in the relevant material on each tort.

Not actionable

The section renders the torts not actionable rather than lawful in all respects.   **4.65**
This had a decisive effect in *Stratford (J. T.) and Son v Lindley* [1965] AC 269. Under the immunity then extant, which was for relevant purposes in the same terms as the current section, the claimant had no action against the defendants for direct inducement of the employees' breach of contract because there was clear immunity. The claimant argued that the defendants had procured breach of the commercial contracts for hire of the boats and that the unlawful means were supplied by the inducement of breach of the

contract of employment. This threatened to render the immunity virtually valueless in any cases affecting commercial contracts, as most disputes would do in one form or another. As the immunities then stood, the fact that the non-actionable inducement of breach of the contract of employment remained unlawful, allowed this to be the necessary unlawful means for the procurement of the breach of the commercial contract. TULRA 1974, s 13(3)(b) provided that a tort which had immunity shall not be regarded as the doing of an unlawful act or as the use of unlawful means or the purpose of establishing liability in tort, thereby nullifying this aspect of the *Stratford* case.

4.66 The subsection was repealed by the Employment Act 1980 and the effect of this can be seen in *Hadmor Productions Ltd v Hamilton* [1983] 1 AC 191. The claimant produced a series about pop music in the 1960s by hiring free-lance members of the Association of Cinematograph, Television and Allied Technicians (ACTT). The ACTT was unhappy about this practice but a letter from the ACTT appeared to suggest a softening of their hard line. Thames TV accordingly agreed in principle (but not by binding contract) to purchase the series, at which point ACTT shop stewards threatened to 'black' the programmes and the company withdrew from transmitting them. The Court of Appeal ([1981] ICR 690) decided that the defendant shop stewards had interfered with the claimant's business by unlawful means and that the repeal of s 13(3)(b) had restored the *Stratford v Lindley* position. The House of Lords did not agree, so that acts in contemplation or furtherance of a trade dispute as defined cannot be unlawful means in other torts.

The relief restrained

4.67 The section protects the appropriate defendants against an the grant of an injunction as well as in an action for damages (*Torquay Hotel Co. Ltd v Cousins* [1969] 2 Ch 106, 141, 144–6; *Camden Exhibition and Display Ltd v Lynott* [1966] 1 QB 555). It does not, however, give immunity against contractual remedies or criminal prosecutions.

The torts not covered

4.68 There are also a number of torts for which there is *no* protection within the golden formula. There is no immunity in respect of conversion (*Royal London etc Society v Williamson* (1921) 37 TLR 742), and there has been some doubt about trespass since *Plessey plc v Wilson* [1982] IRLR 198 where the Court of Session thought it arguable that the section gave protection in the case of a sit-in (see p 248).

The section does not protect against inducement of breach of statutory duty. **4.69** This proposition was accepted in *Meade v London Borough of Haringey* [1979] ICR 494, where unions persuaded the council to close schools in arguable breach of its duty to provide education. Since the local authority was acting ultra vires it was argued that there was a remedy at the suit of a person who had suffered special damages. In that case this would be by the parents of children at the relevant schools for the wrongful closure of the schools by local authority in breach of its duty to secure that sufficient schools should be available. However, it has subsequently become clear that the principle should only apply where there is a right of action for the complainant; see further at pages 36, 44 (see also *Barrett & Baird (Wholesale) Ltd v Institution of Professional Civil Servants* [1987] IRLR 3).

In *Prudential Assurance v Lorenz* (1971) 11 KIR 78, union officials persuaded **4.70** their members not to send returns to the company headquarters. This was a breach of their fiduciary duty as agents to account for profits made and was accordingly not protected with immunity.

Another possible flanking movement was considered in *Universe Tankships* **4.71** *Inc. of Monrovia v International Transport Workers' Federation* [1982] 2 All ER 67. The claimant claimed to recover money paid to the defendant Federation's Welfare Fund on the ground that it had been paid under duress. This was an action in restitution rather than tort but the House of Lords paid regard to the intent of TULRA 1974 to exempt all forms of industrial action from liability. Thus where there were alternative remedies of restitution and damages available the claimant should not be able to circumnavigate the Act by claiming in restitution what they could not claim as damages. On the facts of this case however, the claim for restitution was granted.

In a case where industrial pressure is applied overseas and an agreement **4.72** would be void for duress because the pressure is deemed illegitimate according to English law (though the pressure may be legitimate according to the law of the jurisdiction) the claimant may recover in quasi contract though the claim by way of damages in tort cannot be made (*Dimskal Shipping SA v International Transport Workers' Federation* [1992] IRLR 78; ICR 37).

The protection in respect of interference with commercial contracts does not extend to cases where the interference was committed by way of nuisance and intimidation. (*News Group Newspapers Ltd v SOGAT 82 and others* [1986] IRLR 337, para 121).

I. Secondary Action

Background

4.73 The immunity that a union can gain in respect of a strike or other industrial action can be withdrawn or suspended in a number of situations, as laid down by TULR(C)A 1992:

(1) where a strike ballot has not been held before a strike (see Chapter 5);

(2) where proper notice is not given in accordance with statute (s 224A);

(3) where action is taken to enforce union membership (s 222);

(4) where unofficial strikers are dismissed and action is taken in support (s 237);

(5) where action is taken to encourage or compel a contractor to impose union membership (s 222(2)(a)) or recognition (s 225(1)(a));

(6) where secondary action is taking place;

(7) where picketing which is not lawful within s 220 is being carried out. This remains the only 'gateway to freedom' in respect of secondary action as the lawful picketing within the meaning of s 220, although some secondary action, to the surprise of many, still has the benefit of the immunity.

4.74 The Employment Act 1980, s 17 as originally enacted contained three 'gateways to freedom' in respect of secondary action. It was possible for secondary action to be lawful where:

(1) blacking took place at the premises of the immediate supplier or customer of the employer in dispute;

(2) the blacked job was transferred elsewhere within the same company or group;

(3) there was lawful picketing.

Thus the first two exceptions meant that the immediate supplier or customer or associated companies could be subjected to industrial action without loss of the immunity. However, the Employment Act 1990 took away the first two gateways so that there is only immunity in respect of lawful picketing. The considerable body of case law that was generated in relation to the first two gateways is thus now academic.

The principle

By TULR(C)A 1992, s 224, 'secondary action' is defined as follows: **4.75**

(1) An act is not protected if one of the facts relied on for the purpose of establishing liability is that there has been secondary action which is not lawful picketing.

(2) There is secondary action in relation to a trade dispute when, and only when, a person—

    (*a*) induces another to break a contract of employment or interferes or induces another to interfere with its performance, or

    (*b*) threatens that a contract of employment under which he or another is employed will be broken or its performance interfered with, or that he will induce another to break a contract of employment or to interfere with its performance,

and the employer under the contract of employment is not the employer party to the dispute.

(3) Lawful picketing means acts done in the course of such attendance as is declared lawful by section 220 (peaceful picketing)—

    (*a*) by a worker employed (or, in the case of a worker not in employment, last employed) by the employer party to the dispute, or

    (*b*) by a trade union official whose attendance is lawful by virtue of subsection (1)(*b*) of that section.

(4) For the purposes of this section an employer shall not be treated as party to a dispute between another employer and workers of that employer; and where more than one employer is in dispute with his workers, the dispute between each employer and his workers shall be treated as a separate dispute.

In this subsection 'worker' has the same meaning as in section 244 (meaning of 'trade dispute').

(5) An act in contemplation or furtherance of a trade dispute which is primary action in relation to that dispute may not be relied on as secondary action in relation to another trade dispute.

Primary action means such action as is mentioned in paragraph (*a*) or (*b*) of subsection (2) where the employer under the contract of employment is the employer party to the dispute.

(6) In this section 'contract of employment' includes any contract under which one person personally does work or performs services for another, and related expressions shall be construed accordingly.

Sections 224(1) and (2) thus make it clear that the immunity will not apply at all to secondary action. The focus now is not so much on whether the action is of a type that will be immune but merely whether the employer is the primary or secondary employer to attract immunity. The employer which is the party to the trade dispute will naturally be regarded as the primary employer for the purpose of the action (s 224(5)). The organizing or threatening of industrial action by the workers of an employer who is not a party to the trade dispute will be secondary action.

Primary and secondary employers

4.76 Sections 224(4) and 224(5) contain deeming provisions which are designed to make it clear which employer will be regarded as the primary or secondary employer.

Section 224(4) makes it clear that one employer cannot become a party to a trade dispute between another employer and that employer's workers. Where there is a dispute with A Ltd, the primary employer, and B Ltd assists, for example by supplying goods to A Ltd it may be argued, as a matter of fact, that B Ltd has entered into the dispute and should be a party. However, B Ltd is not a party to the dispute so that both A Ltd and B Ltd may have a cause of action against the union if the union were to instruct its members to black B Ltd.

However, primary action in relation to one dispute will not be treated as secondary action in relation to another dispute (s 224(5)). This would mean that, in the above example, a separate dispute may arise between the union and B Ltd for which the union would have immunity (provided that the dispute came within ss 219 and 244). If the union took action which meant that B Ltd could no longer supply A Ltd, the action against B Ltd would still be primary action so that A Ltd would not have a cause of action based upon there being unlawful secondary action. Because the action is primary against B Ltd it cannot be counted as secondary action for A Ltd.

Where there are several employers who are parties to the same dispute they will nevertheless be deemed to be parties to separate disputes. If there was a national dispute about terms and conditions, in which A Ltd and B Ltd were parties, and A Ltd was particularly targeted then selective action against A Ltd would be primary action. If, in these circumstances the union instructed its members to take action against B Ltd in order to cut off the supplies to A Ltd this would be regarded as secondary action, since, although there is a national aim, the dispute with A Ltd must be regarded as a separate dispute. If B Ltd was also targeted so that there was a dispute with B Ltd being regarded as a primary employer the fact that this incidentally cut off the supplies to A Ltd would not make the action secondary (s 244(4)).

The employers will, however, be deemed to be separate even if they are part of a group and are associated companies.

Workers

The definition of contract of employment in s 224(6) covers those who work **4.77** under any contract to provide personal services, so that it will include independent contractors (cf. *Shipping Co Uniform Inc v International Workers' Federation* [1985] IRLR 71; ICR 245, prior to the amendment contained in the EA 1980 where inducing independent contractors to break their contracts did not constitute secondary action as they were not then covered by the definition).

Liability for secondary action

Section 224 does not operate to create liability for secondary action but takes **4.78** away the immunity so that the trade dispute defences cannot be used. The primary and secondary employer will thus have a cause of action. In a case where the union causes loss to A Ltd by inducing employers at B Ltd to break their contracts so that A Ltd is not supplied with goods the tort contained in *Lumley v Gye* will be made out as against B Ltd. The union may have also committed the tort of interfering with A Ltd's contract with B Ltd by unlawful means. Threats to do any of the above may amount to intimidation. There would be a defence to any of the above under s 219. However, this is taken away since there has been secondary action.

Liability for the torts of both interfering with business by unlawful means and interfering with contract by unlawful means are restored.

The only exception that now exists in relation to picketing is that there is liability for picketing which is not lawful. By s 224(3) the picketing may be carried out by a worker employed or last employed by the primary employer or by a trade union official whose attendances are lawful under s 220(1)(b) and the picketing must be done in the course of attendance as is lawful under s 220. The picket must be picketing in furtherance of his own trade dispute so that a sympathetic picket, who is picketing his own place of work, but is not involved in dispute with his own employer will not be covered. The union official who peacefully pickets with members whom he represents will be protected provided his members are picketing their own place of work.

Picketing

4.79 Picketing, which is secondary action, may be lawful under TULR(C)A 1992, s 220 where it is carried out by a worker employed by a party to the dispute, or by a trade union official whose attendance is lawful by virtue of the section. This is discussed in Chapter 8 on picketing and is the only one of the three gateways to remain intact.

5

BALLOTS

A minefield in which it is all too easy to stray from the paths of safety and legality

PO v UCW [1990] IRLR 143 *per* Lord Donaldson MR

A. Background

The Thatcher Government was firm in its belief in the efficacy and desirability of ballots taking place before industrial action and a move away from the days of mass meetings in the open air voting to strike or indeed no democratic opportunity at all being given to employees before a strike took place. The Green Paper, *Trade Union Immunities* 1983 argued that they would ensure that the strike weapon would be used 'sparingly, responsibly and democratically'. It professed particular concern with 'the spectacle of strike decisions being taken by a show of hands at stage-managed mass

5.01

meetings to which outsiders may be admitted and where dissenters may be intimidated'.

Previous official voices had not been so convinced. The Donovan Commission on Trade Unions and Employers' Associations had found 'little justification in the available evidence for the view that workers are less likely to vote for strike action than their leaders . . .' (para 428).

When first enacted the provisions in the Trade Union Act 1984 gave the right to restrain strikes held without the appropriate ballots only to employers. Many cases were brought under the provisions of the 1984 Act in the early stages, since most unions failed to hold ballots at all as a matter of principle. Important early injunctions were those brought by:

(1) Wolverhampton Express and Star against NGA;
(2) Solihull Borough Council against NUT;
(3) Austin Rover against TGWU, AUEW and others; and
(4) the Post Office against the UCW.

In case (1) the result was that the action was suspended; in cases (2) and (3) a new ballot was held; and in case (4) a ballot was held for the first time.

This rigid union position of refusal to hold a ballot at all soon changed. All unions concerned in the 'Wapping dispute' in 1986 for example held ballots, and there gradually developed a consensus in trade union circles that ballots would become and would remain a part of the trade union scene. Indeed there is a strong case for saying that they give greater legitimacy to a union's campaign in the mind of the employer and the general public and thus have strengthened the position of unions in waging disputes.

Recent injunctions have been gained by employers only by reason of a lack of a *proper* ballot because of some defect in the balloting procedure. Under the Thatcher/Major Government's legislation, there were many balloting traps for the unwary but these have been gradually whittled down by New Labour amendments to those statutes, especially the reforms ushered in by the Employment Relations Act 1999.

Most ballots have in fact resulted in majorities for strike action. The requirement to hold one has, however, slowed down the calling of that industrial action, and reduced the element of surprise which used to be a vital weapon in 'industrial warfare'. This may restrain a union from striking whilst the iron is hot and making most use of an element of surprise. No such restraint arises in the case of unofficial action, and the walk out by BA ground staff in July 2003 at Heathrow Airport was a reminder of the havoc which might be caused by sudden 'wildcat' action.

A union armed with a successful ballot result may however have a stronger moral force than one without, a lesson that many unions took from the ill-fated miners' strike of 1984/5 led by Arthur Scargill when no ballot was held even though the union leadership may well have 'won' it for a strike vote.

The provisions on ballots before industrial actions were coupled in the Trade Union Act 1984 with two other reforms broadly aimed at 'giving the unions back to their members': balloting for members of the principal executive committee and regular approval of the union's political fund. These have been much amended since.

B. Scope of the Ballot Provisions

The strike balloting provisions in the Industrial Relations Act 1971 gave the Government the key role in activating ballots, but under the 1984 legislation it has no such role. The effect of not having a vote (or a properly conducted vote) is instead to strip away the immunity with which the union's action and the action of its officials and members would otherwise be cloaked pursuant to the 'golden formula'. **5.02**

The terms of the 1984 Act differed substantially from the initial Bill. The first draft proposed that a certain proportion of the membership should be able to trigger a ballot, but this was not implemented. Moreover, the original Bill merely required that a vote be held for a union to have immunity, whether the result was in favour of, or against the action proposed. This somewhat illogical provision was tightened up in the House of Lords under political pressure connected with the then continuing miners' strike. **5.03**

The mechanics of the ballot provisions do indeed have the effect of removing the trade dispute immunity if 'official' industrial action is taken 'without the support of a ballot'. There is, however, no parallel requirement that a ballot be held before the action can be called off, nor that there be ballots in relation to unofficial action. The important dividing line between official and unofficial action is laid down in detail in the statute, now TULR(C)A **5.04**

103

1992, s 20 which is applied by s 233(4) 'for the purpose of determining whether a call, or industrial action, is to be taken to have been . . . authorised or endorsed'.

5.05 The section applies only to the torts of: inducing an employee to break his contract of employment; inducing an employee to interfere with the performance of his own contract of employment; and indirectly procuring a breach of or interference in a commercial contract by the unlawful means of inducing a breach of a contract of employment (s 20(1)). Therefore it does not apply to intimidation or conspiracy to injury, but then neither does the golden formula itself.

5.06 The Act covers all trade unions irrespective of what their own rules may provide and regardless even of their ability to perform their obligations under the statute by reason of their constitution. This has been highlighted by its effect on federations of trade unions which have no individual members, such as the International Transport Workers' Federation ('ITF'), but which fall within the definition of 'trade union' provided by the Trade Union and Labour Relations (Consolidation) Act 1974, s 29 (now s 1 1992 Act). Thus, in *Shipping Company Uniform Inc. v International Transport Workers' Federation* [1985] IRLR 71, the ITF claimed that for this reason it could not hold a ballot. Its members were the constituent unions themselves. Staughton J, however, enforced the full rigour of the Act and granted an injunction restraining industrial action which did not have the support of a ballot which *ex hypothesi* the Federation (not being itself a union with individual members) could not hold. The judge advised the Federation to change its rules in order to comply with the Act.

5.07 The ballot requirements operate in three ways:

- An injunction may be gained by the relevant employer(s) if the ballot is not held or is improperly conducted (s 226)
- A member of a union may require the union to hold a ballot (s 62) (see para 7.02)
- A member of the public may seek an injunction if the ballot is not held or is improperly conducted (s 235A)

There is a Code of Practice on Industrial Action Ballots.

There is also a link with the rules on dismissal of strikers because if there is a breach of the balloting rules, the strike may cease to be lawful and employees cannot claim unfair dismissal in respect of such a strike (see p 190).

C. When is a Ballot Needed?

As mentioned above, a ballot is required only in respect of 'an act done by a **5.08** trade union', that is, if it is authorized or endorsed by the principal executive committee, the president or general secretary, an employed official, a committee to whom an employed official regularly reports, or some other person in accordance with the rules of the union. This derived from the codification which governs the vicarious liability of a union in tort actions under TULR(C)A 1992, s 20: see Chapter 3. If the 1992 Act serves to strip away the immunity, however, it removes it from everyone who might be sued under the economic torts including the individual strike organizer, since s 20 provides that an action which has been authorized or endorsed by the union is actionable in tort 'whether or not against the trade union'. Thus in respect of an official strike, an injunction may be brought against a strike organizer(s) and he may not rely on the immunity he would otherwise have had since his union has not held a ballot complying with the Act.

For the purposes of the ballot provisions, strike is specially defined as 'any **5.09** concerted stoppage of work' (s 246). Whilst there is no definition of other industrial action, it clearly extends beyond action in breach of contract.

D. Duration of the Ballot

An affirmative vote is not usually valid for more than four weeks from the **5.10** date (or final date if more than one) on which it is taken. The affirmative vote must be fresh at the point of action being taken. The union thus does not have the flexibility to hold a ballot at the start of negotiations and then wait until the result of those negotiations is known (say) six weeks later before putting it into effect. In the event, however, that unofficial action is later given official backing, a ballot must be held before (but not more than four weeks before) the union declares it official. This is the significance of the words 'continue to act' in s 226(1).

A difficult question concerns when a strike begins and ends in the context of **5.11** 'lightening' strike action. If, for example, a teachers union were to call out its members in Grimsby for two days in week one, Hartlepool for one day in week two and Dorking for three days in week six, is it necessary to have a separate ballot for each strike and does an initial ballot in week one protect the Dorking action? The better view appears to be that the courts should treat all these acts as one strike, but these are issues of fact and degree for the court to determine in the particular factual circumstances.

In *Monsanto plc v Transport and General Workers' Union* [1986] IRLR 406, the Court of Appeal had to consider the position of suspended and then reimposed industrial action (a not atypical pattern). The union initially imposed an overtime ban on 22 April 1986 without a ballot. An injunction was accordingly granted on 30 April 1986, and normal working was resumed. A ballot held on 6 May 1986 resulted in a firm vote in favour of the industrial action. On the day following the announcement of the result, an overtime ban commenced which was then broadened into a ban on training in certain areas, and a restriction on the loading or unloading of the company's trailers. Pending negotiations, both sides agreed to lift the sanctions imposed against the other. When those talks broke down, the union reimposed its various bans, and introduced a cut in production by 50 per cent. The company sought further injunctions on the basis that the reimposed action was not supported by a ballot, and these were granted by Gatehouse J. The Court of Appeal reversed this result essentially on policy grounds. Dillon LJ said that:

> The union may be prepared to suspend industrial action while negotiations take place, but the intention throughout would be that this is not a discontinuance of the industrial action but a temporary suspension for the purposes of negotiation so that the industrial action will be resumed if the negotiations fail. I do not see that in such circumstances the statute or good industrial relations require a further ballot if there is a suspension for negotiations.

It was thus likely that the union would succeed if the matter went to trial, and the union's appeal against the grant of the injunction was upheld.

In *Newham London Borough Council v NALGO* [1993] ICR 189 the facts were quite complex and most easily understood by a chronology:

7.1.92—there was a strike over payroll staff being made redundant;
11.5.92—the rent and benefits section started their own strike action;
22.6.92—officers in the central grants section had a branch wide ballot for

an indefinite all out strike in opposition to compulsory redundancies in the poll tax section and the council's threat to sack workers;
3.8.92—there was a general strike of union members.

The employers contended that their disputes with the union were resolved.

It was held that it was no contravention of the Act to include those already on strike; the further ballot did not relate to the industrial action already taking place although the earlier action was subsumed in the later action. As to whether there was a continuing dispute at all, that was resolved on the basis that if one party honestly and genuinely thinks that it is still in dispute that is sufficient and the court need not decide that it was reasonable in so thinking.

E. Retrospective Ballots

Although it is clear that a union may endorse what was previously 'unofficial' industrial action provided it has a ballot *before* that endorsement, it is doubtful whether a union may endorse the action and then *later* hold a ballot to clothe itself with immunity. **5.12**

F. The Right to Vote

The aim of TULR(C)A 1992, s 226 in effect is to adapt the general democratic principle to the franchise of a union ballot. There is, however, one important difference. While a parliamentary electorate remains generally stable, a union may change its views from time to time on the workers to call out on strike. The situation may alter rapidly as negotiations proceed and one group of workers perhaps secures satisfactory concessions which are denied to others or not acceptable to them. The statute itself accords entitlement to vote to 'all those members of the trade union who it is reasonable at the time of the ballot for the union to believe will be induced to take part or as the case may be to continue to take part in the industrial action in question and to no others' (s 227(1)). This focuses attention on the time of the ballot rather than the onset of the trade dispute which gives rise to it. **5.13**

One issue is the meaning of the words 'induced to take part' in the industrial action. It was commonly thought that this meant induced *by the trade union* **5.14** to take part in order to make sense of the provision but this was thrown into confusion by the controversial Court of Appeal decision in *RMT v Midland Mainline Ltd* [2001] IRLR 813. The court held that it meant those members whom the union reasonably expects will participate in the industrial action whether called out by the union or not. This would include people whom it considers will in fact come out in support. In the case itself the union sent ballot papers to 90 members who were guards or drivers but not to 11 who were not recorded as guards or drivers in the union's records and a further 10 members who were in arrears with their subscriptions. The strike notice to the employer stated that the union would be calling out *all* of its members who were guards or drivers but the strike call was issued only to those who had been balloted. It was held that the industrial action did not have 'the support of a ballot' because the union ought to have balloted all its members who were guards or drivers and not only those it intended to call out. The curious result is surely not what Parliament intended.

5.15 The basic principle is that the union must ballot those whom it reasonably expects to call on to participate in industrial action and no others (s 227(1)). Each such person must have one and only one vote. There must be no weighted voting. A person accidentally omitted from the ballot may not, however, be held to have been *denied* his entitlement to vote within the meaning of the Act. The statutory test is reasonableness and a court may well in practice waive incidental mistakes in the make-up of the franchise.

5.16 Out of caution, the union should clearly err on the side of the widest possible view of the voters eligible to take part in the ballot. If the class of workers to be involved in the action substantially changes, it may be incumbent on the union to hold a new ballot. The union can, however, disenfranchise overseas members, that is, those abroad throughout the currency of the ballot, if it so chooses. There are special provisions for merchant seamen defined as a person 'whose employment or the greater part of it, is carried out on board sea-going ships' (s 230(2C)). If a trade union reasonably believes that the seaman will be employed either in a ship at sea or at a place outside Great Britain at some time in the period during which votes may be cast and it will be convenient for him to receive a voting paper and to vote while in the ship or at a place where the ship is then, he must if it is reasonably practicable have a voting paper made available to him whilst on the ship or at that place (s 230(2A), (2B)).

There may thus be difficulties as to the exact constituency of voters who may take part in a ballot. This can have important consequences on the question whether there is a majority vote for industrial action. The union may call out members who had joined since the date of a ballot, and to do so it does not lose the union its immunity which it would otherwise have. The Court of Appeal so decided in *London Underground Ltd v RMT* [1996] ICR 170 on the basis that it was the industrial action which required to be supported by a ballot, not industrial action in which a particular person has been induced to take part. Their Lordships rejected the proposition put forward by the employers that the industrial action which had been called was thus different from that on which the ballot had been held. They disapproved some comments of Lord Donaldson MR to this effect in *Post Office v UCW* [1989] IRLR 144.

5.17

The support of the ballot

The industrial action loses 'the support of the ballot' if the union calls out a member or ex-member who ought to have been given the right to vote but was not so given it. Section 232A reads in full (as amended by the Employment Relations Act 1999):

5.18

> Industrial action shall not be regarded as having the support of the ballot if the following conditions apply in support of *any person*—
> (a) he was a member of the trade union at the time when the ballot was held;
> (b) it was reasonable at that time for the trade union to believe he would be induced to take part or, as the case may be, to continue to take part in the industrial action;
> (c) he was not accorded entitlement to vote in the ballot; and
> (d) he was induced to take part or, as the case may be, to continue to take part in the industrial action

In *P v NASUWT* [2001] IRLR 532; [2003] IRLR 307, however, the union did not lose immunity when it inadvertently failed to send ballot papers to two members.

Until 1990 the ballot requirements applied only to persons engaged in industrial action who were employees. Section 5 of the 1990 Act, however, extended the provisions of the Trade Union Act 1984, s 10 (no immunity in tort for industrial action without a ballot) and the Employment Act 1988, s 1 to whose who work pursuant to contracts for services. By s 226(1):

5.19

an act done by a trade union to induce a person to take part or continue to take part in industrial action

(a) is not protected unless the industrial action has the support of a ballot and

(b) where section 226A [that is about notice of ballot and sample voting paper for employers] falls to be complied with in relation to the person's employer is not protected as respects the employer unless the trade union has complied with s226A in relation to him.

This crucially requires construction of the words 'industrial action' in cases where there is arguably more than one strike or piece of industrial action. If, for example, employees of 12 different toymakers throughout Britain decide to go on strike, there may be difficult issues as to whether there is in truth one strike, or 12 different strikes. This may have a vital effect on the immunity for industrial action, since there may be a majority in favour of ballots held in say Dorking, Cleethorpes and Louth, but an overall minority throughout the country. The definition of the 'strike' probably raises a matter of fact and degree on which no overall definition can be given, but it is another problem still to be fully worked out.

G. Conduct of the Ballot

5.20 The basic principles are:

(1) Although the union may not include non-members in a ballot, it may call on them to participate in the industrial action (*London Underground Ltd v RMT* [1995] IRLR 636).

(2) On the other hand, the union must be careful not to call out a member without balloting him since the industrial action called by the union does not have the support of a ballot if it was reasonable to expect that the person would be called on to participate in the industrial action but was denied the right to vote (s 232A). The only way out for the union would be falling back on the *de minimis* principle which has received statutory enactment in s 232B.

(3) There is a major distinction between mistakes in the ballot where minor errors may be excused if they are accidental and insignificant (ie they are 'on a scale which is unlikely to affect the result of the ballot') and a case in which the entitlement to vote was improperly denied (s 232A, s 226(2)(bb)).

(4) A union may persuade members who become members after the date of the ballot to participate in industrial action.

(5) A union may call out new employees since those would not be persons whom at the date of the ballot it reasonably expects to call on to participate in the industrial action (Code of Practice para 22).

The reasonable expectation as to who is going to take part is to be determined 'at the time of the ballot' (s 227(1)) which must mean the date on which the ballot papers are sent out as the Court of Appeal has twice determined in *London Underground Ltd v RMT* [1995] IRLR 636 and *P v NAS* [2001] IRLR 532.

The question

The statute requires that the ballot question ask 'whether [the member] is **5.21** prepared to take part, or as the case may be to continue to take part, in a strike' (s 229(2)). A statement to the effect that 'if you take part in a strike or other industrial action you may be in breach of your contract of employment' must be included by s 229(4). There must be no qualification or comment on this 'by anything else on the voting paper'. Further there must be no rolled up question such as was asked in *Post Office v UCW* [1989] IRLR 144 on the lines of whether employees were 'willing to take industrial action up to and including strike action'.

The question must be so phrased even though a ban on overtime may be **5.22** industrial action but not involve a breach of contract (see *Faust v Power Packing Casemakers Ltd* [1983] IRLR 117). Since the amendment by the Employment Relations Act 1999, s 4, Sch 3, paras 1, 6(1), (3) as from 18 September 2000, there is a counterweight to this because the following statement must also appear: 'If you are dismissed for taking part in a strike or other industrial action which is called officially and is otherwise lawful, the dismissal will be unfair if it takes place fewer than eight weeks after you started taking part in the action and depending on the circumstances may be unfair if it takes place later' (s 229(4)).

There appears nothing to prevent the union posing a further question loaded **5.23** in favour of the industrial action (although this would not be binding), nor from including tendentious campaigning material with the ballot, and several unions have done this. For example, in *Express & Star Ltd v Bunday* [1986] IRLR 477, the National Graphical Association sent out an accompanying notice stating that: 'You will be aware that as a result of legal action by the company under the new employment legislation the Association has been required by the court to hold a ballot in respect of continuing our action in response to the company's arbitrary introduction of single key stroking without agreement'.

The key point is that the ballot may not, however, merely ask whether the members agree with the union's negotiating position. Rather, it must put the individual member on the spot as to whether *he* is prepared to *participate* in the action proposed.

5.24 The voting paper must:

- state the name of the independent scrutineer;
- clearly specify the address to which and the date by which it is to be returned;
- be given one of a series of consecutive whole numbers; and
- be marked with that number (s 229(1A)).

5.25 There may be some doubt whether courts will grant an injunction to prevent industrial action if there are only minor defects in the voting procedure, but it seems likely that a judge would intervene if the question caused genuine confusion among voters as to the question(s) to be answered.

5.26 For the purposes of the ballot wording (but for no other purpose) an overtime or call-out ban will be treated as industrial action short of a strike (new TULR(C)A 1992, s 229(2A), reversing the effect of the Court of Appeal's decision in *Connex South Eastern Ltd v National Union of Rail Maritime and Transport Workers* [1999] IRLR 249). In that case, the union called for an overtime ban and ban on rest day working. Smooth operation depended on overtime being worked. Connex contended that the ban on overtime and rest day working was not a strike. Popplewell J considered that if work was available and men did not do it, that was indeed a concerted stoppage of work and therefore a strike. On appeal, Connex argued that this was an artificial meaning but the Court of Appeal found that it was indeed a period across the board of unqualified non-performance of all or any duty (and thus a strike) as opposed to refusal to do certain types of work (which would qualify as action short of strike). In the phrase 'concerted stoppage of work', concerted meant mutually planned; and stoppage of work was not specific; rather any stoppage of work would suffice (Aldous LJ at para 33). An overtime ban was a refusal to work certain periods of work at times required to be worked under the contract of employment. A rest day ban was a refusal to work on days which would normally be worked. Both thus qualified under the definition as a strike. The confusion which this might cause to trade union members led to speedy corrective legislation.

The Code of Practice also recommends not confusing a ballot on industrial **5.27** action with a ballot on other unconnected matters (para 10) and that where several unions are holding ballots on the same dispute they should seek to co-ordinate balloting arrangements.

H. Protection of the Voter

There are many provisions protecting the voter similar to those found in **5.28** TULR(C)A 1992, Part I, Chapter IV, relating to the election for the principal executive committee. The voter must not be interfered with or constrained in exercising his right to vote, nor should he have to bear any direct costs in so doing (s 230(1)(b)). The union is however only to lose immunity if such constraint is 'imposed by the union on any of its members, officials or employees'. The dictionary defines 'constraint' as 'the exercise of force to determine or confine action; coercion, compulsion'. It would be possible to charge for transport to convey members to some central voting place from an extensive or scattered workplace.

Interference here means *improper* interference (*RJB Mining (UK) Ltd v NUM* **5.29** [1997] IRLR 621). The union may thus be partisan and seek a positive vote for a strike or industrial action; any other view would be inimical to the appropriate role of the union and very difficult to police.

There must be security against ballot rigging in the voting arrangements **5.30** (para 38 of the Code of Practice). The Code of Practice recommends the appointment of (a) Returning Officer(s) to facilitate the proper publication of the result. It is an unresolved question as to how postal voting can be achieved if the employees of the Royal Mail are on strike. It is thought that in such a case it would be open to the union to postpone the closing date for the ballot since there is no restriction on the union so doing whether in the statute or the Code of Practice.

Voting at home

Every person entitled to vote must have a voting paper sent to him at the **5.31** address which he has requested the trade union in writing to treat as his postal address and be given an opportunity to vote by post (s 230(2)). Before 2000, there was an option for the union to make the ballot paper available so far as reasonably practicable to the potential striker immediately before, immediately after or during his working hours but this has been removed. A merchant seaman may still be given the opportunity to vote whilst at sea 'on the ship or while at a place where the ship is' (s 230(2A), (2B)). Merchant seaman is defined as 'a person whose employment or the greater part of it is carried out on board sea going ships' (s 230(2C)).

Again, subject to the reasonable practicability defence, the voting must be in secret (s 230(4)(a)).

Overseas members

5.32 A trade union may decide whether or not to accord overseas members entitlement to vote in a ballot (s 232(1)). Such an overseas member is one 'who is outside Great Britain throughout the period during which votes may be cast'. A member who is throughout this period in Northern Ireland is not treated as an overseas member where there are workplace ballots and his place is in Great Britain or there is a general ballot which relates to industrial action involving members in both Great Britain and Northern Ireland.

Industrial action at different workplaces

5.33 A union intending to organize industrial action must conduct separate ballots for each place of work, subject to certain important exceptions (s 228(3)). Industrial action may not be taken at a particular workplace unless the union has obtained a majority vote for the action at that workplace.

5.34 By TULR(C)A 1992, s 228, a separate ballot must be held for each workplace and entitlement to vote must be accorded equally to and restricted to members of the union who have that workplace (s 228(3)). This provision does not apply, however, where 'according to the union's reasonable belief [the union members] have an occupation of a particular kind or have any of a number of particular kinds of occupation'.

5.35 Before 1999 there had to be common features between workplaces, that is some factor:

(a) which relates to the terms, conditions, or occupational description of each member entitled to vote; and

(b) which that member has in common with some or all members of the union who have the same employer.

The High Court held, in *University of Central England v NALGO* [1993] IRLR 81 that it is not necessary for entitlement to vote in a ballot to be restricted to employees of only one employer. This is because while it would have been easy for reference to be made to a restriction to one employer in TULR(C)A 1992, s 288, none was made.

'Workplace' means if the person works at or from a single set of premises, **5.36** those premises and in any other case the premises with which the person's employment has the closest connection (s 228(4)). If the union fails to comply with these provisions, it will:

(1) lose its immunity from action in pursuance of a trade dispute; and

(2) be open to a claim by a member of the union under TULR(C)A 1992, s 235A(1).

Independent scrutiny

The ballot must have independent scrutiny (s 226B) unless it is a small ballot in **5.37** which no more than 50 are entitled to vote (ss 226(2)(a)(i), 226C). The scruti-neer must satisfy the terms of the Trade Union Ballots and Elections (Independent Scrutineer Qualifications) Order 1993 SI No 1909 as substituted by the similarly named amendment order SI 2002 No 2267) and the particular trade union must have 'no grounds for believing either that he will carry out [his] functions . . . otherwise than competently or that his independence in rela-tion to the union or the ballot might reasonably be called into question' (s 226B(2)). The Order states that practising solicitors and qualified accountants may act as may four named bodies: Electoral Reform Ballot Services Ltd; Election.com; Popularis Ltd and the Involvement and Participation Association. Further a person is treated as disqualified if he or 'any existing partner of his' has during the preceding 12 months been a member, an officer or an employee of the trade union proposing to hold the ballot' (reg 5(1)(a)).

There must be no interference by the union on his conduct of these duties (s 226B(3)) and the union must 'comply with all reasonable requests made by the scrutineer' (s 226B(4)).

5.38   The scrutineer has the duty to ensure the ballot is lawfully and efficiently conducted and must satisfy himself and report whether the security of the arrangements for the production, storage, distribution and return of the voting papers and for the counting of the votes minimize the prospect of malpractice.

5.39   To be valid there must be produced a scrutineer's report which gives the ballot a clean bill of health and copies must be made available to interested parties. He must state whether or not he is satisfied in these matters (s 231B):

(1)   the ballot has been conducted lawfully and 'there are no reasonable grounds for believing that there was a contravention of any requirement imposed by or under any enactment';

(2)   the balloting arrangements were as secure as was reasonably practicable; and

(3)   he was able to carry out the duties without interference from the union or those for whom it was responsible that is its members, officials or employees.

Should the scrutineer not be so satisfied, he must give the reasons why not. A person entitled to vote in the ballot or the employer of any such person may request a copy of the scrutineer's report within six months from the date of the ballot.

5.40   The Code of Practice states that the scrutineer might be given additional tasks to perform on the union's behalf such as supervising the production and distribution of voting papers; acting as the person to whom voting papers are returned by those voting; and retaining custody of the returned voting papers for a set period after the ballot.

5.41   The court may intervene to restrain a defective ballot even though the scrutineer has given it a clean bill of heath (*RJB Mining (UK) Ltd v NUM* [1997] IRLR 621), without the employer demonstrating that the scrutineer was perverse in his conclusion.

Notice of the ballot

5.42   A further important requirement for the validity of a ballot is found in TULR(C)A 1992, s 226A. The trade union must 'take such steps as are reasonably necessary to ensure that not less than the seventh day before the opening day of the ballot' (that is 'the first day when a voting paper is sent to any person entitled to vote in the ballot' (s 226A(4)) there is received, by every person whom it is reasonable for the union to believe will be the employer of those persons who will be entitled to vote in the ballot, a written notice to the effect that the union intends to hold a ballot, specifying the opening date of the ballot and describing the category of employees who will be entitled to vote therein (s 226A(1)). This means that a notice received on a Thursday would be valid for a ballot to commence in the next Friday but not before.

The burden of notifying the employer was reduced somewhat by provisions **5.43** contained in the Employment Relations Act 1999. Under these, it is no longer necessary for the union's notice to describe all the individuals who are being balloted; the duty is merely to include 'such information in the union's possession as would help the employer to make plans and bring information to the attention of those of his employees' (s 226A(2)(c)). Where the union possesses information as to the number, *category* or workplace of the employees, the notice to the employer should communicate this, but there is specifically no requirement to name individuals (new s 226A(3A)). Notices served on the employer by the appellant union relating to the pay strike action by 'all members of the union employed in all categories at all workplaces' did not comply with the requirements of ss 226A and 234A of the 1992 Act (*National Union of Rail, Maritime and Transport Workers v London Underground Ltd* [2001] IRLR 229). It was, however, sufficient for a union to tell the employer of its intention to ballot 'all Assessment and Advice Unit workers at Harrow Road who pay their union dues via the deduction of contributions at source scheme' (only about 45 workers). This was a category of employees (*Westminster* CC *v UNISON* [2001] IRLR 524). The court held that 'category' is a very broad word which means no more than a reference to the general type of workers. In *BT plc v CWU* [2003] EWHC 937 the CWU informed the employer that it was calling on 'all Engineering members currently in BT Customer Services Field Operations and BT Northern Ireland (MJE1 4 5)'. It was known that some 90 per cent of those affected by the voluntary introduction of the self-managed teams (the reason for the industrial dispute) were members of the union. Although many pay their dues by deduction from their salaries, others pay in other ways. There were various ways in which the employer might wish to 'make plans', for example to notify customers of the unavailability of services during the period of a strike or to organize teams of non-striking employees to carry out work having the greater priority. The union did give the employer the total number of those to be called out on strike. The judge found however that BT had raised a triable issue because although there were 90 per cent in union membership, this could not be assumed to be uniform across the UK. It would be of practical assistance to BT to have those numbers broken down on a local basis. There was a triable issue that the union indeed possessed information as to the number and category of employees beyond that which it had communicated and an injunction was granted.

Information is in a union's possession under s 226A(2)(c) if it is possessed by any official of the union who, in accordance with the union's rules, and normal operating procedures, is concerned with maintaining records kept for the union's purposes. This includes senior officials at union headquarters and branch secretaries (*NURMT v London Underground*, above). *Willerby Holiday Homes Ltd v UCATT* [2003] EWHC 2608 is an unusual case in that it was a full trial as opposed to an interim determination. Employees at Willerby were given a choice whether to pay union dues by direct debit or through check-off. The strike notice stated 'I understand that we have 397 members involved and I would identify them as being on your check-off list'. When the employers received the check-off list they found that it included 20 names of former employees and excluded two names of persons who were in fact union members before the ballot and were still employed. Also missing from the list were seven further members who had become members since the ballot was called.

The union said that the votes of individuals who were not on the list would be disregarded.

The judge found as an incontrovertible fact that the figure given in the notice was wrong and that the union at regional office level was aware it was wrong. The union could not say that it was prevented from ascertaining the true position by the employer obstructing attempts to inspect its records. The judge found that the union was in possession of more information than it gave to the employer and he could not regard the failures as accidental.

The judge also rejected the union's arguments under the European Convention on the basis that the financial penalty of damages for failing to give the proper notice indirectly discouraged members from exercising their right to associate and penalize them for so doing. It is possible for the state to derogate from Article 11 including to protect the rights of others and this included not only the rights of the employer but also the rights of others directly or indirectly affected by strike action.

The employer must be sent not later than the third day before the opening date of the ballot a sample voting paper (s 226A(1)). Any employer whom it was 'reasonable for the trade union to believe (at the time when the steps are taken) was at the time of the ballot the employer of any persons entitle to vote' must also be informed of the ballot result as soon as reasonably practicable after the holding of the ballot (s 231A(1)). **5.44**

The Code of Practice states that the union should in order to comply use a suitable method of delivery (first class post, courier, fax, e mail, or hand delivery) and obtain proof of delivery (para 15). It goes on to recommend that the union should check whether the employer accepts that the notice complies with the statute and controversially adds that a reasonable employer would immediately take the matter up with the union if it considered that the notice did not comply (para 16). In fact some employers would be tempted to wait to see if the ballot resulted in a yes vote and not so tell the union that it had an Achilles heel. **5.45**

If the union fails to notify the employer of the result of the ballot, it does not have the support of the ballot in respect of that employer so that an injunction could be gained (s 226(3A)). **5.46**

I. Counting the Votes

A majority of the voters must be in favour of the action in question for the union to have immunity from actions in tort. The union must take reasonably practicable steps to inform those entitled to vote of the complete result of the ballot, although here again it can exempt overseas members (s 231). Any inaccuracy in counting the votes is to be disregarded if it is accidental and on a scale which could not affect the result of the ballot (s 232B(1)). **5.47**

A majority vote

An unusual (if not unique) ballot result occurred in *West Midland Travel Ltd v TGWU* [1994] ICR 978. 1,265 votes were for strike action and 1,225 against, a majority of 40. There were 147 spoiled votes; if these were taken into account only 48 per cent had voted positively for strike action. The **5.48**

Court of Appeal ignored the spoiled votes. The union balloted its members on both a strike and other industrial action. 2,490 voted on the strike question but only 2,215 on the accompanying question of action short of a strike. It was discovered that 2,642 had cast at least one valid vote. The employer's argument was that the 1,265 voters for a strike were only a minority of those voting in the ballot. The Court of Appeal construed each question as a separate matter 'which has to be voted on individually' (Sir Stephen Brown P).

First authorization of strike

5.49   The general rule is that the first authorization or endorsement of the strike or other industrial action must be given within four weeks from the date the ballot is taken. Since 1999, the union and the employer may extend this period by agreement between them for up to another four weeks. This gives the union the flexibility to hold a ballot at the start of negotiations and then, with the employer's agreement, wait until the result is known up to eight weeks later before putting it into effect (s 234(1)). This may give more valuable time for negotiation. The Code recommends that an agreement should be reached in writing to avoid misunderstandings (para 46). In the event that unofficial action is later given official backing (ie endorsed, in the language of the statute), the ballot must be held before, but not more than four weeks before, the union declares it official.

5.50   There is, however, no need for the inducement of members to be successful for it to be such a relevant act (s 226(4)). The Court of Session in *Secretary of State for Scotland v Scottish Prison Officers' Association* [1991] IRLR 371 had to consider whether the instruction by the Association's executive to hold meetings of members during working hours without permission was a relevant act. It was held to be such a relevant act even though in the event no breach of contract occurred in fact because the meetings called by the POA were authorized by the employers.

5.51   Authorizing or endorsing by the union does not, however, extend to communicating the decision to authorize a ballot with a view to more extensive industrial action, and it was entitled to be partisan in this respect (*Newham London Borough Council v NALGO* [1993] ICR 189). The union was demonstrating that it wanted industrial action to be extended to members in addition to those already on strike but it was not calling on them to strike.

In the national docks dispute in 1989 the TGWU was prevented from call- **5.52** ing industrial action during this period of four weeks after the result of the ballot was announced because of an injunction granted by the High Court. In similar circumstances the union may now apply to the court for an exten- sion of time of up to 12 weeks, but no such application may be made more than eight weeks after the ballot (TULR(C)A 1992, s 234(6)). If on the basis of evidence presented to the court the ballot no longer appears to represent the views of the members, the court may not grant the extension (s 234(4)) if it considers that 'an event is likely to occur as a result of which those members would vote against industrial action if another ballot were to be held'. This means that the courts are to some extent drawn into the merits of the dispute and into hypothetical areas. The application must be made forth- with on the prohibition by injunction of the action ceasing to have effect. It must be made to the court which made the decision or on the lapsing of an undertaking given in lieu of an injunction. There may be no appeal against such an order (s 234(5)).

The call

The industrial action will not be treated as supported by the ballot if there **5.53** has been a 'call' for such action *before* the date of the ballot (TULR(C)A 1992, s 233(3)). 'Call' means that the actual action is positively announced. However, the Court of Appeal held in *Newham London Borough Council v National and Local Government Officers Association* [1993] I CR 189 that s 233(3) does not require the union to take a neutral stance in relation to the ballot. A union can thus indicate its desire for industrial action to be held without that amounting to a call for, or authorization or endorsement of, such action.

There are various rules about the call to participate in industrial action:

- The call must not be made until after the ballot (s 233(3)(a)).
- A call is not constituted by urging members to vote in favour of industrial action (*Newham LBC v NALGO* [1993] ICR 189).
- The call must be made by a specified person (s 233(1)) who is specified in the voting paper as having the authority to call for the particular industrial action pursuant to s 229(3).
- The specified person may delegate the communication of the call (*Tanks and Drums Ltd v TGWU* [1992] ICR 1).

- There must be one call for each piece of industrial action so that the court may have to determine when one piece of industrial action begins and terminates, and there may be different methods of industrial action within the course of a single dispute so that the union may start with an overtime ban and escalate the action to a strike (*Newham LBC v NALGO* [1993] [1993] ICR 189).

J. Ballots and Injunctions

5.54   The only reported case which has yet weighed the balance of convenience in giving an injunction when there has been no ballot is *Solihull Metropolitan Borough v National Union of Teachers* [1985] IRLR 211. The NUT issued guidelines to its members to refuse to cover for absences of colleagues known in advance and various other tasks. No ballot had been held and Warner J granted an injunction that the union must rescind its instructions. Whilst he accepted that there would be detriment to the plaintiff in the harm done to the children in their schools, which could not be remedied in damages, he thought that on the other side, there would be little inconvenience to the union. It was merely a matter of choosing between holding a ballot and accepting arbitration.

In another case in chambers a judge refused to grant an injunction when one group of workers had voted heavily in favour of a strike and there was no reason to dispute that the group which had not balloted would not do the same (*Morfax v TASS*, unreported).

6

INDUSTRIAL ACTION LESS THAN A STRIKE

A. Background

Professor Clegg has commented that: 'The strike is not the only method of **6.01** bringing industrial pressure to bear on the employer, and indeed it is the most expensive from the employees' viewpoint'. (*The Changing System of Industrial Relations in Britain* (3rd edn, Blackwell, 1979).) Donaldson P said in 1973: 'The forms of industrial action are limited only by the ingenuity of mankind'. Ironically enough, the employer may be more at risk from guerilla action where he cannot identify the culprits than from a general strike by his workforce. The advantages for the union in sponsoring such tactics are that:

- It is likely to be more difficult for the employer to identify the union as having 'authorised or endorsed' such action, which is essential for the union to be liable under TULR(C)A.
- Employers may be at risk if they deduct wages. It may require only a small amount of disruption by unidentifiable persons for example to bring a television station to a standstill whilst other employees will rightly claim to have been ready, willing and able to work and that they should therefore be paid in full. The employee may claim a deduction from wages under the Employment Rights Act 1996, Part II.

- There may be a greater compatibility with the employees' professional code of conduct or ethics. Thus, a full-scale strike by hospital staff is now almost impossible to envisage, but a work-to-rule or overtime ban are regular features of industrial relations in the health service.
- Forms of industrial action short of strike may not alienate public sympathy for those involved.

The Department of Employment Workplace Industrial Relations Survey between 1980 and 1984 found that non-strike industrial action was growing at the expense of strikes. The Labour Research Department Survey (*Unions at Work*, 1986) found that stoppages of work were the most common form of industrial action, followed by overtime bans, although these were more likely to be used in the private sector (36 per cent of action) than the public sector (10 per cent). Works-to-rule, on the other hand, were more common in the public sector—14 per cent compared with 6 per cent in the private sector.

We will now consider the most common British forms of industrial action other than strikes.

B. The Work-to-Rule and Go-Slow

6.02   Employees here meticulously follow work rules, the rationales for many of which have been lost in the mists of time. Forms are filled in with punctilious care. Usually ignored safety provisions are re-activated and relied on to excess. Remote risks to employees' safety are emphasized and the factory inspector may be called in without any real need. This slows down the rate of work in a manner wholly unacceptable to employers, who may then be tempted to stress to their employees that if they are not prepared to work normally they should not work at all, which is a high risk strategy for all. Most employers will not face the prospect of a lock out (which this would amount to) with equanimity.

6.03   This method has traditionally had a particular vogue on the railways, and one of the leading cases not surprisingly arises from that industry. *Secretary of State for Employment v ASLEF (No. 2)* [1972] 2 All ER 949 was actually an exercise by the Court of Appeal in statutory construction of the Industrial Relations Act 1971, but it also revealed fundamental underlying issues of relevance here. Their Lordships had to construe the phrase 'industrial action involving a breach of contract' for the purpose of determining whether the Secretary of State for Employment had jurisdiction, under the then current Industrial Relations Act 1971, to order a cooling-off period and strike ballot. The union banned Sunday and rest-day working, restricted overtime and decreed a work-to-rule. The first two were not contractual duties and so did not qualify; the overtime ban, on the other hand, clearly was a breach of contract. Most controversial was the work-to-rule.

The Court of Appeal did not in fact deal with the matter head on by deciding that the rule book was an integral part of the contract; rather they said that it was a collateral set of instructions. The action of the union, however, emptied the general work obligation of its meaning, so that it was a breach of an implied term of the contract to work in accordance with lawful instructions and not to disrupt the employer's undertaking. There were, nonetheless, three distinct rationales for the decision which to this day have not been clarified by later case law:

(1) Lord Denning MR thought that there was an implied duty not to obstruct the employer wilfully. The employee need not offer his goodwill nor do more than was required by contract, but there was a breach where he 'with the others, takes steps wilfully to disrupt the undertaking, to produce chaos so that it will not run as it should'. The very object of the action rendered it unlawful, and he provided a 'homely example' of a breach in the man employed to take the hirer to the station: 'If he deliberately drives slowly so as to make the hirer miss the train the contract is broken even though the letter of the contract is carried out'.

(2) Buckley LJ defined the duty differently as 'to serve the employer faithfully with a view to promoting those commercial interests for which he is employed'.

(3) Roskill LJ's rationale was the narrower principle that each employee should not 'in obeying his lawful instructions, seek to obey them in a wholly unreasonable way which has the effect of disrupting the system'.

In *Drew v St. Edmundsbury Borough Council* [1980] ICR 513 the EAT **6.04** considered the implied undertaking to be 'that in so far as [the employee] is capable of doing so, he should work at a reasonable speed; if he deliberately slows down his work, he breaks his contract'.

Departure from normal performance may be a breach of the implied duty to give faithful service and/or to maintain trust and confidence. (See also *Miles v Wakefield Metropolitan District Council* [1987] IRLR 193; ICR 368, HL; *Wiluszynski v Tower Hamlets London Borough Council* [1989] IRLR 259; ICR 493.)

6.05   The position was considered further in *Ticehurst v British Telecommunications plc* [1992] IRLR 219. The employee claimed for loss of wages in respect of days on which she was not permitted to work by the employers because she refused to sign an undertaking that she would no longer participate in industrial action in the form of a withdrawal of goodwill. Ralph Gibson LJ's leading judgment stated:

> It is, in my judgment, necessary to imply such a term in the case of a manager who is given charge of the work of other employees and who therefore must necessarily be entrusted to exercise her judgment and discretion in giving instructions to others and in supervising their work. Such a discretion, if the contract is to work properly, must be exercised faithfully in the interests of the employers.

His Lordship further found that:

> There is a breach of the implied term of faithful service when the employee does an act, or omits to do an act, which it would be within her contract and the discretion allowed to her not to do, or to do, as the case may be, and the employee so acts or omits to do the act, not in the honest exercise of choice or discretion for the faithful performance of her work but in order to disrupt the employer's business or to cause the most inconvenience that can be caused.

Although it would be open to the employer to treat the employee's breach of contract as grounds for dismissal, this is not the only option available. Applying *Miles v Wakefield Metropolitan District Council* to this case, Ralph Gibson LJ stated that:

> if on her return to work Mrs Ticehurst was evincing an intention to continue to participate in the action of withdrawal of goodwill, BT was in my judgment entitled on that ground, and without terminating the contract of employment, to refuse to let her remain at work.

The employer was therefore entitled to lock-out, and not pay, an employee who refused to work normally. It was argued on behalf of BT that the principle went even further such that an employee's evinced intention to take part in future in strike action was sufficient ground for the employer to refuse to let her continue to work. The Court of Appeal distinguished, however, between participating in a withdrawal of goodwill and an intention to take part in a rolling campaign of strikes. The former was a continuing breach of the obligation to serve the employer faithfully and thus an intention not to perform the full range of contractual duties. In contrast, although participation in strike action would be a breach of contract, a mere intention to respond to a strike call, if and when it is issued, could not be so regarded, since the employee is assumed to be intending to fully perform the contract unless and until called out on strike. This means that a performance that is apparently lawful may become unlawful if it is done with an intent to disrupt the employer's business. Nevertheless, as the next case makes clear an employee does not have to do all that his employer may wish provided that he performs what he can be required to perform under the contract.

In *Burgess v Stevedoring Services Limited* [2002] UKPC 39; [2002] IRLR 810, **6.06** the Privy Council considered the issue of whether a ban on voluntary overtime was a breach of the contracts of employment of participating employees. The *ASLEF* case had for 30 years been treated as authority for the proposition that concerted action by workers keeping to the strict rules of their contract amounts to a breach of contract where the object was wilfully to disrupt the business of the employer. The principle has now been limited by the Privy Council in the important case of *Burgess*.

Like the *ASLEF* case the issue arose on an exercise in statutory construction. The court had to consider whether an overtime ban by port workers fell within the definition of 'industrial action' in the Bermuda legislation as being a 'concerted course of conduct . . . which, in contemplation or furtherance of a labour dispute . . . is carried on by a group of workmen . . . in breach of their contracts of employment.' The Privy Council held that the overtime ban was not in breach of the contracts of employment of the participants.

Lord Hoffmann's decision addressed the statement by Lord Denning in the *ASLEF (No. 2)* case that an employee who 'takes steps wilfully to disrupt the undertaking . . . is guilty of a breach of his contract'. He pointed out that this does not support the proposition that even if the employees were *not* under a contractual obligation to report for overtime duty, their failure to do overtime was a breach of contract because it was done wilfully to disrupt the business of their employer. He took the view that Lord Denning must have:

> had in mind that employees may legitimately perform their duties in a way which does not suit the employer . . . if they have a bona fide reason but not if their purpose is to be wilfully obstructive. But that does not mean that they are in breach for refusing to do things altogether outside their contractual obligations . . . merely because they do not have a bona fide reason for refusal. They do not have to have any reason at all.

The Privy Council went on to state that:

> It is in any case, difficult to see how the motives of individual employees, as employees, can be relevant when their action is simply to stay at home because they have not been assigned any overtime work. If they had been assigned work and, as part of a concerted action, all claimed to be sick or have some other reason for declaring themselves not available . . . the *ASLEF* case might have some relevance.

6.07 However, performance that is deliberately bad such as a go-slow may be a breach of contract. This was considered by the Privy Council in *General Engineering Services v Kingston and St Andrew Corporation* [1989] IRLR 35, which was an appeal from a decision of the Court of Appeal of Jamaica. The Privy Council ruled that firemen were not acting in the course of their employment when, because they were operating a go-slow in pursuance of an industrial dispute, they took so long to reach the scene of a fire that the property was destroyed. The firemen's conduct could not be categorized as a wrongful and unauthorized mode of carrying out the authorized act of driving to a fire. Their mode and manner of driving—a slow progression of stopping and starting—was not so connected with the authorized act as to be a mode of performing that act. Lord Ackner added that:

> the unauthorised and wrongful act by the firemen was a wrongful repudiation of an essential obligation of their contract of employment, namely the decision and its implementation not to arrive at the scene of the fire in time to save the building and its content. This decision was not in furtherance of their employers' business. It was in furtherance of their industrial dispute, designed to bring pressure upon their employers to satisfy their demands, by not extinguishing fires until it was too late to save the property. Such conduct was the very negation of carrying out some act authorised by the employer, albeit in a wrongful and unauthorised mode.

Such action would therefore be a breach of the contract of employment.

C. Overtime Ban

6.08 These have occurred most frequently in newspapers, local government and the electricity supply industry. The contractual position is more clear-cut if the overtime is compulsory but this is rarely in fact formally the case. A concerted refusal to carry out overtime may, however, constitute 'industrial action' for the purposes of TULR(C)A (*Faust v Power Packing Casemakers Ltd* [1983] IRLR 117, see p 192). However, an overtime ban may not be a breach of contract where there was no obligation to carry out overtime as the Privy Council in the *Burgess* case have recently found.

D. Ban on Particular Duties

Employees may work normally save that they refuse to perform particular **6.09** duties about which they are complaining. Thus drivers on one-man buses may refuse to collect fares or teachers may refrain from supervising dinner duties (*Gorse v Durham County Council* [1971] 2 All ER 666). There may be more argument about whether such refusal constitutes a repudiatory breach. It depends in each case primarily on the importance of the duty not carried out. In *Bowes & Partners v Press* [1894] 1 QB 202, for instance, the court found that there was a repudiatory breach when miners refused to go down a pit cage with a non-trade unionist. The main issue in such cases will be the extent to which the employer may refuse to pay for imperfect service.

The thrust of the teachers' industrial action in their long-running pay dispute **6.10** in 1985–86 was refusal to cover for absent teachers. In *Sim v Rotherham Metropolitan Borough Council* [1986] IRLR 391, four teachers, backed by the National Union of Teachers, sought to recover from their respective employers sums deducted for such refusal to cover. This threw into relief the question whether the obligation to cover was contractual or voluntary, a matter on which the conditions of service were silent. Scott J was not surprised by this. He thought that teachers were professionals and like other professionals their contractual obligations were 'defined largely by the nature of their respective professions and the obligations incumbent on those who follow those professions'. Professionals are employed to provide a particular service and have a contractual obligation to do so properly and 'teachers' duties were not necessarily confined to their obligations to be on school premises during school hours and to take classes during those hours'. It was 'a professional obligation of each teacher to cooperate in running the school during school hours in accordance with the timetable and other administrative regulations or directions from time to time made or given'. The evidence left his Lordship in no doubt but that teachers had always accepted a professional obligation to comply with cover arrangements. The claimants were thus held not to be entitled to repayment of monies deducted from their salary for refusal to cover. The issue for determination therefore remains whether or not the employee is obliged to carry out the particular duties.

E. Disruptive Meetings

6.11   Another form of industrial action is the holding of a disruptive union or chapel meeting. This was a commonly used tactic in national newspapers, where even a short meeting in the middle of the evening may lead to the loss of millions of copies of the paper. Its use has declined with the rapid reduction in union strength in the newspaper industry. Where the action takes place during employees' working hours it may be a breach of contract.

F. Sit-in

6.12   The sit-in or work-in was developed as a tactic to great effect in the renowned Upper Clyde Shipbuilders' dispute in the early 1970s. This arose when there was a proposal to close the shipyards which were major local employers. The advantages to the workers of this form of action are that it may be easier to maintain morale during a sit-in than in the case of a strike, where the striking workforce are spread in different towns and communication is less immediate. Further, it will give to the occupiers control over the employer's machinery, tools and stock.

6.13   Employees who participate in such action will normally be in breach of their contracts of employment since they are not ready and willing to work at the appropriate time. They are also likely to commit trespass, since employees normally only have a contractual licence to remain on the premises of the employer while they are at work, and such a licence can be terminated by reasonable notice, being sufficient time for the person to remove their effects from the premises (see *GLC v Jenkins* [1975] 1 All ER 354; *City and Hackney Health Authority v National Union of Public Employees* [1985] IRLR 252).

6.14   Various offences may also be committed by persons taking part in a sit-in. As we saw in relation to picketing TULR(C)A 1992, s 241 delineates a number of specific offences which may be committed by 'every person who performs certain acts, with a view to compel any other person to abstain from doing or to do any act which such other person has a legal right to do or abstain from doing, wrongfully and without legal authority'. There are offences relating specifically to the hiding of tools, or factory property or preventing the employer having access to them, and to 'watching and besetting' the place where a person works. Both have been applied to employee occupations. In

Gait v Philp [1984] IRLR 156, for example, the Scottish High Court found criminally liable laboratory technicians who conducted a 'work-in'. Medical laboratory scientific officers had convened a meeting in their laboratory in response to the suspension of a colleague for alleged breach of guidelines. The police broke in and arrested the officers who were convicted under what was then s 7 of the 1875 Act. 'Watching and besetting' was not, it was held, limited to action outside property. Control of access from within was equally within the ambit of the section. The defendants could not rely on what is now TULR(C)A, s 219 as providing immunity since the trade dispute defence did not cover criminal acts.

Most commentators were surprised by the decision of the Court of Session **6.15** in *Plessey plc v Wilson* [1982] IRLR 198, in which an injunction was refused in Scotland to restrain a sit-in at the petitioner's Bathgate factory. The court concluded that, albeit that trespass was not included within the torts specifically immunized against by the trade dispute defence, the immunity extended to any tort which constituted an interference with the trade or business. Even if the reasoning were sound at the time the case was decided, it is unlikely that such a case would be decided the same way.

G. Lock-out

An employer may be so determined not to accept imperfect performance of **6.16** the contract of employment in the case of disruptive work that he refuses to allow the employee to work at all unless he is willing to perform his normal duties. Such a course may have its hazards for the employer. For it to be lawful, the employee locked out must be in breach of contract himself. In *Bond v CA V Ltd* [1983] IRLR 360, one of the employees refused to perform tasks mentioned in an ad hoc agreement (a collective bargain) which could, according to the judge, only be terminated on giving reasonable notice. Since the claimant in fact was ready and willing to operate the machines in accordance with the rest of his contract and it was the act of the defendants which prevented him from doing so, the lock-out was in breach of contract and he was thus entitled to wages during the period of lock-out.

It is ironic that in this situation of lock-out, whether or not contractually **6.17** valid, the employer can manufacture for himself immunity under TULR(C)A from unfair dismissal. A dismissal of an employee where there is a lock-out is automatically fair as in the case of 'industrial action' or a strike (see the section on unfair dismissal at p 187 ff).

6.18   Moreover, employees cannot normally gain an injunction to restrain employers from terminating the contracts of employment of those locked out. In *Chappell v Times Newspapers Ltd* [1975] ICR 145, Lord Denning MR based this on the unwillingness of the courts to order specific performance of a contract of employment and because 'no employers can be expected to continue to employ a body of men or any of them who assert through their union that they intend to disrupt the business and bring losses on their employer'.

7

CONSUMER ACTIONS

A. The *Falconer* Case

The prospect of a growth in consumer litigation against strikers was opened **7.01**
up by the county court judgment in *Falconer v ASLEF and NUR* [1986]
IRLR 331. It is rare that a county court case should gain as much publicity
as this one did, but it was the first of its kind. The rail unions decided not to
appeal against the decision and thus robbed the principle of the authority it
might have had with approval by the Court of Appeal.

Mr Falconer claimed damages for expenditure incurred and for inconvenience caused by the rail unions who went on strike on 17 January 1986 leaving him stranded in London. He had gone south on a business trip and
wished to return to Sheffield that evening. The claim was based on the developing tort of interference with the contract, in this case the agreement of
carriage between Mr Falconer and British Rail, by unlawful means (see para
3.7). The unlawful means adopted were the unions' respective calls to their
membership to strike in breach of their contracts of employment. The defendants accepted that they would have no immunity for actions in tort since
no ballot had been held. The argument centred on the existence of a tort, and
the thrust of the unions' defence was that the claimant was unknown to them
and they did not act deliberately or wilfully to harm *him*, and therefore he
had no cause of action.

Judge Henham followed the statement of the law by Jenkins LJ in *Thomson
(D.C.) & Co. v Deakin* [1952] Ch 646. The first question was whether the

defendants knew of the existence of Mr Falconer's contract and intended to interfere with its performance. His Honour concluded that 'the plaintiff was one of a definite and identifiable group of people in a contractual relationship with the BR Board. The fact that his actual name and description were unknown to the Defendants at the time does not preclude him from beginning the action . . . '. To suggest, as did the defendants, that the effect on passengers was merely consequential was 'both naïve and divorced from reality', since 'it was clearly the intention of the defendants in calling the strike to direct its effect on the plaintiff and others and that by so doing create pressure upon the Board by the plaintiff and others and thus to induce the Board to accede to the defendants' wishes'.

The second and third hurdles in Jenkins LJ's test were clearly established. These were that the defendants induced or procured the British Rail employees to break their contracts of employment with the Board and that the employees did in fact break their contracts. The fourth was more problematic, namely whether the interference with the performance of the contract between the BR Board and the claimant ensued as a 'necessary consequence' of the employees' breaches of their contracts. The judge rejected the defendants' contention that the contract with BR merely created an *expectation* to provide transport without any primary obligation. The defendants could not avail themselves of the exclusion clause in British Rail's conditions of carriage since it was their unlawful action which brought about a breach of the primary contractual obligation. As damages, the judge awarded special damages claimed of £53 and general damages of £100.

The judge was not impressed by the arguments of the unions that a decision in favour of the plaintiff would open the floodgates of liability. If so, that was a matter for Parliament and not for the courts. The ambit of liability demonstrated by the *Falconer* decision is indeed wide, and one may expect to see actions by disgruntled businessmen cut off from their post by a post strike, by electricity consumers blacked out, or by airline passengers hit by a lightning strike at the airport of departure.

B. TULR(C)A 1992, s 235A

7.02 There is also a little used provision in TULR(C)A 1992, s 235A which was introduced in order to give statutory recognition to the right of a person affected by industrial action to claim against the union. The action arises when an individual claims that 'any trade union or other person has done or is likely to do an unlawful act to induce any person to take part or to continue to take part in industrial action and an effect or a likely effect of the industrial action is or will be to prevent or delay the supply of goods or services or reduce the quality of goods or services supplied' to the individual making the claim. The action is unlawful if it is actionable in or by one or more persons or it could form the basis of an application by a member under TULR(C)A, s 62. It is not a prerequisite that 'the individual is entitled to be supplied with the goods or services in question'. The court may on such an application:

> make such order as it thinks appropriate for requiring the person by whom the act of inducement has been or is likely to be done to take steps to ensure that no or no further act is done by him to induce any person to take part or continue to take part in the industrial action and that no person engages in conduct after the making of the order in such industrial action (s 235A(4)).

This may include the granting of an interim injunction.

8

PICKETING, CRIMINAL OFFENCES AND STATUTORY RESTRICTIONS

A. Introduction

In an age when the television camera can be mightier than the pen the meth-   **8.01**
ods by which a trade union, or its members, execute a strike can very often
be witnessed by the general public from their armchairs. The battle is as
much for public support as industrial strength itself. One particular method
of execution which may receive widespread media coverage, and which may
help to gain or lose public sympathy for those taking industrial action, is
picketing. The concept of picketing, and the term itself, are not new.
Statutory regulation has been in evidence since 1875, and from time to time

the courts have been called upon to determine whether the picketing that has been carried out has been lawful.

In the 1980s strikes called by the larger trade unions, such as the mineworkers and the print unions, relied for their success upon large-scale, or 'mass' picketing, and that has on occasions led to violent confrontations between picket and strike-breaker, and between picket and police. There is, however, evidence that the incidence of picketing is diminishing. The Department of Employment Workplace Industrial Relations Survey between 1980 and 1984 found that the overall extent of picketing declined by nearly a half between 1980 and 1984, excluding the miners' strike, and in manufacturing the drop was from 18 per cent of plants to three per cent.

In recent major disputes employers have successfully obtained injunctions to limit the numbers of pickets, frequently rendering the pickets' protest ineffective. Unions and workers are left facing the spectacle of the 'right' to demonstrate and to picket peacefully being regulated by statute. The Industral Relations Survey of 1998 shows the continuing trend in the reduction of industrial action with other means of asserting pressure being taken (although 2001 did show a total of 525,000 working days lost through labour disputes which was the highest since 1996). Nevertheless, unions have sought other means to take disruptive action in pursuit of their goals (such as work to rule: see pp 124–8).

Although the introduction of the Human Rights Act 1998 may have an effect upon picketing the Blair Government has not altered the picketing legislation since it came to power.

8.02 Picketing is regulated by both the civil and criminal law although in practice the latter is far more important as it is much more likely to have an impact during the strike where protestors may be arrested for breach of the peace. In this chapter, we will consider the following aspects of picketing:

- historical development;
- the definition of picketing;
- civil liability;
- the statutory immunity;
- the Code of Practice on Picketing;
- the criminal law.

Historical development

The present law starts from the premise that picketing is not of itself unlaw- **8.03** ful. It does not constitute a tort. This was the clear view of the Court of Appeal in *Ward Lock & Co. Ltd v Operative Printers' Assistants' Society* (1906) 22 TLR 327. That case concerned the 'watching and besetting' provision of TULR(C)A 1992, s 141(1)(d) (formerly of the Conspiracy and Protection of Property Act 1875, s 7(4)). The picketing arose in the context of a printing dispute. Members of the defendant union were stationed outside the claimant's printing works. Their intention was to persuade the claimant's employees to join the union and then lawfully to terminate their employment with the claimant. There was no evidence that the pickets invited the workmen to act in breach of their contracts of employment, and the picketing was carried out without violence and without causing any obstruction or other common law nuisance. The court thus held that nothing had occurred which was unlawful. Moulton LJ said that: '. . . in my view, that which decides the question is that there is no evidence of any improper or illegal acts or indeed of any acts whatsoever, by any pickets sent by the defendants during this period. There can, therefore, be no pretence that the Claimants have established anything that would give them a good cause of action in respect of the picketing complained of . . .'.

The picketing was not of itself actionable. It was necessary that some tort or crime had been committed before the claimant could succeed in an action.

Therefore, the mere fact that men were stationed as pickets outside an employer's premises (where no torts of trespass or nuisance were committed) with a view to persuading employees no longer to work for him was not something of which, by itself, the employer could complain. The decision in the *Ward Lock* case was however at variance with a previous decision of the Court of Appeal in *Lyons (J.) & Sons v Wilkins* [1896] 1 Ch 811 (affirmed [1899] 1 Ch 255), where it was held that the mere watching and besetting of a man's house was conduct which seriously interferes with the ordinary comfort of human existence and ordinary enjoyment of the house beset, and such conduct would support an action on the case for a nuisance at common law (*per* Lindley MR at [1899] 1 Ch 267). The issue which was decided differently in the two cases was not strictly whether picketing was of itself lawful, but (and it is an important distinction) whether or not it amounted to a common law nuisance. In the *Ward Lock* case it was held that it did not amount to a common law nuisance. To be actionable the picketing had to be carried out in such a manner as to constitute a nuisance, or be otherwise unlawful.

8.04   Whilst the decision in *Lyons v Wilkins* is still correct with regard to the picketing of a person's home (see *Thomas v National Union of Mineworkers (South Wales Area)* [1986] Ch 20), subsequent statutes and judicial decisions (the *Thomas* case; *News Group Newspapers Ltd v SOGAT 82 and others* [1986] IRLR 337) have firmly established that the *Ward Lock* decision is an accurate statement of the law with regard to picketing of a workplace.

8.05   The present statutory regulation of picketing is to be found in TULR(C)A 1992, s 220. As will be seen, it provides a rather limited cloak of legality for acts carried out in the course of picketing, yet does not render acts falling outside the scope of the section necessarily unlawful. Those acts must be shown to constitute either a criminal offence or tortious conduct.

8.06   Furthermore, picketing is always subject to the overriding control of the police, who are normally present at the picket line in order to keep the peace, but who, to many pickets, seem to act on the side of the employer. In the 1970s and 1980s industrial unrest indeed saw much of the pickets' frustration and anger being levelled at the police. Many pickets view the police as preventing them exercising the pressure they wish to exert on the employer. The police have the power to halt any picketing which they reasonably anticipate will lead to a breach of the peace and this confers a wide discretion on the police as to how they control a picket, which may be violent and a threat to public order.

The Human Rights Act 1998

8.07   The incorporation of the European Convention on Human Rights into UK law by the Human Rights Act 1998 as a matter of law would appear to create a right to picket in so far as the right to peaceful assembly is guaranteed by Article 11 of the Covention. By s 6(1), acts of public authorities, it is unlawful for a public authority to act in a way which is incompatible with a Convention right. This provision extends to the courts. Articles 10 and 11 are most important in this respect.

Under Article 10:

> 1 Everyone has the right to freedom of expression. This right shall include freedom to hold opinions and to receive and impart information and ideas

without interference by public authority and regardless of frontiers. This Article shall not prevent States from requiring the licensing of broadcasting, television or cinema enterprises.

2 The exercise of these freedoms, since it carries with it duties and responsibilities, may be subject to such formalities, conditions, restrictions or penalties as are prescribed by law and are necessary in a democratic society, in the interests of national security, territorial integrity or public safety, for the prevention of disorder or crime, for the protection of health or morals, for the protection of the reputation or rights of others, for preventing the disclosure of information received in confidence, or for maintaining the authority and impartiality of the judiciary.

Under Article 11:

1 Everyone has the right to freedom of peaceful assembly and to freedom of association with others, including the right to form and to join trade unions for the protection of his interests.

2 No restrictions shall be placed on the exercise of these rights other than such as are prescribed by law and are necessary in a democratic society in the interests of national security or public safety, for the prevention of disorder or crime, for the protection of health or morals or for the protection of the rights and freedoms of others. This Article shall not prevent the imposition of lawful restrictions on the exercise of these rights by members of the armed forces, of the police or of the administration of the State.

It was held in *Steel v UK* (1998) EHRR 603 by the European Court of Human Rights that the Article created a right of peaceful picketing albeit in a non-industrial case. The applicant, Mr Steel disrupted a grouse shoot by jumping up and down in front of the shooter to prevent him from firing. Mr Lush stood in front of a mechanical digger to prevent work being carried out on a motorway extension. Mr Needham held a banner and Messrs Polden and Cole distributed leaflets outside an armament conference. All were arrested and charged with breach of the peace. Messrs Steel and Lush were convicted but the prosecution offered no evidence in relation to the other three. Complaints were made to the European Court of Human Rights by the applicants of breaches of Article 5 (freedom from unlawful arrest), Article 10 (freedom of expression) and Article 11 (right of peaceful assembly). **8.08**

So far as Article 5 is concerned, the court found that the Article protected the citizen from arrest on vague and unspecified charges but that the law on breach of the peace was sufficiently precise. There was sufficient evidence against Steel and Lush but a breach in relation to the other three.

The court held that Article 10 was applicable to the actions of all five and that the real issue to be determined was whether the interference with their expressions of opinion was lawful. It found that it was lawful in the case of Messrs Steel and Lush but not in the case of the other three given that no evidence was offered against them. The restriction on the right was lawful against the two in pursuance of a legitimate aim in a democratic society. A degree of latitude was to be allowed to individual states but the overriding consideration was that the means used had to be proportionate to the end to be achieved. Steel and Lush were both intent upon disruption so that their detention was proportionate but the detention of the other three was not as there had been no significant obstruction or attempt to provoke violence.

The court took the view that it was not necessary to consider the effect of Article 11 as the issues had been sufficiently considered under Article 10. However, it is apparent that the same approach would be adopted as with Article 10 so that there will be a line between peaceful assembly and obstruction. The courts will have to consider the purpose and acts of the pickets as against the disruption that is being caused and where an offence is being committed it is not likely that there will be a breach of the Convention.

Definition of picketing

8.09   In domestic law TULR(C)A 1992, s 220 is the key regulation. It is the successor to TULRA 1974, s 15 which was drafted specifically to describe lawful picketing. There is a Code of Practice on Picketing which is intended to guide the courts in deciding whether pickets' conduct is lawful, although breaches of the Code are not themselves unlawful. The Code was issued under the power given to the Secretary of State by the Employment Act 1980, s 3 (as amended by the Employment Act 1988, s 18) with the authority of Parliament (resolutions passed on 19 February 1992 by the House of Commons and on 21 February 1992 by the House of Lords). It is continued in force as if made under TULR(C)A 1992, s 203 by TULR(C)A, Sch 3, para 1. It was brought into force on 1 May 1992 by the Employment Code of Practice (Picketing) Order 1992, SI 1992/2176 and remains the operative Code. The Code does not contain a definition of picketing and there is no statutory definition of the term.

In the *Ward Lock* case Moulton LJ, drawing on the manner in which s 7(4) **8.10** of the 1875 Act had been drafted, described picketing as 'a convenient term for what is included in the phrase "watching and besetting or causing to be watched or beset the Claimants premises or the approaches thereto".' The Oxford English Dictionary defines pickets as: 'men acting in a body or singly who are stationed by a trade union or the like, to watch men going to work during a strike or in non-union workshops, and to endeavour to dissuade or deter them' and picketing as: 'the posting of men to intercept non-strikers on their way to work and to prevail upon them to desist'.

This definition was the one cited by Stuart-Smith J in *News Group* **8.11** *Newspapers Ltd v SOGAT 82 and others* [1986] IRLR 337 (the Wapping picketing case). Picketing normally consists merely of the attendance of two or more persons outside premises 'in connection with an industrial dispute' (for an example of a case not involving an industrial dispute but in which the term was used, see *Hubbard v Pitt* [1976] QB 142). The extent to which picketing is lawful is determined by the combined provisions of the existing common law as modified by statute. In so far as picketing is carried on unlawfully, liability may be incurred under both civil and criminal law and they will be considered in turn.

B. Civil Liability

Although an employer could undertake a private prosecution for criminal **8.12** offences committed during picketing, it is more likely to wish to bring civil proceedings claiming an injunction and damages. If it can establish that tortious conduct is occurring it will often be able to obtain an interim injunction which may effectively end the picketing and be the final relief in the case, since disputes are usually resolved before the employer proceeds to a full trial (see Chapter 11). If matters do come to trial the employer will usually be seeking damages as well as an injunction, and will also be able to recover the cost of measures taken in reasonable anticipation of tortious picketing (see *Messenger Newspapers Group Ltd v National Graphical Association* [1984] IRLR 397 on injunctive relief).

We now consider the most important torts for present purposes which are as **8.13** follows: *Lumley v Gye* and other economic tort claims; public nuisance; private nuisance; trespass to the highway; intimidation; and harassment.

Lumley v Gye and other economic torts

8.14   Such torts will be committed if the pickets succeed in dissuading strike-breakers from continuing working, or suppliers from delivering supplies, or if they succeed in interfering with the employer's commercial contracts. In order to be able to qualify for the general trade disputes immunity provided by TULR(C)A 1992, s 219(1) the pickets' conduct will have to come within s 220.

8.15   Whilst there are factual distinctions between attendance/trespass and persuasion/inducment or interference, the mere attendance of pickets is likely to be persuasion and may be more than persuasion, amounting to an inducement or interference with contract. If it can be shown that the picket had the intention to induce a breach of contract and the presence on the picket line did have that effect, then the tort of *Lumley v Gye* will normally be made out and there may be liability if the immunity does not apply because the picketing goes beyond that which is effectively licensed to be carried on. In *Union Traffic Ltd v Transport and General Workers' Union* [1989] IRLR 127, the former employees' place of work had been closed down so that it was pointless to picket there. Instead, they picketed other premises of their employer. The Court of Appeal rejected the premise that everyone must have somewhere where he can effectively picket. Bingham LJ stated:

> It is inescapable that the defendants' object was to bring the Claimants' business at the two depots to an immediate halt. That could be achieved only if those seeking to enter and leave the depots were effectively deterred from doing so at once. That is something which could not be achieved forthwith without breaches of contract of employment by those persons, whether the Claimants' own employees or the employees of their customers, as the defendant would be very well aware. I do not think that it is very important what, if anything, was said by the defendants. In my judgment, persuasion is enough, but the verb 'persuade' has a wide range of meaning as exemplified by the secondary meaning of the noun 'persuader'. Presence alone at the site would in my judgment be enough if it were clear, as I think it is, that that presence was intended and was successful in its object of inducing breaches of contract. I bear in mind of course that this is an interlocutory application and one should not and cannot take a final view, but on existing materials the Claimants in my judgment show a strong case, subject to the question of statutory immunity, of inducing breach of contract.

The court took account of the reluctance of the lorry drivers to cross the picket line. An interim injunction was considered by the Court of Appeal to be appropriate since there was no statutory protection because the pickets were not at their own place of work.

Public nuisance

As well as being a criminal offence, public nuisance is also tortious. There **8.16** must for this purpose be 'an unlawful interference with the enjoyment of a right common to all Her Majesty's subjects', although the persons affected need only constitute a particular class of the public (*Attorney-General v PY A Quarries Ltd* [1957] 2 QB 169 *per* Romer LJ at 184). One such public right is that of free passage along the highway, and in the context of picketing the nuisance will generally consist of an interference with or obstruction of that right. However, to be actionable the obstruction must form an unreasonable use of the highway (*Lowdens v Keaveney* [1903] 2 IR 82). A march or meeting on the highway will not necessarily constitute a public nuisance simply because there is some obstruction (*R v Clark* [1964] 2 QB 315). An orderly and peaceful march along the highway is likely to be lawful, but uncontrolled, disorganized and possibly violent gatherings on the highway will probably amount to a public nuisance. In *News Group Newspapers Ltd v SOGAT 82 and others* [1986] IRLR 337 the conduct of pickets and daily demonstrators at the News International plant during the Wapping dispute was an unreasonable obstruction of the highway, as were the twice weekly rallies and demonstrations which ended there.

In *Hubbard v Pitt* [1976] QB 142, an unusual case of non-industrial picket- **8.17** ing which has had a major impact in the industrial sphere, a small group of Islington residents, complaining about the policies of a firm of local estate agents, walked up and down on the pavement outside the firm's office carrying placards and distributing leaflets. At first instance, Forbes J granted the estate agents an interim injunction on the grounds that it was likely to be established at trial that the conduct amounted to a nuisance, and that the balance of convenience favoured the claimants. He said: 'As picketing is a use of the highway wholly unconnected with the purposes of dedication for the public's right of passage and is, in fact, designed to interfere with the rights of an adjoining owner to have unimpeded access from the highway, it is likely to be found to be an unreasonable use unless it is so fleeting and so insubstantial that it can be ignored under the *de minimis* rule'.

The majority of the Court of Appeal (Stamp and Orr LJ) upheld his decision, but only on the basis of the principles governing the grant of an interlocutory injunction set out in *American Cyanamid Co. v Ethicon Ltd* [1915] AC 396. Lord Denning MR dissented vigorously pointing out that, on the facts, no tortious conduct had occurred. He stated: 'Picketing is not a nuisance in itself. Nor is it a nuisance for a group of people to attend at or near the Claimants' premises in order to obtain or to communicate information or in order peacefully to persuade. It does not become a nuisance unless it is associated with obstruction, violence, intimidation, molestation or threats'.

8.18 Save in the unlikely event that the Attorney-General brings a relator action, a public nuisance is only actionable as a civil wrong if the claimant can show that he has suffered particular damage over and beyond that suffered by the general public. 'Such particular damage must be substantial, but it is not limited to special damage in the sense of provable pecuniary loss' (*News Group Newspapers Ltd v SOGAT 82 and others* (above)).

8.19 In *Thomas v National Union of Mineworkers (South Wales Area)* [1986] Ch 20, Scott J held that since the working miners' entry and egress from the relevant collieries was not in fact being physically prevented by the pickets, they could not establish the necessary special damage which would entitle them to sue in respect of public nuisance. Those who wished to work were transported in special buses at no cost to themselves. In *News Group Newspapers Ltd v SOGAT 82 and others* (above), it was held that there was special damage where those employees who continued to work were forced to travel to and from the premises by taxi, and were unable to leave in the middle of the day for fear of being subject to the pickets' abuse and threats. They also complained of feeling drained by the pressure created by the situation. The claimant companies also succeeded in establishing special damage in the extra cost of having to transport their employees in specially adapted buses, and of employing extra security.

It is important to note that the claimant does not need to show a proprietary interest in order to succeed.

Private nuisance

8.20 A private nuisance occurs when there is unreasonable use which interferes with the enjoyment of land over which another has a proprietary interest. Such nuisance is likely to occur in relation to the entrances and exits of an employer's premises:

The owner of land adjoining the highway has a right of access to the highway from any part of his premises. . . . The rights of the public to pass along the highway are subject to the rights of access [of adjoining landowners].
(Lord Atkin in *Marshall v Blackpool Corp.* [1935] AC 16.)

If the interference with the right is alleged to be an obstruction, it must be shown that the obstruction was an unreasonable use of the highway, at it was in *News Group Newspapers Ltd v SOGAT 82 and others* (above). News International was entitled to sue since it owned the Wapping plant close by. The mere attendance of pickets without any other tortious conduct is not an actionable nuisance (*Ward Lock & Co Ltd v Operative Printers Assistants Society* (1906) 22 TLR 327 and see *Hubbard v Pitt* above). **8.21**

Although Scott J in *Thomas v NUM (South Wales Area)* [1985] IRLR 136; [1985] ICR 886 thought that the tort of nuisance could be extended to wider tort of harassment (as to which see below) it is submitted that this proposition is erroneous because the tort of private nuisance protects the ownership or exclusive possession of land and the common law does not have a wider tort of harassment. It was indeed confirmed in *Hunter v Canary Wharf Ltd* [1997] AC 655; 2 All ER 426 that a mere licensee or occupier cannot bring proceedings for nuisance. Nor can the union be primarily liable in nuisance where its members have picketed. **8.22**

The union may be vicariously liable for the acts of the members if they constitute a nuisance but the union has no responsibility to abate the nuisance (as a landowner would have), and dicta of Stuart-Smith J to the contrary in *News Group v SOGAT 82* are not correct.

Trespass to the highway

Forbes J in *Hubbard v Pitt* [1976] QB 142 stated that: 'The highway is a piece or strip of land dedicated to the use of the public over which each member of the public has a right to pass or repass and do things reasonably incidental thereto'. Wherever a person is using the highway other than purely as a means of passage, he is only entitled to use it for the purpose which is reasonably incidental and any unreasonable use beyond this use will constitute a trespass (*Hickman v Maisey* [1900] 1 QB 712). The trespass will only be actionable at the suit of the owner of the subsoil, which will usually be the local authority. **8.23**

A meeting or demonstration on the highway is not necessarily an obstruction **8.24**

(*Burden v Rigler* [1911] 1 KB 337). In *News Group Newspaper Ltd v SOGAT 82 and others* [1986] IRLR 337, however, Stuart-Smith J thought the marches organized by the defendants outside the Wapping Print Works were not a reasonable use of the highway, since they got out of control and then there were attacks on the police, the claimants' employees who were working and TNT Roadfreight which was transporting the claimants' newspapers around the country (para 130).

8.25 It is also possible for pickets to commit a trespass if they walk in a continuous circle in front of factory gates which has the effect of obstructing the entrance (cf. *Tynan v Balmer* [1967] 1 QB 91; [1966] 2 All ER 133).

8.26 The law was reviewed most recently in *DPP v Jones* [1999] 2 All ER 257, a non-industrial case in which the House of Lords redefined the scope of trespass. The demonstrators protested at a roadside verge that they had been excluded from Stonehenge. Two of them were arrested and charged with participating in a trespassory assembly in breach of the Public Order Act 1986, ss 14A and 14B. It was necessary to show that they were members of a group of 20 or more who had exceeded the public's rightful use of the highway. The House of Lords held that the prosecution must fail. Lord Irvine LC was of the view that the public's right on the highway was not confined to passage and repassage and purposes that were incidental thereto. He could not:

> . . . attribute any hard core of meaning to a test which would limit lawful use of the highway to what is incidental or ancillary to the right of passage. In truth very little activity could accurately be described as 'ancillary' to passing along the highway; perhaps stopping to tie one's shoe lace, consulting a streetmap, or pausing to catch one's breath. But I do not think that such ordinary and usual activities as making a sketch, taking a photograph, handing out leaflets, collecting money for charity, singing carols, playing in a Salvation Army band, children playing a game on the pavement, having a picnic, or reading a book, would qualify. These examples illustrate that to limit lawful use of the highway to that which is literally 'incidental or ancillary' to the right of passage would be to place an unrealistic and unwarranted restriction on commonplace day-to-day activities. The law should not make unlawful what is commonplace and well accepted.

Lord Irvine concluded:

> . . . the law to be that the public highway is a public place which the public may enjoy for any reasonable purpose, provided the activity in question does not amount to a public or private nuisance and does not obstruct the highway

by unreasonably impeding the primary right of the public to pass and repass; within these qualifications there is a public right of peaceful assembly on the highway . . . Provided an assembly is reasonable and non-obstructive, taking into account its size, duration and the nature of the highway on which it takes place, it is irrelevant whether it is premeditated or spontaneous; what matters is its objective nature. To draw a distinction on the basis of anterior intention is in substance to reintroduce an incidentality requirement. For the reasons I have given, that requirement, properly applied, would make unlawful commonplace activities which are well accepted. Equally, to stipulate in the abstract any maximum size or duration for a lawful assembly would be an unwarranted restriction on the right defined. These judgments are ever ones of fact and degree for the court of trial.

Nor was there any basis for distinguishing highways on publicly owned land and privately owned land. The nature of the public's right of use of the highway could not depend upon whether the owner of the subsoil is a private landowner or a public authority.

Lord Clyde was of the view that in any case where there is a peaceful non-obstructive assembly it will necessarily exceed the public's right of access to the highway. The question then is whether on the facts the limit was passed and the exceeding of it was established. The test then is not one which can be defined in general terms but has to depend upon the circumstances as a matter of degree. It requires a careful assessment of the nature and extent of the activity in question. If the purpose of the activity becomes the predominant purpose of the occupation of the highway, or if the occupation becomes more than reasonably transitional in terms of either time or space, then it may come to exceed the right to use the highway. However:

> The fundamental element in the right is the use of the highway for undisturbed travel. Certain forms of behaviour may of course constitute criminal acts in themselves, such as a breach of the peace. But the necessity also is that travel by the public should not be obstructed. The use of the highway for passage is reflected in all the limitations, whether on extent, purpose or manner. While the right to use the highway comprises activities within those limits, those activities are subsidiary to the use for passage, and they must be not only usual and reasonable but consistent with that use even if they are not strictly ancillary to it.

On this basis, it would be necessary that a picket on the highway be of temporary duration.

Lord Hutton thought that the law had previously been more restrictive but that it should be extended as set out by Lord Irvine. Lords Slynn and Hope dissented, taking the traditional view that the public had the right to use the highway as a highway, for the purpose of passage and re-passage so that demonstrators who were intent upon staying on the spot were not exercising a right of passage along the highway.

It is therefore, following the majority approach, not possible to say that picketing is necessarily lawful or unlawful at common law but it depends upon whether the pickets exceeded their common law right to use the highway, and *per* Lord Clyde, such pickets should be of temporary duration.

8.27 The Human Rights Act 1998 and the Convention may impact upon peaceful picketing as Article 11 gives a *right* of peaceful assembly which will necessarily include picketing. In the *Jones* case, Lord Irvine had disagreed with the Divisional Court's conclusion that all peaceful assemblies on the highway were tortious but Lord Irvine pointed out that:

> Unless the common law recognizes that assembly on the public highway *may* be lawful, the right contained in art 11(1) of the convention is denied. Of course the right may be subject to restrictions, for example: the requirements that user of the highway for purposes of assembly must be reasonable and non-obstructive, and must not contravene the criminal law of willful obstruction of the highway. But in my judgment our law will not comply with the convention unless its *starting-point* is that assembly on the highway will not necessarily be unlawful. I reject an approach which entails that such an assembly will always be tortious and therefore unlawful.

Intimidation

8.28 In the *News Group Newspapers* case Stuart-Smith J explained (at 347) that the tort of intimidation is committed:

> when A delivers a threat to B that he will commit an act or use means unlawful against B, as a result of which B does or refrains from doing some act which he is entitled to do or not to do, thereby causing damage either to himself or C. The tort is one of intimidation and the Claimant, whether it be B or C must be a person whom A intended to injure.

The tort could be committed if a picket threatens to use violence against a strike-breaker unless he ceases working. If the strike-breaker gives in, and this affects the employer and causes him loss, the employer may bring an action against the pickets. The tort is not complete unless the person threatened succumbs to the threat and damage is suffered, although injunctive relief can be obtained to restrain the unlawful act and threats to commit the unlawful act since 'it is both the threats and the assault that should be restrained' (see also *Messenger Newspapers Group Ltd v National Graphical Association* [1984] IRLR 397, paras 48–9). On the other hand, idle abuse by pickets not meant to be taken seriously would not amount to intimidation. There was evidence in the *News Group Newspapers* case that those of the claimants' employees who passed both the pickets at the main gate of the Wapping plant and also those who demonstrated each day a few hundred yards away at the intersection of the Highway and Virginia Street were 'almost invariably subjected to abuse, and frequently, to threats. They are called scabs, but that is the least of the insults. Vile and obscene language is used particularly to women. . . . There are also threats, such as "We'll get you" and "You can't hide forever"' ([1986] IRLR 337, para 49). There were also 'rushes' on the main gate of the plant in order to prevent lorries from leaving the plant.

Harassment

In *Thomas v National Union of Mineworkers (South Wales Area)* [1986] Ch 20 **8.29** (for facts see pp 146–7 and 168) Scott J found that the harassment which the claimants suffered as they went to and from work was tortious. He held that, although the claimants could not bring an action for public nuisance because they could not show that they had suffered particular damage, the law should protect the enjoyment of other rights relating to land and, in particular, the right of every citizen to use the highway. He concluded: 'In the present case, the working miners have the right to use the highway for the purpose of going to work. They are in my judgment entitled under the general law to exercise that right without unreasonable harassment by others. Unreasonable harassment of them in the exercise of that right would in my judgment be tortious'.

Seeking to bring the tort within established boundaries of liability, the judge said that it could be classified as: 'a species of private nuisance, namely unreasonable interference with the victim's rights to use the highway. But the label for the tort does not in my view matter'. Scott J summed up the evidence that: 'the picketing at the colliery gates is of a nature and is carried out in a manner that represents an unreasonable harassment of the working miners. A daily congregation on average of 50 to 70 men hurling abuse and in circumstances that require a police presence and require the working miners to be conveyed in vehicles do not in my view leave any real room for argument'.

The decision was criticized as being an unwarranted extension of the law or an erroneous view of the current law. His Lordship had already stated in his judgment that the claimants could not establish that they had suffered particular damage and could therefore not sue in respect of a public nuisance. Private nuisance involves interference with the enjoyment of land which the claimant owns or over which he has some proprietary right. Therefore, to have held that the harassment was a private nuisance, Scott J would have had to find some proprietary right which the working miners had in relation to the highway or in relation to access to the collieries by virtue of being employed there. The existence of either of these proprietary rights would be a wide extension of the law never before sanctioned.

Strenuous efforts were indeed made by the print unions in the *News Group* case to persuade the judge to disapprove of Scott J's judgment, arguing that the actions found could not constitute a nuisance and that the judge was therefore creating an unwarranted new tort. The judge did not consider it necessary to express a final view on the matter but indicated that he found force in the union's arguments. It is thought unlikely that the Court of Appeal will uphold the existence of the tort of harassment in the sense defined by Scott J, and an employer would be better advised to rely on the established torts such as intimidation, which was revealed to be an effective cause of action in this context in, for example, the *News Group* case.

8.30   The traditional view was indeed reaffirmed in *Hunter v Canary Wharf Ltd* [1997] AC 655. There is thus no common law of harassment. Parliament has however, enacted a statutory crime and tort of harassment by the Protection from Harassment Act 1997.

By s 1 of the Act:

> (1) A person must not pursue a course of conduct—
>   (a) which amounts to harassment of another, and
>   (b) which he knows or ought to know amounts to harassment of the other.
> (2) For the purposes of this section, the person whose course of conduct is in question ought to know that it amounts to harassment of another if a reasonable person in possession of the same information would think the course of conduct amounted to harassment of the other.

8.31   The test of harassment set out in the Act is objective, the question being whether a reasonable person would take the view that the acts in question amounted to harassment. Section 1(3) contains three defences, the third of which is only likely to be relevant in the picketing context, although it may follow that where the picketing has become unlawful the conduct would not be regarded as reasonable:

(3) Subsection (1) does not apply to a course of conduct if the person who pursued it shows—
   (a) that it was pursued for the purpose of preventing or detecting crime,
   (b) that it was pursued under any enactment or rule of law or to comply with any condition or requirement imposed by any person under any enactment, or
   (c) that in the particular circumstances the pursuit of the course of conduct was reasonable.

Section 3 specifically provides a civil remedy to the person who alleges that he has been harassed or is in fear of harassment. By s 3(1) an actual or apprehended breach of s 1 may be the subject of a claim in civil proceedings by the person who is or may be the victim of the course of conduct in question. By s 3(2) damages may be awarded for (among other things) any anxiety caused by the harassment and any financial loss resulting from the harassment. **8.32**

The court may grant an injunction to restrain harassment and, by s 3(3), where the High Court or a county court grants an injunction for the purpose of restraining the defendant from pursuing any conduct which amounts to harassment, and the claimant considers that the defendant has done anything which he is prohibited from doing by the injunction, the claimant may apply for the issue of a warrant for the arrest of the defendant. The application is to be made to a High Court judge if the injunction was granted in the High Court and to a judge or district judge of the county court in which it was granted or another county court where the injunction was first granted in the county court (s 3(4)). By s 3(5) the judge or district judge to whom an application under subsection (3) is made, may only issue a warrant if the application is substantiated on oath and the judge or district judge has reasonable grounds for believing that the defendant has done anything which he is prohibited from doing by the injunction. Breach is also a criminal offence (see para 8.80). **8.33**

Section 7 provides that, for the purposes of the interpretation of the Act, references to harassing a person include alarming the person or causing the person distress; a 'course of conduct' must involve conduct on at least two occasions and 'conduct' includes speech. The aggressive picket line, which for example included the comments referred to in the *Messenger Newspapers* case, is likely to be covered by the Act. **8.34**

C. The Right to Picket and the Statutory Immunity

8.35   The 'right' to picket, so far as it exists (particularly given the impact of the Human Rights Act 1998, see p 140) is now contained in TULR(C)A 1992, s 220. The section provides as follows:

> (1) It is lawful for a person in contemplation or furtherance of a trade dispute to attend—
>> (a) at or near his own place of work, or
>> (b) if he is an official of a trade union, at or near the place of work of a member of the union whom he is accompanying and whom he represents,
>
> for the purpose only of peacefully obtaining or communicating information, or peacefully persuading any person to work or abstain from working.
>
> (2) If a person works or normally works—
>> (a) otherwise than at any one place, or
>> (b) at a place the location of which is such that attendance there for a purpose mentioned in subsection (1) is impracticable,
>
> his place of work for the purposes of that subsection shall be any premises of his employer from which he works or from which his work is administered.
>
> (3) In the case of a worker not in employment where—
>> (a) his last employment was terminated in connection with a trade dispute, or
>> (b) the termination of his employment was one of the circumstances giving rise to a trade dispute,
>
> in relation to that dispute his former place of work shall be treated for the purposes of subsection (1) as being his place of work.
>
> (4) A person who is an official of a trade union by virtue only of having been elected or appointed to be a representative of some of the members of the union shall be regarded for the purposes of subsection (1) as representing only those members; but otherwise an official of a union shall be regarded for those purposes as representing all its members.

8.36   Recognition was first given to the acceptability of *peaceful* picketing in the Conspiracy and Protection of Property Act 1875, s 7 which provided for an exception from the criminal liability otherwise imposed by the section. Section 2 of the Trade Disputes Act 1906 replaced the 1875 exception with a wider immunity, based on the concept of 'attendance' rather than 'watching and besetting', by providing that attendance for, inter alia, the purposes of peacefully persuading any person to work or abstain from working would be lawful in civil as well as criminal law. Such attendance had to be carried out in contemplation or furtherance of a trade dispute.

Section 2 of the 1906 Act was in turn replaced by s 134 of the ill-fated Industrial Relations Act 1971. That section was structured rather differently from its predecessor, although the only significant change was to remove attendance at a person's residence from the scope of lawful picketing. The section also expressly provided that picketing carried out in accordance with its provisions would not of itself constitute a criminal offence or civil tort.

The incoming Labour Government soon repealed the 1971 Act, replacing it with TULRA 1974. Section 15 of that Act, as originally enacted, provided for lawful attendance at a place where a person worked or carried on business, or at any other place where another person happened to be, except that other's place of residence.

The section was amended by the 1980 Employment Act and is now contained in the 1992 consolidating Act as set out above. The section is supplemented by the Code of Practice, which may be admitted into evidence in any proceedings (s 207).

There are three principal factors which will determine the lawfulness or otherwise of the action, and all three must be satisfied for the pickets to be acting lawfully.

- Context: A trade dispute must be in existence and the picketing must be in contemplation or furtherance of it. The meaning of trade dispute is considered in detail in Chapter 4.   **8.37**
- Location: The picketing must take place at or near the pickets' place of work (except in the case of a trade union official; see p 159). Pickets will usually congregate around the entrance to and exits from the employer's premises, since the people whom they are seeking to influence are inevitably the strike-breakers and the employer's customers and suppliers who will use those entrances and exits. Statute cannot and does not specify the distance away from the entrance at which a person may be and yet remain within the definition. This has to be decided on the particular facts of the case. In *Thomas v National Union of Mineworkers (South Wales Area)* [1986] Ch 20, striking miners who congregated on the opposite side of the road to the colliery where they worked came within s 220. In *News Group Newspapers Ltd v SOGAT 82 and others* [1986] IRLR 337, the defendant print unions stationed six official pickets at the gates of the Wapping plant to which the claimants had moved their business shortly after the strike was declared. It was not disputed that the pickets were attending 'at or   **8.38**

near' those premises. In addition, a crowd of between 50 and 200 demon-strators would gather daily at a road junction approximately 50 yards from the gates of the plant. That junction had to be passed by anyone going to or from the plant.

Stuart-Smith J held that, despite the distance from the gates, those people attended for the purpose of persuasion of their views and communication of information, and s 220 therefore applied to them. Furthermore, twice a week a much larger crowd would march to the plant and rally near it. It was held that the participants were not picketing as they progressed to the plant and therefore the provisions of s 220 were not referable to the walk. On the other hand, once the marchers dispersed, those who went to the plant with a view to persuasion and communication were thereupon held to be picketing (see *McCarthy and Stone (Developments) Ltd v TGWU and UCATT*, High Court, December 1986).

8.39   A precise geographical definition of what constitutes being 'at or near' is of course unrealistic. Moreover, although in one case it may be feasible to describe a person who is 50 yards away from the factory gates a picket, in another it might not. It is thought that this issue will generally be resolved (as it was in the *News Group* case) by reference to the purpose and actions of the persons involved rather than merely by strict notions of geographical proximity.

8.40   The interior of private premises does not fall within the phrase 'at or near'. In *Larkin v Belfast Harbour Commissioners* [1908] 2 IR 214, it was held that the Trade Disputes Act 1906, s 2 did not confer a right to enter upon private premises, against the will of the owner. That decision was approved of and followed in *British Airports Authority v Ashton* [1983] IRLR 287 where it was decided that picketing could not take place within the perimeter of Heathrow Airport which was the property of BAA (see also *Galt v Philp* [1984] IRLR 156, a decision on the 'watching and besetting' provision of the Conspiracy and Protection of Property Act 1875, s 7(4) and *Norbrook Laboratories v King* [1982] IRLR 456).

The issue was also considered in *Rayware Limited v Transport and General Workers' Union* [1989] IRLR 134 in which the Court of Appeal took a broad and purposive approach to the words 'at or near his own place of work' in particular. The former employee's place of employment was on a trading estate some 7/10ths of a mile down a private road from the entrance to the estate. Since they would have been trespassing by picketing on the private road, the pickets were set up on the highway at the entrance to the estate. The Court of Appeal, overruling the judge at first instance, held that the pickets were 'at or near' their place of work. Both May and Nourse LJJ took the view that s 220 was intended to establish (*per* May LJ) 'a right to picket' and (*per* Nourse LJ) 'a liberty to exert peaceful persuasion over fellow employees'. Accordingly, Nourse LJ held that: 'It is not consistent with that purpose to construe the section so as to make it impracticable . . . for many groups of employees to maintain pickets at all'.

May LJ stated that 'the mere fact that the Claimants are on a private trading estate . . . is not in my view of itself sufficient to prevent the nearest point where pickets can lawfully stand from being at or near the Claimants' premises'.

The decision is of great relevance for determining the picketing rights of employees in a similar position as it is common for factory units to be on such estates. Indeed, Nourse LJ emphasized that 'if this conclusion establishes a precedent for other comparable industrial and commercial developments, we should not flinch from that result' and Woolf LJ expressly associated himself with this view. The *Rayware* decision was followed in *Timex Electronics Corpn v Amalgamated Engineering and Electrical Union* [1994] SLT 348 where it was held that an interim interdict (the Scottish form of injunction) restraining persons from attending 'at or near' the main gate of the factory was not too vague but had to be interpreted in relation to its purpose and the pickets knew they were enjoined from picketing near the main gate.

Section 220 of TULR(C)A 1992 is very restrictive in relation to the premises **8.41** which a person may lawfully picket. Picketing at the premises of an associated employer of the employer involved in the dispute is not lawful, nor is picketing other premises of the same employer. The section, therefore, does not protect the so-called 'flying pickets' such as those who operated in the 1984–85 miners' strike, who picketed collieries in different coalfields and in different counties, other than their own. Indeed, the only injunction gained by the National Coal Board during the course of that strike was to restrain Yorkshire miners picketing collieries in Nottinghamshire. Although there was evidence of disobedience to this order, the Board did not pursue the issue with enforcement proceedings.

8.42 Special provision is made in s 220(2) for workers who work at more than one place and those for whom it is impracticable to picket at their own place of work because of its location. These workers are entitled to picket at any premises of their own employer from which they work or from which their work is administered. Mobile workers may picket their Head Office or the office from which their work is administered. The wording of TULR(C)A appears to say that it may be any one of several premises but in the *Union Traffic* case (see below) Lloyd LJ inferred that the intention must have been to allow workers to picket that one workplace which was their principal workplace or base or from which the work was administered. This restrictive interpretation is not clear from the wording of the Act and such an interpretation becomes meaningless when one considers the issue of impracticability.

8.43 Where it is impracticable for the employee to picket his place of work (for example, a North Sea Oil Rig) the employee may picket at premises from which his employer works or from which the employee's work is administered. In *Union Traffic Ltd v Transport and General Workers' Union* [1989] IRLR 127; ICR 98, Lloyd LJ did not think that the 'impracticability' test was made out where the employee's depot had closed down. However, if it was not practicable for drivers to picket a closed depot it did not give the pickets the right to close the depot. The right conferred was to picket the principal place of work or from where the work had been administered. The wording, thus interpreted, defeats its purpose as it is precisely because it is impracticable to picket the principal workplace that the picket wishes to picket some other workplace. The restrictive interpretation turns on the definition of 'impracticable'; the purpose of attendance at a workplace that has closed down, that is peaceful persuasion, is impossible because the factory is closed. However, it is not *physically* impracticable for the pickets to attend at the closed premises and Lloyd LJ thought that the section was so limited.

8.44 Often a strike will result from, or shortly lead to, the dismissal of some or all of the workforce. Their former employer's premises could then no longer strictly be described as their own place of work, since they would not have a place of work at all. Section 220(3) therefore provides that during the dispute in relation to which the workers were dismissed, s 220(1) should be read as if instead of 'his own place of work', it referred to 'his former place of work'.

The precise wording of the phrase should be noted; it does not say his 'place of former work'. The distinction was exemplified in *News Group Newspapers*

Ltd v SOGAT 82 and others [1986] IRLR 337. The claimants dismissed members of the defendant unions who were employed by them. The dismissals were effected shortly after the unions had called a strike, and the claimants at once transferred their business to new premises in London. The sacked printers picketed the new premises but since they had never been employed at those premises none were entitled to seek the immunity provided by s 220. The new plant was the place to which *their former work* had been transferred, but was not *their former place of work*. Such a factual situation was unlikely to have been in the contemplation of the statute's draftsman, but the words of the section provide a clear answer to the issue. This interpretation was so held in *Union Traffic Ltd v Transport and General Workers' Union* [1989] IRLR 127. In this case, the former employees' place of work had been closed down so they picketed other premises of their employer. The Court of Appeal rejected the premise that 'everyone must have somewhere where he can effectively picket'. Bingham LJ stated:

> That is, in my judgment, not so, as a reading of s 15 makes plain. One need only take the case of an employee who works . . . at one place which is closed; it may then be futile to picket at that place, but it may nonetheless be the case that there are no other premises of his employer from which he works or from which his work is administered, and in that event there is nowhere he can effectively picket.

Taking the two decisions together, the *Rayware* case [1989] IRLR 134 holds that a purposive interpretation must be given to what is 'at or near' the employee's place of work so as to allow picketing at the nearest practicable point, but as is clear from the *Union Traffic* case [1989] IRLR 127 also reminds us that this is subject to the overriding proviso that the place of work must be the employee's own and that s 15 cannot be stretched to permit picketing at a different premises on grounds of practicability.

Although picketing which takes place other than at one's place of work or **8.45** former place of work ('secondary picketing') cannot be declared lawful under s 220 it is not thereby automatically unlawful (see *Thomas v National Union of Mineworkers (South Wales Area)* [1986] Ch 20, *News Group Newspapers Ltd v SOGAT 82 and others* (below)). To be unlawful, a nuisance or some other tort must be committed.

A trade union official has, by virtue of his office, a slightly less restricted right **8.46** to picket. By TULRA 1974, s 220(1)(b) he may attend 'at or near the place of work of that union whom he is accompanying and whom he represents'.

The purposes for which he may attend are no different. A person who is an official by virtue only of having been elected or appointed to be a representative of some of the members of the union shall be regarded as representing only those members; otherwise he shall be taken to represent all the union's members (s 220(4)).

8.47   • Purpose: This is the factor which most often denies pickets the opportunity to claim the s 220 immunity. It allows pickets to set up placards and banners (provided they do not cause an unreasonable obstruction) and, to an extent, to chant or call out. It allows them to approach strike-breakers and to seek to persuade them to join the strike. However, it does not entitle pickets to force anyone to stop and listen to their views. In *Broome v DPP* [1974] AC 587, Lord Reid said: 'I see no ground for implying any right to require the person whom it is sought to persuade to submit to any kind of constraint or restriction of his personal freedom. . . . If the driver stops, the picket can talk to him, but only for so long as the driver is willing to listen'.

8.48   Protection is lost by shouting abuse or threats, as well as by the use of violence. The courts have also held that the sheer weight of numbers of pickets may be inconsistent with the notion of peaceful picketing. In the *Thomas* and *News Group* decisions, the judge expressed the view that mass picketing could never, by its nature, be lawful, particularly when it necessitated a large police presence and caused those who continued to work in defiance of the strike to have to be brought to work in specially constructed buses whose windows were protected from attack by missiles (see also *Broome v DPP* (above)). In *Messenger Newspapers Group Ltd v National Graphical Association* [1984] IRLR 397, para 48, Caulfield J described the action of the defendants and 'outsiders desirous of violence' as 'mobocracy at its worst'.

8.49   The insertion of the word *only* in s 220(1) means that it is not sufficient that peacefully obtaining or communicating information, or persuading others to work or not to work, is *one* or even the *main* purpose of the action. In *Tynan v Balmer* [1967] 1 QB 91, the court held that although the aim of peaceful protest was present, the additional intent to cause vehicles approaching the factory premises to stop, took the picketing outside the immunity. In *Mersey Dock and Harbour Co. v Verrinder* [1982] IRLR 152 Judge Fitzhugh had regard to the intentions and states of mind of the pickets, in addition to the actual consequences of their acts, and he felt that on the facts those matters displayed: 'an attempt on the part of the defendants to regulate and control the container traffic to and from the company's terminals,' and therefore fell outside s 220(1).

The pickets will lose the protection of s 219 if the picketing is other than peaceful as required by s 220, so that all of the torts that have been discussed may potentially be claimed. **8.50**

A further factor which will affect the legality of the picketing is the number of persons involved. This does not appear on the face of s 220(1) but must be implied from the requirement that the picketing be peaceful. Theoretically, hundreds of pickets could attend at the entrance to the employer's premises and, provided they were at their own place of work and were there only for the lawful purposes specified in the section, their attendance could not be challenged. Lord Reid said in *Broome v DPP* [1974] IRLR 26: **8.51**

> If a picket has a purpose beyond those set out in the section [now section 15], then his presence becomes unlawful and in many cases . . . it would not be difficult to infer as a matter of fact that pickets who assemble in unreasonably large numbers do have the purpose of preventing free passage. If that were the proper inference then their presence on the highway would become unlawful.

However, regardless of the question whether such numbers must necessarily cause an obstruction or nuisance, the courts have held that a massive presence is inconsistent with any notion of peaceful picketing, falls outside s 220(1), is likely to be tortious and can therefore be restrained by an injunction. Support for this course of judicial action has been drawn from the Code of Practice on Picketing which, at para 51, states that six pickets will usually be a sufficient number at a workplace entrance, and that 'frequently a smaller number will be appropriate'. The Code states: **8.52**

> 51. Large numbers on a picket line are also likely to give rise to fear and resentment amongst those seeking to cross that picket line, even where no criminal offence is committed. They exacerbate disputes and sour relations not only between management and employees but between the pickets and their fellow employees. Accordingly pickets and their organizers should ensure that in general the number of pickets does not exceed six at any entrance to, or exit from, a workplace; frequently a smaller number will be appropriate.

The Code, however, is not of binding legal effect although account can be taken of its provisions in certain proceedings. Scott J referred to it in *Thomas v National Union of Mineworkers (South Wales Area)* [1985] IRLR 136, 151, and then drafted the terms of his order so that only six pickets would be able to attend lawfully at the colliery gates. Similarly, in the *News Group* case, Stuart-Smith J prohibited picketing by more than six persons. It should be noticed that both of these cases arose out of mass picketing involving hundreds, sometimes thousands, of people and which on occasions disintegrated into violence. The limits imposed by the judges may be seen as a reaction to this. It does seem, however, that so long as the present legislative scheme operates, the figure of six will continue to be adopted. A limit to the number of persons who may picket can only be justified at law if the picketing had previously been unlawful; an employer should not be able to curb the numbers merely on the grounds that more than six persons were at the gates of his premises, since such an approach would revert back to the stance taken by the Court of Appeal in *Lyons (J) & Sons v Wilkins* [1899] 1 Ch 255 (cf. para 51 of the Code of Practice).

8.53 A further issue arises as result of the incorporation of the European Convention. Since Article 11 provides that 'Everyone has the right to freedom of peaceful assembly . . .' it is arguable that an order that restrains a picket of more than six is in breach of the seventh picket's fundamental rights under the Convention so that any order should be drafted with the circumstances of the case in mind as to what is likely to amount to an unlawful picket by virtue of weight of numbers.

The scope of the immunity

8.54 Pickets whose attendance is declared lawful by s 220 will not be wholly immune from liability for their conduct, under either civil or criminal law. Provided that their attendance is not declared unlawful, the pickets will be able to invoke the immunity contained in s 219(1) to protect them from liability, where they are successful in persuading any of the employees who were still at work to cease working, in breach of their contracts of employment or in persuading or causing suppliers or customers to break their commercial contracts with the employer. Normally these acts would be tortious but s 219 will provide immunity from liability where the acts are in contemplation or furtherance of a trade dispute. If these acts are brought about by picketing which is not declared lawful by s 220(1), the immunity of s 219 will not be available.

Furthermore, secondary action will be immune from liability in tort if carried out in the course of attendance declared lawful by s 220 and by a worker employed (or in the case of a worker not in employment, last employed) by a party to the dispute, or by a trade union official whose attendance is lawful. The secondary action is immune only if brought about by picketing at the picket's own place of work as TULR(C)A 1992, s 220 does not declare lawful picketing which occurs at the premises of an immediate supplier or customer of the employer in dispute, or at the premises of an associated employer of the employer in dispute.

Is there a right to picket?

Although the opening words of TULR(C)A 1992, s 220 are: 'It shall be **8.55** lawful', it is clear that the section provides no right to picket in the sense of an ability to take a course of action which will always be upheld by a court as being a positive right. The so-called 'right to picket' is simply the right to do whatever has not been proscribed by law and s 220 merely acts as an immunity. The Code of Practice enunciates this approach in terms stating 'There is no legal "right to picket" as such, but attendance for the purpose of peaceful picketing has long been recognized to be a lawful activity'. Similar sentiments have also been expressed by the courts. In *Kavanagh v Hiscock* [1974] QB 600 it was held that the Industrial Relations Act 1971, s 134 (a predecessor of TULRA 1974, s 15) does not confer on a picket a right which is capable of being infringed; rather its sole effect is to confer immunity from action in specified circumstances. In *Broome v DPP* [1974] AC 587, the House of Lords emphasized that the right, in so far as it exists, is one to attend in order to persuade, not to attend and persuade. The overriding power of the police to take action where they apprehend a breach of the peace further reduces the 'right' of the striker to express his view by picketing. Even if Articles 10 and 11 of the Convention are brought into play so that there is a right to freedom expression or peaceful assembly this will be subject to the provisos in the Articles and the perpetration of civil wrongs or criminal offences are likely to override the picket's rights.

D. The Code of Practice on Picketing

The Code of Practice on Picketing was issued under the power given to the **8.56** Secretary of State by the Employment Act 1980, s 3 (as amended by the Employment Act 1988, s 18) with the authority of Parliament (resolutions passed on 19 February 1992 by the House of Commons and on 21 February

1992 by the House of Lords). It is continued in force as if made under TULR(C)A 1992, s 203 by TULRA, Sch 3, para 1. It was brought into force on 1 May 1992 by the Employment Code of Practice (Picketing) Order 1992, SI 1992/2176.

The avowed intention of the Code is 'to provide practical guidance on picketing in trade disputes' and to outline the law on picketing (although it is of course for the courts and employment tribunals to interpret and apply the law in particular cases).

Although TULR(C)A 1992, s 203 provides that: 'A failure of any person to observe any provision of the Code of Practice . . . shall not of itself render him liable to proceedings . . .' notice has been taken of one of its provisions, especially where no similar statutory or case law guidance exists. Paragraph 51 of the Code is set out above.

In *Thomas v National Union of Mineworkers (South Wales Area)* [1986] Ch 20, Scott J was sufficiently impressed by this provision to draft his injunctions so as to order that pickets at the colliery gates should not exceed six, and in *News Group Newspapers Ltd v SOGAT 82 and others* [1986] IRLR 337, Stuart-Smith J imposed a limit of that number. Yet TULRA 1974, s 15 now TULR(C)A, s 220 imposes no such limit. A limit to the number of pickets has only been granted where complaint has been made of violent mass picketing.

The Code seeks to provide guidance upon the legal consequences of and the organization of picketing, the role of the police and the manner in which secondary action can lawfully result from picketing.

E. Criminal Law

8.57 In this section we consider: offences under TULR(C)A 1993, s 241 (previously under the Conspiracy and Protection of Property Act 1875); obstruction of the highway; obstruction of a police constable; public nuisance; offences under the Public Order Act 1986; and the role of the police, breach of the peace and bindovers.

TULR(C)A 1992, criminal offences (s 241)

Intimidation or annoyance by violence or otherwise

8.58 Section 241 provides that:

(1) A person commits an offence who, with a view to compelling another person to abstain from doing or to do any act which that person has a legal right to do or abstain from doing, wrongfully and without legal authority—

   (a) uses violence to or intimidates that person or his wife or children, or injures his property,

   (b) persistently follows that person about from place to place,

   (c) hides any tools, clothes or other property owned or used by that person, or deprives him of or hinders him in the use thereof,

   (d watches or besets the house or other place where that person resides, works, carries on business or happens to be, or the approach to any such house or place, or

   (e) follows that person with two or more persons in a disorderly manner in or through any street or road.

(2) A person guilty of an offence under this section is liable on summary conviction to imprisonment for a term not exceeding six months or a fine not exceeding level 5 on the standard scale (now £5,000), or both.

(3) A constable may arrest without warrant anyone he reasonably suspects is committing an offence under this section.

The offences contained in s 241 are of ancient pedigree having previously been contained in the Conspiracy and Protection of Property Act 1875, s 7. The section is of great significance since it contains offences which may be committed by a picket merely by his presence unless the presence is legalized by TULR(C)A, s 220. The defence in s 220 was in fact originally enacted as a proviso to the offences in s 7.

Section 241 of the 1992 Act contains five offences which may be committed **8.59** in the course of picketing. Of these, only one—watching and besetting—is likely to arise in the ordinary course of events, but prosecutions even for that offence were rarely brought until recent strikes. The police have generally preferred to bring charges for offences involving obstruction or a breach of the peace. The other four offences will generally only arise out of conduct that is incidental to the actual picketing. The section as originally drafted in 1875 contained the important exception to liability that where a person attended or happened to be at a person's house, workplace or place of business or at the approach thereto in order 'merely to obtain or communicate information', he would not be deemed to be watching or besetting within the meaning of the section. This exception was replaced and extended by the Trade Disputes Act 1906, s 2 and now forms the basis for the statutory concept of lawful peaceful picketing which is to be found in TULR(C)A 1974, s 219.

The effect of s 241 was described by Moulton LJ in *Ward Lock & Co. Ltd v Operative Printers' Assistants' Society* (1906) 22 TLR 327, 329 in the following terms:

> I cannot see that this section affects or is intended to affect civil rights or civil remedies. It legalises nothing, and it renders nothing wrongful that was not before. Its object is solely to visit certain selected classes of acts which were previously wrongful, i.e. were at least civil torts, with penal consequences capable of being summarily inflicted. . . . The restriction that the acts referred to must in themselves be at least civil torts is plainly expressed by the presence of the word 'wrongfully'.

Therefore, conduct is not capable of amounting to an offence under the section unless that conduct would, regardless of the provisions of s 241, have amounted to a civil tort. The section only serves to impose criminal liability upon conduct which is already actionable as a civil wrong.

In *Thomas v National Union of Mineworkers (South Wales Area)* [1986] Ch 20, counsel for the claimant mineworkers sought to persuade the court that the picketing in that case constituted a criminal offence under s 241 and was therefore tortious. Reliance for this contention was placed on certain passages in *Lyons (J) & Sons v Wilkins* [1896] 1 Ch 811, in which the members of the Court of Appeal, both at the interim stage and at trial, appeared to suggest that picketing which was an offence under s 241 was also tortious. However, in the *Thomas* case, Scott J reaffirmed the correctness of the *Ward Lock* decision thus:

> The purpose of section [241] was to make certain acts unlawful in the criminal sense. It seems to me a complete *non sequitur* to say that picketing which was within the exception, and so was not an offence under the Act, was therefore not tortious. It equally seems to me a *non sequitur* to say that picketing which was an offence under the Act was therefore tortious. . . . no new right of action is given by section 7, and no conduct not actionable without the section becomes so by virtue of it.

(See also *Fowler v Kibble* [1922] 1 Ch 487.) It will therefore not advance a claimant's case in a civil action to argue that because the conduct in question amounts to an offence under s 241 and because conduct must first consist of a tort in order to amount to such an offence, the conduct must *necessarily* also be tortious; in other words, because he can establish the greater he will thereby have established the lesser. That, in the words of Scott J in the *Thomas* case (at 147), 'puts the cart before the horse'. It will always be necessary to show first that the acts are tortious, and then that they also amount to an offence under the section.

Section 241 commences by providing that in respect to industrial action every **8.60** person who, with a view to compel any other person to abstain from doing or to do any act which such a person has a legal right to do or abstain from doing, wrongfully and without legal authority and then proceeds to set out the elements of the five offences. It is to be noted that there must be an act carried out in order to *compel* another to abstain from doing an act which he or she otherwise had a right to carry out. If the accused did not act with a view to compel, the offence will not be made out (*R v McKenzie* [1892] 2 QB 519, 521). Acting for the purpose of persuasion rather than compulsion is not an offence under the section. In *DPP v Fidler* [1992] 1 WLR 91, non-industrial pickets gathered outside an abortion clinic and tried to dissuade people from entering. Several of the clients of the clinic were distressed and it was held that the purpose was to shock, shame and embarrass clients but the pickets did not act with a view to compel so that the offence was not committed. The conduct must also be wrongful and without legal authority, so that at least a civil wrong must have been committed (see the cases of *Ward Lock & Co*; *Hubbard*; *Thomas*).

Intimidation of another person or his family, or injuring that person's property

8.61

Intimidation may amount to a tort, but for the purposes of this criminal offence, it consists of causing another person to be afraid. The fear which is caused need not be violence to the person (*R v Jones* [1974] ICR 310). In *Judge v Bennett* (1887) 4 TLR 75 it was held that a written threat which was so worded as to cause fear that violent picketing was intended, constituted intimidation in this context. A. L. Smith LJ described it as 'the using of language which causes another man to fear'. (See also *Connor v Kent* [1891] 2 QB 545, *Young v Peck* (1912) 107 LT 857.)

Persistently following another person about from place to place

8.62

In *Eisey v Smith* [1983] IRLR 292, the Scottish High Court of Justiciary held that this offence was made out where a union official and other pickets followed in a motor car, two working employees who had continued working during a strike, driving closely behind their car, repeatedly overtaking it and changing places with other pickets' cars so as to dictate the speed of the car being followed. The car had been followed in such a manner as to amount to conduct calculated to harass and annoy the working employees, so that the union official charged was guilty of wrongfully and, without lawful authority, persistently following the employees in a disorderly manner (see also *Smith v Thomasson* (1890) 62 L T 68).

Hiding any tools, clothes or other property owned or used by such other person, or depriving him or hindering him in the use thereof

8.63 Since this conduct has to be tortious in order that it may constitute a criminal offence, it will be necessary that it amounts to conversion or causes the other person to act in breach of a contract of employment or a commercial contract. Usually, the employee will not own the tools which he uses, and so the latter torts will have to be established. For a discussion of the difficulties in establishing liability for this offence, see *Fowler v Kibble* [1922] 1 Ch 487.

Watching or besetting the house or other place where such other person resides, or works, or carries on business, or happens to be, or the approach to such house or place

8.64 Of the five offences, this is most likely to be committed in the course of picketing. As has already been stated, the watching or besetting must be such as to amount to a tort in itself (eg trespass or nuisance) before it can lead to criminal liability. In *Thomas v National Union of Mineworkers (South Wales Area)* [1986] Ch 20, Scott J rejected a contention that a body of men who simply stood glowering at the gates of a factory would be acting unlawfully, but he did suggest that obstructing the highway was a tort other than nuisance (see discussion below and para 8.29).

Follows another with two or more persons in a disorderly manner in or through any street or road

8.65 As explained in *R v McKenzie* [1892] 2 QB 519, the essence of this offence is not the following in a disorderly manner, but doing so with a view to compel a person to do or abstain from doing some act. Under this and the other offences the conduct will still be unlawful even though it does not achieve its aim (*Agnew v Munro* (1891) 28 Sc LR 335).

Obstruction of the highway

8.66 By the Highways Act 1980, s 137: 'If a person without lawful authority or excuse in any way willfully obstructs the free passage along the highway he is guilty of an offence and liable to a fine'.

This offence may be committed not only by a picket who stands in front of a lorry and prevents it proceeding along the highway or entering the employer's premises (*Broome v DPP* [1974] AC 587), but also by one who takes part in a march along, or a demonstration on, the highway. It is no defence that an obstruction was not intended if one did in fact occur (*Arrowsmith v Jenkins* [1963] 2 QB 561, but cf. *Eaton v Cobb* [1950] 1 All ER 1016). To constitute an unlawful obstruction, the defendant's use of the highway must be unreasonable. This will depend upon all the circumstances, including the length of time it continues, the place where it occurs and the purpose for which the obstruction has arisen (*Nagy v Weston* [1965] 1 WLR 280). In *Hirst v Chief Constable of West Yorkshire* (1986) 85 Cr App R 143, the Divisional Court set out the criteria for commission of this offence. Unless it is *de minimis* any stopping on the highway is, prima facie, an obstruction. The second question is whether the obstruction is wilful or deliberate. The prosecution then has to prove that the obstruction is without lawful authority or excuse. Otton J cited with approval Lord Denning's dicta in *Hubbard v Pitt* [1976] QB 142, 178 in relation to demonstrations, that: 'As long as all is done peaceably and in good order, without threats or incitement to violence or obstruction, it is not prohibited. . . . So long as good order is maintained, the right to demonstrate must be preserved. . . .' (see also *Waite v Taylor* (1985) 149 JP 551, *Hipperson v Newbury District Electoral Registration Officer* [1985] QB 1060, 1075E). See the House of Lords in *DPP v Jones* [1999] 2 All ER 257 and compare *Broome v DPP* [1974] ICR 84; IRLR 26.

Obstructing a police constable in the execution of his duty

Section 89(2) of the Police Act 1996 (formerly the Police Act 1964, s 51(3)) now sets out the criteria for this particular offence. A constable is under a duty to prevent the occurrence of a breach of the peace. The offence of obstruction is frequently committed by pickets who attempt to push past police officers who are trying to restrain pickets from approaching a particular person or location (see, for example, *Kavanagh v Hiscock* [1974] QB 600; *Moss v McLachlan* [1985] IRLR 77). In *Piddington v Bates* [1960] 1 WLR 162 the Divisional Court held that there must be shown to have been a real, rather than a remote, possibility of a breach of the peace occurring, and this would require proof of the existence of facts from which a constable could reasonably have anticipated a breach of the peace. If a person obstructs a constable who is taking action to prevent a breach of the peace, he will

8.67

commit an offence under s 51(3) (*Duncan v Jones* [1936] 1 KB 218). The police officer must have a reasonable belief that a breach of the peace was likely to occur (*Kelly v Chief Constable of Hampshire* The Independent, 25 March 1993) and is believed to be imminent and the police should take into account the source of any threat (*Foulkes v Chief Constable of the Merseyside Police* [1998] 3 All ER 704, CA; *Bibby v Chief Constable of Essex* (2000) 164 JP 297).

8.68   Pickets have indeed been arrested some considerable distance away from the site of the proposed picket line on the ground of an apprehended breach of the peace (the *Moss* case) and paragraphs 45–47 of the Code emphasize the discretion which the police have whilst noting that they are under no duty to enforce the civil law.

Public nuisance

8.69   The offence of public nuisance will be committed where members of the public generally are obstructed in the exercise or enjoyment of rights which are common to all subjects. Such rights include the right of passage along the highway, and the acts which cause the offence of public nuisance will often also give rise to an offence under the Highways Act 1980, s 137. The use of the highway which causes the obstruction or interference must be unreasonable or unlawful (*R v Clark* [1964] 2 QB 315). In *Tynan v Balmer* [1967] 1 QB 91, about 40 pickets formed a circle outside the entrance to their employer's factory, and thereby obstructed the highway and access to the premises. It was held that this was an improper use of the highway and therefore unreasonable. Furthermore, the statutory immunity then in force (Trade Disputes Act 1906, s 2) did not afford a defence, since on the facts the pickets' purpose included obstructing the highway and this was not a lawful activity within the scope of the section.

The Public Order Act 1986

Introduction

8.70   The Public Order Act 1986 was the most extensive reform in the area of public order law for 50 years and the law has had a considerable impact upon the way the police regulate picketing. The avowed intention of the Conservative Government of the time in promoting the legislation was to 'ensure that the law provides the police with adequate powers to deal with disorder, or where possible prevent it before it occurs, in order to protect the rights and freedoms of others', whilst at the same time recognizing that: 'The right of peaceful protest and assembly are numbered among the touchstones which distinguish a free society from a totalitarian one'. For this reason the Government was 'concerned to regulate these freedoms to the minimum extent necessary to preserve order and protect the rights of others' (White Paper, *Review of Public Order Law*, Cmnd 9510, paras 1.7–8). There were, however, many who believed at the time of its introduction that aspects of the Act represented an unwarranted encroachment upon civil liberties by unnecessarily reducing the right to assemble and protest whilst providing no adequate safeguards for the peaceful protestor. The relevant parts of the Act in the context of an industrial dispute will be considered in the following order:

- riot;
- violent disorder;
- affray;
- fear or provocation of violence;
- harassment, alarm or distress;
- advance notice of public processions;
- imposing conditions on public processions and on public assemblies; and
- prohibiting public processions.

Riot

Riot is the most serious of the public order offences. As a common law **8.71** offence it carried a maximum penalty of life imprisonment, although it was rare that the maximum sentence was imposed. Section 1(6) of the 1986 Act now provides for a maximum possible penalty of 10 years' imprisonment or a fine or both. A common law charge of riot has been frequently pressed in circumstances where there has been violent picketing; 137 charges of riot were laid during the 1984 miners' strike, 95 of them as a result of picketing at the Orgreave Coke Depot which was a major victory for Arthur Scargill's use of flying pickets. It was partly as a result of the collapse of the Orgreave picketing prosecutions that the Government decided to reform the offence of riot. The new definition of riot is contained in the Public Order Act 1986, s 1(1):

> Where twelve or more persons who are present together use or threaten unlawful violence for a common purpose and the conduct of them (taken together)

is such as would cause a person of reasonable firmness present at the scene to fear for his personal safety, each of the persons using unlawful violence for the common purpose is guilty of riot.

The constituents of the statutory offence are significantly different from those of the common law offence before its repeal. This only required the presence of three persons who executed a common purpose with intent to help one another by force if necessary, and displayed force or violence in such a manner as to cause alarm to one person of reasonable firmness and courage (*Field v Receiver of Metropolitan Police* [1907] 2 KB 853). The statutory requirement that 12 persons come together for a common purpose is intended to reflect the gravity of the offence and is derived from the minimum number of people who were required to be present to justify the reading of the Riot Act (White Paper, para 3.18). The common purpose may be inferred from the conduct of the persons so attending (POA 1986, s 1(3)). It is not, however, necessary for the 12 persons to use or threaten violence simultaneously (s 1(2)). The statutory offence is broader than its common law counterpart in an important respect, since it is not necessary for a person of reasonable firmness actually to be present at the scene of the alleged riot (s 1(4)). The statutory offence can be committed in a private as well as a public place (s 1(5)).

The definition of violence in s 8 of the 1986 Act, which applies generally to all the Public Order Act offences where violence is a necessary constituent, is as follows:

> 'violence' means any violent conduct, so that—
> (a) except in the context of affray, it includes violent conduct towards property as well as towards persons, and
> (b) it is not restricted to conduct causing or intended to cause injury or damage but includes any other violent conduct (for example, throwing at or towards a person a missile of a kind capable of causing injury which does not hit or falls short).

The new definition of violence is considerably wider than that at common law, where a breach of the peace or assault was necessary.

Violent disorder

8.72   By the Public Order Act 1986, s 2(1) the offence of violent disorder is committed in the following circumstances:

> Where three or more persons who are present together use or threaten unlaw-

ful violence and the conduct of them (taken together) is such as would cause a person of reasonable firmness present at the scene to fear for his personal safety, each of the persons using or threatening unlawful violence is guilty of violent disorder.

This offence of violent disorder represents an attempt by the Government to rationalize the public order offences according to the gravity of the violence or threatened violence involved. In its wake, the offences of unlawful assembly and rout were abolished (see *R v Caird* (1970) 54 Cr App R 499 for a definition of the offence of unlawful assembly). The offence is similar to riot in that it is immaterial whether or not three or more persons use or threaten violence simultaneously (s 2(2)), no person of reasonable firmness need actually be present at the scene (s 2(3)), and the offences may be committed in private as well as public (s 2(4)). The maximum possible penalty is five years' imprisonment or a fine or both on trial on indictment, or on summary conviction six months' imprisonment or a fine not exceeding £5,000 or both.

Affray

The statutory offence of affray is contained in s 3(1) of the 1986 Act: **8.73**

> A person is guilty of affray if he uses or threatens unlawful violence towards another and his conduct is such as would cause a person of reasonable firmness present at the scene to fear for his personal safety.

The definition in the Act is considerably wider than that which existed at common law. This is because, if the common law offence was to be committed in private it was necessary that there be *present* at least one person who was terrified (*Button v DPP* [1966] AC 591). As with the other offences, the Act specifically provides that affray may be committed in private as well as public (s 3(5)) and no person of reasonable firmness need actually be or be likely to be at the scene (s 3(4)). However, the threat of unlawful violence cannot be by the use of words alone (s 3(3)) and since the essence of affray is that innocent people are put in fear, violence towards property will not suffice. Since the maximum sentence on trial on indictment is three years' imprisonment or a fine or both, and on summary conviction a sentence of imprisonment of six months and/or a fine not exceeding £5,000 (s 3(7)), the Act provides that a constable may arrest without warrant a person suspected of committing this offence.

The wording of s 3(1) imports mixed notions of *actus reus* and *mens rea*.

Fear or provocation of violence

8.74　The most commonly charged public order offence before 1986 was that contained in the Public Order Act 1936, s 5 of threatening, abusive or insulting words or behaviour with intent to cause a breach of the peace or whereby a breach of the peace was likely to be occasioned. This section has been repealed, modified and extended by the Public Order Act 1986, ss 4 and 5.

Section 4(1) provides that:

> A person is guilty of an offence if he—
>> (a) uses towards another person threatening, abusive or insulting words or behaviour, or
>> (b) distributes or displays any writing, sign or other visible representation which is threatening, abusive or insulting,
>
> with intent to cause that person to believe that immediate unlawful violence will be used against him or another by any person, or to provoke the immediate use of unlawful violence by that person or another, or whereby that person is likely to believe that such violence will be used or it is likely that such violence will be provoked.

The section therefore covers the person who behaves in a threatening, abusive or insulting manner which is likely to provoke other people to use or threaten violence. It is not, however, necessary that the violence be provoked against the person carrying out the insulting behaviour. Thus the definition will cover the 'rabble rouser' who whips up violent opposition against, for example, workers attempting to cross a picket line. It will be no defence for a defendant to say that he did not intend to provoke the violence, since a speaker must take his audience as he finds it (*Jordan v Burgoyne* [1963] 2 QB 744).

The offence may be committed in a public or private place, but it cannot be committed where both parties are inside the same or different dwelling-houses (s 4(2)). The maximum sentence is six months' imprisonment on summary conviction and/or a fine not exceeding £5,000 (s 4(4)). A constable may arrest without warrant a person reasonably suspected of committing the offence (s 4(3)).

The meaning of the word 'insulting' was considered by the House of Lords in *Brutus v Cozens* [1973] AC 854. Their Lordships held that the interpretation of the word 'insulting' was a question of fact for the magistrates deciding the case. Lord Reid thought that the word was intended to have its ordinary meaning and '[A]n ordinary sensible man knows an insult when he sees or hears it. . . . Insulting means insulting and nothing more'.

Harassment, alarm or distress

The new 'disorderly conduct' offence represented the widest extension of the proscription of conduct in the public order field for many years. The offence is defined in s 5(1) of the 1986 Act in the following terms: **8.75**

> A person is guilty of an offence if he—
> (a) uses threatening, abusive or insulting words or behaviour, or disorderly behaviour, or
> (b) displays any writing, sign or other visible representation which is threatening, abusive or insulting, within the hearing or sight of a person likely to be caused harassment, alarm or distress thereby.

Again, although the offence may be committed in public or private, there is no offence where both persons are inside the same or different dwelling-houses (s 5(2)). The maximum sentence on summary conviction is a fine on level three of the standard scale, currently £1,000. The offence may have a very considerable impact upon the conduct of picketing. The picket who yells 'scab' to strike-breakers as they cross the picket line will quite clearly come within the terms of the section, since the words are likely to be regarded as abusive and cause distress to the persons abused. Similarly, offensive placards are likely to fall foul of the section. The police have a power which is considerably wider than the common law breach of the peace powers and it is probable that these powers will be used to regulate picketing to a greater extent than previously.

The disorderly conduct provisions were an innovation in English law, although a similar offence has existed in Australia for a number of years. The Government thought that the new provision was particularly necessary to deal with acts of hooliganism (White Paper, para 3.22), but it can be used equally to control disorderly conduct on the picket line. 'Disorderly conduct' is not defined in the 1986 Act but in an Australian case it was held to mean conduct which, while sufficiently ill-mannered or in such bad taste as to meet with the disapproval of well-conducted men and women, was something more, in that it must tend to annoy or insult persons faced with it sufficiently deeply to warrant the interference of the criminal law (*Dillon v Byrne* QJPR 112; see also *Melser v Police* (1967) NZLR 437; Andrew Hiller, *Public Order and the Law*, Law Book Company Limited, Sydney, 1983, pp 98–104). The offence thus goes beyond violence or the threat of a breach of the peace. **8.76**

8.77 The test of intention is a subjective test so that even if bystanders were likely to suffer alarm, harassment or distress as a result of conduct and subjective intent or awareness is not shown then no offence is committed (*DPP v Clarke* (1991) 94 Cr App Rep 359). However, if the defendant had the necessary intent he or she may be convicted even if it was only the arresting officer who suffered alarm, harassment or distress (*DPP v Orum* [1988] 3 All ER 449).

8.78 The requirement that the conduct be in the sight or hearing of a person likely to be caused alarm, harassment or distress may reduce the scope of the offence, but there is no requirement that the person present actually suffers alarm, harassment or distress. The accused will however have a defence if it is proved (s 5(3)):

(1) that he had no reason to believe that there was any person within hearing or sight who was likely to be caused alarm, harassment or distress, or

(2) that he was inside a dwelling and had no reason to believe that the words or behaviour used, or the writing, sign or other visible representation displayed, would be heard or seen by a person outside that or any other dwelling, or

(3) that his conduct was reasonable.

In the context of the picket line, it is unlikely that the first two grounds will provide a defence to a charge of disorderly conduct, since the conduct will be in public and a strike-breaker will in all probability be able to say that he was caused alarm, harassment or distress. The scope of the third defence is uncertain. A picket might claim that his conduct was reasonable when he has called the strike-breaker names such as 'scab', because it is in the collective interest that the strike is successful and his conduct sought to achieve that result. One cannot, however, imagine the courts normally being very sympathetic to such a plea.

8.79 A constable may arrest a person without warrant, but only where the person has engaged in offensive conduct which the constable has warned him to stop, and the person has engaged in further offensive conduct immediately or shortly after the warning (s 5(4)). Offensive conduct is conduct which the constable reasonably suspects to constitute an offence under s 5, although the initial and further conduct need not be of the same nature before an arrest may be made (s 5(5)). The arresting power is curious, in that a warning must already have been administered and ignored before an arrest may be effected. This may reduce the effectiveness of the offence in the context for which it was primarily designed, since it is likely that the rowdy hooligan in the housing estate who is warned about his conduct will desist, at least whilst the police officer is still present. On the picket line, however, the offence may prove to be of more impact since the picket is unlikely to be prepared to desist from conduct which he will regard as the whole point of his picketing.

The similar offence of harassment in s 4A, as inserted by the Criminal Justice   **8.80**
and Public Order Act 1994, applies an objective test.

Where the offence is racially or religiously aggravated the penalties are more   **8.81**
severe (Crime and Disorder Act 1998, s 31). An on the spot fine may be imposed (see The Penalties for Disorderly Behaviour (Amount of Penalty) Order 2002 SI 2002/1837).

Advance notice of processions

The 1986 Act contains a general requirement that advance notice be given to   **8.82**
the police where a procession is to be held. Written notice must be given to a police station in the police area where it is proposed the procession will start (s 11(5)) if the procession is one: (a) to demonstrate support for or opposition to the views or actions of person or body of persons; (b) to publicize a cause or campaign; or (c) to mark or commemorate an event save that notice is not required where it is not reasonably practicable to give an advance notice of the procession (s 11(1)). Whilst picketing will *normally* involve a static assembly on the highway at factory gates, marches are now a frequent feature of an industrial dispute and the requirements of s 11 must be complied with. In *News Group Newspapers Ltd v SOGAT 82 and others* [1986] IRLR 337 for example, twice a week a large crowd would rally and march to the Wapping plant to express their views against the actions of News International companies in dismissing some 5,500 employees. The requirement does not apply to a procession which is commonly or customarily held (s 11(2)), so that it would not apply to, for example, an annual gala.

The notice must specify the date when it is intended to hold the procession, the time when it is intended to start, its proposed route and the name and address of the person proposing to organize it (s 11(3)). Notice must be given not less than six clear days before the date on which it is intended to hold the procession or as soon as reasonably practicable (s 11(6)) and may be by recorded delivery service if delivered not less than six clear days before (s 11(5)). Failure to give such notice as is required or to hold the procession in accordance with the notice given will amount to a criminal offence on the part of the organizers (s 11(7)). However, it will be a defence if the accused can prove that he did not know of and neither suspected, nor had reason to suspect, the failure to satisfy the requirements or the different way in which the procession was held (s 11(8)). In respect of the procession being held differently it is a defence to show that the difference arises from circumstances beyond his control or from something done with the agreement of a police officer (s 11(9)). A person found guilty under s 11 is liable to a fine not exceeding level three on the standard scale, currently £1,000 (s 11(10)).

Imposing conditions on public processions and public assemblies

8.83   Sections 12 and 14 of the Public Order Act 1986 are concerned with the power of the police to impose conditions on processions and assemblies. Conditions may be imposed where the senior police officer, having regard to the time or place at which and the circumstances in which any public procession or assembly is being held or intended to be held, and in the case of a procession to its route or proposed route, reasonably believes that:

- it may result in serious public disorder, serious damage to property or serious disruption to the life of the community, or
- the purpose of the persons organizing it is the intimidation of others with a view to compelling them not to do an act which they have a right to do, or to do an act which they have a right not to do.

Where these circumstances are satisfied in relation to processions, the senior police officer may give directions imposing on the persons organizing or taking part in the procession such conditions as appear to him necessary to prevent such disorder, damage, disruption or intimidation, including conditions as to the route of the procession or prohibiting it from entering any public place specified in the directions (s 12(1)). In relation to assemblies, directions may be given to the persons organizing or taking part in the assembly which impose conditions as to the place at which the assembly may be (or continue to be held, its maximum duration, and the maximum number of persons who may constitute it, as appear necessary to prevent such disorder, damage, disruption or intimidation (s 14(1)).

8.84   A public procession is defined as 'a procession in a public place' (s 16). More helpfully, a public assembly is defined as 'an assembly of 20 or more persons in a public place which is wholly or partly open to the air' (s 16). Public place is also defined as being a highway or any place or any section to which the public has access on payment or otherwise by reason of an express or implied permission. This is in accordance with the previous definition under the Public Order Act 1936 (see *Cawley v Frost* [1976] 1 WLR 1207). The senior police officer identified by the Act to give directions is, in relation to a procession or assembly being held, and in relation to a procession intended to be held where persons are assembling with a view to taking part in it, the most senior police officer in rank present at the scene. In the case of a procession or assembly intended to be held, it is the chief officer of police (ss 12(2),14(2)). The direction given by the chief officer of police in relation to an assembly or procession intended to be held must be in writing (ss 12(3), 14(3)).

A person who organizes or takes part in a procession or assembly who know- **8.85** ingly fails to comply with a condition, is guilty of an offence, but it is a defence to show that the failure arose from circumstances beyond the person's control (ss 12(4) and (5),14(4) and (5)). A person who knowingly incites another to take part in breach of a condition will also commit an offence (ss 12(6), 14(6)). A constable may arrest without warrant any person contravening these provisions (ss 12(7), 14(7)). Organizers and inciters will be liable to a fine not exceeding level four or three months' imprisonment or both (ss 12(8) and (10), 14(8) and (10)), whilst a participant will be liable to a fine up to level three on the standard scale (ss 12(9), 14(9)).

Section 14, in particular, is important in relation to picketing, since it gives **8.86** to the police the power to regulate the place, time and duration of static pickets. It is arguable that the police already possessed such powers by reason of their common law power to control a breach of the peace. The inclusion of the criterion of 'serious disruption to the life of the community' goes beyond violence or breach of the peace as a yardstick to what action should be proscribed. The intimidation leg of the section was clearly drafted with mass picketing in mind.

Prohibiting public processions

Section 13 of the Act empowers the chief officer of police to prohibit public **8.87** processions from taking place. There is no similar power with regard to public assemblies, although s 14 gives to the police power to direct that a procession must take place elsewhere. By s 13(1), if the chief officer of police reasonably believes that because of particular circumstances existing in the district or part of a district the powers under s 12 will not be sufficient to prevent serious public disorder, he may apply to the council of the appropriate district for an order prohibiting for up to three months the holding of all public processions (or any class of public procession so specified) in the district or part concerned. The council may then with the consent of the Secretary of State make an order as requested or with such modifications as approved by the Secretary of State (s 13(2)). Section 13(4) concerns the City of London and provides that the Commissioner of Police for the City of London or the Commissioner of Police of the Metropolis may apply to the Secretary of State bypassing the council. An order may be varied or revoked by a subsequent order (s 13(5)).

8.88   A person who organizes a procession the holding of which he knows is in breach, is guilty of an offence and potentially liable to a fine on level four or three months' imprisonment or both (s 13(7), (11)). A person who knowingly participates in a banned procession commits an offence for which he may be fined on level three of the standard level of fines (s 13(8), (12)). A person who incites another to commit an offence under s 13(8) commits an offence for which he may be liable to a fine on level four, currently £2,500 or three months' imprisonment or both (s 13(9)). A constable may arrest without warrant a person committing an offence under these sections (s 13(10)).

The role of the police in strikes

8.89   When picketing is organized in the midst of an industrial dispute, the police will almost invariably be present. Sometimes one or two constables may be present to watch over half a dozen pickets at a seldom used gateway of a factory. On other occasions, hundreds of officers will be required to control an even larger number of pickets. Ostensibly their role is to keep the peace, but many pickets argue that their presence frequently fuels the tension and frustration, leading to disorder and violence. It is significant that in the 1984–85 miners' strike and the Wapping dispute the most violent confrontations occurred not between picket and employer or picket and strike-breaker but between picket and police.

8.90   It is not only in the context of mass picketing that the police may intervene. They have powers to take whatever steps are necessary where they have reasonable cause to anticipate a breach of the peace. In such circumstances it will not avail any picket who is asked by a constable to 'move along' to point out that he is in fact picketing in accordance with TULR(C)A. Thus, the High Court has upheld the decision of a police constable to limit the number of pickets to a particular location, and in the circumstances of the case (albeit before the Picketing Code of Practice was introduced), to two (*Piddington v Bates* [1960] 3 All ER 660). In *Kavanagh v Hiscock* [1974] QB 600, the police physically prevented pickets from even approaching lorries and cars. One picket who attempted to break through the police line was arrested and charged with obstructing a police officer in the execution of his duty. His conviction was upheld on appeal. These two decisions confirm that the courts will not lightly interfere with the exercise of police discretion in this area. For a constable lawfully to arrest a picket on the grounds that he apprehended a breach of the peace, there need only be shown to be proved facts from which a constable could reasonably anticipate that a breach of the peace would occur, together with a real, rather than just a remote, possibility of its occurrence (*Piddington v Bates* (above) at 663). One of the landmark features of the miners' strike of 1984–85 was the decision of the police to intercept the convoys of flying pickets who were travelling great distances to picket coalfields in different counties. In *Moss v McLachlan* [1985] IRLR 77, the police stopped a convoy of cars on a motorway which was easily identifiable as transporting miners by the stickers with which the cars were decorated. The miners were travelling to picket coal pits in Nottinghamshire, and the police believed that a breach of the peace would be caused when they reached their destinations. The police therefore formed a cordon at a motorway junction two and a half miles from the pit which was the pickets' destination, and refused to allow the miners to proceed. Some miners attempted to push through the cordon and were arrested for obstruction of a police officer in the execution of his duty contrary to the Police Act 1994, s 89(2) (previously the Police Act 1964, s 51(3)). Their convictions and the action of the police were upheld on appeal. A similar, and now notorious, incident involved miners from Kent collieries, also travelling to picket Nottinghamshire pits, who were stopped at the Dartford Tunnel in London. In the *Moss* case and the other cases, a very loose approach appears to have been taken to the notion of proximity to the scene where the breach was likely to take place and the requirement that a breach of the peace be *reasonably* apprehended.

Trade unions have tried to turn the fact that the police have wide preventive **8.91** powers on its head and persuade the courts that in the context of picketing, the conduct of the pickets should be regulated by whatever action the police on the spot deem it necessary to take, and not by the civil courts granting injunctions to employers. This was rejected by Stuart-Smith J on the ground that the function of the police is to uphold the criminal law; the employer, on the other hand, comes to the court to seek relief from tortious acts which are of no concern to the police. Accordingly, the courts are extremely unlikely ever to accede to such an argument (see also *Barber v Penley* (1893) 2 Ch 447). It is unlikely that the provisions of the European Convention on European Rights will change the position in this respect.

F. Statutory Restrictions on Specific Industrial Action

Particular statutory prohibitions

8.92 Britain has nothing to compare with the wide restrictions on strikes as enacted in respect of the *Beamter*, established public servants, in Germany. There are, however, several statutory restrictions on the right to strike, some of more consequence than others, but mainly concerning the public sector (see Gillian S Morris, *Strikes in Essential Services*, Mansell 1986). They are as follows:

- Armed forces: Any member of the armed forces who engages in 'disruptive action' in order to redress a grievance may be disciplined under the Army Act 1955, s 29A, Airforce Act 1955, s 29A or Naval Discipline Act 1957, ss 7–18 respectively. Section 1 of the Incitement to Disaffection Act 1934 makes it an offence 'if anyone maliciously and advisedly endeavours to seduce any member of Her Majesty's forces from his duty or allegiance to Her Majesty'.
- Merchant seamen: All merchant seamen are restricted in calling industrial action by the Merchant Shipping Act 1995. Merchant officers will not be liable under TULR(C)A, s 240(4) as the Merchant Shipping Act 1995, s 58 provides that there may be liability for acts that cause or are likely to cause:

  (1) the loss or destruction of or serious damage to their ship or its machinery, navigational equipment or safety equipment; or
  (2) the loss or destruction of or serious damage to any other ship or any structure; or
  (3) the death of or serious injury to any person.

Section 58 provides for liability where a seaman employed in a United Kingdom ship combines with other seamen employed in that ship:

(1) to disobey lawful commands which are required to be obeyed at a time while the ship is at sea; or

(2) to neglect any duty which is required to be discharged at such a time; or

(3) to impede, at such a time, the progress of a voyage or the navigation of the ship.

- Police: The Police Act 1996, s 91 provides that a person who causes, or attempts to cause, or does any act calculated to cause, disaffection amongst the members of any police force, or induces or attempts to induce, or does any act calculated to induce, any member of a police force to withhold his services, shall be guilty of an offence.

- Postal workers: By the Postal Services Act 2000, s 83 there is an offence of intentionally delaying the mail by a person engaged in the business of a postal operator where this is done contrary to his duty and without reasonable excuse. However, by s 83(4) the section does not apply to the delaying of a postal packet as a result of industrial action in contemplation or furtherance of a trade dispute. Section 84 enacts a general offence of interfering with or delaying the mail but s 83(4) also applies to this section. In *Gouriet v Union of Post Office Workers* [1978] AC 435, it was made clear that private citizens were not able to obtain injunctions because they feared a breach of the criminal law. That was the sole prerogative of the Attorney-General, who had complete discretion whether to proceed in such an action. If the Attorney-General had given his authorization, the selective blacking of mail to South Africa by Post Office workers would have been a breach of the Post Office Act 1977.

The sections supersede the Telegraph Act 1863 although it does have impact in the area of industrial action as seen from time to time. The operation of this statute arose indirectly in *Stephen (Harold) & Co. v Post Office* [1978] 1 All ER 939. The Post Office locked out sorters who refused to handle post addressed to Grunwick Ltd, the scene of a bitter strike over trade union recognition. The Court of Appeal would not intervene on the application of local residents who complained that they also had not received their post because of the action of the postal unions. They had sought an injunction on the ground that the Post Office was, by locking out its employees, condoning criminal offence. In *Mercury*

Communications Ltd v Scott-Garner [1984] Ch 3 (for facts see p 80), the employers alleged a breach of the 1863 Act where the Post Office Engineers Union threatened disconnection of the British Telecom system. However, the Court of Appeal did not feel it necessary to consider the submission which the defendants' counsel had no time to rebut.

• Prison officers: The Criminal Justice and Public Order Act 1994, s 127 makes it unlawful to induce prison officers to go on strike. The Government announced in May 2003 that this provision is to be repealed following the success of a Voluntary Agreement signed by the Prison Officers' Association, the Prison Governers' Association and the Prison Service in 2001. At present, however, any person who induces a prison officer to commit a breach of discipline will commit a tort against the Home Secretary. Under s 127(5) 'a breach of discipline by a prison officer is a reference to a failure by a prison officer to perform any duty imposed on him by the prison rules or any code of discipline having effect under those rules or any other contravention by a prison officer of those rules or any such code'.

• Aliens: Probably the least known statutory restriction is the Aliens Restriction (Amendment) Act 1919, s 3(2) which makes it a crime punishable by three months' imprisonment for an alien to promote industrial unrest unless he has been bona fide engaged in the same industry for two years. The section remains on the statute book and was enacted because of fears of unrest after the Russian Revolution.

Endangering life

8.93 There is also a more general provision which must be noted although it is of little effect. The Conspiracy and Protection of Property Act 1875, s 5 created an offence punishable by a fine or imprisonment for a period of up to three months and this is now re-enacted in TULR(C)A, s 240 which provides:

(1) A person commits an offence who wilfully and maliciously breaks a contract of service or hiring, knowing or having reasonable cause to believe that the probable consequences of his so doing, either alone or in combination with others, will be—

(a) to endanger human life or cause serious bodily injury, or

(b) to expose valuable property, whether real or personal, to destruction or serious injury.

(2) Subsection (1) applies equally whether the offence is committed from malice conceived against the person endangered or injured or, as the case may be, the owner of the property destroyed or injured, or otherwise.

(3) A person guilty of an offence under this section is liable on summary conviction to imprisonment for a term not exceeding three months or to a fine not exceeding level 2 on the standard scale or both.

(4) This section does not apply to seamen.

Section 5 was repealed by the Industrial Relations Act 1971 in so far as it **8.94** used to apply to gas, water and electricity work. The possible scope of the existing provision, however, reaches doctors, firemen, dustmen, nurses and lorry drivers. In fact, there is no recorded instance of a prosecution under the section. It is necessary that the contract is broken before the section applies so that due notice to terminate the contract would avoid liability. During the firemen's dispute in 2002–3 it was reported that the Attorney-General was considering taking action under this section but none materialized.

Emergency provisions

A state of emergency may be declared where events threaten 'by interfering **8.95** with the supply and distribution of food, water, fuel or light or with the means of locomotion, to deprive the community or any substantial proportion of the community, of the essentials of life' (Emergency Powers Act 1920, s 1(1)). The Government may in such a situation make regulations 'for securing the essentials of life to the community'. Twelve states of emergency have been declared under this provision, five of which were during the course of the Heath Government between 1970 and 1974 which saw much sustained industrial action in different sectors of the economy. While regulations promulgated during such an emergency may not alter existing criminal procedure or institute any penalty without trial, they do permit summary trial for breach of the regulations with a fine or imprisonment for up to three months, or both (Emergency Powers Act 1920, s 2(3) as amended by Criminal Justice Act 1982, s 41). The procedure under the Defence (Armed Forces) Regulations 1939, para 6, is that the Government may request the assistance of the armed forces and the Defence Council may order men under them to be employed temporarily in 'civilian urgent work of national importance'. Any command is treated as lawful for the purpose of military discipline. The Energy Act 1976, s 3 also gives power, if an emergency exists which affects fuel or electricity supplies that an Order in Council may regulate the production, supply or acquisition of all forms of fuel.

The armed forces have been used in disputes on nine occasions since the

Second World War. During the ambulancemen's strike in 1979 the police ran an emergency service.

Proposals on strikes in essential services

8.96   It has been frequently mooted that there should be a complete removal of trade dispute immunity from action by public sector workers in essential industries. This concern may be traced back, in particular, to the so-called 'winter of discontent' of 1978–79, when workers in the health service and even gravediggers were on strike. At that time the TUC issued guidance to its affiliated unions on the conduct of industrial disputes and called on them to ensure that their members maintained supplies and services essential to the health and safety of the community or otherwise required to avoid causing serious hardship or exceptional pollution. Many wish to see legislative action and the matter was touched on by the Green Paper, *Trade Union Immunities* (Cmnd 8218, 1981 paras 330–4) which identified the chief problem as isolating the industries to be covered. It went on (at para 330) to state that: 'It can be argued that it is not an unreasonable condition of employment in an essential service for the employee to be required to waive his right to abrogate that contract at will if the consequence is to threaten the continued function of that service with grave effects on the country.'

A majority of the House of Commons Employment Committee have stated that 'industrial action which puts public health or public safety at risk poses a very serious problem which must be tackled without delay'. One of the proposals which has received favour in some quarters is that such workers should have a system of binding arbitration, but it is doubted that at present this is a realistic possibility.

9

INDUSTRIAL ACTION AND UNFAIR DISMISSAL

The policy is 'to give a measure of protection to the employer if his business   **9.01**
is faced with ruin by a strike. It enables him in those circumstances, if he
cannot carry on the business without a labour force, to dismiss the labour force
on strike; to take on another labour force without the stigmas of its being an
unfair dismissal'.

(*Heath v J F Longman (Meat Salesmen) Ltd* [1973] 1 All ER 1228, 1230).

Industrial disputes are often very complex, having a long history and involving many contributory factors. In no area of English law of which we are aware
are courts ever entrusted with the determination and allocation of blame in
relation to industrial disputes.

(Browne-Wilkinson J in *Courtaulds Northern Spinning Ltd v Moosa*
[1984] IRLR 43, 46).

187

A. The General Nature of TULR(C)A 1992, s 238

9.02 There is a special unfair dismissal regime for strikes, lock-outs and other forms of industrial action. The provisions of the Trade Union and Labour Relations (Consolidation) Act 1992 concerning them are a borderline where collective and individual labour law meet. The interconnection is not altogether happy, and the tensions are apparent in the case law. One can see, in particular, the natural desire of the tribunals to avoid determining the merits of industrial disputes. Section 238 was indeed conceived as a form of 'collective *laissez-faire*', a system to keep tribunals away from the political minefield of adjudicating on strike issues. The section achieved increasing prominence in several 'high profile' disputes, including those involving the News International Wapping plant and the Kent Messenger newspaper. The provisions have been amended by different Governments and are now a complex patchwork since there are separate provisions for official, unofficial and protected action. Some are jurisdictional provisions, some render a dismissal automatically unfair.

The history

9.03 By s 238(2) of the 1992 Act, which reflects the unfair dismissal scheme as originally enacted, a tribunal has no jurisdiction to determine whether a dismissal is unfair if at the time of the dismissal, the employer was conducting a lock-out or the employee was taking part in a strike or other industrial action if all who were so participating are dismissed, and none are re-engaged within three months of the dismissal. The employer does not have to prove that the industrial dispute was the *reason* for the dismissal for the jurisdiction of the tribunal to be taken away, but merely that such termination coincided with the industrial action. It appears that the employer may even deliberately provoke the stoppage to remove his workforce with financial impunity.

There were significant changes to the section by the Employment Act 1982 because of concern that they were too wide, which considerably facilitated reliance by the employer on the immunity and, in particular, that:

(1) an employer need only dismiss all employees at one particular establishment rather than his whole company even though other establishments are also on strike; and

(2) an employer may re-engage with impunity within three months of a rele-

vant employee's dismissal, and this does not depend on when the strike actually commenced and ended.

The Conservative Government in 1993 introduced the principle that those engaged in unofficial strikes could be dismissed with impunity whether all or only some taking part were so dismissed.

Further radical changes were made in the Labour Government's Employment Relations Act 1999, which again changed the balance of power in industrial disputes, making it impossible for the employer to dismiss fairly in the first eight weeks of the dispute and thus taking away one of the primary weapons in the employer's armoury.

The sense of these sections is thus highly complex, and the risks of making a wrong decision are high. In *Hindle Gears Ltd v McGinty* [1984] IRLR 477, Waite J thought that the general immunity: **9.04**

> is subject . . . to stringent sanctions, designed to deter employers from abusing the immunity by treating a strike as a pretext for dismissing the unwanted elements in their workforce and retaining the remainder . . . Motive is irrelevant. Inadvertence makes no difference. The rule is wholly rigid and inflexible. The result (as the authorities show) has been to turn the process of dismissal of a striking workforce into something like a game of hazard in which the winner takes all, in which defeat or victory turns upon the fall of a single card and in which the stakes increase dramatically according to the number involved. It is a game requiring intense concentration, each side closely watching the other. It is also, one suspects, a game in which no one does half so well as the lawyers who have become indispensable as its croupiers.

It thus behoves employers to be very wary before embarking on dismissal of their workforce. Some of the possible 'hard cases' are dealt with at paras 9.21 and 9.55.

It is particularly unfortunate that the Employment Appeal Tribunal have failed to define fully the central concepts of ss 237–9 but rather leave them to tribunals to consider as matters of fact and degree on the circumstances of the case. As Browne-Wilkinson P said in *Coates v Modern Methods and Materials Ltd* [1982] ICR 763, in such cases 'it is of great importance to employers that they should so far as possible know the consequences of their acts before they decide who to dismiss and who to retain or re-engage'. The costs of getting it wrong, from the employer's point of view, may be colossal, especially if the tribunal were to decide that the employees were not dismissed in the course of a strike and that the reason for dismissal was the trade union activities of the workforce. **9.05**

The basic questions for official action

9.06   To consider whether the employer's immunity from claims under s 238 that is whether official action is established, the tribunal must decide in turn:

(1) the date and time of dismissal;
(2) the existence at that time of a lock-out, strike or other industrial action;
(3) whether all relevant employees have been dismissed;
(4) whether any relevant employees have been re-engaged within three months of the time of dismissal;
(5) if (4) is established whether the employer has acted reasonably in discriminating between those dismissed or re-engaged and those not dismissed or not re-engaged, as the case may be.

The basic vocabulary of the sections must be considered first since it is not as clearly defined as it might be.

B. Strike, Lock-out or other Industrial Action

What is a strike?

9.07   Strike is not separately defined for the purposes of ss 237–8. In two cases *Fisher v York Trailer Co Ltd* [1979] ICR 834 and *Express & Star Ltd v Bunday* [1986] IRLR 477; [1988] ICR 379, the Employment Appeal Tribunal incorporated by reference its definition for continuity purposes in Sch 13 of the 1978 Act (now the Employment Rights Act 1996, s 125(5)) but the Court of Appeal disagreed in the *Bunday* case albeit that the section could be turned to for guidance (see para 10.02). Lord Denning's definition in the contractual case of *Tramp Shipping Corp. v Greenwich Marine Inc* [1979] ICR 261, has also been applied in this context and this is rather more appropriate. The then Master of the Rolls considered that a strike was 'a concerted stoppage of work by men done with a view to improving their wages or conditions or giving vent to a grievance or making a protest about something or other or sympathising with other workmen in such endeavours'. See also *Connex SE v RMT* [1999] IRLR 249.

9.08   The ballot provisions define strike as 'any concerted stoppage of work' which clearly derives from Lord Denning's formulation (TULR(C)A, s 246). An individual protest would not normally qualify (*Bowater Containers Ltd v Blake* EAT 522/81) but it did in *Lewis and Britton v E. Mason & Sons* [1994]

IRLR 4 when an employer told the employee that he would not drive from Wales to Edinburgh without an overnight heater. The decision reflected the EAT upholding the decision of the employment tribunal on a matter of fact alone, rather than indicating a general principle. Tuckey J held that it was open to the tribunal to decide that in order to constitute industrial action there must be conduct designed merely to coerce the employer to improve terms and conditions of employment. The refusal of the employee to carry out an instruction which the employer was entitled to give was sufficient.

What is a lock-out?

The only definition of lock-out throughout labour law is for the purposes of **9.09** continuity of employment, where the Employment Protection (Consolidation) Act 1978, Sch 13, para 24(1) (now Employment Rights Act 1996, s 235(4)) defines it as 'the closing of a place of employment, suspension of work, refusal by an employer to continue to employ any number of persons employed by him in consequence of a dispute done *with a view to compelling those persons to accept terms or conditions of or affecting employment'.* This was applied in the unfair dismissal case of *Fisher v York Trailer Co Ltd* [1979] ICR 834. The italicized words would appear to exclude the case where the employer has made it clear that the dismissal is once and for all and that the employees will not be re-engaged under any circumstances.

Some further guidance was offered in *Express & Star Ltd v Bunday* [1986] **9.10** IRLR 477; [1988] ICR 379. The Employment Appeal Tribunal overturned a tribunal decision that there was no lock-out because the employer was not acting in breach of contract in refusing to continue to employ the applicants. The relevant facts were that in a dispute over new technology in a local newspaper, employees found access to the premises closed with the exception of a management-manned door. On arrival, employees were shepherded to a meeting where those who refused to work with the new machinery were suspended without pay. Popplewell J thought that 'lock-out' merely meant that an employer was taking steps to enforce what he believed to be his legitimate rights to persuade the workforce to comply with what he believed to be their conditions of contract. What had to be decided was who in fact stopped the work continuing. Here it was a lock-out

> because it was the management who said to the workforce unless you are willing to do what you have not done before you will be suspended, and then suspended them, that constitutes the lock-out; whereas it might equally as well

have happened that the workforce said if you want us to do this work we shall take industrial action, and have taken industrial action. In the latter case it would have constituted strike or other industrial action (para 60).

The Court of Appeal took a different view; the continuity provisions were of assistance in defining a lock-out, and whether the employer was in breach of contract was a relevant factor but not an essential ingredient. Here the view of the tribunal that there was not a lock-out but rather that there was industrial action could not be faulted. Whether the presence of a particular element or ingredient in a given state of affairs is necessary before there can be a lock-out may be a mixed question of law and fact or pure fact.

The distinguishing factor between a lock-out and a strike or industrial action will indeed often be marginal even though it may have a major significance for liability.

What is the other industrial action?

9.11   Not only are the words strike and lock-out undefined, but tribunals and appeal bodies have also been reluctant to place a specific limit on the activities which might constitute 'other industrial action' for the purposes of s 238. Again they see it as a question of fact in each case; the categories are certainly not closed. It may clearly include a go-slow, work-to-rule, concerted non-cooperation, and probably a picket of the employer's premises. Most such activity will break the implied contractual duty that an employee must not disrupt the employer's enterprise (*Secretary of State for Employment v ASLEF (No. 2)* [1972] 2 QB 455).

9.12   The phrase is not, however, restricted to such a breach; thus a concerted withdrawal of cooperation over admittedly voluntary overtime was 'other industrial action' according to the Court of Appeal in *Faust v Power Packing Casemakers Ltd* [1983] IRLR 117. It was sufficient that the action applied pressure against management and was designed to extract some benefit from the employer for the benefit of the workforce. The characterization of industrial action was a question of fact for the employment tribunal. It depended on the motive of the employee for not working the overtime. Stephenson LJ thought that if the reason for absence was 'a private commitment to visit a sick friend or a personal preference for a football match, the employee was not taking industrial action'. The opposite was true if the aim was to, for example, 'extract an increase of wages'.

This means that one employment tribunal may treat concerted action as industrial action, whereas another presented with the same facts would not. This was a situation which Browne-Wilkinson J found unfortunate in an obiter dictum in *Coates v Modern Methods and Materials Ltd* [1982] ICR 763.

9.13

In the most esoteric forms of employee action, it becomes, moreover, difficult to draw the line between legitimate trade union activity on the one hand, for which dismissal is automatically unfair, and taking part in industrial action on the other hand, where the tribunal may have no jurisdiction at all. This issue is most acute in complaints made to management about health and safety matters which the union claims, are quite genuine but which management considers frivolous, because, for example, such matters are raised only at times of dispute about pay, and disruption of production. To one tribunal they may amount to trade union activities, to another a work-to-rule.

9.14

Another explanation for what appears to management to be disruptive action is collective disobedience to an unnecessary and unreasonable instruction. The employer may justify dismissal in those circumstances on the ground of misconduct but if this is the correct analysis, he is not entitled to blanket immunity. In *South East Kent Health Authority v Gillis* EAT 927/83 employees refused a management instruction to accept a flexible shift rota. The employees refused to attend a briefing meeting on the new rota with the Authority's personnel manager. They wanted such a meeting to take place in their own lodge. Their refusal to attend was met by summary dismissal. The tribunal rejected the employer's contention that the employees were thus participating in industrial action. Rather, they were found to be expressing their resentment at what they considered to be a petty, officious and unnecessary requirement. The dismissal so peremptorily carried out was held to be unfair, but the employees were found to have contributed to the dismissal to the extent of 75 per cent (for consideration of contributory fault see para 9.50).

9.15

Controversy has also arisen over participation in unauthorized mass meetings, although these are not so common a phenomenon as they were. In some businesses, especially television and newspapers, the disruptive union meeting at the peak point of production used to be a well-worn disruptive tactic because of the irrecoverable loss it could cause to the employer at minimum impact to the employee (*Lookers of Bradford v Marvin* EAT 332/80). In

9.16

Rasool v Hepworth Pipe Co. Ltd (No. 1) [1980] ICR 495, the tribunal decided that this did amount to industrial action, and the Employment Appeal Tribunal were not prepared to overturn the decision. The EAT refrained from setting out any general guidance but did consider that it was 'probably incorrect to attempt to interpret the expression "industrial action" mainly in terms of specific intention and that the nature and effect of the concerted action are probably of greater importance'.

9.17 It may also be difficult in some cases to distinguish between a strike and other industrial action, although to do so is less crucial to the result of the case than that between a strike and a lock-out. In *Thompson v Eaton Ltd* [1976] ICR 336, for example, employees stood round a new machine for a short time to prevent their employers from testing its operation. The EAT held that this could qualify under either hearing (see also *Connex South-Eastern Ltd v RMT* [1999] IRLR 249).

Can an employer provoke industrial action and then dismiss those who participate in it?

9.18 It appears, as a general principle, that an employer may deliberately engineer a dispute and then dismiss without compensation those who participate in it (although now, save for unofficial action, he would have to wait for eight weeks to do so). The test is merely whether the employee was dismissed in the course of the action. Whether the action was the real reason for the sacking is irrelevant to this issue (see *Faust v Power Packing Casemakers Ltd* (above)). This principle has, however, the advantage of keeping tribunals away from deciding on the merits of the dispute. Moreover, as Phillips J said in *Thompson v Eaton* (above):

> The argument that the section does not apply to provoked strikes is tantamount to saying that the provisions . . . do not apply to a case where the employer is wholly or substantially to blame for the occurrence of the strike or other industrial action. There is no warrant for this proposition in the words. Furthermore, it would introduce a test . . . which it would be impossible to apply in practice. It is rare for a strike or other industrial action to be wholly the fault of one side or the other. Almost always there is some blame on each side.

(See also *Marsden v Fairey Stainless Ltd* [1979] IRLR 103.)

9.19 Employers who follow a strategy of provoking a strike and then dismissing, must be careful not to repudiate the contracts of employment of their employees in so doing, since the workforce might accept such a breach as constructive dismissal, and then claims would be made on grounds not of the employer's choosing. This is all the more real a problem given the recent expansion in the implied term of trust and confidence (eg *Malik v BCCI* [1997] ICR 606). The question for the employment tribunal would then be whether in breaching the contract, the employer acted reasonably in all the circumstances of the case (the normal test for unfair dismissal). The fact of going on strike will not, however, be treated in itself as the acceptance by the employee of the employer's repudiation (*Wilkins v Cantrell & Cochrane (GB) Ltd* [1978] IRLR 483; see also *Hindle Gears Ltd v McGinty* [1984] IRLR 477 at para 16).

C. Is the Employee a 'Relevant Employee'?

An employee is only a 'relevant employee' for the purposes of the section if he was himself participating in the strike or other industrial action on the date of dismissal. A different regime applies in the case of lock-outs, which we consider below. The proper question is not whether there was a relevant employee who at the time of his dismissal was taking part in industrial action but was subsequently re-engaged, but rather whether that employee was taking part in industrial action at the date of dismissal of the complainants (*Express & Star Ltd v Bunday* [1986] IRLR 477). The reason for dismissal is irrelevant; the exclusion of the unfair dismissal jurisdiction applies even if the employee was also redundant because the employer decides not to replace him (*Baxter v Limb Group of Companies* [1994] IRLR 572).

9.20

Was the dismissed employee participating in the action?

Stephenson LJ in *Coates v Modern Methods and Materials Ltd* [1982] ICR 763 considered that this vital issue on which the jurisdiction of the tribunal depended, was 'just the sort of question which an industrial jury is best fitted to decide' (see to the same effect *Hindle Gears Ltd v McGinty* [1984] IRLR 477). This position was criticized with great force by the EAT in *Naylor v Orton & Smith Ltd* [1983] IRLR 233. There, 33 employees were dismissed for participating in an overtime ban. Two others had voted in favour of such action at a meeting but later signed a form initiated by the employers, stating that they would work normally. The tribunal decided that these two were not to be taken as participating in industrial action, and the EAT President

9.21

considered that the appeal body could not intervene in the light of the Court of Appeal's pronouncements in the *Coates* case.

9.22   It is, however, clear that participation must be personal and direct and not made vicariously through the agency of a shop steward (*Dixon v Wilson Walton Engineering Ltd* [1979] ICR 438).

9.23   Participation in a strike need not, however, necessarily be known to the employer before it can amount to 'taking part in the action'. In *Hindle Gears Ltd v McGinty* (above), after stating that Parliament had intended to leave such an issue to the good sense of the tribunal, Waite J said (at para 23):

> It would in our view be wrong, and would place an unwarranted limitation upon the freedom of decision given advisedly by Parliament to the Industrial Tribunals, if we were to go to either of the alternative extremes of holding on the one hand that the employer's knowledge is essential or on the other hand that it is altogether irrelevant.

9.24   In *McKenzie v Crosville Motor Services Ltd* [1989] IRLR 516, the EAT decided that the employer had immunity if he dismissed all those whom he reasonably believed to be participating in the industrial action. However in *Manifold Industries Ltd v Sims* [1991] IRLR 242, another division of the EAT preferred the approach taken in *Bolton Roadways Ltd v Edwards* [1987] IRLR 392, so that the matter was one of objective fact, and not the knowledge of the employer at all (see also *Jenkins v P&O European Ferries (Dover) Ltd* [1991] ICR 652).

9.25   A genuine belief by the employer that the employee took part in a strike is not enough to justify the employer's action in dismissing (*Thompson v Woodland Designs Ltd* [1980] IRLR 423).

9.26   It would appear that on the strict wording of s 238(2) if an employee who was taking part in the strike or industrial action resigns between the date of dismissal of the applicant and the hearing of the unfair dismissal applications, he may put the employer's immunity in jeopardy. Section 238(2) provides that the employment tribunal has jurisdiction where it is shown that 'one or more relevant employees . . . have not been dismissed'. If an employee has resigned he has not been dismissed.

Browne-Wilkinson J said:

> We reach this conclusion without any satisfaction and would be relieved if it were found that we had misinterpreted the law as laid down in the *Coates* case.

In the realm of industrial relations, it is particularly undesirable to draw fine legal distinctions; for that reason we have sought to follow the decision of the Court of Appeal in the *Coates* case. But in industrial relations terms the consequences are unfortunate. As it seems to us, on the primary facts as found by the Industrial Tribunal in this case, another Industrial Tribunal could reasonably have found that the imposition of the immediate ban on overtime itself constituted industrial action without protest for whatever reason are to be regarded as having crossed that line to take part in the strike. In the field of industrial action those who are not openly against it are presumably for it.

In *Coates*, Kerr LJ said: **9.27**

> Of course if the employee does not go to work for reasons which have nothing to do with the strike, such as illness or being on holiday, then the position would be different. But when the employee's absence from work is due to the existence of the strike in some respect, because he or she chooses not to go to work during the strike, then I think the employee should be regarded as taking part in the strike.

Two categories of employee—the frightened and the sick—have naturally engaged the particular attention of tribunals.

The frightened employee

In the *Coates* case, a Mrs Leith went on strike not (she said) because of her **9.28** support for the cause in dispute but, she said, because she was frightened that she would be abused by her fellow workers if she did not. The tribunal decided that she was nevertheless participating in the strike, so that it had jurisdiction to hear the claims of other workers who had been dismissed while she had been re-engaged after the end of hostilities. Kerr LJ did not think that the employee's reasons or motives for participating in the strike were of any moment. Such an enquiry would not be 'correct or practicable'. It would not be relevant 'to consider whether [the employee's] utterances or actions, or silence or inaction showed support, opposition or indifference in relation to the strike'. He went on:

> When it is necessary to determine the question whether an employee does or does not take part in a strike which is admittedly in progress, but which does not prevent the employee from going to work in defiance of the manifold pressures which the existence of the strike is bound to exert, then it seems to me that this question can in practice only be answered on the basis of his or her action by staying in or going out.

Stephenson LJ took the direct view that: 'In the field of industrial action those who are not openly against it are presumably for it'. Eveleigh LJ, however, dissented on the ground that an employee must act in concert with the strikers to be participating in the strike, and this Miss Leith did not do.

The sick employee

9.29 An employee genuinely on sick leave or holiday during a strike could not normally be said to be participating in it, since he would be absolved from working at the time, even though he might have spoken to pickets when attending work to present his sickness certificate (*Hindle Gears Ltd v McGinty* (above)). The position is, however, different if the employee has already taken part in the action before he goes off sick. In *Williams v Western Mail and Echo Ltd* [1980] ICR 366, members of the NUJ were given an ultimatum to discontinue industrial sanctions by a certain day or face dismissal. The applicant was off sick at the time but made clear that he would not have submitted to the ultimatum had he been well. Slynn J was not impressed by the argument that he was not to be considered as taking part in industrial action (see also *McKenzie v Crosville Motor Services Ltd* [1989] IRLR 516).

9.30 A genuine belief by the employer that the employee took part in a strike is not enough to justify the employer's action in dismissing (*Thompson v Woodland Designs* [1980] IRLR 423). Moreover, the onus is on the employer to prove that the employee took part in the strike.

Relevant employee in relation to lock-out

9.31 A relevant employee in relation to a lock-out is one who is 'directly interested in the dispute in contemplation or furtherance of which the lock-out occurred' (TULR(C)A), s 238(3) . This is a much wider concept than in relation to a strike or other industrial action and owes its provenance to the social security legislation (see para 10.08 ff).

9.32 In *Presho v DHSS (Insurance Officer)* [1984] IRLR 74, the House of Lords in interpreting 'directly interested in a trade dispute' in the Social Security Act 1975, s 19(1) as amended, said, *per* Lord Brandon at para 18:

> where different groups of workers, belonging to different unions are employed by the same employers at the same place of work . . . and there is a trade dispute between the common employers and one of the unions to which one of the group of workers belong, those in the other group of workers belonging to other unions are directly, and not merely indirectly, interested in that trade

dispute provided that two conditions are fulfilled. The first condition is that, whatever may be the outcome of the trade dispute, it will be applied by the common employers not only to the group of workers belonging to the one union participating in the dispute, but also to the other groups of workers belonging to the other unions concerned. The second condition is that the application of the dispute 'across the board', as it has been aptly described, should come about automatically as a result of one or other of three things: first, a collective agreement which is legally binding; . . . or, thirdly, established industrial custom and practice at the place (or possibly places) of work concerned.

D. The Importance of Date of Dismissal

The employee must be taking part in the appropriate action on the actual **9.33** date of dismissal for the employer to remain immune from an unfair dismissal claim. The 'date of dismissal' has somewhat surprisingly been construed as the actual *time* of dismissal. This has had important consequences in many cases. In *Heath v Longman (J.F.) (Meat Salesmen) Ltd* [1973] ICR 407, a dispute about overtime payments for Saturday working provoked the employer to declare that if the employees did not work on the following Saturday, they would be dismissed. The applicant and two colleagues went out on strike in response to this ultimatum, but, after seeing their union representatives, one of them told the employer that the strike of all of them was at an end. Even though he knew of this change of heart, the employer announced that all three were dismissed. The National Industrial Relations Court was of the view that 'once the men had telephoned and told the employer that they no longer wished to withdraw their labour and wanted to come back to work, they had in our view clearly ceased to be on strike'. The general rule of law and statutory construction that a part equalled the whole day was not appropriate in this context. The essence of the decision was that the return to work had been communicated to the employer.

The employer may not, moreover, dismiss with impunity those employees **9.34** who have announced their intention of going on strike but have not yet begun their action (*Midland Plastics Ltd v Till* [1983] IRLR 9). If, on the other hand, a strike has already begun, and an employee who is off duty states a clear intention to become involved in the action as soon as his shift starts, he is treated as participating from the time at which he makes his intention clear, even if his shift has not started at the time of dismissal (*Winnett v Seamarks Brothers Ltd* [1978] ICR 1240).

9.35 Three further points must be considered:

(1) *By what time does the tribunal decide whether all relevant employees have been dismissed?* It appears that the dismissal of all those on strike at the same time as the applicant must have taken place by the time of the tribunal hearing if the employer is to have immunity.

In *P&O European Ferries (Dover) Ltd v Byrne* [1989] IRLR 254, the Court of Appeal determined that the question had to be asked at the *conclusion* of the tribunal hearing. If only some have been dismissed by this time, the tribunal must examine whether the employer was fair or unfair in deciding who was to remain and who was to go. This introduces a certain arbitrary element since the length of time between dismissal and hearing can vary greatly. Moreover, the reason for dismissal of the comparative employees need not be by reason of the strike but may be, for example, because of redundancy.

The date of dismissal for the purposes of s 238 has the same meaning as 'effective date of termination' in unfair dismissal generally (see J Bowers, *Bowers on Employment Law*, 6th edn, OUP 2002 284–7). There is, however, one modification to this by s 238(5), which provides that it means 'where the employee's contract of employment was terminated by notice, the date on which the employer's notice was given'. This is intended to remove the argument that the employee did not *receive* notice until a later stage.

(2) *What is the position if participants in action have returned to work by the time of the applicant's dismissal?* Following the amendments introduced by the Employment Act 1982 (now Trade Union and Labour Relations (Consolidation) Act 1992, s 238(1)) any participant in strike action who has returned to work at the time of the applicant's dismissal does not qualify as a relevant employee. Thus, the employer need not dismiss all those on strike at any time but merely all those participating in the disruptive action at the time of the applicant's dismissal. He may issue an ultimatum to his employees on strike to return or else. Moreover, only those participating in the action at the particular *establishment* 'at or from which' the complainant worked are to be considered.

(3) *Must all the employees be involved in the same strike?* This issue was

considered in *McCormick v Horsepower Ltd* [1981] IRLR 217, where the appellant was one of a number of boilermakers who went on strike for increased pay. A fitter's mate in a different department (before the restriction to establishment was introduced in 1982) refused to cross the picket lines of the boilermakers. The appellant claimed that the other employee was a relevant employee for the purposes of s 238 who had not been dismissed. The Court of Appeal disagreed on the ground that there was no agreement between the parties to take industrial action and so this was not participation in the same strike.

E. Re-engagement

As already mentioned it is necessary to consider whether all those participating in a strike or other industrial action have been dismissed *and* whether some have been re-engaged. If not all have been dismissed *or* some but not others have been re-engaged, the tribunal has jurisdiction to consider the reason for the non-dismissal or re-engagement of some but not others on its merits in each case. **9.36**

Time of re-engagement

Before the Employment Act 1982 came into force, the tribunal had to consider whether any employee had been re-engaged by the time of the hearing. The statute limited the tribunal's view to the three months following dismissal of the relevant employee. Thereafter the employer could re-engage without any effect on unfair dismissal claims at all. **9.37**

In *Highlands Fabricators Ltd v McLaughlin* [1985] ICR 183, the EAT in Scotland decided that the tribunal had no jurisdiction where all the striking employees, including the applicant, had been offered re-engagement before the end of three months even though in an original offer of re-engagement, the applicant was one of 400 employees who did not receive the offer and had gained work elsewhere. Lord MacDonald considered that 'it would wreck all chances of negotiations in what is frequently a delicate and tense situation if a limited offer of re-engagement were to confer immediately on employees to whom the offer was not directed a vested right to complain of unfair dismissal'. The three months was in effect a 'cooling-off' period before re-engagements could take place and spoil the employer's defence. An **9.38** employee who has not yet received his dismissal notice which has been delayed in the post, cannot be re-engaged when he goes back to work since he has not yet been dismissed (*Hindle Gears Ltd v McGinty* [1984] IRLR 477).

Suitable terms of re-engagement

9.39 An offer of re-engagement is defined as an offer in the same job as that held before dismissal or in a different job which would be reasonably suitable in the case of the employee. The job concept focuses on the nature of the work and the place where it is to be carried on. An offer may so qualify even though by its terms it requires that the employee be treated as on the second warning stage of the disciplinary procedure (*Williams v National Theatre Board Ltd* [1982] ICR 715).

9.40 The re-engagement need not however be at the same site as that from which the employee was dismissed, nor need the employer realize that it was re-engaging an employee previously dismissed from one of its sites (*Bigham v GKN Kwikform Ltd* [1992] ICR 113). There was, however, no offer of re-engagement within the meaning of the statute when the employer placed notices at their bus depot, made press and local radio announcements that they were recruiting, and so advised local job centres (*Crosville Wales Ltd v Tracey* [1993] IRLR 60). What was made available to employees in this case was merely the *opportunity* of having an offer made to them, not an offer of re-engagement itself. If not all have been discussed *or* some but not others have been re-engaged the tribunal has jurisdiction to consider the reason for the non-dismissal or re-engagement of some but not others on its merits in each case. Similarly if the offer is not effectively communicated because for example the employee is deaf it will not amount to a relevant offer (*Tomczynski v K Millar Ltd* (1976) 11 ITR 127).

F. Discriminatory Selection

9.41 Where there is a selective dismissal or re-engagement, the employer must reveal the genuine criteria on which he made his choice as to who should go and who should stay. He must show that the selection criteria used are fair in all the circumstances of the case, so that if the reason for picking and choosing would be invalid if there were no strike, it is likely to be invalid in this situation. The fact that the employee was on strike may, however, be taken into account as a relevant matter in the fairness equation. The EAT, in *Laffin and Callaghan v Fashion Industries (Hartlepool) Ltd* [1978] IRLR 448, said that 'a valid matter to be considered is the loyalty of those who served during the strike but . . . by the same token to give *carte blanche* to the loyalty of those who did work is likely to cause indignation among those . . . who did not stay loyal to the management'.

Where there has been discriminatory selection, it is not proper for a tribunal to reduce compensation on the ground of contributory fault, since to do so would require the tribunal to assess the merits of participation in the dispute (*Courtaulds Northern Spinning Ltd v Moosa* [1984] IRLR 42, see further below para 9.50). **9.42**

Unofficial action

The rendering lawful of selective dismissals in unofficial strikes was one of the Conservative Government's central planks in seeking to outlaw and discourage wildcat strikes (see *Unofficial Action and the Law*, Cm 821, 1989). **9.43**

The question of whether a person is engaged in official or unofficial action is decided in relation to that person rather than in relation to the strike generally. **9.44**

The principles are these:

- The authorization or endorsement by the union will determine the nature of the action both for union and non-union members (this is covered at greater length on pp 61–63).
- If a person was a member when he began to take part in the action he is treated as a member even if he subsequently ceased to be so; this is to prevent employees changing the status of the action by resigning from the union.
- If there are no trade union members taking part in the action, it cannot be treated as unofficial, and must be seen as official.

There is a subtle difference between the wording under the unofficial action section where the right to claim unfair dismissal is removed altogether and under s 238A where the action is 'protected' so that the dismissal is made automatically unfair; in practice this does not make any difference. **9.45**

9.46   If the union repudiates the industrial action, so that it becomes unofficial, employees will lose their protection from unfair dismissal if they continue taking action after the end of the working day following the union's repudiation (s 238A(8)). This is designed to give to those who may have their protection removed by the action of their union time to consider their position as to whether they wish to remain part of the industrial action which could lead to their being dismissed without any recourse to the employment tribunal. Working day is defined to exclude major holidays, Saturdays or Sundays even though work may be done on those days (s 237(5)).

9.47   The only exceptions to the inability to claim whilst on unofficial action are where the reason for dismissal was on grounds of pregnancy, health and safety, working time, protected disclosure or by reason of the person being an employee representative.

Provision is made so that applications for reinstatement or re-engagement cannot be heard until the end of the dispute.

'Protected' industrial action

9.48   The Blair Government's primary reform of strike law is the concept of 'protected' industrial action, a period (of usually eight weeks) in which the employer may not dismiss at all. The White Paper, *Fairness at Work* (Cm 3968) paras 4.21–22 stated that the Government wanted to tackle the anomaly that industrial action may be clothed with immunities at the collective level but leave employees exposed to dismissal without remedy. The extensions to the eight-week period are intended to avoid delaying tactics by the employer and to advance the strategy of dealing with disputes by appropriate conciliation.

9.49   Section 16 of and Sch 5 to the Employment Relations Act 1999 inserted a new s 238A into TULR(C)A 1992, which provides that a dismissal is to be treated as unfair if the reason or principal reason for it is that the employee participated in 'protected' industrial action. The action is 'protected' if it has been *lawfully* organized under s 219 of the 1992 Act, which includes the requirement that there is a primary trade dispute and a properly conducted ballot. The dismissal will thus be automatically unfair if:

(1) it takes place within eight weeks of the day on which the employee started to take protected industrial action (s 238A(3)); or

(2) it takes place after the end of this eight-week period, but the employee has stopped taking part in the industrial action before eight weeks has expired (s 238A(4)); or

(3) eight weeks have passed and the employee is still taking part in the industrial action but the employer has not taken 'such procedural steps as would have been reasonable for the purposes of resolving the dispute' (s 238A(5)). Whether such procedural steps have been taken is to be determined without reference to the merits of the dispute but by reference to (s 238A(6)):

(a) whether the employer or union complied with procedures established by any applicable collective or other agreement;

(b) whether the employer or union offered or agreed to resume negotiations after the start of the protected industrial action;

(c) whether the employer or union unreasonably refused, after the start of the protected industrial action, a request that conciliation or mediation services be used.

G. Participation in Industrial Action and Contributory Fault

Participation in industrial action was for many years held to fall outside the **9.50** rubric of contributory fault (*Courtaulds Northern Spinning Ltd v Moosa* (above)) since this would require tribunals to attach blame in industrial disputes, but the EAT departed from this principle in *TNT Express Ltd v Downes* [1994] ICR 1, on the basis that it was not warranted by the statutory language.

This controversial issue was finally resolved by the House of Lords. The broad **9.51** position in *Moosa* was restored in *Tracey v Crosville Wales Ltd* [1997] ICR 862 HL on the basis that this was the presumed intention of Parliament, especially given that many who had been involved in the same industrial action would have been offered re-engagement. There is, however, an important caveat that where complainants have been shown to be responsible for some additional conduct of their own over and above mere participation in the industrial action, the fact that such conduct occurred during and as part of the industrial action does not preclude the tribunal from examining it separately and considering whether it contributed to the dismissal (see especially at p 880G).

H. Applications to the Employment Tribunal

9.52   In order to permit the necessary leeway to the employee to discover whether other persons engaged in the industrial action have been re-engaged he is permitted six months, rather than the usual three, in which to present his claim for unfair dismissal (Trade Union and Labour Relations (Consolidation) Act 1992, s 239(2)). The time runs not from the effective date of termination but rather from the date of dismissal as defined in s 238(5).

9.53   The onus of proof in s 238 cases has never been fully explored, but may be of vital importance in relation to the giving of further and better particulars. Our preliminary view is that:

- the employer must prove that there was a strike, industrial action or lock-out, and that the employee was taking part in the industrial action, but that
- the employee must prove that one or more relevant employees have not been dismissed or that one or more have been offered re-engagement within three months.

9.54   This means that the employer should be obliged to give further particulars of what action by the employee constituted taking part in industrial action. This may be difficult for an employer in mass industrial action dismissals. The employees, on the other hand, have to make a positive case as to who they say has not been dismissed. This can be dangerous for applicants since, as we have seen, the employer may dismiss such persons up to the date of the hearing of the claims. Thus to give such particulars may invite the dismissal of those named.

Examples

Example 1

9.55   A, B and C start action on 1 January. D joins the action on 1 February. All four are dismissed on 3 February for their participation in the industrial action; which is official action. Their dismissal is automatically unfair because in each case it is within the eight weeks.

NB   the relevant date is the date on which the dismissed employee starts action; others might have started earlier. If Y and Z had started taking action on 1 December they might fall outside s 238A if also dismissed on 3 February.

Example 2

E starts action on 1 January; the action is unofficial. If he is dismissed at any time whilst taking part in it, E will (subject to s 237(1A)) have no right to claim for unfair dismissal. However, if he returns to work at 12 noon, but is given a dismissal letter at 3 pm he is protected.

Example 3

F starts action on 1 January; ballot papers do not go to all those entitled to vote in the ballot. F is dismissed on 4 February for industrial action; there is no claim for automatically unfair dismissal under s 238A because of the ballot defect, although a tribunal would have to weigh the importance of that defect. F's claim would only be heard if not all his fellow employees are dismissed and picking and choosing is unfair.

Example 4

G starts action on 1 January. On 5 February the employer discovers G is involved in violent picketing; it is not industrial action alone which is responsible for G's dismissal. The ET would also have to review the case as one of misconduct. Protected action focuses on the *reason* for dismissal.

Example 5

H starts action on 1 January. He is dismissed on 1 March, but his employer has refused to use conciliation by ACAS even though that is provided for in the relevant collective agreement. Dismissal would be automatically unfair under s 238A(6)(c).

Example 6

J starts action on 1 January. The action continues on 4 March, but J is no longer taking part in it. His dismissal on 4 March on grounds of industrial action is automatically unfair.

Example 7

K starts action on 1 January. On Monday 5 February the action loses official union backing. K cannot be dismissed on 5 February but could (perhaps after close of business on 6 February but certainly) on 7 February be dismissed with impunity.

10

EMPLOYMENT PROTECTION RIGHTS AND SOCIAL SECURITY CLAIMS

Industrial action will have an important effect on the entitlement of employees to various employment protection rights. **10.01**

A. Continuity of Employment

Before an employee can claim most employment protection rights it is **10.02** necessary for him to show that he has been continually employed for the requisite qualifying period—for example, one year in the case of unfair dismissal. There are also detailed rules prescribing the situations in which the employee's continuity of employment may or may not be broken. (For details of the calculation of time periods see John Bowers, *Bowers on Employment Law*, 2002 OUP 6th edn, pp 208–220.) If an employee takes part in a strike in a week or part of a week then that week is not to be counted in calculating the period of time the employee has been employed.

However, continuity of employment is not broken where the employee takes part in a strike or there is a lock-out at his place of work. These two principles are to be found in Employment Rights Act 1996, s 216. Dismissal during a strike will not break continuity of employment where the employee is re-employed after the strike (*Bloomfield v Springfield Hosiery Finishing Co. Ltd* [1972] ICR 91). Nor is it possible for an employer to re-engage an employee on the basis that service prior to the dismissal is to be disregarded for continuity purposes (*Hanson v Fashion Industries (Hartlepool) Ltd* [1981] ICR 35).

B. Guarantee Pay

10.03 The Employment Rights Act 1996 gives a limited right to guarantee payments during a lay-off (ss 28–35). Broadly, an employee employed for over one month will be entitled to his daily pay up to a specified limit for up to five days in any three months. However, s 29(2) provides that an employee shall not be entitled to a guarantee payment in respect of a workless day if the failure to provide him with work occurred in consequence of a strike, lock-out or other industrial action involving any employee of his employer or of an associated employer. In deciding whether the lay-off was in consequence of the dispute, the question to be asked is whether there would have been a lay-off but for the dispute. So, in *Thompson v Priest (Lindley) Ltd* [1978] IRLR 99, although there were also a number of economic factors that led to a lay-off, it was the strike that was the immediate reason for the lay-off and without which the lay-off would not have occurred. The employees were therefore not entitled to a guarantee payment.

10.04 Employees who have no interest (and are not involved in any way) in a dispute may be precluded from claiming a guarantee payment where fellow employees have become embroiled in a dispute not of their making. In *Garvey v J & J Maybank (Oldham) Ltd* [1979] IRLR 408, the employer was a paper merchant, and supplies were carried into its works by means of outside haulage contractors and by their own lorries. During a road haulage strike the employer's lorry drivers refused to cross the hauliers' picket lines. No supplies could enter or leave the works and about 50 workers were laid off. It was held that they were not entitled to a guarantee payment since they were laid off in consequence of a trade dispute between the employer and his employees, the lorry drivers. By way of contrast, in *Peplow v Bennett Swiftline*

(Birmingham) Ltd (1982) COIT 1324/30, employees were laid off by their employer, an independent contractor situated at the British Leyland Longbridge plant, in consequence of a strike between BL and its employees. The independent contractor's employees were not concerned in the strike and were prepared to work but their employer told them not to report for work while the strike was in progress. It was held that they were entitled to a guarantee payment.

C. Redundancy

Strikes or other industrial action often occur in response to threatened lay-offs or redundancies by a particular employer. Such action will normally be a breach of contract which will entitle the employer to dismiss without having to make a redundancy payment (ERA 1996, s 140(1)). The same principle will apply where the employee is dismissed for other forms of misconduct. Where the employee is under notice of a redundancy and goes on strike, s 140(2) states that s 140(1) does not apply and the employee remains entitled to a redundancy payment. If the employee's contract is terminated for any other reason during this time a tribunal may award the whole or such part of the redundancy payment as it considers equitable. If the employee goes on strike during notice of redundancy the employer may serve a notice that it will require any time lost during the strike to be made up before he will be entitled to the redundancy payment, stating that any entitlement will be disputed unless the employee complies with the notice (ERA 1996, s 143). **10.05**

There are thus two situations to be distinguished:

(1) If employees go on strike or take other industrial action in breach of their contracts of employment either before they receive redundancy notices or after they receive them but before the obligatory period of notice (that is, the period of minimum contractual and/or statutory notice to which the employee is entitled, reckoning backwards from the date on which the redundancy notice would expire), the employees will not be entitled to redundancy payments.
(2) If employees take other industrial action in breach of contract in the obligatory period and they are summarily dismissed, a tribunal may award all or part of a redundancy payment as it sees fit.

D. Employment Agencies

10.06   There is a curious provision in the Conduct of Employment Agencies and Employment Businesses Regs 1976 SI No 715 reg 4(10) by which an Employment Agency 'shall not supply workers to a hirer as direct replacements of employees who are in industrial dispute with that hirer to perform the same duties as those normally performed by those employees'. The intention is to prevent employment agencies being used to provide what would be seen as 'blacklegs' by strikers.

E. Social Security

10.07   The employee's industrial muscle during an industrial dispute, which is his ability to withdraw his labour, is often considerably weakened by the fact that the employee simply does not have the financial resources to continue to live without a wage packet for a very long period. Although the unemployed are eligible for Jobseeker's Allowance if they have paid sufficient national insurance contributions, and for other benefits if they have not, the State generally refuses benefits to strikers on the ground that it must adopt a neutral stance and not become involved in disputes. It has been claimed that the purpose of the trade dispute disqualification is to 'prevent the insurance fund from being used for financing employees during strikes or lock-outs' (R(U) 17/52). This ostensibly neutral stance has, however, been criticized on the ground that the employer is in any case in a superior economic position and to refuse benefits to strikers further weakens their bargaining position when they may have a legitimate grievance. The subject arouses strong emotions; some of the most acrimonious exchanges in the House of Commons during the miners' strike of 1984–85 were about the non-availability of social security benefits to striking miners. Although the striker himself may not be eligible for benefits, he may be able to claim benefit on behalf of his family. This chapter considers the nature of the trade dispute disqualification and also those areas of social security law where some form of benefits may be available to the striker or his family.

F. Jobseeker's Allowance

The disqualification

The framers of the social security legislation envisaged that the contributory **10.08** benefits would be the primary form of social insurance, with means-tested benefits being available for those who had not made enough contributions or had exhausted their contributory benefit entitlement (see, for example, Beveridge, *Social Insurance and Allied Services*, Cmnd 6404, 1942, paragraph 369). The benefit is available after three workless days for up to 312 days of unemployment in any one year in which sufficient contributions have been made. Complicated linking rules apply where there are intermittent periods of unemployment (for full details, see Ogus and Barendt, *The Law of Social Security*.

Adopting the traditional 'neutrality' approach to the availability of social security benefits to strikers, the Jobseekers Act 1995, s 14 now provides:

> 14.—(1) Where—
> (a) there is a stoppage of work which causes a person not to be employed on any day, and
> (b) the stoppage is due to a trade dispute at his place of work,
> that person is not entitled to a jobseeker's allowance for the week which includes that day unless he proves that he is not directly interested in the dispute.
> (2) A person who withdraws his labour on any day in furtherance of a trade dispute, but to whom subsection (1) does not apply, is not entitled to a jobseeker's allowance for the week which includes that day.

The basic principle that a person who loses employment because of a strike cannot claim benefit nevertheless remains (notwithstanding the change of name from unemployment benefit to Jobseeker's Allowance) and previously decided cases remain relevant.

Once the insurance officer is satisfied that the claimant comes within the **10.09** wording of the section he will not inquire further into the merits of the dispute. Thus, in R(U)27/56, the claimant was disqualified when he became unemployed because of a trade dispute relating to the employer's unilateral decision to reduce workers' wages. In R(U) 5/77, *R v National Insurance Commissioner ex parte Thompson*, it was said to be irrelevant that the trade dispute concerned alleged breaches of the Health and Safety at Work Act 1974 by the employer. This is a similar principle to that in the Employment (Protection) Consolidation Act 1978, s 62 now Employment Rights Act 1996, s 238. The wording of the section has given rise to a very considerable amount of litigation, primarily in the form of Commissioners' decisions, and must be considered in some detail. The onus of showing that the claimant is disqualified is on the insurance officer (R(U) 17/52) and under s 14(1) it is necessary for him to show:

(1) that there was a trade dispute
(2) at the claimant's place of employment
(3) which caused a stoppage
(4) by reason of which the claimant lost employment

Section 14(2) is an addition to the legislation which will disqualify the striker who withdraws his labour, although a stoppage does not occur because the employer is able to carry on his business as normal or sufficient workers do not go on strike to create a stoppage.

Trade dispute

10.10   A trade dispute is defined in the Jobseekers Act 1995, s 35 as:

> any dispute between employers and employees or between employees and employees, which is connected with the employment or non-employment or the terms of employment or the conditions of employment of any persons, whether employees in the employment of the employer with whom the dispute arises, or not.

10.11   The wording was taken from the Trade Disputes Act 1906 and this accounts for the width of the definition, which is perhaps not wholly appropriate in the social security context. For example, in R(U) 2/53, there was held to be a trade dispute between a claimant and pickets who had prevented the claimant from working by unlawful threats of violence. In R(U) 1/74, pickets from another site managed to persuade the claimant and his fellow workers to withdraw their labour. It was held that there was a trade dispute between the pickets and the claimant's employer. As with the definition of trade dispute in TULR(C)A 1974, s 244, there must be more than just a grievance before a difference can be properly categorized as a dispute. The difference must 'reach a certain stage of contention before it may be properly termed a dispute' (R(U) 21/59). Case law on s 244 may be used to assist in deciding what is a trade dispute.

Claimant's place of employment

10.12   The claimant is not required personally to be involved in the trade dispute so long as it is taking place at his place of work, being the place he is employed (s 14(4)). (The claimant may, however, be able to satisfy the provisio to s 14(1) that he is not directly interested in the dispute.) The rule may cause difficulties in large plants or factories where it will be necessary to decide whether separate works amount to one place of employment. However, s 14(5)(a) gives a wide definition to the meaning of place of employment:

> where separate branches of work which are commonly carried on as separate businesses in separate premises or at separate places are in any case carried on in separate departments on the same premises or at the same place, each of these departments shall for the purposes of subsection (4) be deemed to be . . . separate premises or (as the case may be) a separate place . . .

It will be for the insurance officer to show that the premises in question are the claimant's place of employment. Once he has shown this, the onus is on the claimant to show that his employment premises constitute a separate business (R(U) 1/70). Large factories or work premises are often held to be one single place of employment. In R(U) 8/71, the whole port of Port Talbot comprised the place of employment, while in R(U) 1/70, the whole of the Ford Dagenham plant constituted the claimant's place of employment. However, in UD 5145/26, an engineering works attached to a group of collieries but separated physically was not part of the colliery premises. It is difficult for a claimant to argue that he is within the exception because, as well as showing that his work was carried out as a separate branch, he must show that such work was commonly carried out as a separate business in separate premises elsewhere, and that it was so carried out at the premises in question as a separate department. He will not be able to show that his work was carried out as a separate branch if it was merely one step in an integrated process (R(U) 4/62). The claimant will need to adduce some evidence of the practice of other firms to show that his work was commonly carried out as a separate business elsewhere (R(U) 1/70, R(U) 4/62). **10.13**

Stoppage of work

There must be a *stoppage of work* at the claimant's place of employment, which has been described as a situation 'where a considerable number of men cease to carry on their work' (R(U) 7/58). The stoppage must be part of the dispute, the intention being to resume normal working once the dispute is over. However, if the claimant ceased work because of a trade dispute he will **10.14** be disqualified for the duration of the dispute even though the employer has decided to dismiss him and not re-employ him under any circumstances once the dispute is over. In R(U) 1/65, the claimant went on strike on 30 April 1964, together with 63 fellow welders belonging to two trade unions. The employer sent them each notice of termination of employment the next day, with a conditional offer of re-engagement. None of the claimant's union members was re-engaged and the Commissioner found that the employer did not intend to re-engage any of them after the walk-out on 30 April. He held that they were, however, disqualified until 8 August when the strike ended, stating that: 'If an employer determines to dismiss certain employees for ever it does not follow that the stoppage for them cannot be due to a trade dispute.' The Commissioner distinguished R(U) 17/52 on the basis that, although in that case a trade dispute was taking place, the dismissal of employees was because of a desire to get rid of troublemakers. One must ascertain whether the determination of the employer is a move in the dispute or a different and separate cause of the stoppage.

10.15 Once a dispute is over, it may not be possible for the employees to resume work straightaway, whether because damage has been caused to the work premises, because production levels must first be built up (CS 2/81) or for some other reason. The question then arises whether this continued unemployment is due to a trade dispute so that the erstwhile strikers continue to be disqualified from obtaining unemployment benefit. The question was considered in R(U) 9/80, which was appealed to the Divisional Court, and the judgment of Forbes J was appended to the Commissioner's decision as *R v Chief National Insurance Commissioner ex parte Dawber*. The claimant was one of a number who went on strike at a gasworks, thereby placing the furnace in danger. The employer adopted a number of remedial measures, but the furnace nevertheless suffered damage. The dispute was quickly settled but the employer laid off all its employees whilst repairs were carried out to the furnace. Modifications were carried out to the furnace at the same time. The question arose whether the claimant was disqualified by reason of a dispute, whether the modifications delayed the return to work and whether the remedial measures adopted by the employer should affect benefit claims. Upholding the Commissioner, Forbes J held that the damage to the furnace was reasonably foreseeable by the parties and a natural and probable consequence of the trade dispute. Nor did the measures adopted by the employer break the chain of causation. The decision may be contrasted with R(U)

15/80: a closure was due to bad trade and these economic reasons were not due to a trade dispute. It should be noted that s 19(1)(b), which in effect states that a person is not to be disqualified when his labour is no longer withdrawn, will not help the claimant where the dispute is over but he cannot return to work because of some factor caused by the strike, since the subsection is expressly subject to s 19(1)(a).

Loss of employment due to stoppage

The loss of employment must be *due to* the stoppage which occurred because **10.16** of the trade dispute. If the loss of employment is for some other reason the claimant will *not* be disqualified (R(U) 15/80). However, it may be that the claimant has ceased to be employed at a time just *before* the trade dispute. It is always possible, of course, that the claimant deliberately left his employment so as to avoid disqualification during the dispute. Although in those circumstances the striker may be disqualified for 13 weeks for voluntarily leaving his employment, it is possible that the strike may last a considerably longer period than 13 weeks. In such a situation the approach has therefore been taken that if the employee left his employment within 12 days before the dispute he will be disqualified for the duration of the stoppage (R(U) 30/55, R(U) 20/57). The 12-day limit is a rule of thumb which emanates from decisions under the early social security legislation (UD 18901/31). However, the rule is arbitrary and in R(U) 6/71, Commissioner Shewan thought that it was less readily justifiable than it had been in the past and reserved his opinion as to its continued validity. It appears that it is recent DHSS practice not to invoke the rule.

The 1975 Act also operated to disqualify someone who was under notice of **10.17** dismissal for redundancy when the stoppage of work due to the dispute started, for the whole period of the stoppage not just the relevant notice period (see R(U) 12/72, R(U) 13/72, R(U) 12/80)). These decisions could be harsh in their effect, but were regarded as correct by the Court of Appeal in *Cartlidge v Chief Adjudication Officer* [1986] IRLR 182, where it was held that a miner under notice of redundancy when the 1984–85 miners' strike commenced was disqualified from receiving benefit for the duration of the strike. Because of the perceived injustice that this rule caused, Social Security Act 1975, s 19(1A) as inserted by the 1986 Act, now contained in the Jobseekers Act 1995, s 14(3)(b), provides that a person who would have been disqualified under s 19(1A) shall not be disqualified where his employment has been terminated by reason of redundancy within the meaning of s 81(2) of the Employment Protection (Consolidation) Act 1978.

Length of disqualification

10.18 Disqualification under s 14(a) will last so long as the stoppage continues. The position used to be that a claimant was disqualified for the whole duration of the dispute if he was disqualified at some point in the dispute (R(U) 4/79). This is no longer so where the striker has ceased to be employed because he is under notice of redundancy (see s 14(3)(b) reversing *Cartlidge v Chief Adjudication Officer* (above)).

Withdrawal of labour

10.19 Section 14(2) of the 1975 Act provides that, even though there is no stoppage within s 14(1), a person is disqualified from receiving benefit, where that person has withdrawn his labour, for every day that it is withdrawn. This would seem to cover the position where a strike does not really 'take off' because most employees do not participate so that no stoppage occurs.

The disqualification exceptions

10.20 The width of s 14(1) is mitigated by four exceptions to the general rule, which provide that unemployment benefit will be available where:

(1) the employee's employment terminated because of redundancy;
(2) the employee has become bona fide employed elsewhere;
(3) the employee is not directly interested in the dispute; or
(4) the employee resumed employment with his employer but subsequently left for a reason other than the trade dispute.

The first situation has already been considered and the latter three will be reviewed here. The 1986 reform repealed the previous requirement for the employee to show that he was not participating in the dispute at any stage and has thereby made it easier for the employee to show that he comes within one of the exceptions.

Employment elsewhere

10.21 A claimant will be eligible for benefit if he can show that before becoming unemployed 'he had become bona fide employed elsewhere' (s 14(3)(a)). The claimant used to have to show that the employment elsewhere was in the occupation which he usually followed, or he had become regularly engaged in some other occupation, but this extra condition was removed by the 1986 Act. The rationale is that if a claimant has genuinely sought employment elsewhere, he should not be penalized on account of the trade dispute which affected his previous employment. The onus is on the claimant to show that the new employment was bona fide (R(U) 39/56). The fact that the employment elsewhere was of short duration does not mean automatically that it was not bona fide. However, if the employment was 'a temporary expedient with no permanent severance intended' (R(U) 39/56) the claimant will remain disqualified. In R(U) 6/74, it was held that a claimant who took employment elsewhere was bona fide employed even though he knew that the employment was temporary. What mattered was that the employee was not using the employment as a ploy to escape disqualification but was honest in his intention to seek alternative employment.

Not directly interested

Claimants who can show that they are not affected by the dispute will be able **10.22** to call into aid this exception. The meaning of the word 'directly' has given rise to a considerable amount of litigation, culminating in the House of Lords' decision in *Presho v DHSS (Insurance Officer)* [1984] 1 All ER 97. Employees who were members of the Amalgamated Union of Engineering Workers were in dispute with their employer over a pay rise and went on strike bringing the whole of the works to a standstill. The claimant was a member of the Union of Shop, Distributive and Allied Workers, which was not seeking a pay rise. The House of Lords, nevertheless, held that the claimant was directly interested in the dispute and therefore disqualified, since there was evidence that USDAW members would automatically get the same pay rise as AUEW members if they applied for it. Lord Brandon said that a claimant would be directly interested if 'whatever may be the outcome of the trade dispute, it will be applied by the common employers not only to [those] participating in the dispute, but also to the other groups of workers belonging to the other unions concerned', or if the same rise would automatically come about whether as a result of a collective agreement or industrial custom and practice. (See also para 13.3.2 and *Watt v Lord Advocate* 1979 SLT 137, 141).

The direct interest of the employee may relate to any terms and conditions of employment (R(U) 5/79). In R(U) 4/79, a tribunal of Commissioners held that if a claimant had been interested *at any stage* of the dispute he was disqualified for the whole duration of the stoppage. The same approach was taken by the Court of Appeal in *Cartlidge v Chief Adjudication Officer* (above), although the decision has been overturned by legislation. It is unlikely that the present wording of the legislation will lead to a different approach to that in R(U) 4/79 in cases other than redundancy.

Other reasons for leaving

10.23 The fourth exception applies when the employee can show that he resumed employment with his employer but then left for some reason unconnected with the strike (Jobseekers Act 1995, s 14(3)(c)). This may be seen as an extension of the bona fide employment exception elsewhere. The employee will have to satisfy the tribunal that he genuinely left for reasons other than a dispute.

G. Income Support, Jobseeker's Allowance and Families

10.24 An individual who would be disqualified from the Jobseeker's Allowance will also be disqualified from claiming income support unless, during the same period, he or she is incapable of work by reason of disease, disablement, or pregnancy in which case a claim may be made either side of the expected week of confinement (SSCBA 1992, s 127). After a period of seven days a claimant may make a claim for members of his family and the benefits payable will be by reference to the dependant's allowances that apply from time to time. The sums are subject to deduction for strike pay received by the striker (s 126).

10.25

Income based Jobseeker's Allowance may be payable to the partner of an individual who is on strike but no benefit is payable for the first seven days as the striker is treated as in full-time employment. The applicable amount will be as for income support thus excluding any element for the partners involved in the strike (Jobseekers Act 1995, s 15).

11

INJUNCTIONS

A. Introduction

The employer in almost all cases will be seeking an injunction to restrain **11.01** industrial action rather than damages to compensate for loss caused by it. The threat to his business is immediate, and by the time a claim for damages reaches trial, in most cases the passion will have gone out of the dispute. The only well-known case of recent years to proceed to damages was that involving Messenger Newspapers Ltd, the newspaper publishing business chaired by Eddy Shah. Since speed is essential, the employer will usually wish to seek an interim injunction. It behoves employers to plan carefully their strategy for gaining injunctions if they foresee the possibility of industrial trouble. We first consider the principles applicable to the grant of such injunctions and then look at the relevant practice and procedure. It should be noted that the rules on applying for an interim interdict, the Scottish form of interlocutory injunction, are somewhat different and are not covered here.

B. Granting Interim Injunctions: General Principles

11.02   The law on strike injunctions is intimately linked to the general principles which have developed to govern interim injunctions. Before 1975, the plaintiff (now known as the claimant) had to prove a prima facie case on affidavit in order to gain injunctive relief. The merits would thus have to be tested to some extent at a very early stage in the litigation. This rule was laid down in the industrial case of *Stratford (J. T.) and Son v Lindley* [1965] AC 269. It was, however, inconvenient and to some extent unjust that this should occur before the process of disclosure of documents and without the opportunity for cross-examination. Moreover, the increasing length of such interim proceedings gave cause for concern. The House of Lords thus modified this approach in the leading case of *American Cyanamid Co. v Ethicon Ltd* [1975] AC 396. This arose in the field of patent law but had vital and immediate implications for industrial disputes applications. It is now only necessary for the claimant to prove that there is a 'serious issue to be tried'; that is, that the claim is not frivolous and vexatious, or, to put it another way, that the claimant has a real prospect of succeeding in his claim for a permanent injunction at the trial (see also *Beese v Woodhouse* [1970] 1 WLR 586, 591, *Smith v Inner London Education Authority* [1978] 1 All ER 411, 419). The judge must then at once go on to weigh the 'balance of convenience' on the facts of the case.

Lord Diplock explained the rationale of interim injunctions in the *American Cyanamid* case when he said (at p 398E) that:

> The object of the interlocutory injunction is to protect the plaintiff against violation of his right for which he could not be adequately compensated in damages recoverable in the action if the uncertainty were resolved in his favour at the trial; but the plaintiff's need for such protection must be weighed against the corresponding need of the defendant to be protected

against injury resulting from his having been prevented from exercising his own legal rights for which he could not be adequately compensated under the plaintiff's undertaking in damages if the uncertainty were resolved in the defendant's favour at the trial. The court must weigh one need against another and determine where 'the balance of convenience' lies.

At the heart of this delicate balance is the consideration whether, if no injunction was awarded and the claimant succeeded at the full trial of the action (however unlikely that is to take place), damages would be an adequate remedy for any loss suffered in the meantime. If it would be an adequate remedy, no injunction should normally be granted (see also *Garden Cottage Foods Ltd v Milk Marketing Board* [1984] AC 130). The courts should, if other factors are evenly balanced, preserve the status quo, that is, the state of affairs existing 'during the period immediately preceding the issue of the writ claiming the permanent injunction, or if there be unreasonable delay between the issue of the writ and motion . . . the period immediately preceding the motion' (the *Garden Cottage* case (above)). Lord Diplock in the *American Cyanamid* case stressed that the court was not justified in embarking at that stage on anything resembling a trial of the action on conflicting affidavits in order to evaluate the strength of the respective parties' cases. The Master of the Rolls described this concept as 'the balance of justice' in *Francome v Mirror Group Newspapers Ltd* [1984] 1 WLR 892.

11.03

The *American Cyanamid* principle at once threatened to unbalance matters against defendants in industrial action cases. The cross undertaking in damages which is usually of great benefit to a defendant which is inappropriately restrained by an interim injunction is of little value to the defendant which is a union or union official in an industrial dispute, since the loss which the union would suffer by not striking at a particular time is intangible and not susceptible of ready calculation for damages purposes. Moreover, the status quo usually leans heavily in favour of maintaining production and preventing a strike. The industrial reality is, however, that the impetus of the workers' case may be lost at the point of restraint. Once postponed, enthusiasm for a strike may be difficult to revive when the immediate heat has gone out of the particular situation. The employer will, in any event, have more time to organize to defeat a later strike and the union's momentum may be lost. Lord Diplock recognized this consideration when he realistically said in *NWL Ltd v Woods* [1979] 3 All ER 614: 'It is in the nature of industrial action that it can be promoted effectively

11.04

only so long as it is possible to strike while the iron is hot; once postponed it is unlikely to be revived.' He thus distinguished the *American Cyanamid* case, since it was 'not dealing with a case in which the grant or refusal of an injunction at that stage would in effect dispose of the action finally in favour of whichever party was successful in it'.

11.05 Various cases have sought to explain or create other modifications to the general *American Cyanamid* principle itself (eg *Fellowes & Son v Fisher* [1975] 2 All ER 829, 834, *Dunford and Elliott Ltd v Johnson & Firth Brown Ltd* [1977] 1 Lloyd's Rep 505, 511, *Office Overload Ltd v Gunn* (1976) 120 SJ 147, *Mothercare Ltd v Robson Books Ltd* [1979] FSR 466). The modification which has gained greatest acceptance is shown in the Court of Appeal decision in *Cayne v Global Natural Resources* [1984] 1 All ER 225. Their Lordships were there of the view that in a case which is unlikely to proceed to trial, the court may then indeed be justified in weighing up the rival contentions of the parties, and to balance the risk of doing an injustice to either party. Moreover, Kerr LJ reminded practitioners that 'the grant or refusal of an injunction is ultimately a matter of statutory discretion, and that the powers of the courts in this regard cannot be fettered by decisions in general terms, when the facts of cases will infinitely vary' (see also *Fulwell v Bragg* (1983) 127 SJ 171, *Morris and others v National Union of Mineworkers (Midland Area) and others* (1984)). In the miners' picketing case, *Thomas v National Union of Mineworkers (South Wales Area)* [1986] Ch 20, Scott J was doubtful that the case would ever come to trial and adopted the criteria that he had to be satisfied that 'the relief is necessary to protect the plaintiffs' rights and . . . that the relief does not impede lawful and proper picketing at the collieries . . .'. Stuart-Smith J adopted a similar realistic approach in *News Group Newspaper Ltd v SOGAT 82 and others* [1986] IRLR 337, para 166. In *Barrett & Baird (Wholesale) Ltd v Institution of Professional Civil Servants* [1987] IRLR 3 Henry J said that he would look at 'the respective risks that injustice may result in' in a decision taken at that stage. He cited for this proposition Lord Diplock's speech in *NWL Ltd v Woods* [1979] 1 WLR 1294, 1306G. Further he said that the 'so-called' right to strike, while not absolute, was 'a valuable right' and 'should not be rendered less valuable than Parliament intended by too fanciful or ingenious a view of what might develop into a serious issue to be tried . . .'.

C. Section 221 of TULR(C)A 1992

The unions naturally considered that the decision in *American Cyanamid Co. v **11.06** *Ethicon Ltd* [1975] AC 396 swung the pendulum too far in favour of employers at the vital stage of industrial action proceedings (since very few go as far as a trial) so that Parliament decided that there should be a special exemption in such cases. By TULRA 1974, s 17(2) (introduced by the Employment Act 1975), where the defendant claims or is likely to claim the trade dispute defence for its action, 'the court shall in exercising its discretion whether or not to grant the injunction *have regard to* the likelihood of that party succeeding at the trial' in establishing the defence, now TULR(C)A, s 221. The italicized words are, however, somewhat ambiguous and certainly open to interpretation.

Employers have thus for example argued that the court may 'have regard to' **11.07** the trade dispute argument yet find on the facts of the case that consideration is outweighed by the damaging consequences of the dispute. The three most important analyses have come from Lords Diplock and Scarman in *NWL Ltd v Woods* [1979] 3 All ER 614 and May LJ in *Mercury Communications Ltd v Scott-Garner* [1984] Ch 37. Lord Diplock thought that where the defendant could prove that it was more likely than not that its action would fall within the golden formula of the trade dispute defence, the judge should refuse the relief sought. The likelihood of that defence succeeding was to his Lordship thus simply one element in the 'balance of convenience' test. It was not the paramount or overriding factor. There were other 'practical realities' to be considered, including the facts that:

- the real dispute was not between the employer, claimant and the defendants (individual officers of the union) but between the employer and the union which threatened the industrial action; and
- the injunction stage generally disposes of the whole action (see also *Hadmor Productions Ltd v Hamilton* [1982] IRLR 102, *Mersey Dock and Harbour Co. v Verrinder* [1982] IRLR 152).

These two factors have now to some extent been superseded by the **11.08** Employment Act 1982 and Trade Union Act 1984, as Lord Diplock pointed out in the case of *Dimbleby & Sons Ltd v National Union of Journalists* [1984] 1 All ER 117, since there is more prospect of actions for damages proceeding to trial against a claimworthy defendant. This is, as we have seen, more apparent as a possibility than a real likelihood in fact.

11.09 Lord Scarman's view in the *NWL* case of the proper process of reasoning was that the judge should first consider whether there was a serious issue to be tried, weigh the balance of convenience, ignoring the statutory trade dispute defences and then, if he were still inclined to grant the injunction, consider the likelihood of the defendants establishing the defence.

11.10 According to May LJ in *Mercury Communications Ltd v Scott-Garner* [1983] 3 WLR 914, 954, the subsection requires the judge to look forward to the trial and use his experience of conducting litigation to anticipate the likely outcome of cross-examination on the affidavits sworn. He saw 'no good reason why the industrial action being taken cannot, if temporarily post-poned, be revived if the union does not succeed at trial and revived effectively' (see also Geoffrey Lane LJ in *Associated Newspapers Group v Wade* [1979] 1 WLR 697, 719). This may however underrate the difficulty of mobilizing fresh support for action once the initial furore has died down.

D. Factors in the Discretion

11.11 We now consider how courts have weighed the several factors in exercising their discretion within the *American Cyanamid* rule and s 221. One must, however, bear in mind that Lord Diplock in the *American Cyanamid* case counselled against listing 'all the various matters which may need to be taken into consideration'. Each case must be considered against its own facts.

Exceptional cases

11.12 In the *NWL* case, Lord Diplock thought that there might be cases in which the serious consequences of a strike for the employer, a third party and for the general public were so great that a higher degree of probability of proving a trade dispute defence would be required. This is a very extreme case and the House of Lords, for example, did not rate the situation as sufficiently grave in the nationwide steel strike in 1980 (*Duport Steels Ltd v Sirs* [1980] ICR 161). Lord Fraser thought that there must be 'immediate serious danger to the public safety or health' and no other means available to prevent that danger.

Maximum damages

11.13 A new consideration weighing in the balance of convenience was identified in the *Mercury* case, where their Lordships pointed out that the employer's losses could well exceed £250,000 which was and remains the maximum sum under the Employment Act 1982, now TULR(C)A, s 22, which could be levied against a union in one cause of action. This argued against the notion that damages could be an adequate remedy at all. On the other hand, in the instant case, the union would have suffered no loss by the grant of an injunction if at trial it was held to be improperly granted. There was no suggestion that a temporary halt on union action would hasten the redundancies about which the union, by its strike action, was protesting. In *Mersey Dock and Harbour Co. v Verrinder* [1982] IRLR 152, an interim injunction was granted on the balance of convenience, since the employer had already lost £200,000 and, even if it succeeded at trial, it was unlikely to be fully compensated for loss caused by picketing in the interim. In *News Group Newspapers Ltd v SOGAT 82 and others* (above), Stuart-Smith J weighed in favour of granting an injunction the fact that the expenses incurred for bussing employees through violent picket lines at the Wapping Printing Plant and extra security staff were already greater than the limitation of liability in damages on the defendant unions.

No tangible loss to employees

The consideration which swung the balance against the union in *Solihull Metropolitan Borough v National Union of Teachers* [1985] IRLR 211 (see also para 3.34), was the lack of any tangible loss to the union if the injunction were granted. The NUT issued guidelines to its members, as part of national industrial action over pay, to refuse to cover for absences or supervise during the lunch period, etc. No ballot of members had been held to secure a mandate for this action. Over protests from the defendant, Warner J found that there was an issue to be tried as to whether the functions were contractual obligations. The issue could, however, only be fully tried with cross-examination and after disclosure of documents. Damages would not be an adequate remedy for the local authority since the detriment lay in the harm done to children in its schools, while the detriment to the union, if the injunction were granted, was merely a choice between holding a ballot and accepting arbitration which had been offered by the employer's side. The cost of holding a ballot would be recoverable on the cross undertaking in damages if it were shown in due course that a ballot was unnecessary. It is likely that in most cases under the Trade Union and Labour Relations (Consolidation)

11.14

Act 1992 the courts will find that the unions lose little by, in effect, being forced to hold a ballot of their members if they wish to have immunity from suit.

11.15   Rather more tendentious was the comment of Lord Denning MR in *Star Sea Transport Corp. of Monrovia v Slater* [1978] IRLR 507, when, after concluding that the claimant shipowners were losing money every day of the defendant's blacking of its ship, asked 'if the injunction issues, what damage will be done to these men of the sea? They do not suffer any actual damage. They only lose a bargaining counter which is in their hands'. Modern judges are likely to see such a prospect as real damage to the union.

Damages as an adequate remedy

11.16   In a few cases, it has been successfully argued that damages are an adequate remedy for the employer because, for example, the loss under a particular contract may be quite easily identified. During the News International Wapping dispute, Hutchison J accepted this argument and refused an injunction to the Post Office against the Union of Communications Workers (*Post Office v Union of Communications Workers* (1986 unreported)). This arose when the union, without a ballot, had instructed Post Office employees not to handle *Sun* bingo cards. The judge considered that the loss to the Post Office was easily assessed as the amount that News Group International Ltd would pay to them for distribution of the cards under the contract between the company and the Post Office. One day later, News Group Newspapers Ltd itself gained a similar injunction from the same judge on the basis that their loss was incalculable, since it could be a loss of circulation and goodwill, as well as advertising revenue. It was also argued in the Wapping picketing case, *News Group Newspapers Ltd v SOGAT 82 and others* (above), by the union that damages would be an adequate remedy, but Stuart-Smith J thought that the 'loss or potential loss of journalists and other key staff [by reason of violent picketing] cannot be quantified . . . or adequately compensated'.

11.17   In *Express Newspapers Ltd v Keys* [1980] IRLR 247, Griffiths LJ, however, was not impressed by the argument that an injunction against a TUC day of action, which he decided was a political strike, should not be granted because damages would be an adequate remedy. In his view, the action was clearly unlawful and the defendants should not be given a licence to commit it. There was also the practical difficulty of knowing how to attribute any particular breach of contract to incitement by the defendants as opposed to the voluntary act of the employees.

The public interest in the freedom of the press

The public interest in the 'freedom of the press' has frequently exercised the judges as an aspect of the balance of convenience. In *Beaverbrook Newspapers Ltd v Keys* [1978] ICR 582, 586, Lord Denning said: 'I put on one side the damage to either party or the convenience or inconvenience to either of them. To my mind the public should not be made to suffer at the hands of the contesting parties. Readers ought to be allowed to get a newspaper to read'.

11.18

In *Associated Newspapers Group v Wade* [1979] ICR 664, he said: 'Running through all our cases you will find it implicitly accepted as a fundamental principle of our law that the press shall be free. It shall be at liberty to express opinions and to give news and information to the public at large without interference by anyone inside or outside their organisation'.

This is all the more relevant with the European Convention on Human Rights brought into force by the Human Rights Act 1998.

'Clean hands'

The court will also exercise its discretion on the basis that only those who come to equity with clean hands gain an injunction. This was the reason for the failure of the employer in *Chappell v Times Newspapers Ltd* [1975] ICR 145, who sought to prevent dismissals while they themselves were unwilling to perform their contracts of employment. Lord Denning MR (at 174G) summed up the view of the court that: 'Not being ready and willing to do their part, they cannot call on the employers to continue to employ them. They are seeking equity when they are not ready to do it themselves.'

11.19

Judges will inevitably find it difficult to adjudicate on the 'clean hands' argument, even when, as in the Wapping pickets' case, there is considerable argument about it and much evidence because that evidence will not have been tested by cross-examination at that stage. In *News Group Newspapers Ltd v SOGAT 82 and others* [1986] IRLR 337 (for facts see para 8.28), the defendants argued that the company had substantially misled the court about their plans to produce a London evening newspaper called the *London Post* at the

11.20

Wapping plant, which the defendants said was never the real intention of the company; rather it was a blind to cover over the development of the Wapping plant for News International's four national newspaper titles. They argued that 'the whole operation [of the *London Post*] was part of a callous and calculated plan to dispose of [the company's] existing workforce . . . at minimum cost to themselves, and that since mid-1984 the company have never had any intention of conducting genuine negotiations with the unions'. Stuart-Smith J was not prepared to determine this complaint against the employers at that interim stage—whilst the defendants' contention was 'a possible inference from the facts as they have emerged . . .' he did not 'think that it is the only inference or even the probable explanation'.

Consideration of defence

11.21 In considering the effect of TULR(C)A 1992, s 221 in *Hadmor Productions Ltd v Hamilton* [1983] 1 AC 191, 223, Lord Diplock said that 'the greater the likelihood [of establishing the statutory immunity] the greater is the weight to be attached to it'. In *Duport Steel Ltd v Sirs* [1980] ICR 161, 185, his Lordship also said that: 'If judges were to grant injunctions notwithstanding that they know that it is highly probable that the acts they are enjoining are perfectly lawful, it is unlikely that voluntary respect for the law would continue'.

11.22 Nevertheless, judges are quite naturally reluctant to decide matters on witness evidence without cross-examination and will frequently make assumptions without deciding on legality. Lord Wedderburn gives the example of *Solihull Metropolitan Borough v National Union of Teachers* [1985] IRLR 211 (see para 5.54 for facts), where the union argued that it had not induced breaches of contract by instructing members not to provide cover during a period of industrial action, since there was an implied term that teachers did not need to carry on. Warner J said that this was 'not the sort of conflict one can resolve on motion, on affidavit evidence, without cross-examination and before discovery'.

Delay

11.23 Delay is a factor which may be taken against the grant of an interim injunction but normally only when the delay is such as would cause prejudice to the defendant. It was argued in the Wapping pickets case, *News Group*

Newspapers Ltd v SOGAT 82 and others (above), that the employer had delayed too long in issuing their writ (now claim form). The picketing started in January 1986 on the move by News International to Wapping but the proceedings were not issued until mid-June 1986. The learned judge accepted the company's explanation that they did not want to exacerbate relations with the defendants while negotiations with them were continuing. Moreover, it would have been more difficult at the start of the dispute to show that the unions had authorized the violence.

The risk of further industrial action

11.24 The fact that further industrial action might ensue if an injunction is granted is not a relevant consideration against the grant of an injunction (*Perry v British Rail Board* [1980] ICR 743, 753; cf. *Stephen (Harold) & Co. v Post Office* [1977] 1 WLR 1172).

E. Undertaking in Lieu of Injunction

11.25 The courts will normally accept an undertaking by the defendant in lieu of an injunction, provided that the undertaking offered is clear enough to be enforceable as though it were an injunction. It may then be enforced in precisely the same way by contempt as if the judge had given the injunction sought (*Biba Ltd v Stratford Investments Ltd* [1973] Ch 281).

11.26 If the claimant is not in a position to honour its undertaking in damages and appreciable damage to the defendant is likely, the injunction should be refused (*Morning Star Co-operative Society Ltd v Express Newspapers Ltd* [1979] FSR 113).

F. *Quia Timet* Injunctions

11.27 The court may grant an injunction before damage actually occurs in the event that substantial damage is threatened which could not be adequately remedied (*Litchfield-Speer v Queen Anne's Gate Syndicate (No. 2) Ltd* [1919] 1 Ch 407). In *Proctor v Bayley* [1889] 42 ChD 390, 398, the court said: 'Where a man threatens and intends to do an unlawful act, we will, before it is done, grant an injunction to prevent his doing it, and we will grant it where the act had been done and is likely to be repeated—the jurisdiction is simply preventive'.

(See also *Att.-Gen. v Manchester Corp.* [1893] 2 Ch 87, 92, *Fletcher v Bealey* (1885) 28 ChD 688, 698.) It will not, however, be granted if the risk of injury is merely insignificant or illusory.

11.28 For an injunction to be appropriate, a stage must be reached where there is a substantial fear that unlawful action will occur. In *Shipping Company Uniform Inc. v International Transport Workers' Federation* [1985] IRLR 71, there was a dispute between the owners of the ship *Uniform Star* and the ITF over rates of pay of crew members, and the shipowners feared that the ITF might arrange for the ship to be blacked when it attempted to leave Tilbury docks (see para 3.95). Staughton J refused to grant a *quia timet* injunction on this aspect: it was only proper where there was evidence that the defendant would engage in unlawful action. He cited *Halsbury's Laws of England* (4th edn, vo1. 24, para 932) which stated that: 'no one can obtain a *quia timet* order by merely saying "timeo" . . . it is not sufficient ground for granting an injunction that, if there is no such intention, the injunction will do the defendant no harm'.

11.29 In *News Group Newspapers Ltd v SOGAT 82 and others* [1986] IRLR 337, Stuart-Smith J, however, granted an injunction to restrain intimidation by words and shouts even though he accepted that the tort was not complete until the person threatened succumbed to the threat. An injunction could be granted since such succumbing was reasonably to be anticipated in the circumstances.

G. Mandatory Injunctions

11.30 Employers may seek an injunction ordering the union to withdraw, revoke or cancel a strike call by a certain time and by a certain method. This goes further than a mere restriction on the industrial action, and raises further consideration of when it is appropriate to grant a mandatory as opposed to a prohibitory order.

11.31 The courts are generally reluctant to issue mandatory orders, although one of the reasons for this—that it means that a party will have to spend money—does not realistically apply in trade dispute cases. In *Redland Bricks Ltd v*

Morris [1970] AC 652 the House of Lords required that the claimant show a very strong possibility that grave damage would accrue to him in the future if the injunction were not granted and that damages would not be an adequate remedy (see also *Strelley v Pearson* (1880) 15 ChD 113, 117, *Hooper v Rogers* [1975] Ch 43). The proper rationale is that the court will not compel the defendant to do so serious a thing as to undo what he has done without a full trial save where the case is especially sharp and clear (*Gait v Abbott* (1862) 6 LT 852, *Shephard Homes Ltd v Sandham* [1971] Ch 340, *Hounslow London Borough Council v Twickenham Garden Developments Ltd* [1971] Ch 233). In *Locabail International Finance Ltd v Agroexport* [1986] 1 WLR 657 the Court of Appeal called for a high degree of assurance that at the trial it would appear that the injunction was rightly granted. In the 'Wapping pickets' case Stuart-Smith J, however, distinguished the case from the order sought there that the defendants would inform their members not to carry on any of the prohibited acts, since this was 'merely supplementary to and in aid of the main negative injunction' (*News Group Newspapers Ltd v SOGAT 82 and others* [1986] ICR 1172, 1180). The judge said that 'it can only be in rare circumstances that this court should interfere by way of mandatory injunction in the delicate mechanism of industrial disputes and industrial negotiations'. Moreover, in *Meade v London Borough of Haringey* [1979] ICR 494, the Court of Appeal agreed with the judge in refusing to grant a mandatory injunction that the defendants should keep their schools open notwithstanding strike action by school caretakers. The reason was that on the affidavit evidence the facts were strongly contested. (See also *Nottingham Building Society v Eurodynamics Systems* [1993] FSR 468; *Norbrook Laboratories v National Office of Animal Health Ltd* Aug 2001.)

11.32 In recent years the courts have often granted mandatory orders as an aid to enforcement of a prohibitory order and did so in almost all of the cases arising out of the News International Wapping dispute in 1986. This in particular required the union to inform its own members and the Press Association that the industrial action had been called off.

11.33 The court must however be careful in a mandatory order to ensure that the defendant knows exactly what he must do, not only as a matter of law but also in fact. Moreover, in the case of a mandatory order, personal service is required if the order is to be enforced by committal or sequestration (para 13.07 ff).

11.34 It is good practice in a mandatory injunction sought in a strike case to specify a time by which any strike instruction is to be withdrawn. The danger of too speedy a timescale, however, is that the injunction is useless if it cannot be served before the end of the time limit. A defendant might seek the variation of such a timescale by the court. In *Express Newspapers Ltd v Mitchell* [1982] IRLR 465, no timescale was laid down for the defendants to withdraw their strike threat, but since the injunction was granted in respect of a planned 'day of action' within a week of the order, Leonard J considered it obvious that the mandatory action required was to be done at once.

11.35 The main aim of the employer in seeking a mandatory order is usually to ensure that persons on strike become aware as soon as possible of its grant, and that there is no ambiguity felt by union members that the instructions of their union might override the orders of the court to call off the action. It is normally unrealistic to expect all strikers to be notified individually of the calling-off of industrial action in the short time likely to be available, so that an order to communicate withdrawal of strike instructions through the Press Association or another news agency is more appropriate, and has become the common form in strike injunctions. A variant in a local dispute may be the notification of all relevant local newspapers (eg *Kent Free Press Ltd v National Graphical Association* November 1986, unreported). Nowadays, it may be appropriate to ask the union to send the withdrawal by email to its membership.

H. Application for an Interim Injunction

The division

11.36 An application for an interim injunction may be made to either the Chancery or Queen's Bench Division of the High Court. Interim injunctions in both divisions are governed by CPR, r 25.3 which provides that an application for the grant of an injunction may be made by any party to a cause or matter before or after the trial of the cause or matter, whether or not a claim for the injunction was included in that party's claim as the case may be. It is unlikely that a county court would be an appropriate forum for an action in an industrial dispute; although it did provide the forum for the damages claim in the *Falconer* case (see Chapter 7).

11.37 Whichever division the application is made in, it must be made with all due speed and this is particularly true for a fast-moving matter like an industrial dispute (*Sherwell v Combined Incandescent Mantles Syndicate Ltd* (1907) WN 211, 212).

A High Court master may only grant an injunction with the consent of both parties (Practice Direction—Interim Injuntions 25PD.1.2). This will rarely happen in a trade dispute case on first application but might occur later if the parties agree to the variation of an order after it is obtained.   **11.38**

Without notice applications

In the normal case of an application for an interim injunction, at least three days' notice must be given to the defendants. This may be too late for a strike injunction to have any effectiveness. Much use is thus made of the without notice application, or an application on short notice. An application may be made without notice if it appears that there are good reasons (CPR, r 25.3(1)). It must be supported by evidence unless the court otherwise orders (CPR, r 25.3(2)). There would normally be little difficulty in justifying this in a strike case, especially where there is a continuous production process. A without notice injunction will in most cases provide that the defendant can apply on notice, usually of 24 or 48 hours to the claimant, to discharge or vary the order which has been made, and that costs are to be reserved until a later hearing with both parties present. In the most extreme cases an injunction may be obtained before the claim is issued (*Thornelae v Skoines* (1873) LR 16 Eq 126; *Re N (Infants) (No. 2)* [1967] Ch 512), but in that case the claimant must give an undertaking to issue the claim and to serve the witness statements forthwith.   **11.39**

The ease with which without notice injunctions may be obtained in industrial cases prompted Parliament to enact TULR(C)A, s 221 by which: **11.40**

> where an applicant for an injunction . . . is made to a court in the absence of the party against whom the injunction . . . is sought or any representative of his and that party claims, or in the opinion of the court would be likely to claim, that he acted in contemplation or furtherance of a trade dispute, the court shall not grant the injunction . . . unless satisfied that all steps which in the circumstance were reasonable have been taken with a view to securing that notice of the application and an opportunity of being heard with respect to the application have been made to that party.

It may be argued in some cases that this section does not apply on the basis that no reasonable union could in the circumstances of the case claim to be   **11.41** acting in contemplation or furtherance of a trade dispute. This argument should, however, be treated with some circumspection.

11.42 The subsection also requires the claimant, in any event, only to use reasonable endeavours to contact the other party. Often this is fulfilled merely by a telephone call to the union headquarters, in which the claim form and outline of the witness statement are read over the telephone. The solicitor for the claimant should swear a statement that this has been done.

11.43 Procedure on applications for without notice injunctions is now governed by CPR, Practice Direction 25. The applicant should lodge: the claim form; the application; evidence in support of the application; and a draft order.

11.44 Evidence is given by a witness statement, a statement of case verified by a statement of truth or an application verified by such a statement; Practice Direction—Interim Injunctions 25PD.3.2.

11.45 The application notice, evidence in support and a draft order should be filed with the court two hours before the hearing wherever possible (Practice Direction—Interim Injunctions 25PD.4.3). Where the application is made before issue of the claim form, the applicant must undertake to the court to issue a claim form immediately or alternatively the court will give directions for the commencement of the claim (Practice Direction—Interim Injunctions 25PD.4.4(1)).

(For forms, see Chapter 17.)

11.46 In strike cases involving continuous processes, like newspapers, the claimant will usually be able to take advantage of the exception to these rules which caters for 'the very rare case where the application was of such urgency as to preclude . . . the foregoing procedures'. A telephone call to the judge's clerk should be made, and the case must be certified by counsel as being urgent.

11.47 It is vital that the claimant does not mislead the court on a without notice application in the absence of the defendant. A heavy responsibility rests on the party seeking the injunction to give a full and fair view of the defendant's position, and the injunction may be discharged merely because the claimant has failed to disclose all material facts in such a witness statement (*Edison (Thomas E.) Ltd v Bullock* (1912) 15 CLR 679, 682, *Armstrong v Sheppard & Short Ltd* [1959] 2 QB 384, *Memory Corporation plc v Sidhu* [2000] 1 WLR 1443—this was described as a 'high duty'; *Siporex Trade SA v Comdel*

Commodities [1986] 2 Lloyd's Rep 428, 437). It is not necessary that such matter be decisive, merely that it would be relevant to the cause of action or the court's discretion in granting an injunction. The claimant must in effect exhibit the utmost good faith (*R v Kensington Income Tax Commissioners* [1917] 1 KB 486, 504).

If the defendant has been informed that a without notice application is to be made he may attend and be heard, in which case the matter is described as an 'opposed without notice hearing'. The judge will of course recognize that the defendant in these circumstances is unlikely to have had an opportunity to prepare witness statements (*Pickwick International Inc. (GB) v Multiple Sound Distributors* [1972] 1 WLR 1213) or even fully marshal his arguments, possibly having had only a few hours' or minutes' warning of the application. **11.48**

Applications may be made by telephone 'where it is not possible to arrange a hearing'; Practice Direction—Interim Injunctions 25PD.4.4. **11.49**

Out of hours applications

If the application is made without notice, the order should contain a return date for a further hearing at which the other party may be present (Practice Direction—Interim Injunctions 25PD.5.1(3)). Judges and court staff are very understanding of the need for urgency in strike cases, and are usually obliging in accommodating parties at short notice. It would not, however, be possible to get an order sealed over the weekend so that an unsealed copy should be served with a notice as to why this has been done. Such applications were made, for example, in the claim by News Group Newspapers against SOGAT in May 1985, and applications have been made on Christmas Eve. **11.50**

The witness statement

The claimant's evidence should in most cases deal with, as appropriate, at least: **11.51**

(1) the background to the application;
(2) the failure of the union to indicate the existence of a lawful trade dispute;
(3) the likely losses to the claimant; and
(4) the need for ugency.

Evidence should be served at least three clear days before the application is heard: Practice Direction—Interim Injunctions 25PD.2.2.

11.52 The courts may be prepared to work on the basis of 'tenuous evidence' of commercial contracts allegedly interfered with or breached at the interim stage, which may leave the unions at a great disadvantage (*Daily Mirror Newspapers v Gardner* [1968] 2 QB 762, *Dimbleby & Sons Ltd v National Union of Journalists* [1984] 1 WLR 427). Nothing should however be taken for granted by a claimant and witness statements should be as detailed as the circumstances permit.

11.53 Most strike injunction hearings last only a short time, but there have been several long drawn out applications, in particular in the picketing area where the principles are less fixed (eg *Thomas v National Union of Mineworkers (South Wales Area)* [1986] Ch 20 (10 days) and *News Group Newspapers Ltd v SOGAT 82 and others* [1986] IRLR 337 (10 days)). In those cases, parties have been able with the leave of the court to serve evidence in the middle of the case to deal with new matters.

Particulars of claim

11.54 If the claim is generally endorsed, a full particulars of claim must be served in accordance with the Rules even if an interim injunction has been granted in the meantime, unless the defendant otherwise agrees (*Hytrac Conveyors Ltd v Conveyors International Ltd* [1983] 1 WLR 44). The particulars of claim must be served within 14 days of service of the claim form on the defendant (CPR, r 7.4(1)(b)).

Cross-examination

11.55 There is power to cross-examine the deponent of a witness statement but this is in fact rarely done in such cases at the interim injunction stage. If, however, an order were made and the witness did not then attend, his evidence would not be admissible without the permission of the court.

Undertaking in damages

11.56 Since the court is not able to make a final decision on the merits of the case at the interim stage (having merely seen witness statements), the normal practice is that in order to gain an injunction, the claimant must be given an undertaking in damages (CPR 25PD.6) that he will compensate the defendant if it should turn out when all the facts are examined that the claimant was not entitled to the order sought. Although it will be implied in most cases (*Howard v Press Printers Ltd* (1905) 74 LJ Ch 100) it may be dispensed with in exceptional circumstances (eg *Att.-Gen. v Albany Hotel Co. Ltd* [1896] 2 Ch 696) none of which are likely to arise in trade dispute cases. Enforcement of this undertaking requires the issuing of separate proceedings, and there are no reported cases in the industrial sphere in which such an undertaking has been enforced, reflecting, amongst other things, the fact that few cases ever go so far as to trial when the enforcement of the undertaking would be dealt with. It should be noted that a party may be liable on the cross undertaking even if he succeeds at trial, in the unusual event that even so, he should not have been granted an interim injunction (*Barclays Bank Ltd v Rosenberg*, Financial Times 12 June 1985).

11.57 The normal form of the undertaking is that the claimant 'will abide by any order which this court may make as to damages, in case this court shall be of opinion that the defendant shall have sustained any by reason of this order which the defendant ought to pay'.

Costs

11.58 The normal costs order on an application for an interim injunction is 'costs in the case' (that is whoever succeeds at trial gains the costs of the interim procedure) or costs reserved if it is too early to determine where the costs should fall.

I. Injunctions Against Persons Unknown and Groups

11.59 Having regard to the controversy which the decision engendered and the attempts subsequently made to limit its scope, it is strange and ironic that the case of *Taff Vale Ry Co. v Amalgamated Society of Railway Servants* [1901] AC 426 still rules parts of labour law from its grave. It is, however, authority for the proposition that an unincorporated association may be sued in a representative action if the persons selected as defendants are persons who, from their position, may be taken fairly to represent the body sued.

11.60 In certain circumstances, it is thus possible to gain an injunction against a clearly defined set of persons whose names are unknown to the claimant.

This is particularly useful in picketing cases where the owner of property will often not know the names of persons for example besieging his property, and it was in such a case that one of the first such orders was granted. In *Michaels (M.) (Furriers) Ltd v Askew and others*, The Times 25 June 1983, the claimants owned a fur shop which was picketed by members of Animal Aid, an unincorporated association which opposed the fur trade. The claimant sought an injunction against unknown members of the association who had been involved in the picketing of its shop in Bristol. They relied on RSC, Order 15, r 12(1), which states that 'where numerous persons have the same interest in any proceedings ... the proceedings may be begun ... by or against any one or more as representing all or ... all except one or more of them'.

11.61 The Court of Appeal accepted the argument advanced on behalf of the demonstrators that care must be taken to ensure that the rule was not abused. Nevertheless, their Lordships thought that where a number of unidentified persons were causing injury and damage by unlawful acts of one kind or another, and there was an arguable case that they belonged to a single organization or class which encouraged actions of the type complained of, and their actions could be linked to that organization, the rule enabled the court to do justice in the particular case. Here, an injunction restraining picketing, against Mrs Pink and others on their own behalf and on behalf of all other members of Animal Aid, was upheld (see also *EMI Records Ltd v Kudhail and others*, The Times 16 June 1983).

11.62 If the members of the body sought to be represented may have different defences they do not have the same interest in the proceedings. Apart from this essential requirement, the court has an unfettered discretion to decide whether or not to allow a representative action to continue. Dunn LJ said that:

> The application of the rule is a matter of practical convenience, to enable the plaintiff's rights to be tried fairly and in order to obtain an effective remedy ... where a number of unidentified persons are causing injury and damage by unlawful acts of one kind or another, and there is an arguable case that they belong to a single organisation or class which encourages action of the type complained of, and their actions can be linked to that organisation, then the rule enables the court to do justice in the particular case.

11.63 The principle was narrowly confined in *United Kingdom Nirez Ltd v Barton*, The Times 14 October 1986. Henry J said that such representative proceedings were not proper where there was a clear divergence of interests between members of an organization who would be subject to the injunction, in that some of its members were prepared to take part in tortious actions whilst others were not. Injunctions were granted against all persons belonging to, associated with or affiliated to 'Lincolnshire and Nottinghamshire Against Nuclear Dumping' and 'Humberside Against Nuclear Dumping', who were protesting against the sites chosen for the dumping of low-level nuclear waste. The judge held that even if some or many members of an association broke the law, it should not readily be assumed that such was the policy of the association. On the other hand, if anyone knowing of the injunctions, whether a party to the proceedings or not, were himself to do or cause to be done acts which were forbidden by the injunctions, such acts would prima facie be a wrongful interference with the administration of justice and he would be liable to proceedings for contempt (see also *News Group Newspapers Ltd v SOGAT 82 and others* [1986] IRLR 337). Applications to restrain trespassers may be brought against persons unknown (see Chapter 12).

J. The Role of the Court of Appeal in Injunction Cases

An appeal lies from a decision of a judge to grant or refuse an injunction without permission being needed. This forms an exception to the general principle that an appeal from a interim order requires permission of the initial judge or the Court of Appeal (Supreme Court Act 1981, s 18). The application must be made within 14 days and the appeal set down within seven days after service of the notice of appeal. This notice must be given to other parties within two days. Many strike injunction cases have in fact gone to the Court of Appeal and thence the House of Lords. These two courts have been willing in trade dispute cases to expedite their procedures, with Court of Appeal hearings sometimes following on directly after the determination of the issue by the High Court judge as for example in *Connex SE Ltd v RMT* [1999] IRLR 249. **11.64**

Generally, the appeal courts have a limited role in appeals from discretionary orders. The House of Lords specifically considered this function in *Hadmor Productions Ltd v Hamilton* [1983] 1 AC 191, and decided that the Court of Appeal should not exercise a discretion differently from that of the High Court judge who heard the application. Lord Diplock, with whom the other Lords agreed, said (at 220C): **11.65**

An interim injunction is a discretionary relief and the discretion whether or not to grant it is vested in the High Court judge by whom the application for it is heard. Upon an appeal . . . the function of an appellate court whether it be the Court of Appeal or Your Lordships' House is not to exercise an independent discretion of its own.

The function of the appellate court is initially one of review only. It may set aside the judge's exercise of his discretion on the ground that it was based on a misunderstanding of the law or of the evidence before him or upon an inference that particular facts existed or did not exist, which, although it was one that might legitimately have been drawn upon the evidence that was before the judge, can be demonstrated to be wrong by further evidence that has become available by the time of the appeal; or upon the ground that there has been a change of circumstances after the judge made his order that would have justified his acceding to an application to vary it . . . The right approach by an appellate court is to examine the fresh evidence in order to see to what extent, if any, the facts disclosed by it invalidate the reasons given by the judge for his decision.

11.66 In *Dimbleby & Sons Ltd v National Union of Journalists* [1984] 1 WLR 427, Lord Diplock said that the House of Lords could, however, set aside the judge's exercise of his discretion on the ground that it was based upon a misunderstanding of the law or of the evidence before him or because, even though no error of law or fact can be identified, the judge's decision to grant the injunction was so aberrant that it must be set aside on the ground that no reasonable judge regardful of his duty to act judicially could have reached it.

11.67 The fast-changing circumstances of a strike are pre-eminently appropriate for new evidence to be presented on appeal. In *Mercury Communications Ltd v Scott-Garner* [1984] Ch 37 the Court of Appeal thought that it was proper to review the decision of Mervyn Davies J since he had, according to Dillon LJ, 'misdirected himself in important respects' because of the relevance and importance of fresh evidence before the Court of Appeal of a job security agreement. It cannot, however, be assured that such will be permitted.

K. Form of Injunction

11.68 It is vital that the form of an injunction should be clear to all concerned. It is not enough that the defendant be told merely to desist from unlawful acts. In the American case *Collins v Wayne Iron Works* (1910) 227 Pa 326, the court said that an injunction 'should be as definite, clear and precise in its terms as possible so that there may be no reason or excuse for misunderstanding or disobeying it . . .'.

The injunction is a remedy of enormous flexibility and may restrain third parties, so that the injunction may be effective even though the third party is not necessarily guilty of the tort restrained. **11.69**

The forms of order granted in industrial dispute cases follow a generally similar form. Some examples are given in Chapter 17. It is worth noting the following examples from reported cases of prohibitory and mandatory orders. In a national newspapers dispute, the newspapers were granted the following injunction against the National Graphical Association: **11.70**

> An order restraining the defendants and each of them by themselves, their servants, agents or otherwise howsoever forthwith from (i) inducing, procuring or persuading employees of the plaintiff to break their contracts of employment; (ii) interfering with the business of the plaintiffs by inducing, procuring or persuading employees of the plaintiff to break their contracts of employment.

The mandatory injunction adopted in *Austin-Rover Group Ltd v Amalgamated Union of Engineering Workers (TASS)* [1985] IRLR 162, was that the defendant should: **11.71**

> Withdraw and cancel any instruction, direction or decision which it has issued or made to the effect that its members employed by the plaintiff should withdraw their labour or otherwise refuse to work in accordance with their contracts of employment [and] to take all practical steps to inform its members employed by the plaintiff of such withdrawal and cancellation.

An injunction to restrain an employee from 'acting in breach of his contract of employment . . . by participating in strike or other industrial action' is not, however, appropriate, according to Henry J in *Barrett & Baird (Wholesale)Ltd v Institution of Professional Civil Servants* [1987] IRLR 3. This was because TULRA 1974, s 16 now TULR(C)A, s 236 provides that: 'No court shall, whether by way of . . . (b) an injunction . . . restraining a breach or threatened breach of a contract of employment, compel an employee to do any work or attend at any place for the doing of work.' In such a case, the proper remedy is dismissal. **11.72**

It is common form to find the words 'liberty to apply' included at the end of an interim injunction. This means that if a party finds that the injunction **11.73** gained on first application is insufficiently wide to cover action taken (a common feature of a fast-developing situation like industrial action), the claimant may return to court to seek further relief without issuing a fresh application and without having to contend with the argument that the proper remedy is to appeal.

11.74 A word which is most commonly the subject of argument in a trade dispute injunction is 'forthwith'. A defendant is often required to call off the strike action 'forthwith'. This must be construed according to circumstances but normally means within a reasonable time without delay (*Hillingdon London Borough Council v Cutler* [1968] 1 QB 124, *In re Southam ex parte Lamb* (1881) 19 ChD 169, *Brown v Bonnyrig Magistrates* (1936) SC 258). The only case which considered its meaning in a dispute case is *Kent Free Press Ltd v National Graphical Association* (November 1986) where Henry J said in relation to an order forthwith to restrain 'blacking', that:

> In this context, I can reasonably have regard to the fact that the defendants had had notice that the plaintiffs were seeking this relief since the 28th August [ie three days], that they had—but had not availed themselves of—the opportunity to make representations to the court in opposition to the making of the order, and so had already had ample opportunity to take legal advice on the matter. This being so, it seems to me that on notice of the order all the defendants had to do was to make the appropriate telephone call to each of the [strike leaders] involved, though a defendant who chose to ring his solicitor before doing this would not be criticised.

11.75 The meaning of 'forthwith', when contained in an order in the strikes context, means that the party subject to the order must comply with the order as soon as possible and modern means of communication must be used to give effect to the order without delay. In the instant case, a three-day delay was a breach of the forthwith order.

L. Declarations

11.76 The declaration has in the past had little role to play in the remedial armoury of strike cases. This is for two main reasons: first, it could be granted only at the final trial; and secondly, there were no powers of the court to compel obedience to it. There are signs of movement on both fronts. In the course of the miners' strike, in *Clarke v Chadburn* [1984] IRLR 350, an extraordinary annual conference of the NUM held at the height of the dispute had voted to change the union's rules so as to establish a national disciplinary procedure. This was in defiance of an order obtained two days earlier by the claimants (17 members of the NUM's Nottinghamshire area) that a meeting of the Nottingham Area Council should be held in order to mandate delegates as to how they should vote. The claimant returned to court for a declaration that the conference resolutions were of no effect and did not bind the claimant. With the defendants having chosen not to attend, Megarry V-C said that the motion 'was a matter of such public concern to so many people that it seems to . . . fall within the category of infrequent cases in which the sparing exercise of this jurisdiction [to grant interim declarations] is fully justified'. His Lordship turned for authority to *International General Electric Co. of New York v Commissioners of Customs and Excise* [1962] Ch 784, where the Court of Appeal rejected the concept of an interim declaration but envisaged the possibility that in certain cases it might be proper to make a declaration of rights in interlocutory proceedings, 'though this jurisdiction would be infrequently and sparingly exercised'. Interim declarations were first referred to in the procedure rules in CPR, r 25.1(1)(b).

We shall also see in relation to sequestration that in one rather special case **11.77** the courts have held that a writ of sequestration may be issued to enforce a declaration (*Webster v Southwark London Borough Council* [1983] 2 WLR 217; see para 13.45 ff).

12

RESTRAINING SIT-INS

We have already examined the substantive law on trespass and sit-ins (para **12.01** 8.23). Here we consider the practice and procedure. The employer will probably be able to resort to proceedings under CPR, r 55. This is most normally used against squatters and permits summary proceedings 'where a person claims possession of land which he alleges is occupied solely by a person or persons . . . who entered or remained in occupation without his licence or consent . . .'. The provision has, for example, been used to remove student demonstrators (eg *University of Essex v Djemal* [1980] 1 WLR 1301). Lord Denning MR described the procedure as 'specially designed to deal with squatters and other people who occupy premises without any colour or right whatsoever and still refuse to get out' (*McPhail v Persons Unknown* [1973] Ch 447, 458H). As in squatter cases, there will usually be no argument in trade disputes about who owns the property and that those sitting in have no permission to remain on the premises.

The essence of the procedure, which is not available in Scotland, is its speed. **12.02** Application is made to the High Court or county court. A form of application is included in Chapter 17. One advantage for the employer of using this remedy as opposed to injunctive proceedings is that personal service of the documents is not required. Instead service is deemed to be effective if process is left at the premises occupied or in whatever other manner the court orders. Service against persons unknown may be effected by attaching the claim form to the main door or 'placing stakes in the land in places where they are clearly visible' and attaching to them copies of the claim form (CPR, r 55.6). In *Crosfield Electronics Ltd v Baginsky and others* [1975] 3 All ER 97, this took the form of having the summons pinned to the door of the factory being occupied.

12.03   The order for possession may also be granted to protect not only that part of the employer's property then wrongfully occupied, but also premises which the claimant fears that the defendants will move to in reaction to the making of an order. It does not even matter that the person evicted was not in the workplace at the time when the summons was served (*R v Wandsworth County Court ex parte Wandsworth LBC* [1975] 1 WLR 1314). It is indeed an offence under the Criminal Law Act 1977, s 10 to resist or obstruct the sheriff who is executing the order. By CPR, r 55 PD 2.6 the particulars of claim in a case against trespassers must include details of the claimant's interest in the land, and the evidence should deal with the circumstances in which the land has been occupied and a statement that he does not know the name of any person occupying the land who is not named in the summons. In dispute cases it should also emphasize the danger which may be caused to plant and equipment if possession is not delivered up and the trespassers stay. Moreover, it is prudent to exhibit a letter or instruction to employees in plain terms to vacate the premises forthwith.

12.04   An injunction may also be obtained to restrain trespass. In *Plessey plc v Wilson* [1982] IRLR 198 the Court of Session, however, refused an interim interdict on the basis that TULRA 1974, s 13 might apply to trespass. It is however doubtful whether this would be applied in an English case (see para 8.23).

13

COMMITTAL FOR CONTEMPT

A. Introduction

Employers should be wary lest a committal for contempt needlessly inflames **13.01** an already tense industrial situation. In all contempt cases it is open to the courts to commit the defendant union officials to prison, which would almost guarantee their martyrdom amongst other trade unionists. Although in 1972 several dockers were committed to Pentonville prison for breach of an order made in the bitter dockers' strike, in recent times the courts have been more attracted by fines on the unions who from 1982 lost their immunity from suit, or sequestration of the union's assets. In *Mirror Group Newspapers v Harrison* (November 1986, unreported), however, Mars Jones J fined two lay officials £10,000 and £5,000 respectively. Moreover, once a contempt motion is launched it may be impossible to restrain the tiger unleashed even though the applicant may wish to withdraw the motion because for example the underlying industrial dispute has been settled. Notwithstanding this, there have been several cases in which employers have enforced injunctions by way of committal, often in sensitive industrial relations situations. Moreover, the limits on damages set out in the Trade Union and Labour Relations (Consolidation) Act 1992 do not apply to fines for contempt which are unlimited.

13.02   There are various forms of contempt which may be committed. Sir John Donaldson said in *Howitt Transport v Transport and General Workers' Union* [1973] IRLR 25, applied in *Kent Free Press Ltd v National Graphical Association* (10 November 1986, unreported) that:

> It may, at the top end of the scale, consist of a flat defiance of the Court's authority. Going down the scale, it may not amount to flat defiance but rather to a passive ignoring of the Court's order. Going down the scale still further, it may amount to a half-hearted or, perhaps, colourable attempt to comply with the Court's order. And at the bottom end of the scale, there may have been a genuine, whole-hearted use of best endeavours to comply with the order which nevertheless has been unsuccessful. In each case there is a breach of the Court's order . . . But the quality of non-compliance varies over an enormous range.

13.03   An instruction to members of the National Graphical Association (NGA) that an employer was an unrecognized house and that therefore under the NGA rules no member should do any work bound for that employer, is a breach of an injunction restraining blacking (*Kent Free Press Ltd v NGA*, 10 November 1986, unreported).

B. Procedure: Personal Service

13.04   Not surprisingly, the courts insist that in a matter so serious as contempt all procedural aspects of a committal for contempt are fully complied with. The injunction must be served personally on the defendant with a penal notice endorsed thereon (RSC, Order 52, rule 4), unless the court dispenses with such personal service, which would be an unusual course (see *Beeston Shipping v Bananaft International SA; The Eastern Venture* [1985] 1 All ER 923). The notice of motion for committal must also be served personally two clear days before the hearing. The writ, two copies of the notice of motion and copy affidavits should also be lodged with the court.

The defendant must comply with an order from the time when he hears of it, whether by telephone, telegram or otherwise (RSC, Order 45, rule 7(2)(a)). Where a person gives an undertaking to the court, it was held in *Hussain v Hussain* [1986] 2 WLR 801 that it was not even necessary for a copy of the order recording such an undertaking to be served or to be endorsed with a penal notice where the court is satisfied that the person giving the undertaking knew and understood the effect of the undertaking given (see also *Camden London Borough Council v Alpenoak* (1985) 135 NLJ 1209, cf. *Callow v Young* (1886) 55 LT 543). **13.05**

It is important to consider in some detail what is required as personal service, first on individuals and then on trade unions.

Service on individuals

Service on the defendant solicitor or other agent or relation of the defendant is not good personal service, nor does the appearance of the defendant or his counsel upon the motion waive any objection on his part of lack of proper service (*Mander v Falcke* [1891] 3 Ch 488, *Ellerton v Thirsk* (1820) 1 Jac & W 376, *Frith v Lord Donegal* (1834) 2 DPC 527). It is not, however, necessary that the process be left in the actual corporal possession of the defendant provided that the nature of it is brought clearly to his notice (*Thomson v Pheney* (1832) 1 Dow 441). In *Heath v White* (1844) 2 Dow & L 40, however, it was insufficient that the person seeking to serve a notice saw the defendant standing at a closed window on the ground floor, told him clearly the purpose for which he had come and threw a copy of the writ down in his sight and in the presence of the defendant's wife. Nor was it good enough to level a writ in the crevice of a door (*Christmas v Eicke* (1848) 6 Dow & L 156). The defendant must not only be served with a copy of the notice of motion, but also have the opportunity to view the original (*Parker v Burgess* (1834) 3 N & M 36). **13.06**

Where, however, it is sought to commit persons for aiding and abetting breach of an injunction, it is merely necessary that such persons have notice of the terms of the injunction or undertaking without any requirement for personal service (*Elliot v Klinger* [1967] 1 WLR 1165).

Service on trade unions

13.07 By CPR, r 6.4(4), 'A document is served personally on a company or other corporation by leaving it with a person holding a senior position within the company or corporation'. Section 10 of TULR(C)A 1992 provides that a trade union is 'capable of suing and being sued in its own name', and it is generally understood that a union may be served in the same way as a body corporate, that is, on its senior officers. The only reference to punishment for contempt in the Act is found in s 12(2), that any 'punishment for contempt' may be enforced against 'any property held in trust for the trade union to the like extent and in the like manner as if the union were a body corporate'. Usually now, unions will co-operate to the extent of making a duly authorized officer available to accept service. On the other hand, some union premises in the 1970s had sealed letter boxes and entry was only by means of an 'entry-phone' specifically so as to evade service. Care must be taken that proper service is effected. It is not sufficient to serve on a person who claims to be an officer of the union if he should turn out in fact not to be such an officer.

Dispensing with personal service

13.08 In exceptional circumstances, the court may be prepared to dispense with the personal service of the injunction. (This is a different issue from whether a person may be bound by an order before it has been personally served when it has, before the contempt hearing, been in fact served.) To permit a without notice application without service of the injunction, the matters for which committal is sought must indeed be grave, the need for relief must be urgent and it must be shown that the person sought to be committed had knowledge of the committal proceedings (*Spooner v Spooner* (1962) 106 SJ 1034). An order for substituted service may be made where there is evidence that a defendant is keeping out of the way in order to avoid service (*Re A Solicitor* (1916) 60 SJ 708; see form for substituted service, Chapter 17, form H). It must be clearly proved that the claimant is unable to effect personal service of the order and that the notice is likely to reach the defendant or come to his knowledge if the method of substituted service which is asked for by the claimant is adopted (*Porter v Freudenberg, Kreglinger v Samuel and Rosenfeld, In re Merten's Patents* (1915) 31 TLR 162; *Phillipson & Son v Emanuel* (1887) 56 LT 858). In *Express Newspapers Ltd v Mitchell* [1982] IRLR 465, personal service was dispensed with since it was proved that the injunction had been served on the defendant's wife and had been widely announced in the news media. It was thus highly unlikely that the defendant had failed to hear of it. In *Kent Free Press Ltd v National Graphical Association* (10 November 1986, unreported) Henry J dispensed with service of the order with a penal notice when the defendants had already received notification of its terms in a letter.

Although a mandatory order only matures into an actual obligation when the **13.09** defendant has proper notice of what he has to do, this does not require personal service. When the order is to be obeyed forthwith, as it usually will be in a strike case, this means 'forthwith' from proper notice being given according to Henry J in *Kent Free Press Ltd v NGA* (above). Notice could not be avoided by the defendants' refusing access to the process server, as occurred in the instant case. The time for compliance did not, however, run from a telephone message from the claimant's solicitor to the defendant's secretary, but rather from the time a letter containing the order arrived.

Serving notice of a new hearing date

When a new or adjourned date is fixed for the contempt hearing, that must **13.10** also be notified by personal service to the respondent save in exceptional circumstances, as the Court of Appeal emphasized in *Phonographic Performance Ltd Tsang*, The Times 10 May 1985 (see also *Chiltern District Council v Keane* [1985] 1 WLR 619).

C. Contents of the Notice of Motion

The notice of motion for committal should particularize the precise manner **13.11** in which it is alleged that the contemnor is in breach of the order made against him or undertaking given by him. It is not sufficient that the nature of the breach is clear from the evidence served with the application (*Hipkiss v Fellows* 101 LT 701, *Chanel Ltd v F.G.M. Cosmetics* [1981] FSR 471). The person alleged to be in contempt must know with sufficient particularity of the charge so as to enable him to defend himself. An application may be amended with the leave of the court. A specimen notice of motion is included in Chapter 17, Form J. (See also *Mirror Group Newspapers v Harrison,* 7 November 1986, unreported.)

If contempt is proved, the order should set out the paragraphs of the notice **13.12** of motion which are found proved (see *Chiltern DC v Keane* (above)).

D. Without Notice Applications

13.13 Not only must the order be personally served on the defendants sought to be committed, but also the application seeking committal for contempt should be served in the same way. Only in rare cases will without notice applications for contempt be considered without notice of motion being served. In *Bannister v Bannister* [1948] 2 All ER 133, Roxburgh J stressed that the only proper case was where delay would cause irreparable mischief. One such case was *Warwick Corp. v Russell* [1964] 1 WLR 613. The defendant was enjoined on 6 April from holding a circus on land owned by the corporation. The injunction was brought to his attention on the day on which it was granted but not by way of personal service. The next circus was on the night the injunction was granted, and the claimant sought an order for committal without further notice. Since the defendant had already manifested his attitude of hostility to the law, Buckley J granted the without notice application. This was a proper case, having regard to the gravity of the breach and the fact that unless the respondent was restrained he would fully have achieved his objective and the law would have gone unimposed.

13.14 These decisions may be of great importance in most strike cases involving rapidly developing situations, where the failure to enforce an injunction at once may frequently render it useless (see also *Favard v Favard* (1896) 75 LT 664, *O'Donovan v O'Donovan* [1955] 1 WLR 1086).

E. Can the Court Commit for Contempt of its Own Accord?

13.15 The court has power 'to make an order of committal of its own motion against a person guilty of contempt of court'. The old rule had the extra words 'in the face of the court', but the present wording clearly permits the court to act of its own motion in a wider range of circumstances. In *Att.-Gen. v Times Newspapers Ltd* [1974] AC 273, 308, Lord Diplock thought, however, that 'no sufficient public interest is served by punishing the offender if the only person for whose benefit the order was made chooses not to insist on its enforcement'. In the strike case of *Con-Mech (Engineers) v Amalgamated Union of Engineering Workers* [1973] ICR 620, Donaldson P said that 'it is not open to the parties to settle the matter of the contempt'.

Sir Robert Megarry V-C was rather bolder during the course of the miners' strike. In *Clarke v Chadburn* [1985] 1 WLR 78, 83, he said that the court may feel it necessary to act of its own accord when orders were openly flouted and the administration of justice was thereby brought into disrepute.

Once a contempt application has been launched it is in the discretion of the court whether it may then be withdrawn. On 3 October 1986 Mars Jones J refused to give leave to Mirror Group Newspapers Ltd and two associated companies to withdraw motions for contempt against the National Graphical Association and the father and deputy father of the graphics union chapel at Mirror Group Newspapers, on the grounds that once the court is seized of a contempt motion, it is not up to the parties to decide its disposal (*Mirror Group Newspapers Ltd v Harrison*, November 1986, unreported). **13.16**

F. Standard of Proof

The applicant for a committal order is restricted to the grounds for committal set out in his notice of motion and cannot add to them in his affidavit in support. These allegations must be proved 'with all that strictness that is necessary in such a proceeding as this when you are going to deprive people of their liberty' (*Churchman v Joint Shop Stewards Committee* [1972] 1 WLR 1094). The remedy of committal should be treated as the last resort to compel obedience to an order (*Ansah v Ansah* [1977] Fam 138). If a mental element is alleged, it should be included in the notice. **13.17**

In *West Oxfordshire District Council v Beratec Ltd*, The Times 30 October 1986, Hutchison J thought that the correct standard of proof in relation to the breach of an undertaking given to the court was the civil standard but the court should not regard that burden as discharged unless the evidence adduced was 'cogent and convincing'. On the other hand, in *Bartrum v Healeswood* [1973] FSR 85, the Court of Appeal said that on a contempt motion, 'the evidence must be looked at in the same way and by the same standards as evidence in a criminal case' (see also *Kent County Council v Batchelor* (1976) 75 LGR 151, *Deborah Building Equipment Ltd v Scaffco Ltd*, The Times 5 November 1986). This dispute was resolved by the Court of Appeal in *Dean v Dean* [1987] Fam Law 200, where the court decided that the criminal standard was appropriate, and the *West Oxfordshire* case was overruled. **13.18**

A defendant is not excused from committal on the ground that he did as **13.19** much as he could unless the order merely required this standard, which would be unusual. Sir John Donaldson said, in *Howitt Transport v Transport and General Workers' Union* [1973] ICR 1:

> It is not sufficient by way of an answer to an allegation that a court order has not been complied with, for the person concerned to say he 'did his best'. The only exception to that proposition is where the court order itself only orders the person concerned to 'do his best'. But if a court order requires a certain state of affairs to be achieved, the only way in which the order can be complied with is by achieving that state of affairs.

13.20   When it is alleged that the respondent failed to take a positive step required by a mandatory injunction, however, the applicant must prove that there was something the respondent could reasonably have done but failed to do to secure its enforcement. This was the central issue in *Express Newspapers Ltd v Mitchell* [1982] IRLR 465. The employer gained an injunction against unlawful secondary action by electricians in Fleet Street newspaper industry. They went on strike in support of the TUC's Day of Action for the health service workers who were then on national strike. The order restrained, among others, Sean Geraghty, leader of the the Fleet Street electricians, from inducing workers to breach their contracts, and required him to withdraw the strike instruction. The strike in fact went ahead. When an application was made for his committal, Mr Geraghty argued that there was nothing which he could do to withdraw the strike call since he had not made it in the first place. Leonard J thought, however, that he could have done more in the time available to encourage compliance with the injunction granted and thus fined him £350.

13.21   In *Austin-Rover Group Ltd v Amalgamated Union of Engineering Workers (TASS)* [1985] IRLR 162, the union TASS sought to avoid liability with the similar argument that the act of calling a strike which the order said should be reversed was that of a larger body of which it was part, namely the staff side of the Joint Negotiating Committee, and not the action of TASS. The union, however, had authorized industrial action without a ballot and the company obtained an order that the union should 'withdraw and cancel any instruction, direction or decision' to take strike action. Hodgson J said (at para 29) that: 'In a proper case it may be permissible in the face of a mandatory injunction for someone to sit back and do absolutely nothing but it is obviously highly dangerous because by definition, the court has been satisfied by evidence that there is something he can do'. His Lordship thought that it was obvious here as to what was required and condemned the attitude of the union's General Secretary, that because he did not consider that the order should have been made there was no need to obey it. It was not possible for the union, which indeed had not appeared when the order was made, to claim at this late stage that the injunction should not have been granted.

Moreover, it does not matter in terms of an application for committal that **13.22** an order has been subsequently discharged for some reason. That is no excuse for disobeying the order whilst it was in force (*Hadkinson v Hadkinson* [1952] P 285, *Eastern Trust Co v McKenzie, Mann Co. Ltd* [1915] AC 750 as applied in *Austin-Rover Group Ltd v AUEW (TASS)* (above)).

A union's internal constitution cannot exclude non-compliance with the **13.23** court's orders, nor can the fact that the union's officers do not find time to meet to discuss the order (*Kent Free Press Limited v National Graphical Association* 10 November 1986, unreported).

The breach of an injunction does not cease to be a contempt notwithstand- **13.24** ing that it was done on the basis of legal advice that the acts were lawful (*Re Mileage Conference Group of the Tyre Manufacturers' Conference's Agreement* [1966] 1 WLR 1137). This would, however, be a substantial matter in mitigation of punishment for that contempt (cf. *Austin-Rover Group Ltd v AUEW (TASS)* (above)).

G. Evidence

Evidence on a contempt application is given by witness statements, supple- **13.25** mented, if appropriate, by orders to cross-examine witnesses to determine contested issues of fact. Unusually, the court may call evidence of its own accord if necessary to give full consideration to the issue of contempt raised (*Yianni v Yianni* [1966] 1 WLR 120, *Mirror Group Newspapers Ltd v Harrison*, November 1986, unreported). The judge will exercise this discretion to permit cross-examination in committal applications readily in order to establish the facts. A deponent is not, however, a compellable witness since civil contempt 'partakes of the nature of a criminal charge' (*Comet Products UK Ltd v Hawkez Plastics Ltd* [1971] 2 QB 67).

Committal applications are heard in open court save in highly exceptional **13.26** circumstances where secrecy is essential to the value of the injunctive relief as it would rarely be in strike cases (RSC, Order 52, rule 6(1)). These exceptions are highly unlikely to apply to industrial dispute cases.

H. Manner of Committing Contempt

Interference with administration of justice

13.27 In most cases in the industrial context, the application to commit will arise from the failure of the defendants to obey an injunction or undertakings given to the court. There may also be a contempt where the defendant takes action against a person for bringing proceedings or giving evidence in an action. Examples in the industrial area include 'blacking' an employer because it has brought court proceedings against a union, or withdrawing a union member's union card because he has given evidence against the union. The RSPCA was found guilty of contempt in a similar situation (*Att.-Gen. v Royal Society for the Prevention of Cruelty to Animals*, The Times 2 June 1985). The desire to punish a person need not be the predominant motive of the act done for it to amount to a contempt (*Att.-Gen. v Butterworth* [1963] 1 QB 696, *Chapman v Honig* [1963] 2 QB 502, *Roebuck v National Union of Mineworkers (Yorkshire Area)* [1977] ICR 573, *Hillfinch Properties Ltd v Newark Investments Ltd*, The Times 1 July 1981). The fundamental principle is that 'all citizens should have unhindered access to the constitutionally established courts of criminal or civil jurisdiction for the determination of disputes as to their legal rights and liabilities' (*Att.-Gen. v Times Newspapers Ltd* [1974] AC 273, 309).

Committal of third parties

13.28 An injunction may embrace those not named in it who aid and abet its breach (*Seaward v Paterson* [1897] 1 Ch 545, *Z Ltd v A-Z and AA-LL* [1982] QB 558, *United Kingdom Nirex Ltd v Barton*, The Times 20 October 1986). In *Acrow (Automation) Ltd v Rex Chainbelt Inc.* [1971] 3 All ER 1175, 1181, Lord Denning MR said, 'it seems to me that if a person complied with a direction of another, which he knows or has reason to know is unlawful, then he is acting unlawfully himself. He is aiding and abetting an unlawful act.' It is open to doubt whether a person can be committed if a principal has not himself committed an act of contempt. This issue might arise, for example, if persons continue to picket at a factory where picketing is prohibited. The only persons actually prevented from picketing may be the unions but there may be no evidence that they are liable for organizing the picketing so that they are not themselves in contempt. It is submitted that in such a case, the pickets would not be aiding and abetting a contempt. In the *Nirex* case (above) Henry J, however, appeared to suggest a wider principle, that 'if anyone knowing of the injunctions, whether a party to the present proceedings or not, were to do or cause to be done those acts forbidden by the injunctions, such acts would prima facie be a wrongful interference with justice and he would be liable to proceedings for contempt' (see para 11.63).

A solicitor might also be liable if he advised a course of conduct which he **13.29** knew would be a contempt (*Taylor v National Union of Mineworkers*, The Times 20 November 1985). It must however be stressed that the exercise of this power to commit depends on the person to be committed (a) having knowledge of the terms of the injunction, the breach of which he is aiding, and (b) the requirement that such person knows that what he is doing is inconsistent with the order.

J. Responsibility of Union for Members and Officials

The union may be in contempt of court if it does not act positively to **13.30** prevent its officials from acting in contempt of court. The code of responsibility for authorizing or endorsing industrial action set out in the Trade Union and Labour Relations (Consolidation) Act 1992 does not apply to contempt proceedings, so that one has to go back to the general common law principles of vicarious liability to establish who is responsible for whom (see *Nirez* para 11.63). These have been pursued in industrial dispute cases with great stringency. A high standard was set in *United Kingdom Association of Professional Engineers and Newell v Amalgamated Union of Engineering Workers* [1972] ICR 151, 161. The court stated: 'if a union knows that its officials are acting contrary to the law, it has a duty to assert its authority and to require them to comply with the law. Advising them to comply is not enough.' In *Heaton's Transport (St. Helen's) Ltd v Transport and General Workers' Union* [1972] ICR 308, 404, the union was advised to threaten the withdrawal of shop stewards' credentials from those acting unlawfully. Moreover, Lord Wilberforce said (at 403B):

> To be effective in law a withdrawal or curtailment of an existing actual author-
> ity of an agent must be communicated by the principal to the agent in terms
> which the agent would reasonably understand as forbidding him to do that
> which he had previously been authorized to do on the principal's behalf.

13.31 A plea that the union had not authorized breach of an injunction was the
central issue in *Read (Richard) Transport Ltd v National Union of Mineworkers
(South Wales Area)* [1985] IRLR 67, which arose during the 1984 miners'
strike and the court took a typically robust response to the claim. The
companies were independent road hauliers whose businesses had been
affected by mass picketing by striking miners of the Port Talbot Steel Works,
to which they regularly delivered. The companies gained an order restraining
the union by its servants or agents from 'continuing to instruct or otherwise
encourage its members from stopping approaching or in any way interfering
with the free passage of the employers' vehicles into or out of the Port Talbot
Works . . . or abusing or threatening the drivers thereof'. The defendants
were obliged to 'withdraw any such instruction or encouragement already
given'. The defendants did not appear at the hearing. (Indeed the NUM
resolutely refused to so appear at that stage of their year-long dispute with the
National Coal Board.) The union did, however, write a letter to the court,
assuring the court that it would comply with the order but stressing the difficulty of so doing, since the employers' vehicles travelled in a long convoy of
between 50 and 130 vehicles with those of other companies which did not
have the protection of any such order. The vehicles were still stoned after the
injunction was granted just as they had been before. On the committal application, Park J thought that it was an insufficient response by the defendants
to say that they had not *knowingly* committed breaches of the injunction.
There was evidence that the conduct of the pickets towards the drivers had
been authorized or endorsed by responsible people in the union, who
appeared completely indifferent to the consequences of the pickets' violent
behaviour. The defendants' letter was silent about any instructions given to
the pickets to cease violence against the employers' vehicles.

13.32 In *Express and Star Ltd v National Graphical Association (1982)* [1986] ICR
589 (for full facts see para 3.120), Skinner J found that two branch officials
of the NGA had indicated to members of the union 'by nods and winks' that
they should disobey an injunction made in a dispute about new technology
notwithstanding that the union's formal position was that the order should
be obeyed. His Lordship did not accept that since the officials were employed

by the branch the NGA could not be liable for them. He reached that result by applying the code of vicarious responsibility now set out in the Trade Union and Labour Relations (Consolidation) Act 1992, s 20. The Court of Appeal thought that this was incorrect since this applied only to proceedings in tort, and contempt proceedings could not fall within that definition. Lawton LJ found, however, that:

> If it was a fact that he, as a branch official had been given a nod and a wink [from the union], what the union was doing was putting up a humbugging pretence that they were complying with the law, at the same time doing what they could to ensure that their members did not comply with it.

This was a contempt for which the union was liable.

Where an order is addressed to the defendant 'by his servants or agents', the defendant will only be liable for breach if: **13.33**

(1) the persons who did the acts alleged were his employees or agents;
(2) the acts were done in the course of the service or agency; and
(3) he either:
    (a) authorized the acts; or
    (ii) could reasonably have foreseen the possibility of such acts and failed to take all reasonable steps to prevent them (*Hone v Page* [1980] FSR 500).

J. Punishment

There is no limit on the time that a person may be imprisoned for contempt. He may also be fined or ordered to give security for good behaviour. In a family law case, *Danchevsky v Danchevsky* [1975] Fam 17, Lord Denning MR thought that 'whenever there is a reasonable alternative instead of committal to prison, that alternative must be taken'. The court may also suspend the operation of a committal order for a period. A fine may be enforced by the Queen's Remembrancer (a Master of the Supreme Court) as if it were a judgment debt due to him (Supreme Court Act 1981, s 140). **13.34**

Where the breach of an order is not deliberate, it may be that no penalty will be imposed (*Association of Licensed Aircraft Engineers v British European Airways* [1973] ICR 601). The court will amongst other things clearly bear in mind whether the defendants have shown contrition and made an apology to **13.35** the court. In *Mirror Group Newspapers Ltd v Harrison* (November 1986), Mars Jones J, however, refused to accept a purported apology by the defendants phrased as a non-admission of fault and expression of regret therefor. The court will also consider in mitigation whether the defendants acted on the basis of legal advice (eg *Superstar Australia Pty v Coonan & Denlay Pty (No. 2)* (1982) 65 FLR 432).

13.36   In cases under the Industrial Relations Act 1971, the AUEW was fined £50,000 (*Goad v Amalgamated Union of Engineering Workers (No. 3)* [1973] ICR 108; see also *Con-Mech (Engineers) v Amalgamated Union of Engineering Workers* [1973] ICR 620). In *Howitt Transport v Transport and General Workers' Union* [1973] ICR 1, Donaldson P indicated that in the case of organizations a financial penalty would be more appropriate than imprisonment. In *Austin-Rover Group Ltd v Amalgamated Union of Engineering Workers (TASS)* [1985] IRLR 162 (see para 13.21) the judge did not decree any punishment since the contempt was not serious and the union might have taken sufficiently vigorous steps to dissociate themselves from the industrial action had they taken legal advice at an earlier stage. In *Heaton's Transport (St. Helen's) Ltd v Transport and General Workers' Union* [1973] AC 15, the union was fined £25,000 in each case making a total of £50,000. In *Express & Star Ltd v NGA* (above) a fine of £15,000 was imposed whilst during the Wapping dispute, News Group Newspapers and Times Newspapers Ltd gained fines of £25,000 each against the NGA and SOGAT 82 respectively. The biggest fine so far recorded is £200,000 which was imposed against the NUM on 10 October 1984.

13.37   In considering punishment, the judge will almost certainly wish to have details about the means of a defendant. In the case of a union, this can be best extracted from form AR21 'Annual Return for a Trade Union', which must be submitted by each trade union pursuant to the Trade Union and Labour Relations (Consolidation) Act 1992. This contains details of a union's membership and finances.

13.38   It is only rare that individuals have been fined in industrial dispute cases. Mr Arthur Scargill, however, received a penalty of £1,000 during the miners' strike. Moreover, in *Mirror Group Newspapers Ltd v Harrison* (November 1986, unreported), the father and deputy father of the NGA graphics chapel of the Mirror Group Newspapers were fined £10,000 and £5,000 respectively. The judge indicated that their 'flagrant' contempt in holding a disruptive chapel meeting in defiance of a clear injunction merited immediate imprisonment, but he bore in mind that the men had 'misguidedly' thought that they were acting in the best interests of their members.

In an unprecedented decision, however, in *Clarke v Chadburn* [1985] 1 WLR **13.39**
78 Megarry V-C declared that rule changes passed by the National Union of Mineworkers in defiance of an injunction not to do so, were void and of no effect. The applicant for committal does not, however, have a right of action in damages against the contemnor for loss caused by reason of his contempt (*Re Hudson* [1966] Ch 207).

It is normal to award indemnity costs against a respondent in a successful **13.40**
contempt application. Although the court could so award costs in an unsuccessful application for committal, it should only do so in the most exceptional circumstance, according to the decision in *Knight v Clifton* [1971] 2 WLR 564.

A respondent actually committed to prison may be discharged on application **13.41**
at any time (RSC, O52, r 8). Where it is unlikely that imprisonment will make a person comply with the order, and especially when the contemnor enjoys the publicity of imprisonment, he should be released once sufficiently punished (*Enfield London Borough Council v Mahoney* [1983] 1 WLR 749). The Official Solicitor has the duty to review the cases of imprisoned contemnors and report on them quarterly (Direction of Viscount Dilhorne, 20 May 1963). It was by the use of this procedure that the dockers were released from imprisonment in the celebrated dispute in 1972 (*Churchman v Joint Shop Stewards Committee* [1972] 1 WLR 1094).

Strictly, a party in contempt of court has no right to address the court until **13.42**
that contempt is purged, but the judge has a discretion to allow any such party to address him (see *Clarke and others v Heathfield and others (No. 2)* [1985] ICR 606). Indeed, in the Wapping dispute, Michael Davies J read out in open court a letter from Miss Brenda Dean, the General Secretary of SOGAT, explaining their defiance of the court order.

It will usually be necessary for the contemnor to make an apology to the **13.43**
court in order to have the remedy for contempt lifted. There was much speculation in the miners' strike that the judges would insist on a formal apology from the National Union of Mineworkers. In fact, Scott J in *Read (Richard) Transport Ltd v National Union of Mineworkers (South Wales Area)*, Financial

Times, 15 March 1985, did not so insist but was satisfied that the union 'had recognized the authority of the court by seeking the lifting of the sequestration order'.

K. Receiver

13.44   The unprecedented circumstances of the miners' strike of 1984–85 brought forth an unusual enforcement device in the form of the appointment by the High Court of a receiver of union funds. In *Clarke v Heathfield* (above), the National Union of Mineworkers was in continuing contempt of various orders made by the High Court and had not paid fines of £200,000 imposed for such contempt. Moreover, the union trustees had sent funds abroad precisely in order to frustrate the sequestrators appointed by the court. Sixteen working miners sought, without notice, an order that the court appoint fit and proper persons to be trustees of the union property. Mervyn Davies J applied the test laid down in *American Cyanamid Co. v Ethicon Ltd* [1975] AC 396 and *Higginbotham v MacGilchrist* 1930 SC 625, that a trustee may be removed if he obstinately refuses to acknowledge his legal duty and to discharge his legal responsibility with the result that the affairs of the trust are brought into confusion ([1985] ICR 606, 613E). He thought that this was a proper case to exercise the discretion to appoint new trustees, in particular because: funds had been removed from the jurisdiction in order to frustrate the orders of the court; the union would not undertake to obey future orders; and the 'the trustees have by their own action caused the union funds, for the time being at any rate, to be unavailable for the purposes for which they were contributed by the general membership'.

L. Sequestration

Effects of sequestration

13.45   Sequestration is the remedy of last resort to enforce a judgment requiring a person to do an act within a specified time or to abstain from doing a specified act. Its aim is to compel obedience rather than merely to punish (*Australian Consolidated Presses Ltd v Morgan* [1965] 112 CLR 483, 498). It lies at the top end of the spectrum of severity of the court's orders and can paralyse the affairs of the party in contempt of court. It is thus often used to enforce an injunction in an industrial action case, and is cumulative to other methods of enforcing an order such as committal for contempt. It was the threat of further sequestration, because of breach of picketing orders granted to News International companies, which led the two print unions SOGAT 82 and the NGA to call off their support for the Wapping dispute on 5 and 6 February 1987.

13.46 The writ of sequestration is addressed to not less than four commissioners, of whom at least two must act, and charges them to seize the assets of the defendant until he or it purges his or its contempt to the satisfaction of the court. By the nature of the work involved, chartered accountants are well suited to perform the role of sequestrator, and have invariably been appointed in recent strike sequestration cases. Partners in Price Waterhouse served in this role in the NUM sequestration and partners of Ernst & Whinney in the SOGAT 82 sequestration which resulted from the Wapping dispute.

13.47 The writ of sequestration binds all property of the person sequestered from the date of its issue, and the sequestrators must enter at once to take possession of his real and personal estate. They receive all rents from tenants of property of the defendant. Sequestrators may break open doors or boxes in order to get possession of property affected by the writ (*Lowter v Colchester Corp.* (1817) 2 Mer 395). In *Webster v Southwark London Borough Council* [1983] 2 WLR 217, 225, sequestration was ordered in respect of non-compliance with a declaratory order, but it is likely that this will be confined to its special circumstances.

Application for order

13.48 A party seeking sequestration as a mode of enforcement must issue a writ and (unusually, but because of its dire consequences for the defendant) requires the leave of the court to do so. The application for leave must state the ground of application and should be supported by an affidavit. The general rules for this application are similar to those for committal, and frequently both applications are made together (see Chapter 17). The hearing of the application is usually held in open court save in special circumstances. As with committal for contempt, it is a prerequisite of the granting of leave that the injunction should have been served personally on the person against whom this procedure is sought (see para 13.04). The court must also be satisfied that disobedience to the order made has been more than casual, inadvertent or accidental, save in the event that disobedience is repeated (*Fairclough v Manchester Ship Canal Co.* (1897) 41 SJ 225, *Worthington v Ad-Lib Club Ltd* [1965] Ch 236, *Heaton's Transport (St. Helens) Ltd v Transport and General Workers' Union* [1973] AC 15). There is no requirement, however, that the applicant prove that the defendant has property available to be seized (*Hulbert and Crowe v Cathcart* [1896] AC 470). The applicant should state the names of the sequestrators and there should be some evidence as to their suitability for such appointment. The court may grant an injunction in lieu of sequestration or direct that the writ shall lie in the office for a specified period. Leave is required to withdraw a motion for sequestration (*Showerings Ltd v Fern Vale Brewery Co. Ltd* [1958] RPC 462).

Discretionary remedy

13.49 This mode of enforcement is in the discretion of the court, so that in *Steiner Products Ltd v Willy Steiner Ltd* [1966] 1 WLR 986, for example, the court refused an application because it would adversely affect the livelihood of innocent parties, namely the employees of the defendants. Instead, a fine was imposed for the defendants' contempt. In *Read (Richard) Transport Ltd v National Union of Mineworkers (South Wales Area)* [1985] IRLR 67, the judge ordered sequestration of the assets of the defendant union area 'because from a report in the *Daily Express* . . . it would appear that the defendant may be seeking to avoid payment of any fines imposed by this court by the device of transferring its funds into the private bank accounts of its leaders' (para 26). In the sequestration hearing in *News Group Newspapers Ltd v SOGAT 82* (unreported) Michael Davies J found the case for sequestration 'really unanswerable' since 'there is no hint of any change of attitude on the part of the defendants [in defying the court orders]'.

Third parties

13.50 The sequestrators act as officers of the court, and may from time to time be given directions by the judge. Usually one judge will be appointed to supervise a sequestration in an industrial dispute case. Any resistance or interference by any person with the sequestrators' carrying out of their proper duties is itself a contempt of court. In *Eckman v Midland Bank Ltd* [1973] ICR 71, Sir John Donaldson determined that banks could, in the absence of instructions from the sequestrators to do otherwise, honour cheques and stockbrokers could sell shares on the authority of the party in contempt, unless the transaction were designed to obstruct or prevent the sequestration. The sequestrators cannot trace and seize property which has passed to other persons after the date of the issue of the writ of sequestration if they are bona fide purchasers for value without notice of the writ (*Coulston v Gardiner* (1681) 3 Swan 279, 293).

The defendant union's accountant must give full cooperation to the seques- **13.51** trators. This sensitive issue was explored in *Messenger Newspapers Group Ltd v National Graphical Association* [1984] 1 All ER 293. The assets of the NGA were sequestrated in order to ensure that the union pay a substantial fine imposed on it for contempt in failing to desist from picketing the Warrington premises of the plaintiff. The union's auditors, mindful of the duty of confidentiality which they owed to their union clients, refused to disclose details of the union's assets. The Court of Appeal decided that the accountants must not obstruct the sequestrators' investigations, even though they did not hold any property belonging to the union. Sir John Donaldson MR thought that: 'a sequestration would be quite impossible if it required the consent of, for example, the officers of the company against whom the writ of sequestration is issued.'

In *Taylor v NUM (Yorkshire Area) and National Union of Mineworkers* **13.52** (14 November 1985, unreported) Nicholls J on the discharge of the sequestration order against the NUM said:

> Those who give professional or other advice to a person against whom an injunction has been granted or whose assets are the subject of a sequestration order must be vigilant to see that they are not assisting in a breach of the injunction or an interference with the sequestrators. Solicitors as officers of this court have a particularly heavy responsibility in this regard. . . . Those who assist others to take steps intended to thwart orders which it is anticipated that a court may thereafter make should not regard themselves as necessarily unassailable.

In *Clarke and others v Heathfield and others (No. 2)* [1985] ICR 606, the court **13.53** removed the trustees of the National Union of Mineworkers who had sought to frustrate the efforts of the sequestrators by sending money abroad. Notwithstanding the wide powers possessed by the sequestrators, in the miners' sequestration, by 29 November 1984 the sequestrators had been able to locate only £8,174 out of the union's estimated funds of £10.6 million because the union had transferred money to banks in Luxembourg, Switzerland and Ireland in anticipation of such an order.

Branch funds

13.54 Where there is a dispute about the ownership of property which the sequestrators claim, a party may apply to the court to direct an enquiry as to the
precise nature of the respective interests in the property. Thus, in the course
of the SOGAT sequestration during the Wapping dispute, the sequestrators
sought directions as to whether certain assets belonged to the national union
which was the subject of the sequestration, or the local branches, which were
not. Although Taylor J considered that the sequestrators were entitled to seize
the funds of both national union and local branches, the Court of Appeal did
not. In *News Group Newspapers Ltd v SOGAT* [1986] IRLR 227, their
Lordships carefully analysed the rules of the London Clerical Branch of
SOGAT and the Syndication International chapel (constituent organizations
of the union), and found that the rules clearly stated that branch funds were
the property solely of the branch, were vested in trustees and those trustees
had to comply with the decisions of the branch committee. The branch was
like an ordinary members' club, and property could be held on trust for the
members of such an unincorporated association. There was nothing repugnant in the idea of a club owning its own property and being affiliated to a
central organization. An example might be the Rugby Union. Thus the
sequestrators of assets of the national union could not get their hands on
funds and property belonging to the branches (see, to the same effect,
Messenger Newspapers Group Ltd v National Graphical Association (1982),
Eastham J, 9 December 1983).

Duties of sequestrators

13.55 Sequestrators are officers of the court but are liable for negligence and costs
if they, for example, act wrongfully in sequestering particular property
(*Wiebeck v Told* (1913) 29 TLR 741). Their primary duty is to hold the
contemnor's property until the contempt is purged and the court makes a
further order. Property can be sold by the sequestrator only with the leave of
the court. When the contemnor has purged or cleared his contempt, the
sequestrators will be ordered to be discharged.

13.56 The costs of a union's defiance of a court order may be colossal. In *Taylor v
NUM (Yorkshire Area) and National Union of Mineworkers* (14 November
1985, unreported) Nicholls J tallied up a fine of £200,000 for contempt;
£400,000 as the expenses and costs of the sequestrators and their advisers;
and £800,000 as disbursements and costs of the Receiver.

14

DAMAGES FOR INDUSTRIAL ACTION

A. The Measure of Damages in Contract

The measure of damages in consequence of strikes is an underdeveloped area **14.01** of law, partly because unions were for long immune from such claims, but mainly because employers have not wanted to disturb industrial calm following a dispute by engaging in hazardous and lengthy litigation.

The authorities reject the measure most favourable to employers, a percentage share of overhead expenses or revenue lost during the strike. Instead, the court will ascertain the individual worker's probable output during the absence, convert his productivity to the selling value of the goods made, and then deduct expenses which would have been incurred only if he had performed the contract. In *Ebbw Vale Steel Iron and Coal Co. v Tew* (1935) 79 SJ 593, where this unrealistic calculation was carried out, the court awarded £3 8s 11d to the employer in respect of lost production. The Court of Appeal in *National Coal Board v Galley* [1958] 1 WLR 16, specifically rejected the appellant's submission that they should be awarded a proportional amount of their whole loss arising from a strike against each participant. Pearce LJ said that:

> The measure of damages cannot be different because when he broke his

269

contract in this respect he knew that his fellow deputies intended to commit similar breaches, except in so far as it would then be apparent that any damage likely to flow from the breach could not be avoided or lessened by their presence.

14.02 *Bowes & Partners v Press* [1894] 1 QB 202 is a case with very special facts, but again demonstrates the real difficulties of assessing damages in this area. The respondent workers gave 14 days' notice of refusal to descend the company's mine shaft with non-unionists. On the first day of the industrial action the defendants would not descend in the first cage which was occupied by a solitary non-trade unionist. However when the next cage came up a few moments later they offered to go down, but the under-manager in charge refused to allow them to do so. The employer sued under the Employers and Workmen Act 1875 for damages but the defendant claimed that these could be only nominal because the breach lasted merely a few minutes. The Court of Appeal rejected this contention since 'the men deliberately put themselves in the wrong and ... continuously and persistently refused to work except upon terms which they had no right to dictate'.

The maximum award

There is a maximum level of damages which may be awarded against a trade union in tort by what is now TULR(C)A, s 22. It depends on the membership of the union as follows:

(1) £10,000 when the union has fewer than 5,000 members;
(2) £50,000 when the union has between 5,000 and 24,999 members;
(3) £125,000 when the union has between 25,000 and 99,999 members; and
(4) £125,000 when the union has more than 100,000 members.

Interest may be awarded in addition to the appropriate sum of damages (*Boxfoldia v NGA (1982)* [1988] ICR 752).

The maxima relate to each set of 'proceedings'. What is not entirely clear is the meaning of proceedings.

There may be losses to several parties in one strike. Each would have its own right of action in damages up to the relevant maximum award. In *Duport Steels Ltd v Sirs* [1980] IRLR 116 there were 15 plaintiffs and each could have gained the maximum.

A more difficult question is whether a single employer might issue several claims arising from the same industrial action and seek the maximum in each one. In the case of a strike affecting a newspaper it might be possible to issue one set of proceedings for loss of circulation and another for loss of advertising revenue. It is thought that it would be more consistent with the policy lying behind the provision.

The Act does not specify the date at which it must be determined how many members the union has but in principle it appears that the relevant date should be the date of the commission of the tort.

B. Property Immune from Enforcement

The Trade Union and Labour Relations (Consolidation) Act 1992 protects certain property held by or on behalf of a trade union from the enforcement of any judgment for damages, costs and expenses. This applies outside the area of tort, and to any award whether against the union itself, trustees or members in a representative action. As such, it may be traced back to a recommendation of the Dunedin Report (Royal Commission on Trade Disputes and Trade Combinations) in 1906. **14.03**

The provision does not, however, apply to fines for contempt, or compensation for unfair dismissal. In all other cases, the following property is protected: **14.04**

• property belonging to union trustees themselves otherwise than in their capacity as trustees;
• property belonging to any member of the union otherwise than jointly in common with other members (this protects the ordinary member from losing his house and home);
• property belonging to any union official who is neither a member nor trustee of the union;
• property in the political fund (although under the Trade Union Act 1984 a political fund which is no longer supported by the necessary resolution is transferred to the general fund and so loses its protection);
• the provident funds of the union.

C. Practice in Damages Claims

14.05   This book does not provide a general analysis of the law of civil procedure but we do examine those aspects of procedure which are most relevant to strike cases which go beyond the injunction stage.

Privilege

14.06   Issues may arise as to whether the documents produced by management and passed to their employer's solicitors attract legal privilege. The general principles of legal privilege as explained in the Sixteenth Report of the Law Reform Committee are that the following are covered by privilege:

(1) communications between the client or his agents and the client's or professional legal advisers;

(2) communications between the client's professional legal advisers and third parties, if made for the purposes of pending or contemplated litigation;

(3) communications between the client or his agent and third parties, if made for the purpose of obtaining information to be submitted to the client's professional legal advisers for the purpose of obtaining advice on pending or contemplated litigation.

14.07   It is category (3) which causes most controversy in strike cases, and difficulty in the case law. It is certainly not enough that the document may at some time have been submitted to a solicitor (*Graham v Bogle* [1924] 1 IR 68). There was a difference of opinion in *Birmingham and Midland Motor Omnibus Co. Ltd v LNWR Co.* [1913] 3 KB 850, between Hamilton LJ who considered that the obtaining of legal advice must be the primary and substantial purpose of the document and Buckley and Vaughan Williams LJJ who thought it sufficient if one of the purposes of the communication is that it is to be laid before a legal adviser in relation to contemplated litigation. Where communications are made to solicitors the whole of the document is privileged. In *Re Sarah C. Getty Trust* [1985] 3 WLR 302, Mervyn Davies J held that the separation of parts of those communications said to be unconnected with the giving and receiving of advice from others would erode the protection provided by the law to an unacceptable degree.

15

DEDUCTION OF PAY FOR INDUSTRIAL ACTION

A. Contractual Claims	15.01	B. Judicial Review	15.13

A. Contractual Claims

The employer may decide that a dismissal or injunction during the course of **15.01** disruptive action short of strike will exacerbate a delicate industrial relations situation. His first reaction may instead be to deduct or withhold a proportion or all of the pay for the period of disruption. (See House of Lords decision in *Miles v Wakefield* MDC [1987] ICR 368.)

Lord Denning MR in *Secretary of State for Employment v ASLEF* [1972] 2 QB **15.02** 443, 492 asked rhetorically:

> Is a man entitled to wages for his work when he, with others, is doing his best to make it useless? Surely not. Wages are to be paid for services rendered, not for producing deliberate chaos . . . The breach goes to the whole of the consideration and was put by Lord Campbell, Chief Justice, in *Cuckson v Stones* (1858) 1 E & E 248, 255, and with other cases quoted in Smith's Leading Cases . . .

In the *ASLEF* case, the court had to determine whether a 'work-to-rule' was **15.03** 'irregular industrial action' for the purposes of the ballot provisions of the Industrial Relations Act 1971 (for facts see para 6.03). The issue of payment did not arise directly but Lord Denning's dictum was 12 years afterwards cited in a case where it did: *Royle v Trafford Borough Council* [1984] IRLR 184. The employee followed the instructions of the National Association of Schoolmasters in refusing to accept additional pupils into his class. At the end of term, he refused to take five extra pupils, who accordingly had to be sent home. The council regarded Mr Royle as failing to carry out the terms of his contract and deducted an amount based on the time when he failed to comply with instructions, in his case six months. Park J found this solution too drastic since the claimant had during the relevant period taught 31 pupils. By accepting the employee's imperfect performance of his contract, the council had impliedly affirmed it. The learned judge did not, however, conclude that the employee was entitled to full payment. Rather, the court could make a deduction representing the notional value of the services which Mr Royle did not render. A deduction of 5/6ths would be just in the circumstances.

15.04   One of the problems in reviewing the authority of this case is that Park J relied, inter alia, on the decision of Nicholls J in *Miles v Wakefield*, The Times 22 November 1986, which then went to the Court of Appeal and was reversed (below). Subsequently on 12 March 1987 the House of Lords allowed the appeal by the council. Mr Miles was a superintendent registrar of births, marriage and deaths who was appointed and entitled to be paid by the District Council under the terms of the Registration Act 1953, s 6. Between August 1981 and October 1982, he followed the instructions of his union by refusing to perform marriages on Saturday mornings. The council thus withheld 3/37ths of his pay, and effectively did not pay him for Saturday mornings at all, notwithstanding that he attended on that day to perform other functions. Nicholls J's decision that this was quite appropriate was overturned by the Court of Appeal ([1986] IRLR 108), with Sir Edward Eveleigh dissenting. It is only of persuasive authority for employees, since both sides accepted that Mr Miles was an office-holder whose office was regulated by statute.

15.05   Parker LJ's judgment thus proceeded from his construction of the relevant statute. He found it difficult to accept that Parliament intended that the council should be 'entitled to withhold some part of his salary for any and every part of duty'. The obligation to pay was, while the officer held his office, unqualified. Parker LJ also considered in an obiter dictum that 'in the absence of a breach amounting to a repudiation accepted by dismissal or a specific right to suspend, there appear to me strong grounds for saying that there is no right to withhold payment and take the benefit of all work in fact done during the period in which the refusal to perform a particular function was operative'. His Lordship thought that the proper remedy was to sue the employee for breach of contract. Not only is the loss suffered by disruptive action, particularly in the service sector, difficult to quantify but also employers will be looking for an immediate reaction to disruption, rather than a long drawn out claim for damages. Deduction of pay appears the common sense remedy, but it must be admitted that the direct authority for it is limited. Fox LJ agreed with this view but would 'express no view as to the position if there had been a contract since that does not arise'.

Sir Edward Eveleigh, on the other hand, saw no reason why there cannot be conditions affecting the claimant's right to receive salary imposed by contract, statute or in some other way. He found support for his view in the *ASLEF* case.   **15.06**

It is submitted that in the case of employees, Sir Edward Eveleigh's view is to be preferred because:

(1) It provides the employer with a remedy more realistic than a damages claim, which is difficult to quantify and will be determined long after the event.

(2) It probably represents what most people would consider the common sense view.

(3) It is easier to square with the Court of Appeal decision in *Henthorn and Taylor v Central Electricity Generating Board* [1980] IRLR 361, that in order to be entitled to pay at all, the employee has to prove that he is ready, willing and able to work. It would be a strange position that an employer could refuse to allow the employee to work without assurances of full production, yet if he does permit him to work and he deliberately goes back on such undertaking given, he must be paid in full; a lock-out might exacerbate the industrial relations situation.

It is necessary to analyse the only case cited by Parker LJ for his obiter proposition, *Gorse v Durham County Council* [1971] 2 All ER 666. Mr Gorse claimed his unpaid salary for three and a half days when he was not permitted to attend at his school because he had refused to supervise school meals, which was then a breach of contract before the school meals agreement was reached. Cusack J decided that he was entitled to payment during that period because of a contractual provision that payment of salary must be made for a period of suspension which was followed by reinstatement. The case thus does not provide general authority for those many cases where there is no such agreement.   **15.07**

15.08   The employer must make clear what it is that he regards as a breach of contract. In *Bond v CAV Ltd* [1983] IRLR 360 the employee had refused to work on one of the machines on which he was normally engaged because of a dispute about piecework bonuses. Notwithstanding that it 'was open to the [employers] to . . . insist that the setters cease work and leave the premises if they were not prepared to work' on all four machines, the defendants had waived the breach of contract by facilitating the claimant's work during the days in question. Peter Pain J concluded that: 'Having approbated the plaintiff's contract of employment the employers could not subsequently reprobate it by refusing to pay for what he did.' Moreover, a refusal by union officials to give an assurance of normal production may not be sufficient to amount to a breach of contract and the position of each employee must be considered separately (*Chappell v Times Newspapers Ltd* [1975] ICR 145).

15.09   In *Sim v Rotherham Metropolitan Borough Council* [1986] IRLR 391, the High Court was concerned with claims by teachers for money deducted from their salaries during the lengthy pay dispute in 1985–6. The claimants were secondary school teachers who each refused requests to cover. They each argued on the lines of *Miles v Wakefield* (above) reasoning that no amounts could be deducted, but Scott J did not agree since such amounts were justifiable as equitable set-offs. A contractual claim was clearly impeached by a claim to damages for refusal to carry out some of the services for which the salary is being paid. The defendants accepted that the amount of deduction by the Education Authority in each case was not less than the amount of damages to which the defendants were entitled for breach of contract committed by the relevant claimant. Scott J was influenced in his decision by the fact that Parliament had excluded teachers and other professionals from the protection of the Truck Acts which then prohibited deductions now amended in the Employment Rights Act 1996, Part 1. His Lordship did not consider that Parker LJ's obiter remarks in the *Miles* case were intended to express a view on the applicability of equitable set-off in the employment context. There was no sufficient reason why the doctrine of equitable set-off should not apply where the employee is suing for his contractual salary but in breach of contract has failed to do all or some of the work required by his contract. Any other decision would be manifestly unjust. He thought that 'the aphorism "no work, no pay" expresses the equity of the situation'.

15.10   The Court of Appeal decision in *Wiluszynski v London Borough of Tower Hamlets* [1989] IRLR 259 is the authoritative decision on payment and limited industrial action. There the local authority was held not to be entitled to withhold pay from an estates officer in the Housing Directorate who was merely boycotting inquiries from council members. This was a small part of his job description. Michael Davies J held that the breach was minimal. Moreover, the council had allowed him to perform the substantial part of his services, so that they were not entitled later to withhold his salary for such period. The Court of Appeal overturned this decision of the High Court on the basis that the council could not physically prevent the plaintiff from attending work and performing his duties, and the doctrine of substantial performance was inapplicable since he would be performing a material part of his contractual services. The employer is entitled in response and in advance of his services being undertaken to decide to accept the proffered partial performance. In this case the council had made clear to the claimant that if he was not prepared to comply with his contract he was not required to work and that if he did work he did so voluntarily and would not be paid. There was no waiver. Although the council's senior management knew that the employee was continuing to work, their failure to take any further steps to prevent that did not sensibly lead to the conclusion that the council was to be taken to have chosen to accept partial performance (see also *MacPherson v London Borough of Lambeth* [1988] IRLR 470; *Home Office v Ayres* [1992] ICR 175).

In an interesting case, but one devoid of any binding authority, a District **15.11** Judge sitting at Dartford County Court decided that lecturers engaged on terms that they had a 190-day working year should suffer a deduction of 1/190th of their year's salary for each day on strike even though they in fact worked longer than those 190 days per year (*Smith and Others v London Borough of Bexley*, unreported, 5 April 1991). The lecturers had contended that the proper deduction was 1/365th of a year's pay (see also *Thames Water Utilities Ltd v Reynolds* [1996] IRLR 186).

The issue of employer remedies for disruptive action short of a strike is **15.12** controversial. The principles appear to be that where the action is such as to disrupt seriously the business of the employer, the employer may:

(1) deduct from the wages of employees participating in the action the notional value of the services performed;
(2) suspend employees without pay unless they are ready and willing to work;

(3) dismiss with impunity those engaged in such action, provided that all are dismissed.

Industrial action is one of the exceptions where an employee cannot complain of deductions from wages (Employment Rights Act 1996, s 14(5)).

B. Judicial Review

15.13   In *R v Liverpool Corp. ex parte Ferguson and Ferguson* [1985] IRLR 501, the Divisional Court made a declaration that teachers who were ready, willing and able to work on a 'day of action' in support of Liverpool Council's policies should be paid. About 2,000 members of the National Union of Teachers reported for work but found that their schools were closed since the caretakers were on strike. The local authority decided not to pay those who attended and officials of the NUT sought judicial review of the decision. Counsel for the local authority did not argue that the decision was reasonable but rather that the applicants had no *locus standi* and that the decision was not justifiable as a matter of public law. Mann J rejected both contentions.

16

INTERNATIONAL STANDARDS

A. European Convention on Human Rights

Article 11 of the Convention (given direct effect in English law by Human Rights Act 1998) states that everyone has a right to freedom of association, including the right to form and join trade unions for the protection of his interests. Restrictions on that right, if they are to be lawful, must be prescribed by law, and be necessary in a democratic society in the interests of national security or public safety, for the prevention of disorder or crime, for the protection of health or morals, or for the protection of the rights and freedoms of others (Article 11(2)). The restriction must be proportionate to the interest pursued. Contracting States are given a margin of appreciation to determine what measures are necessary and proportionate.

16.01

Article 11 does not expressly include a right to strike, and the European Court of Human Rights when the issue has been raised has stopped short of implying such a right. Article 11 safeguards the freedom of trade unions to protect the occupational interests of their members. While the ability to strike represents one of the most important of the means by which trade unions can fulfil this function, there are others. Contracting States are left a choice of means as to how the freedom of trade unions ought to be safeguarded (*Schmidt and Dahlström v Sweden* 6/2/76 Series A no. 21; *Gustafsson v Sweden* (1996) 28 EHRR 409; *Schettini v Italy* Application no 29529/95 9 Nov 2000)).

16.02

16.03   In 2002 the court twice considered the scope of Article 11 in the context of strikes, and has dismissed the application in each case.

Unison v UK [2002] IRLR 497 concerned an injunction to prevent strike action by Unison members at University College Hospital (see *UCLH v Unison* [1999] ICR 204). The Strasbourg Court considered that the prohibition of the strike must be regarded as a restriction on the union's power to protect those interests and therefore disclosed a restriction on the freedom of association. However, the court went on to decide that the restriction was justified under Article 11(2). The court was satisfied that UCLH could claim that its ability to carry out its functions effectively, including the securing of contracts with outside bodies, might be adversely affected by the actions of the union so that measures taken to prevent the strike may be regarded as concerning the 'rights of others', that is UCLH (para 39). The State had not exceeded the margin of appreciation accorded to it in regulating trade union action (para 42).

16.04   The court reached a similar result in *Federation of Offshore Workers' Trade Unions v. Norway* (App 38190/97, 27/6/02). The Norwegian Government had issued an ordinance preventing a strike of workers on offshore gas platforms, and compelling the disputing parties to participate in a compulsory arbitration process. The court held that restrictions imposed by a Contracting State on the exercise of the right to strike do not in themselves give rise to an issue under Article 11. The question is whether the law of the Contracting State, looked at as a whole, adequately protects the freedom of trade unions to pursue their members' interests.

On the assumption that the restriction in the case did amount to an interference with a right guaranteed by Article 11(1), the interference was justified under Article 11(2). The court had regard to the very serious repercussions of the strike: a strike would halt all gas output from Norway, with serious effect on the Norwegian economy and on countries dependent on Norwegian gas. There was evidence that a halt of any length risked damage to technical installations and the environment. The court was at pains to state that it found these circumstances to be exceptional, and was not saying that a system of compulsory arbitration would be considered proportionate in all cases in which economic pressure is being exerted.

The decision leaves open arguments to justify restrictions on strikes by 'key' workers where strike action would have a very serious effect on national economic interests. Public safety and protection of health are themselves grounds of justification under Article 11(2). It seems likely that if the court is prepared to countenance an economic disruption justification in this manner, the court will allow a wide margin of appreciation in relation to restrictions on strikes based on protection of public safety.

Applications to the court under Article 11 have been almost universally unsuccessful but an exception is *Wilson, Palmer & Doonan v UK* [2002] IRLR 568 which concerned the payment of sweeteners to employees to give up their union recognition and is thus beyond the scope of this book. The relevance is the apparent recognition of a right to strike in some circumstances in para 46 that 'the essence of a voluntary system of collective bargaining is that it must be possible for a trade union which is not recognised by an employer to take steps including if necessary organizing industrial action with a view to persuading the employer to enter collective bargaining with it on those issues which the union believes are important for its members' interests'. **16.05**

B. International Labour Standards

The right to strike is recognized by other international treaties to which the UK is a signatory. The UK has been the subject of repeated criticism by the bodies responsible for monitoring particular treaties, although of course such instruments, and decisions upon them, are not binding in English law. **16.06**

The International Labour Organization Convention 87 provides that workers shall have the right to establish and join organizations of their own choosing (Article 2); and that 'workers and employers' organisations shall have the right to draw up their constitutions and rules, to elect their representatives in full freedom, to organise their administration and activities and to formulate their programmes' (Article 3). Whilst there is no express right to strike, the Committee of Experts of the ILO has for many years said the right to strike is impliedly protected, as being one of the essential means available to workers and their organizations for the promotion and protection of their social and economic interests. Such interests are extensive, including seeking solutions to economic and social policy questions and to labour problems of any kind which are of direct concern to the workers. This is a broader approach than is permissible under the English law definition of trade disputes, and **16.07** the ILO Committee of Experts has stated on a number of occasions that English law fails to provide adequate protection of the right to strike by its limited definition of trade disputes, and by the restrictions on secondary action.

16.08 The ILO does however recognize that restrictions upon the right to strike may be justified. Strike action may be prohibited in respect of public servants engaged in the administration of the state, if it would affect essential services thereby jeopardizing the life, health or personal security of the life of the entire population or parts of it, and the harm was clear and imminent. However, harmful economic effects (such as in the Norwegian gas workers case) have not been regarded as sufficient reason for prohibition.

16.09 The European Social Charter of 1961 does expressly recognize the right to strike:

> with a view to ensuring the effective exercise of the right to bargain collectively the Contracting Parties . . . recognise . . . .. the right of workers and employers to collective action in cases of conflicts of interest, including the right to strike, subject to obligations that might arise out of collective agreement previously entered into (Article 6(4)).

The Committee of Independent Experts has repeatedly reported that the power to dismiss the workforce for striking means the UK is not in conformity with Article 6(4).

17

SAMPLE FORMS AND PRECEDENTS

A. Claim Form to Restrain Strike Action by the Claimant's Own Employees

The claimants' claim is for:

17.01

(1) An order that the Defendants by themselves, their employees, officers, agents or otherwise howsoever be restrained forthwith from inducing, procuring, persuading, assisting, encouraging, organising and/or facilitating in any manner whatsoever employees of the Claimants to break their several contracts of employment with the Claimants or to threaten to do so by:

  (a) refusing to work in accordance with their contracts of employment in connection with the Claimants' installation and operation of [   ] and/or

  (b) interfering in any way with the business of the Claimants and/or procuring breaches of the contracts between the Claimants and [   ]

[Unless and until the majority of the relevant employees engaged or to be engaged in such industrial action against the Claimant shall have voted in favour of such strike and/or industrial action in a ballot held by the First Defendant in accordance with Part II Trade Union and Labour Relations (Consolidation) Act 1992].(1)

(2) An order that the Defendants forthwith:

  (a) withdraw and cancel any order, instruction, decision, direction or advice given or communicated whether directly or indirectly to employees of the Claimants to the effect that the said employees should do any act or acts in breach of their contracts of employment and in particular [(2)   ]

  (b) take all practicable steps to inform forthwith members of the First Defendant of the said withdrawal and cancellation and in particular to inform the . . . . .forthwith of the said withdrawal and cancellation(3)

  (c) direct that any such order, instruction, direction or advice hereinbefore mentioned be disregarded.

(3) Damages for:

  (a) Wrongfully interfering with contracts between the Claimants and [   ] by unlawful means, namely procuring employees of the Claimants to break their several contracts of employment with the Claimants.

  (b) Wrongfully and with intent to injure the Claimants interfering with the trade or business of the Claimants.

  (c) Conspiracy to interfere with the said contracts by unlawful means.

  (d) Conspiracy to procure such breaches of contract.

  (e) Intimidation.

(4) Interest on the amount found to be due to the Claimants at such rate and for such a period as the Honourable Court thinks fit pursuant to Section 35A of the Supreme Court Act 1981.(4)

Notes

(1) See para 5.08 ff.

(2) State here the precise form which the blacking takes.

(3) In the case of a local dispute, it may be more appropriate to inform all local newspapers, which should be named in the order; see para 000.

(4) See on pleading interest, CPR 7.0.12–18.

B. Claim to Restrain Occupation by Employees

Since the employees are likely to be trespassing on the employer's land the appropriate procedure would be that set out in CPR r 55 using standard form N121. See CPR r 55.1(b). **17.02**

C. Claim for Possession Against Unlawful Trespassers

Particulars of claim	In the	Claim No.	**17.03**
for possession			
(trespassers)		Claimant	
		Defendant(s)	

1. The claimant has a right to possession of:

   which is occupied by the defendant(s) who entered or (has)(have) remained on the land without the claimant's consent or licence.

2. The defendant(s) (has)(have) never been a tenant or sub-tenant of the land.

3. The land mentioned at paragraph 1 does (not) include residential property.

4. The claimant's interest in the land (or the basis of the claimant's right to claim possession) is
   Give details:

5. The circumstances in which the land has been occupied are
   Give details:

6. The claimant does not know the name(s) of (all) the defendant(s).

7. The claimant asks the court to order that the defendant(s):
   (a) give the claimant possession of the land;
   (b) pay the claimant's costs of making this claim.

Statement of Truth

*(I believe)(The claimant believes) that the facts stated in these particulars of claim are true.
*I am duly authorised by the claimant to sign this statement.

signed _____ date_____
*(Claimant)(Litigation friend (*where claimant is a child or a patient*)
(Claimant's solicitor)
delete as appropriate

Full name_____

Name of claimant's solicitor's firm_____

position or office held_____
             (*if signing on behalf of form or company*)

D. Particulars of Claim: Secondary Action

IN THE HIGH COURT OF JUSTICE   **17.04**

QUEEN'S BENCH DIVISION

BETWEEN

[Newspaper publisher]

Claimants

and

(1) [Union]

(2) [Branch secretary]

(3) [Assistant branch secretary]

Defendants

PARTICULARS OF CLAIM

---

1. The Claimant publishes eight editions of a free newspaper known as 'Cleethorpes Post'.

2. The First Defendant is an independent trade union with a membership of approximately [   ].(1)

3. The Second Defendant is the Branch Secretary of the Cleethorpes Branch of the First Defendant and the Third Defendant is one of the Assistant Secretaries of that Branch. The Second and Third Defendants are employed by the First Defendant and/or by the said Branch on behalf of, or alternatively as a Branch of, the First Defendant.

4. By a[n oral] contract [in writing] dated [   ] between the Claimants and Waltham Offset Limited (henceforth 'Waltham'), Waltham agreed to print the said newspapers each week [in consideration of].

5. By a[n oral] contract [in writing] dated [   ] between Waltham and Humberstone Setters Limited (henceforth 'Humberstone'), Humberstone agreed to provide typesetting services to Waltham in

287

respect of the said newspapers as and when required and to meet the reasonable deadlines laid down by Waltham.

6. By a[n oral] contract [in writing] dated [   ] between Waltham and Louth Printers Limited (henceforth 'Louth'), Louth agreed to provide typesetting services to Waltham in respect of the newspapers as and when required and to meet the reasonable deadlines laid down by Waltham.

7. The Claimant has numerous contracts with advertisers by which contracts the Claimant agrees to carry advertisements in the various newspapers. The value of such contracts is based, inter alia, on the circulation of the newspaper in question.

8. The following were, inter alia, express and/or implied terms of the respective contracts of employment between Humberstone and its respective employees and between Louth and its respective employees, that

   (a) the employees would work the full shifts they were instructed to work;
   (b) the employees would obey the lawful and reasonable instructions of Humberstone and Louth as appropriate;
   (c) the employees would not disrupt the production of the newspapers.

9. On or about [   ], the Second and Third Defendants for and on behalf of the First Defendant instructed members of the First Defendant employed by Humberstone not to handle typesetting work for the Claimant and thereby induced them to break their contracts of employment with Humberstone.

10. On or about [   ] the Third Defendant for and on behalf of the First Defendant instructed members of the First Defendant employed by Louth not to handle typesetting work for the Claimant, and thereby induced them to break their contracts of employment with Louth.

11. At some time on or before [   ] the Second and Third Defendants together with persons unknown agreed to give the instructions in order to injure the Claimant and to damage its trade and business.

12. The Defendants gave the instructions and/or agreed as aforesaid, notwithstanding that they knew or ought to have known that the same would breach and/or interfere with the contracts set out in paragraphs 5 and 6 hereof in that Humberstone and Louth respectively would not be able to provide typesetting services to Waltham by the required deadline or at all, whereby the contract set out in paragraph 4 hereof would be breached and/or interfered with.

13. By reason of the unlawful acts, the Claimant has suffered loss and damage.

PARTICULARS OF LOSS AND DAMAGE

Loss of circulation   £

Loss of advertising revenue   £

14. Unless restrained by this Honourable Court, the Defendants intend to continue the unlawful acts.

15. Further, pursuant to section 35A of the Supreme Court Act 1981, the Claimant is entitled to and hereby claims to recover interest on the amount found due to it at such rate and for such period as to the Honourable Court may appear just.

And the Claimants claim

(1) An Order that the Defendants and each of them whether by themselves, their employees, officers, agents or otherwise howsoever be restrained forthwith from interfering with the trade and business and contracts of the Claimant by inciting, inducing, procuring, persuading, assisting, encouraging, organising, financing and/or facilitating in any manner whatsoever employees of Waltham Offset Limited and Humberstone Setters Limited (hereinafter called 'the Companies') to break their several contracts of employment with the Companies by in particular (but without prejudice to the generality of the foregoing) withdrawing their labour and/or refusing to handle and/or to typeset and/or to 'black' newspapers and/or parts thereof and/or magazines and/or printed matter published and/or printed and/or produced and/or distributed by the Claimant.

(2) An Order that the Defendants and each of them forthwith:

(a) withdraw and cancel any resolution, order, instructions, decision, direction or advice given and/or communicated whether directly or indirectly and/or by their employees, officers, agents, or otherwise howsoever to employees of the Companies to the effect that the said employees should do any act or acts in breach of their contracts of employment with the Companies and in particular (but without prejudice to the generality of the foregoing) to withdraw their labour or to refuse to handle and/or typeset newspapers and/or magazines and/or printed matter published and/or produced and/or printed and/or distributed by the Claimant;

(b) take all practical steps to inform members of the First Defendant employed by the Companies of the withdrawal and cancellation and in particular to inform the Press Association or all relevant local newspapers forthwith of the said withdrawal and cancellation;

(c) direct that any such resolution, order, instruction, decision, direction, or advice mentioned hereinbefore be disregarded.

(3) Damages for:

(a) Wrongfully interfering with contracts of the Claimant namely with its advertisers and the Companies;

(b) wrongfully interfering with the trade or business of the Claimant;

(c) wrongfully and with intent to injure the Claimant procuring or inducing breaches of contract between the Claimant and the Companies;

(d) conspiracy to interfere with the said contents by unlawful means;

(e) conspiracy to procure such breaches of contract;

(f) intimidation.

(4) Interest on the said damages to be assessed pursuant to Section 35A of the Supreme Court Act 1981.

Notes

(1) This should be pleaded by reason of the limitation on damages (see para 14.04).

E. Particulars of Claim: To Restrain Meeting in Working Time

IN THE HIGH COURT OF JUSTICE

QUEEN'S BENCH DIVISION

BETWEEN

(1) GOLDERS NEWS LIMITED

(2) HEMSTAL PRINTING LIMITED

(3) HEMSTAL SERVICES LIMITED

Claimants

and

(1) THOMAS WILLIAM FRANKS

(2) PRINTERS UNION

Defendants

PARTICULARS OF CLAIM

---

1. The First Claimant publishes the Golders Hill Gazette (henceforth 'the newspaper').

2. The Second Claimant prints the newspaper.

3. The Third Claimant carries out ancillary services on the newspaper.

4. The First Defendant is and was at all material times:

   (a) a member of the Second Defendant, and the Golders Hill Park Chapel thereof (henceforth 'the Chapel');
   (b) an employee of the First Claimant; and
   (c) the Father of the Chapel.

5. The Second Defendant is an independent trade union with a membership of approximately 30,000.

6. By a[n oral] contract [in writing] dated [   ] between the First Claimant and the Second Claimant, the Second Claimant printed the newspaper.

7. By a contract in writing dated [   ] between the First Claimant and the Third Claimant, the Third Claimant provided ancillary services to the First Claimant.

8. The First Claimant has numerous contracts with advertisers by which contracts the First Claimant agrees to carry advertisements in the newspaper. The value of such contracts is based, inter alia, on the circulation of the newspaper.

9. The following were, inter alia, express and/or implied terms of the said respective contracts of employment between the First Claimant on the one hand and its employees including the First Defendant on the other hand, that:

    (a) the employees would work the full shifts they were instructed to work;

    (b) the employees would obey the lawful and reasonable instructions of the First Claimant;

    (c) the employees would not disrupt the production of the said newspaper.

10. Further it was agreed between the First Defendant on behalf of its members and the First Claimant and/or was a reasonable instruction by management that no Chapel might hold a meeting for whatever purpose within the hours of work except with the express permission of the Managing Director of the First Claimant.

11. At some time before 1 January 2004, the First Defendant agreed with members of his Chapel committee to hold a meeting at 4 p.m. on 5 January 2004 notwithstanding that they knew or ought to have known that:

    (a) attendance at such meeting would be in breach of the respective contracts of employment of persons so attending;

    (b) the period between 4 p.m. and 6.30 p.m. is the busiest period of the day for setting the newspaper;

(c) as a necessary consequence of the holding of that meeting the contracts set out in paragraphs 6 to 8 hereof would be broken or interfered with.

12. Further in pursuance of the said agreement, the First Defendant posted and/or caused to be posted notices at the First Claimant's premises at [   ] (henceforth 'the premises') inviting employees to attend such a meeting.

13. By reason of the unlawful acts, the First to Third Claimants and each of them have suffered loss and damage.

PARTICULARS OF LOSS AND DAMAGE

[Insert special damages claimed]

14. Further pursuant to section 35A of the Supreme Court Act 1981, the Claimants are entitled to and hereby claim to recover interest on the amount found due to them at such rate and for such period as to the Honourable Court may appear just.

And the Claimants claim that

(1) The Defendants and each of them, whether by themselves, their employees or agents or otherwise howsoever be restrained from:

(a) instructing, directing, advising, procuring or inducing employees of the Second and Third Claimants to act in breach of their contracts of employment, whether by refusing or failing to work, refusing or failing to work normally or otherwise; and

(b) interfering with the performance of the contracts between the First, Second and Third Claimants for the printing and production of the Golders Hill Gazette by any of the acts referred to in (a).

(2) The Defendants and each of them do forthwith revoke, cancel and withdraw:

(a) any instruction, direction or advice given by them to employees of the Second and Third Claimants to act in breach of their contracts of employment, whether by refusing or failing to work, refusing or failing to work normally or otherwise; and

(b) any instruction, direction or advice given by them to employees of the Second and Third Claimants likely to interfere with the performance of the contracts between the First, Second and Third Claimants for the printing of The Golders Hill Gazette by any of the acts referred to in (a).

(3) The First and Second Defendants do forthwith cancel a meeting of the Golders Hill Park Chapel of the Printers Union employed by the Second and Third Claimants scheduled to be held at 4 p.m. on 5 January 2004 and

(a) do forthwith display and distribute notices of cancellation in the same manner and with the same prominence as notices convening the meeting were displayed and distributed; or

(b) do forthwith inform every member of the said Chapel that the said meeting is cancelled.

(4) Damages for inducing breach of contracts of employment and interfering with commercial contracts and interest thereon to be assessed pursuant to the said section 35A of the Supreme Court Act 1981.

F. Order Restraining Unlawful Picketing

17.06 Upon hearing Counsel for the Claimant and the Defendants and upon reading the statements of [   ] sworn on [   ] and upon the Claimants [and each of them] by their Counsel undertaking to abide by any Order this Honourable Court or Judge may make as to damages in case the Court or Judge shall hereafter be of the opinion that the Defendants or any one or more of them shall have suffered any which the Claimants (or any of them) ought to pay,

IT IS ORDERED that until trial or further order:

(1) The Defendants and each of them be restrained forthwith whether by themselves, their employees, officers, agents or otherwise howsoever from inciting, inducing, procuring, persuading, assisting, encouraging, financing and/or in any other way organising (save that it is hereby declared for the avoidance of doubt that nothing herein shall prevent the Defendants from paying strike, lock-out or victimisation benefit pursuant to their respective rules) at or near the premises of the Claimant at [   ] demonstrations, and/or marches and/or picketing (1)

which involves the commission of any tortious act or acts (2), in particular but without prejudice to the generality of the foregoing, nuisance and/or obstruction of the highway, interference with the commercial contracts of the Claimants, intimidation and/or assault of the Claimants' employees or visitors, save and except as the Defendants may organize

(i) pickets, provided they do not exceed six in number (3) at each entrance to the main gate of [   ] for the purpose of peacefully obtaining or communicating information; (4) and

(ii) peaceful, disciplined and orderly marches [   ] save and except as the police may otherwise direct.(5)

(2) The Defendants shall as soon as practicable and in any event within seventy-two hours instruct members of their respective unions not to carry on any of the activities restrained by paragraph 1 above and shall inform the Press Association of such instruction.

Notes

(1) For the distinction see *News Group Newspapers Ltd v SOGAT 82 and others* [1986] IRLR 337 at para 120-5.

(2) This reflects the fact that picketing is not *per se* tortious (see Chapter 8).

(3) See *News Group Newspapers Ltd v SOGAT 82 and others* [1986] IRLR 337 at para 129; *Thomas v National Union of Mineworkers (South Wales Area)* [1986] Ch 20.

(4) This follows the wording of s 220 of the Trade Union and Labour Relations (Consolidation) Act 1992.

(5) See *News Group Newspapers Ltd v SOGAT 82 and others* [1986] IRLR 337.

G. Order Restraining Trespass on the Employer's Premises

Upon hearing Counsel for the Claimant and upon reading the witness statements made by [   ] on [   ]   **17.07**

AND upon the Claimants by its Counsel undertaking

(1) to abide by any Order the Court may make as to damages in case the Court shall hereafter be of opinion that the Defendants shall have sustained any by reason of this Order which the Claimant ought to pay and

(2) not to enforce these proceedings against any of the Defendants who may be lawfully on the premises

IT IS ORDERED that

(1) The Defendants be restrained forthwith from entering or remaining on the Claimant's premises at [   ] until further order save with the express consent in writing of the Claimant;

(2) the Claimants have leave to serve copies of the witness statement made in support of the Application herein without serving copies of the exhibits thereto;

(3) both parties have liberty to apply.

H. Order for Substituted Service of Injunction on Trade Union

[Title of action]

17.08   Upon hearing Counsel for the Claimant and upon reading the witness statement of [   ] on [   ] and the

IT IS ORDERED that service of a copy of the Order herein made on [   ] be made as to the Defendant by delivering a copy of the same to the premises by posting a copy of the same through the post box of the [name of trade union] at [address] and affixing the same on the door thereof [or to the office of the [   ] at [   ]]

AND THAT such service shall be good and sufficient service of the Order.

DATED [   ]

Notes

See Chapter 11 for details.

I. Penal Notice to be Inserted on Injunction Order

(a) If you [trade union] the within-named Defendant disobey this Order, **17.09**
you will be liable to process for execution (including by an order of
committal) for the purpose of compelling you to obey the same.

[Name of
solicitors]

(b) In the case of an order against a trade union when it may be sought to
take enforcement proceedings against a particular officer, the notice
should read:

If [trade union] by the time therein limited (or in the case of a restraining order: If [trade union] disobey this order) you [officer] will be liable
to process of execution for the purpose of compelling the said [trade
union] to obey the same.

J. Motion to Commit for Contempt and Sequestration in Respect of Breach of Order Made in Form D

IN THE HIGH COURT OF JUSTICE   **17.10**

QUEEN'S BENCH DIVISION

BETWEEN

[NEWSPAPER PUBLISHER]
                                                    Claimants

and

(1) [UNION]

(2) [BRANCH SECRETARY]

(3) [DEPUTY BRANCH SECRETARY]

                                                    Defendants

In the matter of an application on behalf of the Claimant for leave to issue a
writ of sequestration against the First Defendant the [union] and/or that
such order be made in relation to the [union] and/or the Second Defendant

[name the branch secretary] and/or the Third Defendant [name the Deputy Branch Secretary] as the Honourable Court shall deem fit for their respective contempts of this Honourable Court in disobeying an Order dated [   ] and made herein

TAKE NOTICE that the High Court of Justice Queen's Bench Division sitting at the Royal Courts of Justice, Strand, London WC2A 2LL will be moved at [   ] of the [   ] day of [   ] 2004 or so soon thereafter as Counsel can be heard by Counsel on behalf of the Claimant for orders that the Claimant be at liberty to issue a writ of sequestration directed to the Commissioners therein named to sequester all the real and personal property of the First Defendant, the [union] and/or that such order shall be made in relation to the [union] and/or the Second Defendant [name the branch secretary] and/or the Third Defendant [name the Deputy Branch Secretary] as the Honourable Court shall deem fit for their respective contempts of this Honourable Court in disobeying an Order dated [   ] and made herein in that

(1) The Defendants and each of them have failed forthwith or at all to withdraw any resolution, order, instruction, decision, direction or advice given and/or communicated whether directly or indirectly and/or by their employees, officers, agents or otherwise howsoever to employees of Waltham Offset Limited and Humberstone Setters Limited to the effect that the employees should do any act or acts in breach of their contracts of employment with those Companies in particular (but without prejudice to the generality of the foregoing) to withdraw their labour or to refuse to handle and/or typeset newspapers and/or magazines and/or other printed matter published and/or distributed by the Claimant;

(2) The Defendants and each of them have failed forthwith or at all to inform members of the First Defendant employed by the said Companies of the said withdrawal and cancellation;

(3) The Defendants and each of them have failed forthwith or at all to inform the Press Association or all relevant local newspapers of the said withdrawal and cancellation;

(4) The Defendants and each of them have failed forthwith or at all to direct that any such resolution, order, instruction, decision, direction or advice mentioned hereinbefore be disregarded;

(5) When asked by an employee of Humberstone Setters Limited, John Smith about the currency and status of the instructions to black newspapers published by the Claimant, the Second and Third Defendants on behalf of the First Defendant failed to indicate that the instructions had been withdrawn and cancelled;

NOTWITHSTANDING and in breach of the Order of the Hon Mr Justice [   ] dated [   ] and personally served on

(a) the First Defendant the [union] by [state means of service]
(b) the Second Defendant [name the Branch Secretary] by [   ]
(c) the Third Defendant [name the Deputy Branch Secretary] by [   ]
[set out the full terms of the order]

AND FOR AN ORDER that the costs of and incidental to this Application and of an order made herein be paid on an indemnity basis by the [union] and/or the Second Defendant [name the Branch Secretary] and/or the Third Defendant [name the Deputy Branch Secretary]

AND FURTHER TAKE NOTICE that the Claimant intends to read and use in support of this Application the witness statements of [   ] dated [   ] proving the contempts, copy of which witness statements and exhibits are served with this Notice of Motion

Dated [   ]

Messrs [name of solicitors]

To [name of Defendants]

K. Letter to Persons Occupying Employer's Premises

17.11   Dear Sir,

We are instructed by [   ].

You have already been required to vacate the premises you are occupying at [   ] and you have refused to do so notwithstanding that you have no right to remain on the premises.

Please note that [   ] will be issuing proceedings against you for an injunction to require you to leave the said premises and to restrain your re-entry thereto, and for damages. The application for an injunction against each and every one of you will be heard by a Judge sitting in Chambers at [   ] on [   ] at the Law Courts, Strand, London. If you wish to oppose such application you should and are entitled to attend the hearing.

This letter will be produced at the Court as evidence that you have notice of said application having regard to.

Yours faithfully,

[   ]

L. Draft Dismissal Letter

17.12   Dear Sir/Madam,

The industrial action in which you have participated today has disrupted production of the Company's [   ].

By participating in that industrial action you have been and are in repudiatory breach of your contract of employment. The Company accepts your breach as terminating your employment with immediate effect. It is also accepting breaches of contract by other employees, who have also been and are participating in the industrial action, as terminating their employment.

Your employment having ended, your Form P45 and any money due to you will follow shortly.

Yours faithfully,

[   ]

18

TRADE UNION RECOGNITION: THE APPLICATION

A. Introduction

In this and the following chapters we consider the recognition of unions for **18.01** collective bargaining purposes and in particular the statutory scheme for compulsory recognition of trade unions contained within the Trade Union and Labour Relations (Consolidation) Act 1992, TULR(C)A, Schedule A1. That schedule was introduced by the Employment Relations Act 1999 and came into effect on 6 June 2000. In February 2003 the Government published its review of the recognition and derecognition procedures under the Act in accordance with a commitment it first made in its White Paper *Fairness at Work*. In the brief summary the review stated that:

> The review has found that the Act is working well. It therefore concludes that there is no case for making wholesale changes to the legislation. However, the review has identified some areas where there are problems and anomalies in the way the Act works. In many of these areas, the review puts forward firm proposals for change. On other issues, the review identifies a case for change but the Government wishes to reflect further before finalising its proposals.

The review invited further submissions by May 2003. The TUC submitted its response to the review, having made submissions as part of the review process, advocating various changes in the statutory scheme. Where appropriate in the following chapters we highlight the proposals for change and the issues which have prompted this debate. Before addressing the statutory scheme it is firstly necessary to consider some fundamental principles.

B. Recognition

18.02   Recognition is the status of an independent trade union having a negotiating voice with the employers on behalf of its members for the purposes of collective bargaining. This goes beyond merely being informed or consulted about decisions. The core statutory definition of recognition is to be found in TULR(C)A, s 178:

> **178 Collective agreements and collective bargaining**
> (1) In this Act 'collective agreement' means any agreement or arrangement made by or on behalf of one or more trade unions and one or more employers or employers' associations and relating to one or more of the matters specified below; and 'collective bargaining' means negotiations relating to or connected with one or more of those matters.
> (2) The matters referred to above are—
>   (a) terms and conditions of employment, or the physical conditions in which any workers are required to work;
>   (b) engagement or non-engagement, or termination or suspension of employment or the duties of employment, of one or more workers;
>   (c) allocation of work or the duties of employment between workers or groups of workers;
>   (d) matters of discipline;
>   (e) a worker's membership or non-membership of a trade union;
>   (f) facilities for officials of trade unions; and
>   (g) machinery for negotiation or consultation, and other procedures, relating to any of the above matters, including the recognition by employers or employers' associations of the right of a trade union to represent workers in such negotiation or consultation or in the carrying out of such procedures.
> (3) In this Act 'recognition', in relation to a trade union, means the recognition of the union by an employer, or two or more associated employers, to any extent, for the purpose of collective bargaining; and 'recognized' and other related expressions shall be construed accordingly.

These are broad definitions of recognition as it may in practice take many forms. An employer may recognize a union only for specific purposes or only upon certain issues. For example a union may be recognized only for the purposes of the negotiation of disciplinary procedures. Full recognition of a union would include negotiation of all terms and conditions including remuneration. Unions may be recognized at different levels within an organization. They may for example be recognized at a national level for the purpose of the negotiation of terms and conditions across the entire workforce of an employer. A union may, however, be recognized only at a local level for the purpose of negotiation of specific issues relating to a particular site.

18.03

Whatever the scope of the recognition it is important to appreciate the limitations of recognition. Whilst recognition will carry with it an obligation to listen to the union on the issues for which they are recognized there is no compulsion on the employer to accept what is said by the union. It takes two willing parties to reach an agreement. Although it may thus appear to be something which imposes no (or relatively little) limitation on management prerogative, there is in some industries and regions great resistance to union recognition and the very idea is treated as an anathema. Putting aside political reasons why this may be so, recognition does carry with it certain practical consequences in industrial terms which may present a disincentive to recognition.

18.04

As a consequence of recognition within the meaning of s 178(3) the union will also enjoy the following rights under employment legislation:

18.05

(1) A right to the disclosure of information from the employer for the purpose of the collective bargaining for which it is recognized: TULR(C)A, s 181;

(2) A right to be consulted on collective redundancies: TULR(C)A, s 188;

(3) A right to information and consultation in connection with the transfer of undertakings: Transfer of Undertakings (Protection of Employment) Regulations 1981;

(4) A right for its officials to take time off work to carry out trade union duties: TULR(C)A, s 168;

(5) A right for members of the union to take time off work to take part in certain trade union activities: TULR(C)A, s 170;

(6) A right for its learning representative to take time off for the purpose of the carrying on of its duties towards members of the union: TULR(C)A, s 168A;

(7) A right to information and consultation on occupational pension schemes: Pensions Schemes Act 1993, s 11(5) and the regulations created thereunder;

(8) A right to information and consultation with its appointed safety representatives on health and safety at work: Safety Representatives and Safety Committees Regulations 1977;

(9) A right to initiate negotiations for the establishment of a European Works Council: Transnational Information and Consultation of Employees Regulations 1999.

18.06   The above rights arise simply by reason of recognition to any degree within the definition of s 178. This is the case whether that recognition arises voluntarily or as a consequence of the statutory procedure.

There is one further right which arises only in circumstances where a union has been recognized under the statutory scheme set out in Schedule 1A and the method for collective bargaining has been specified by the Central Arbitration Committee (CAC). This is a right to be consulted about training for the workers in the bargaining unit for which the union has been recognized: TULR(C)A, s 70B.

C. Voluntary Recognition

18.07   Outside the statutory recognition process the corner stone of union recognition remains voluntary recognition, that is the employer voluntarily agreeing to recognize a union for collective bargaining purposes. Before the scheme for statutory recognition was implemented in 2000 trade unions had been widely recognized in many industries for the purposes of negotiation. This voluntary recognition may arise from a formal agreement recognizing the union, a recognition agreement, or may be implied from the employer's conduct in their dealings with the union: *National Union of Gold, Silver and Allied Trades v Albury Bros Ltd* [1978] IRLR 504; [1979] ICR 84, CA. The essence of the voluntary form of recognition is that the employer may withdraw recognition at any time without incumbrance or penalty. Even if there is a recognition agreement which stipulates a notice period for the withdrawal of recognition or provides for a fixed period for recognition there will be, unless the agreement was expressly stated to be intended to create a legally binding agreement, no actionable consequences of the employer's unilateral withdrawal. This is a consequence of the long standing presumption that collective agreements are not intended by the parties to be legally enforceable: TULR(C)A, s 179. There may of course be practical industrial consequences flowing from the rupture to the employer's relationship with the union; disputes as to recognition are trade disputes so the union may contemplate industrial action or it may take a more militant stance to the conduct of disputes over pay and conditions.

The statutory scheme, as we will see, has introduced a different status of **18.08** recognition which an employer cannot unilaterally terminate. This is true both where the employer has been required to recognize the union consequent upon the operation of the schedule, or there has been a voluntary recognition during the process of the implementation of compulsory recognition under the scheme. The latter has been described as semi-voluntary recognition because whilst it reflects an agreement made voluntarily between the parties, restrictions apply to it under the schedule because it has been reached as a consequence of a request for recognition initiated under the schedule.

The statutory scheme might at first be thought to remove the role of volun- **18.09** tary recognition, but experience in practice appears to be different. Faced with a union which is actively canvassing members and is positioning itself for an application for compulsory recognition, voluntary recognition has its attractions for the employer especially if the employer thinks that there is a union around which may be more compliant than that which is presently recruiting its employees. In the case of the recruiting union itself, recognizing it will avoid the statutory process and leave the employer with a recognition agreement which may be terminated at will if commercial considerations dictate this course later. If another union is recognized, as we will see, then even though that recognition is voluntary it will prevent the recruiting union from seeking compulsory recognition. Thus the employer may be able to use voluntary recognition of a union it could bear dealing with so as to avoid being compelled to recognize a union it could not.

These factors, and the potential inevitability of recognition being imposed by **18.10** the CAC in some cases, have greatly stimulated voluntary agreements since the statutory arrangements came into force. Thus, one of the perhaps surprising consequences of the introduction of the statutory scheme for compulsory recognition is an increase in the number of voluntary recognition agreements.

A record of the applications to and decisions of the CAC, which operates the statutory scheme, can be found at www.cac.org.uk. A consideration of these decisions in fact reveals a substantial number of applications being withdrawn during the process. Up to 31 December 2002 the CAC had received 236 applications for recognition. Of these only 69 had completed the process to a decision of the CAC with unions being recognized in 52 cases. When the application is withdrawn the parties are not required to notify the CAC of the reasons for the withdrawal and consequently it is not possible accurately to determine the number of cases in which the withdrawal is consequent upon the parties having reached a voluntary recognition agreement. This may be a fruitful area for further research. The Government's review reported that the CAC was only aware of 40 voluntary agreements being reached. In its Annual Report for 2002/2003 the CAC itself reported that the level of applications withdrawn as a consequence of a voluntary agreement continued to be approximately 20 per cent of the submitted applications. The Government's review concluded, however, that the evidence supported the conclusion that the number of voluntary agreements being reached was greater. Evidence to the review from ACAS, which has a role in conciliating between the parties before an application is made to the CAC, supported this view. In the period to 31 December 2002, ACAS was asked to conciliate in 99 cases. Conciliation took place in 85 of these cases, leading to recognition in 55 of them. The TUC's own surveys have recorded 1,000 new instances of voluntary recognition since 1998 with three times as many agreements reached in 2000/1 as in 1999/2000.

The CAC

18.11   The Central Arbitration Committee (CAC) is a permanent independent body with statutory powers whose main (but not sole) function is to adjudicate on applications relating to the statutory recognition and de-recognition of trade unions for collective bargaining purposes, where such recognition or de-recognition cannot be agreed voluntarily.

18.12   The present Chairman of the CAC is Sir Michael Burton, a High Court Judge who is also President of the Employment Appeal Tribunal. The Committee consists of 10 Deputy Chairmen, 16 members experienced as representatives of employers and 16 members experienced as representatives of workers. The Committee sits as a panel of three, the Chairman or Deputy Chairman and two members, one with experience as a representative of employers and the other as a representative of workers. Many of the Deputy Chairmen are experienced industrial relations and legal academics.

When sitting as a panel to make determinations it may convene an oral hearing and take evidence. If it does so, the procedure to be adopted is a matter for the Chairman, typically a Deputy Chairman. Written submissions and witness statements will be used and whilst the evidence is not taken on oath there is an opportunity for cross-examination of witnesses through the Chairman. The decision-making process operates within a tightly defined timetable although there is provision for the CAC to extend time. The decisions of the CAC are decisions on each particular application and they are not binding upon another CAC panel in another case. Decisions of the CAC are referred to in the course of applications for guidance as to the manner in which issues have been resolved. There is no right of appeal against the decisions of the CAC. The only redress therefore is an application for judicial review of the CAC's decisions.

18.13 As noted above the CAC has a web site at www.cac.gov.uk. This is a particularly valuable resource. A full list of the members of the committee can be found at the site as well as copies of its annual review. Application forms for recognition and a guide to the recognition process can be downloaded from the site. In addition there is a database of past decisions of the CAC and a record of pending applications. All the decisions of the CAC which are referred to in the following chapters can be found on this site.

D. Statutory Recognition

18.14 The core effect of statutory recognition is that the employer must recognize the union as a bargaining agent for a specified group of workers in respect of pay, hours and holidays: TULR(C)A, Sch 1A, para 3(3). (All the subsequent references to paragraph numbers are references to the paragraphs of that Schedule.) Paragraph 3(3) then identifies the limit of the negotiating scope of a statutory recognition. The parties may agree recognition for other purposes (para 3(4)) but statutory recognition embraces these minimum issues: pay, hours and holidays.

18.15 Pay has been widely interpreted by the CAC in this context to include pension contributions where those were regular pension contributions made through the pay roll: *UNIFI v Bank of Nigeria* [2001] IRLR 712. The union had been recognized under the statutory procedure and had been able to agree a method of collective bargaining with the employer with the exception of one issue which was whether it could include pensions within collective bargaining as to pay. In the absence of a definition under the schedule, the CAC determined the issue and concluded that pay should not be interpreted narrowly. In the context then of what was a pension scheme with defined employer contributions the CAC concluded that collective bargaining as to pay embraced all matters relating to the level and amounts of the employer's contribution. An artificial line was therefore drawn as to the scope of the bargaining in that the CAC concluded that pay did not include the right to bargain as to the administration or management of the pension scheme. In this decision, the CAC did not reflect the Parliamentary intention of introducing only a limited number of topics for statutory recognition.

As with other decisions of the CAC it is open for it to come to a different conclusion in another case but as a consequence of the *Bank of Nigeria* case the scope of bargaining as to pay was considered at some length in the Government's review. The review's conclusion was that as most voluntary recognition agreements do not include collective bargaining as to pensions it was not appropriate for it to be included in the core statutory scheme as this would risk the statutory recognition scheme being wider than most voluntary arrangements. The review's proposal therefore is that the schedule should be clarified so that pay does not include collective bargaining as to pensions. The review however outlined the possibility of a change in this underlying position, possibly as a consequence of the Government's future proposals for pensions or implementation of the EU Directive on Information and Consultation. To recognize the possibility of future change in recognition agreements, the review further proposed that there would be a power for the Secretary of State to add pensions to the list of core issues for collective bargaining when there was evidence that it was typical practice for pensions to be included in recognition agreements as a bargaining topic. Future CAC panels may be reluctant to take the bold interpretation taken in the *Bank of Nigeria* case.

Initiation of the statutory scheme

18.16 The statutory scheme is initiated by a request for recognition. This will usually be preceded by correspondence from the union asking for voluntary recognition by the employer. The initiation of the scheme is, however, itself an important step. It triggers the strict timetable under the schedule. This further has consequences for the possible creation of semi-voluntary agreements. These may only be reached once the statutory scheme has been commenced. It is therefore important for all parties to be clear as to when the scheme has been initiated.

There is no prescribed form for a request for recognition. It may consist of   **18.17** nothing more formal than a letter although usually unions will use the CAC standard application form. In order to be effective as a request for recognition, however, certain requirements under the schedule must be complied with.

- The request must be in writing (para 8(a)).
- It must identify the union or unions (para 8(b)). It should be noted that in certain circumstances (considered in greater detail below) joint applications by unions may be made. In such circumstances wherever there is reference to the union this, in the case of a multi-union application, should be read as including all unions making the application.
- It must identify the bargaining unit proposed by the union, and this is a critical issue which will be examined in detail below (para 8(b)).
- The request must be received by the employer. It may then be necessary for the union to be able to prove delivery of the request for example by the provision of a recorded delivery receipt. Indeed where the workforce is fluctuating in size it may additionally be critical to determine when precisely the request was received by the employer in considering the application of the small employer exemption referred to below. The employer is defined to be the employer of workers constituting the bargaining unit concerned. The definition of employer has not proved to be without difficulty and this will be considered in greater detail below. The union must identify the correct employer in order to make the request. It is the identity which matters, so consequently an error as to the correct title of the employer will not in itself invalidate the request. Where an employer had changed its name, the applications and the request having been made to its previous name, the application was allowed to proceed: *GPMU v DSR Ltd* (TUR1/101/01).
- The union making the request (or in certain circumstances considered below where a joint request may be made, each of the unions making the request) must have a certificate under TULR(C)A, s 6 that it is an independent union (para 6).

The small employer exemption

18.18 The request is not valid unless the employer, taken with any associated employers, employs at least 21 workers (para 7). Submissions were made to the Government as part of its review that the number of workers should be changed. The unions were keen to see the exemption removed or reduced because of the number of workers employed by small employers who fell outside the scope of the statutory scheme. The review's conclusion was, however, that there should be no change in this provision. There are two aspects to this exclusion, the meaning of worker in the context and how that number is calculated.

The meaning of 'worker'

18.19 'Worker' is defined by TULR(C)A, s 296(1) to mean an individual who works, or normally works or seeks to work—

> (a) under a contract of employment, or
> (b) under any other contract whereby he undertakes to do or perform person-ally any work or services for another party to the contract who is not a professional client of his, or
> (c) in employment under or for the purposes of a government department (otherwise than as a member of the naval, military or air forces of the Crown) in so far as such employment does not fall within paragraph (a) or (b) above.

18.20 Thus individuals who are not within the normal definition of employees are included, for example independent contractors. There are difficult factual and legal issues to be determined here under subsection (b) in the context of any particular group of individuals as to whether they fall within the scope of the definition or not. Subsection (b) can be seen to have four elements. First that the individual must work or seek work under a contract. Secondly the indi-vidual undertakes by the contract to do or perform personally any work or services for another party to the contract. A similar definition of worker under the Working Time Regulations 1998 has led to contracts being drafted so as to seek to avoid obligations as to personal service for example by providing the individual with the ability to provide a substitute to perform the work or services; see by way of example *Byrne Bros (Formwork) Ltd v Baird* [2002] IRLR 96. The third element arises if the preceding requirements are met in that the individual will not be a worker if he is undertaking to do or perform the work or services for a professional client of his.

The schedule provides no definition of a profession. There are clearly individuals who are excluded, so that for example a contract with your dentist is certainly one which you anticipate will be performed personally; dentists are not workers because of their professional standing. The edges of the definition are however less clear. BECTU made an application for recognition to the BBC in respect of a bargaining unit containing wildlife camera people who worked for the BBC Natural History Unit. An issue arose then as to whether the relationship between the camera people, who were not employees of the BBC, and the BBC was that of professional and client. The CAC concluded that the exception for professionals should be narrowly construed and without seeking to advance a definition considered that some form of regulation of a professional's field of activity by a body covering those engaged or seeking to be engaged in that activity is required. In the case then of the camera persons the absence of such a regulatory authority meant that they were not providing their services as professionals.

The BBC sought judicial review of the CAC's decision. The High Court held that the CAC had erred in law in their approach to the issue of professional status, *R (on the Application of the BBC) v Central Arbitration Committee* [2003] IRLR 460. The imposition of the requirement that there be a regulatory body was found to be an error of law. The general question of whether the individuals were engaged in a profession was however one of fact for the CAC having considered all the features which it considered relevant. One factor would be the exercise of special skill or the possession of special qualifications or training. The existence of a regulatory body may itself be a powerful indicator pointing to the exercise of a profession and equally its absence may be significant in concluding that this of itself will not be determinative. There will remain then, in the absence of any further definition, an area where the question is one of degree. On remission, a differently constituted CAC found that the camera persons were workers by looking at all the facts, treating none as decisive.

If there is no contract for service or otherwise, then the individuals will not **18.21** be workers. Thus in *GPMU and Keely Print* (TUR1/98/01) the application turned on whether directors of the company were workers and, there being no evidence of their working under a contract of service, it was held that they were not.

18.22　The fourth condition relates to the relationship with the employer who is the subject of the recognition application. There the requirement is that the putative worker works under or seeks to work under a contract with the employer. 'Seeks to work' carries with it the implication that an individual may be a worker for the purposes of the section even though no contract is in place at the point of the application for recognition in that they may then be seeking to work under a contract rather than working under one. This issue arose too in the *BBC* case. The Wildlife unit maintained a 'contact list' of camera people not all of whom were under contract at any one point in time. It was contended by the union that the individuals on the list were potentially part of the bargaining unit as workers since they were seeking to work. The CAC found on the evidence that as everyone on the contacts list wanted to be offered work, they were 'seeking to work' under contracts which otherwise met the conditions. This was not diminished by the fact that other individuals not on the 'contact list' were also offered work.

This finding was also the subject of challenge by the BBC in the High Court on the alternative basis that it was necessary to consider more closely the position of putative workers in that the circumstances of some individuals within the group may be different. There may be some who remained on the contacts list who were no longer seeking work. An argument was also advanced that the consideration of the question of professional status required a similar closer analysis of the position of subsets within the putative group of workers. Thus, when considering qualifications, some may have qualifications and experience which others did not. Moses J on the judicial review held that the CAC was entitled to look at the definition as it applied to the group of individuals as a whole and there was no requirement to look at every member of the group. Similarly in the context of professional status it is the position of the proposed group which must be considered and not the position of individuals. It is suggested that this decision takes the simplification of the question for the CAC too far and adopts too much of a 'broad brush' approach to the question. While it is clearly correct that in most cases it would be impracticable to embark upon a consideration of the circumstances of each individual, the need to consider the number of workers and to identify them may require a more detailed consideration than that of the status of the group as a group. The definition of the bargaining unit proposed by the union may embrace a group of individuals which is so eclectic that the position of subsets within that group is so markedly different that application of the definition to those subsets has to be considered. The way in which this will be applied on a case by case basis remains to be seen.

The status of worker is not dependent upon the hours or permanence of the **18.23** contract under which the individual worked. Consequently part-time workers and temporary workers, working at or during the relevant period of calculation, will be counted as workers for the purpose of the calculation although whether they are appropriate members of a bargaining unit is another issue.

The width of the definition of worker may incidentally cause problems for **18.24** the union. The union may have difficulty with establishing the necessary membership of the bargaining unit, or fear that if a ballot eventually takes place on the question of recognition, the union recognition may be refused by the wider constituency. As the union defines the bargaining unit it proposes to the employer, the definition may embrace the status of the individuals as part of that bargaining unit. Thus in *RMT and ISS Transport Division* (TUR1/135/01) 21 November 2001 the bargaining unit proposed by the RMT related to those 'employed' by the employer within certain roles. Similarly in *NUJ and Gloucestershire Newspapers Ltd* (TUR1/66/01, 16 July 2001) the union defined the bargaining unit by reference to journalists employed by the employer thus producing a bargaining unit which did not include the wider group of freelance journalists used by the newspapers who would have been workers. It will still be necessary for the CAC to consider subsequently, if the application is accepted, if this is an appropriate bargaining unit.

When the condition must be fulfilled

Having identified the meaning of worker the second question is when the **18.25** calculation of the number of workers is determined. There are two methods of determining this question. First whether there are at least 21 workers on the day the employer receives the request, and hence the possible need for the union to be able specifically to show the date of receipt. Secondly, if that condition is not satisfied, whether there was an average of 21 workers in the 13 weeks ending with the day on which the request was made. The schedule stipulates the formula for the calculation of that average (para 7(2)).

In calculating the number of workers, certain workers will be disregarded. These are workers employed by an associated company incorporated outside Great Britain unless the worker was ordinarily working in Great Britain at the date of the request, in the case of calculation based upon the number of workers on that date (para 7(3)). In the case of the average number of workers over the 13-week period, the worker is disregarded, save for those weeks where in whole or in part he ordinarily worked in Great Britain (para 7(4)). It should be noted that these exclusions only apply to associated employers incorporated outside Great Britain. Thus the worker, even though he works wholly outside Great Britain, will be included where he works for the employer or an associated employer incorporated in Great Britain. Special rules are provided for those employed on merchant ships (para 7(6)).

The employer

18.26 The employer for the purpose of the calculation only includes any associated employer. An associated employer is a company of which the other (directly or indirectly) has control or both are companies of which a third person (directly or indirectly) has control: TULR(C)A, s 297. If an application is made in respect of A Ltd, with only 15 employees, but A is a wholly owned subsidiary of A Group Ltd which additionally owns two other subsidiaries the application will be valid if the total number of employees including A Group and all the subsidiaries is 21 or more.

It is of note that 'employer' is used in the singular throughout the schedule and the only occasion on which the definition of associated employer is adopted is under para 7. This raises an issue where the proposed bargaining unit embraces workers of more than one employer. This arose in *Graphical Paper and Media Union v Derry Print Ltd and John Brown Printers* [2002] IRLR 380. The GPMU presented two separate applications to the CAC in respect of two Nottingham print companies. The proposed bargaining units were production workers employed by the companies at a particular site. The companies argued that they were not associated companies and that each had less than 21 employees. The CAC panel found that the two companies had a common shareholder who held more than 50 per cent of the shares in each company. The CAC concluded that they were associated employers and together they had more than 21 workers so that the small employer exemption did not apply. The CAC had thus far considered the applications as separate applications but then proceeded to consider whether the proposed bargaining unit could include more than one employer. (As a procedural side note the CAC panel having established that none of the parties were intending to be legally represented instructed one of the authors as Counsel on its own behalf to attend the hearing.) The CAC's conclusion was that the schedule was not intended to embrace a single application proposing a bargaining unit embracing more than one employer. In part this view recognized the problems created in the operation of the schedule where none of the procedures, such as de-recognition, are apt for multi-employer situations. This conclusion, which it is suggested is correct, does carry with it the risk that employers would organize their business by the use of subsidiary companies so as to fragment any appropriate bargaining unit across separate employers.

The CAC proceeded in the *Derry Print* case to consider whether in excep- **18.27** tional cases two employers, or more, could be considered to be a 'single employer' for the purposes of the application. The CAC panel concluded that it could. The panel had heard submissions about the limited occasions in which the 'corporate veil' might be lifted but the panel's approach was not to lift the corporate veil as such but rather to fuse the independent corporate identity of the separate employers and treat them as a single identity. The panel concluded that: 'In our view, however, outside the area of corporate liability, it is permissible to view two companies as one in reality if there is overwhelming evidence that, in respect of all the elements of the area to which the relevant law applies, they are actually one.'

On the facts of the case in *Derry Print*, the CAC panel concluded that the reality of the situation was that the controlling shareholder was the employer employing what was, in reality, a unified workforce which had only as a legal technicality been assigned to different companies. The decision does however create the problems which the CAC panel recognized for the subsequent procedures, such a de-recognition, particularly if there has been some change in the factual unity over the passage of time. Further factual issues are created by the decision as to when a factual situation exists in which two legal entities can be considered to be a single employer. This will be worked out on a case by case basis. In *GMB and Northbourne* (TUR1/183/02) 20 June 2002 for example the GMB's proposed bargaining unit included workers who were employed by a limited company and by a partnership. The partners were however the controlling shareholders of the limited company. The union sought to argue a case based upon the claimed integration of the businesses with the consequence that they were in reality a single entity. Having considered this evidence, the CAC panel concluded that there was insufficient evidence to establish this. The decision serves well to illustrate the factual issues which the decision in the *Derry Print* case opens.

18.28   The Government's review has invited submissions on the question of whether the procedure should be amended so that it may expressly deal with multi-employer bargaining units where those are associated employers and how that practically could be achieved. It is to be hoped that the product of that consultation is a definition which affords greater clarity than the approach in the *Derry Print* case. It is of course perfectly possible for the parties to agree to a voluntary recognition agreement which extends across more than one employer.

Union or unions

18.29   An application may be jointly made by two unions. The unions may even change their identity in the process. In *Amicus & GMB v Alan Worswick* (TUR1/57/02) 23 January 2002 the initial application was jointly made by AEEU and GMB. During the progress of the application, AEEU merged with MSF and became Amicus. The application was therefore amended. The change of identity here was not merely a change of name or an occasion when members were transferred on the merger of one union into another but the creation of a new union. A rather more focused consideration of the consequences of the merger of AEEU and MSF was undertaken by the CAC panel in *MSF and Unipart* (TUR1/94/01) 7 February 2002. Here the employer argued, at the stage of consideration of whether a ballot should take place, that the consequence of the merger was that MSF had ceased to exist and that the application could not be continued. The CAC panel concluded that this treated the union as a distinct economic entity rather than, what it was, a voluntary association of its members. The panel conclusion was that the merger was not fatal to the application. Other panels in other applications by these unions at the time of merger appear to have allowed the applications to proceed, such as *Amicus v GE Caledonian Ltd* (TUR1/120/1) 5 April 2002 and *Amicus v Britton Gelplas Ltd* (TUR1/17/02) 22 April 2002.

18.30   There is however force in the employer's argument and it is one which has not been tested by judicial review. Whilst not a legal entity in the nature of the company it is a requirement for recognition that it is an independent trade union holding the appropriate certificate of independence. That certificate in the name of the union will be cancelled if it merges or ceases to exist. In that sense, a new entity does come into existence, albeit that it is a new voluntary association of members, and it can thus be argued that the application should not continue. This of itself may not be a fundamental problem as, consistent with that approach, the new union ought not to be blocked from a new application and the practical consequence of an employer succeeding in the argument that the union has ceased to exist is that the application for recognition will merely be delayed while the union makes a new request for recognition. It may be that until this has been conclusively resolved the safest course is for a new application to be brought. This is because it is arguable that if it had been an error of law for the CAC to allow the applications to proceed in the Amicus example and statutory recognition was apparently achieved this would be a recognition which was not effective in law and did not enjoy the protections afforded by the schedule.

The Government's review has considered this issue and it is proposed that the schedule will be changed to deal with this type of situation to allow the original application to proceed. **18.31**

A joint application by two or more unions is treated as a single application **18.32** but there are specific requirements which must be complied with in such a case. As part of the application the unions must seek to satisfy the CAC that the unions are able to cooperate in a manner which is likely to secure stable and effective collective bargaining arrangements (para 37(2)(a)). Secondly the unions must show that they are prepared, if the employer requests this, to enter an arrangement where they negotiate together (para 37(2)(b)). The first joint application made was withdrawn before a decision on admissibility (*Amicus & GMB v Alan Worswick* (TUR1/57/02) 23 January 2002). The CAC panel concluded that the requirements of para 37(2) were met, although the employer does not appear to have contested this point. As these were unions in the process of merging, this may not be surprising. In the subsequent application, *ISTC and Amicus v Polypipe Buildings Products Limited* (TUR1/278/03) 26 August 2003 the CAC panel found the requirements of para 37(2) were met. The employer unsuccessfully argued that a history of previous competing applications showed that the unions would not cooperate. The unions, however, provided several examples of where they had already cooperated, both nationally and locally, and stated clearly that they would work together at a single table. The CAC accepted this evidence as showing that the requirements were met. An agreement between the unions agreeing the method by which they will cooperate and for the creation of a single negotiating voice and a mechanism for achieving this would appear to be likely to be sufficient material upon which to satisfy the schedule's requirements.

19

TRADE UNION RECOGNITION: THE BARGAINING UNIT

A. The Bargaining Unit

The bargaining unit is a central concept in the scheme of statutory recogni- **19.01**
tion and is usually the most contentious in practice. It is the grouping of
workers for whom the union seeks to be recognized for the purpose of collective bargaining. The bargaining unit requiring a definition which enables the
workers within the proposed bargaining unit to be identified in a clear and
workable way. By way of example this could be workers in a geographical
region or by reference to grades or job roles. At this stage the union is proposing the bargaining unit for which it wishes to bargain. The proposed bargaining unit must be defined in the request for recognition. The definition needs
only sufficient precision for the employer to be able clearly to recognize the
bargaining unit and which workers fall within it. Equally, it needs to be one

319

which the CAC can apply in considering whether the statutory tests for a valid application (ie the 10 per cent test) are met.

19.02   The question of the bargaining unit has proved to be the subject of a number of contested applications before the CAC. In the course of the statutory scheme the CAC has to decide on whether the bargaining unit proposed by the union is appropriate, if it has not been possible to reach agreement between the parties as to the bargaining unit. The number of disputes as to the composition of the bargaining unit usually reflects an underlying tactical agenda of the parties to the application. As we will see it becomes a critical issue as the application progresses for the union either to command a majority of members or a majority of support for recognition in the bargaining unit. Consequently the union ought practically to have regard to the formulation of the bargaining unit it proposes in the light of its membership or support. While a national bargaining unit embracing all the hourly paid staff of an employer may appear superficially attractive to a union if its membership nationally is small, this may prove to be a difficult unit upon which to succeed in a ballot.

19.03   The selection of a narrower unit may however compel recognition and force an employer to recognize the unit which may then provide the springboard for a wider recruitment of members and the subsequent enlargement of the scope of its statutory recognition. This is particularly the case if the employer has excluded the unions from the workplace and it is necessary to get a toehold upon which to recruit membership. For the employer reluctant to recognize a union the reverse position of course applies. An employer in the circumstances explained would wish for the process to be focused upon a larger bargaining unit where the prospects of defeating the application are enhanced. The employer would then wish to argue that the bargaining unit proposed by the union is not appropriate. This underlying agenda has led to the large number of decisions of the CAC on this issue. Any earlier decisions of the CAC on the composition of the bargaining unit must, however, now be considered in the light of the decision of the Court of Appeal in *R (On the application of Kwik-Fit Ltd) v CAC* [2002] ICR 1212. We will consider this decision in detail on the issue of the determination of the bargaining unit by the CAC at the appropriate stage of the process. The facts of the *Kwik-Fit* decision do however provide a useful practical example of the issue of the bargaining unit at work at the stage of the formulation of the request for recognition. Kwik-Fit GB is a company operating throughout Great Britain.

It specializes in the replacement of tyres, brakes and exhausts on cars. At the time of the decision the company operated some 646 centres in Great Britain, of which 110 were located in London (ie within the M25 boundary). The TGWU had been for some two years actively seeking to organize and recruit Kwik-Fit employees in the London area. It had on a number of occasions represented employees in disciplinary and grievance procedures in that region. We pause to note that the representation at grievance and disciplinary procedures consequent upon the rights granted to employees by the Employment Rights Act 1999 is a common method of advancing the cause of union membership within an unfriendly, if not openly hostile, employer. The TGWU made a request for recognition by Kwik-Fit in relation to the company's London employees, who were organized into two divisions.

The London employees of Kwik-Fit were advanced as the bargaining unit for which the union wished to be recognized. The practical working definition was that of the employer's workers within the two London divisions. It is possible to divine in this that the union's thinking would have been that, bearing in mind the active recruitment of members within that area, this bargaining unit secured the necessary majorities in support of recognition. The reverse strategy may have been apparent to Kwik-Fit and it sought to argue before the CAC that this was not an appropriate bargaining unit and that the appropriate unit was a national one. We will return to the *Kwik-Fit* decision below on the issue of how the CAC determines this issue. For present purposes it is important simply to recognize that the formulation of the request for recognition and in particular the formulation of the bargaining unit proposed is a critical tactical stage in the union's strategy in seeking recognition.

B. The Employer's Response to the Request for Recognition

On receipt of a request the employer has a period of 10 working days, start- **19.04** ing on the day after that on which it received the request (para 10(6)), to consider its response to the request. The definition of working days which is used here is that which is used throughout the schedule and means weekdays, other than bank holidays, Christmas day and Good Friday (para 172).

Once the employer has received the request there are four possible positions **19.05** it may take. Firstly it may agree to recognize the union for the bargaining unit proposed. That is the end of the process and there is voluntary recognition, although this is strictly described as a semi-voluntary recognition with the consequences considered further below. The second position is that the employer may inform the union within that 10-day period that it does not agree to the request. If it does so, the union may then apply to the CAC (para 11(2)(a)) for a determination. The third option is that the employer may in the 10-day period refuse the request but indicate a willingness to negotiate with the union about the appropriate bargaining unit. If it does so a second time period arises which is 20 working days starting with the day after that on which the first period ends or such longer period as the parties may from time to time agree (para 10(7)). In this period the parties may request ACAS to assist them in conducting their negotiations. As set out above ACAS has been successful in conciliating complete or partial agreement in a high proportion of the cases in which it has been asked to act for this purpose. Even the most reluctant employer is then likely to indicate a willingness to negotiate if only to delay the application. If the negotiations fail to reach agreement over that second period the union may again apply to the CAC (para 12(1)). The fourth option is inaction, so that the employer neither communicates acceptance nor refusal of the request. In these circumstances the union may apply to the CAC (para 11(1)).

C. The Union's Application to the CAC

19.06   Assuming that no agreement has been reached it falls to the union to consider the next step, whether to make the application for recognition to the CAC or not. This is not, or ought not to be, an automatic step. As we will see the consequences of the refusal of an application, once it has been accepted, for the union are significant because it blocks out a further application in respect of the same or substantially the same bargaining unit for a period of three years. If legitimate issues have been raised by the employer as to the appropriateness of the bargaining unit these should be considered at this point. It should be noted that the employer does not strictly have to put forward an alternative bargaining unit to that proposed by the union but most will do so and give reasons at this stage. There is the risk that the CAC may determine a modified bargaining unit in the light of the objections with consequent problems for establishing the necessary membership and majority within that bargaining unit. The union can at this stage re-formulate its bargaining unit and simply make a new request for recognition in respect of the modified bargaining unit with adverse consequences.

It should be noted that there is a further intermediate step before the union is committed to an application and the consequences of failure. This arises because the CAC has to decide whether to accept the application and before it is accepted the union may withdraw the application and make a fresh request without a three-year waiting period. If the application is accepted the CAC may have to decide two questions:

(1) whether the proposed bargaining unit is appropriate or some other bargaining unit is appropriate; and
(2) whether the union (or unions in the case of a joint application) has the support of a majority of the workers constituting the appropriate bargaining unit.

It is possible that the parties have agreed that appropriate bargaining unit, in which case the first question does not arise, but the employer may not accept that the union commands majority support in that unit. In these circumstances the union may apply for that question alone to be determined (para 12(3)). The above analysis has assumed that the union is willing to negotiate at the employer's behest. If, however, the union rejects the employer's proposal that ACAS be requested to assist negotiations or fails to respond to that proposal within 10 working days of its being made, the union is unable to apply to the CAC (para 12(5)). This appears to bar proceeding upon that request. It would not appear to prevent the union from making a new request for recognition, although the time limits would apply from that date and the employer could once again propose that ACAS be invited to assist.

The form of the application to the CAC

The union is not under a time constraint as to when it makes the application to the CAC. This is not surprising as it is always open to it at this stage to initiate the process again by a new request. Practically, assuming that the union has formulated a request on its best assessment of a successful conclusion to an application, there would appear to be little purpose to delay. Indeed as part of the Government's review submissions were made by some employers that there should be some time limitation on the period in which an application could be made following a request. An analysis of the average period between the request and the application revealed that there was no

19.07

significant issue here and the review's conclusion was that no change was necessary.

19.08   The union makes the application in the form stipulated by the CAC. A copy of the form can be obtained from the CAC or downloaded from the CAC web site, www.cac.gov.uk. It is additionally possible to download *Statutory Recognition—A guide for the parties*, a CAC publication to assist in the preparation and progress of applications. The CAC may additionally stipulate that such supporting documentation as it requires be served with the application (para 33). An application will not then be admissible unless it is made on the specified form and accompanied by any stipulated information. On the present form no specific documentation is identified but it does provide for details of the evidence upon which the union will rely to establish that its application is admissible. As this relates to evidence of membership levels and levels of support for recognition within the *employer* there may be issues of confidentiality here. For example the union will have to show, as we will see, a level of membership in the proposed bargaining unit for which a list of members is appropriate. The CAC's position is clear that if this information is included in or annexed to the application it must be served on the employer. The application is not valid unless the entirety of the application is served and the schedule requires the application to be served on the employer. Where confidentiality is an issue (as it usually will be) then the CAC invites the union to seek guidance. In the case of numbers of members, for example, the appropriate course will be to identify that there will be evidence that a certain numbers of workers within the bargaining unit are members of the union but that the individual names of members would be supplied separately in confidence to the CAC, thus indicating the evidence upon which the union will rely but not annexing the documentation. In *AEEU and Control Techniques Drives Ltd* (TUR1/109/01) 22 October 2001 the CAC panel considered that it was proper for the union to take this approach and that it could not compel the union to disclose the names of individuals to the employer. We will see how that process is operated in practice below.

D. The CAC Procedural Response to an Application

19.09   On receipt of the application a case manager is assigned by the CAC. Their role is to be the main point of contact for the parties, to do all they can to explain the procedures and help both parties understand the implications of the legislation, as well as resolve difficulties. A panel of three CAC members will be convened to deal with the application. The panel will consist of the CAC Chairman or, more usually, one of the deputies and one member with experience as a representative of employers and one member with experience as a representative of workers. The composition of the panel will normally remain the same throughout an application. If changes are necessary they will only be made after one of the stages in the statutory process, and not during a stage unless exceptional circumstances prevail. Both the parties are informed of the names of the panel members, and of any changes in the composition of the panel.

On receipt of the application the CAC has to be satisfied that a number of   **19.10** conditions have been met before the CAC can accept the application. The period in which the CAC has to decide whether the application is admissible is a period of 10 working days from the receipt of the application. The CAC panel is able to extend this acceptance period by notice to the parties with reasons for the extension (para 15(5)).

Conditions for a valid application

Firstly the CAC will have to be satisfied that the pre-application process has   **19.11** been correctly followed, that is the union did make a valid request to the employer. This involves the CAC considering whether the conditions outlined above for a valid request have been complied with. If a valid request had been made then the CAC proceeds to consider whether the application itself is admissible. A number of decisions are noted above and it will be apparent that the employer may raise an issue about an aspect of the validity of the request or the admissibility of the application. If it does so a hearing may be convened by the CAC panel.

Whilst the CAC panel must be satisfied that the application is admissible it   **19.12** is not obliged to convene a hearing if it has clear evidence upon which to conclude that the application is admissible. So for example in *GMB and AJ Cheetham Ltd* (TUR1/159/02) 14 February 2002 the employer submitted no evidence to contradict the material submitted by the union that its application was admissible. The CAC panel still considered without an oral hearing whether the material submitted by the union established that the application was admissible. Even if they have submitted material the parties cannot compel the CAC to hold an oral hearing. For example in *BALPA and Ryanair*

Ltd (TUR1/70/01) 25 May 2001 despite the parties having requested a hearing the CAC panel considered that it had sufficient information to decide the question of admissibility and proceeded to do so without an oral hearing. It ensured however that both parties had the opportunity to comment on the material supplied by the other in writing. There may be some cases in which a party may only have its rights to a fair hearing under Article 6 of the European Convention on Human Rights if there is an oral hearing but these will be few and far between.

An admissible application

In order for the application to be admissible a number of conditions must be satisfied.

Service on the employer

19.13 First the union must have served the application on the employer (para 34). As with the request it will be desirable for the union to be able to prove the service of application on the employer. As set out above the entirety of the application and the documents annexed must be served.

Existing collective agreements

19.14 Secondly there is the more complex question of existing collective bargaining arrangements. Here the definition of the proposed bargaining unit becomes again of critical importance. The CAC has to consider whether there is in force a collective agreement under which a union is (or unions are) recognized as being entitled to conduct collective bargaining on behalf of the workers falling with the relevant bargaining unit (para 35(1)). If so the application, subject to some caveats considered further below, is not admissible.

19.15 By way of example if union A makes an application for recognition in respect of the workers in a particular factory but union B is already recognized in respect of all of the workers of that employer for the whole country A's application is inadmissible. If there is any overlap between any of the members of the proposed bargaining unit and workers for whom another union is recognized, that is fatal to the application. An important factor is that the existing recognition agreement does not have to be for pay, hours and holiday. It can be recognition for collective bargaining on *any* issue. It follows that some employers have recognized that if a union they perceive as one they are able to deal with more readily is recognized for the whole of the workforce, ideally in respect of collective bargaining on a non-contentious area such as disciplinary procedures, other unions are effectively frozen out from statutory applications. It does however have to be the recognition of a union for collective bargaining purposes. Thus in *TGWU v Grosvenor Casinos Ltd* (TUR1/188) 12 July 2002 the existence of an 'Employee Council' which had no collective bargaining rights but existed for purposes of consultation did not block the application. To have this blocking effect, the union involved need not be an independent trade union; it need only be a trade union falling within the definition under TULR(C)A, s 1. This may be a matter of argument in the case of a body without a certificate of independence. Thus in *TGWU and W Jordan (Cereals) Ltd* (TUR1/258/03) the employer argued that it had collective bargaining arrangements with a staff association called 'the Voice', which, on the basis of its constitution, it contended was a trade union. The CAC panel applying the statutory test concluded that it was not a trade union specifically because it could not be considered to be an organization consisting of workers within TULR(C)A, s 1. Factors which it considered relevant were that the workers did not have contracts of membership with it, could not join or refuse to join it, could not resign from it, and could not dissolve it. In addition they did not elect any officers. Further it considered that the fact that the Voice staff association could not, as then constituted, comply with the legal duties imposed on a trade union in respect of membership which was a further indication suggesting that it was not a trade union. Consequently it could not block the application of the TGWU.

19.16 The recognition which blocks the application may not be as well defined as being contained in an existing express voluntary recognition agreement. There may be factual issues as to whether there is an existing recognition which the CAC will have to determine. For example in *POA v Wackenhut [UK] Limited Escort Services* (TUR 1/108) (2001) the POA sought recognition but the workers had been transferred to the employer under a TUPE transfer and their previous employer had had a recognition agreement with another union, the GMB. The issue was whether this blocked the POA application. It was held on the facts that the previous agreement was no longer alive and that the POA could be recognized.

19.17 The recognition agreement thus must be an active one: in *TSSA and Rail Europe Ltd* (TUR 1/154/02) 4 March 2002 the CAC panel considered evidence from the parties and concluded that the last collective bargaining under a previous agreement had occurred four years before and that this did not block the application. Equally the recognition may arise from the course of dealing with the union rather than a specific recognition agreement. This is because TULR(C)A, s 178 defined collective agreements as including any 'arrangement' between the union and the employer embracing any of the specified issues. Thus in *NUM and RJB Mining Ltd* (TUR1/32/00) 16 February 2001 the CAC found on analysis of the dealings of RJB with NUM that it had recognized it, although there was no specific voluntary agreement for collective bargaining purposes on pay, hour and holiday thus blocking the NUM's own application. In such circumstances it is open to the union to regularize the position by terminating the voluntary recognition arrangements.

19.18   While as noted there is an attraction for the employer to put in place a voluntary agreement so as to block the application of another union the caveats to this principle give the employer pause for thought.

The first exception occurs when the existing collective agreement, which might in principle bar the application, is one with the union (or unions) which itself is bringing the application. That union may still bring the application if certain conditions are met. The existing agreement must be one which does not include pay, hours or holiday (para 25(2)). This means that, in the example above, if a union is recognized for the purpose of the collective bargaining of disciplinary processes it may itself make an application for statutory recognition, even for a smaller bargaining unit within the employer. This then becomes the attraction for a union to enter into a voluntary collective agreement for negotiation on other issues because it clears the applications of other unions and gives a toehold upon which to recruit with the objective of broadening the basis of recognition.

19.19   In the *NUM and RJB Mining* case the CAC also considered that where a number of unions were voluntarily recognized for collective bargaining as a bargaining unit this did not prevent an application to enlarge bargaining rights to include pay, hours or holidays if the union concerned was not recognized for these issues. What barred the NUM's application was the fact that it had from the course of dealings been recognized on the issue of pay, hours and holiday.

19.20   It should be noted that there is presently an unresolved ambiguity on this question of 'top-up' recognition. The construction of the exception would suggest that if the collective agreement includes *one* of the three elements, and the least intrusive is holidays, then even this union is barred from an application. Consequently it is unclear whether the union which is recognized for one of the issues of pay, hours and holiday may apply to extend its recognition to the other issues. The Government's review has made clear its intention that it should be able to do so and it therefore proposes to clarify the law on this point.

The second caveat is where the CAC has made a declaration because of a **19.21** change in the bargaining unit in respect of a collective agreement (para 35(3)). This has the consequence that the bargaining unit which has been the subject of that declaration ceases to have effect to the extent of that declaration. Changes in bargaining units and possible consequent declarations in the bargaining unit are considered further below. This has the consequence that an application in respect of the workers who have fallen out of the scope of the changed bargaining unit can be the subject of an application.

The third caveat relates to the nature of the collective agreement which is said **19.22** to bar the new application. A collective agreement in respect of which three conditions are met will not block the new application (para 35(4)). The CAC has interpreted the clause as requiring all three sub-conditions to be satisfied, *Prison Officer Association and Securicor Custodial Services* (TUR1/5/00) 21 August 2000. Those sub-conditions are:

(1) that the agreement (the existing agreement) is with a union (or unions) which do not have certificates of independence under s 6 of the Act (para 35(4)(a));
(2) & (3) the second and third conditions are more easily understood together and relate to attempts by an employer to block an application by terminating one agreement and recognizing another union to block an application by the first (para 35(4)(b) and (c)). Thus say union A has voluntary recognition by the employer but the employer would prefer another union, union B. It terminates the agreement with A and immediately enters into an agreement with B. Is A blocked from an application? The first consideration is whether the old agreement with A covered the same or substantially the same group of workers as are covered by the agreement which the employer has entered into with B. Finally if it did so and the agreement with A ceased to have effect in the period of three years preceding the date of the agreement with B, then B's agreement will be disregarded and the application is still brought.

Thus the workers will be able to decide the union of their choice for the purposes of collective bargaining.

19.23 One can see that the thrust of this caveat is to deal with the following specific factual situation. The employer has a voluntary recognition agreement with union A. It wishes to extract itself but knowing that A commands a majority of support and a high level of membership it wishes to block a statutory application by A. The employer therefore recognizes B which is not an independent union. The caveat means that A is not blocked from making its application. The caveat is narrowly defined and leaves it open to the employer to voluntarily recognize an independent union in preference to A. That is despite the fact that it does not have a majority of workers in the bargaining unit. De-recognizing the union in order for an application to proceed, against the wishes of the employer, is not an easy task. The present procedure, which is considered below, involves the worker or workers themselves seeking de-recognition. There is no basis upon which union A in our example could seek de-recognition of the sitting union. The TUC's proposals to the Government's review were that the recognition of a non-independent union should not block an application by an independent union or that an independent union itself should be able to apply for de-recognition. The Government's proposals have not acceded to that view and propose no change in the existing system.

The membership condition

19.24 The third condition for the admissibility of the application brings the membership of the bargaining unit into particular focus. The CAC has to consider, in order for the application to be admissible, that at least 10 per cent of the bargaining unit are members of the union (or unions) and further that a majority of the workers within the bargaining unit would be likely to favour recognition if asked (para 36). It will have been necessary for the union to have indicated on its application the evidence upon which it intends to rely in establishing this condition of admissibility.

19.25 There are of course two, but related, aspects to the requirement of at least 10 per cent membership. One is the number of workers within the proposed bargaining unit and second is the number of those who are members of the union. There could be issues as to both of these matters. The employer is able to provide lists of the number of employees within the bargaining unit and the union to provide lists of its members. There may be reluctance on the part of each party to reveal this information to the other. The consistent practice has therefore developed of the case manager undertaking a comparison of the lists supplied to the CAC in confidence (although this remains untested on judicial review). This enables overlapping workers to be clearly identified, and indeed the comparison is undertaken by the case manager and the convened CAC panel does not see the information itself. The CAC has not then compelled the disclosure of the material to the other party, whilst noting again that if the information was annexed to the application it must be served on the employer. Where there continue to be questions raised about the veracity of the documentation a suggestion raised by parties is that their documentation be open to scrutiny by ACAS on a confidential basis to verify the accuracy. The process has evolved out of voluntary agreements between the parties to supply the necessary information. There is no specific obligation to supply the necessary information. The Government's review proposals contemplate amendments to the procedure to compel both parties to co-operate with the membership check. It is intended that safeguards for confidentiality would be included as part of the procedure. It is additionally intended for there be a statutory basis for ACAS to carry out the membership check. ACAS does carry out membership checks as part of its role in assisting parties to reach agreement but this is with the consent of the parties.

One issue which has arisen here is the question of membership status. First **19.26** it should be noted that although later in the process the union has to be afforded access to the workers at this stage, and previously, it does not. Where the employer has closed its doors on the union it will be difficult for the union to have recruited members to achieve the necessary 10 per cent. One method which has been employed is reduced or free membership of the union for workers in the target employer, this obviously being in the nature of a limited offer until recognition is established. The issue of whether the individuals concerned are then members of the union is strictly determined by the union's rule book but employers have expressed disquiet about this practice insofar as employees may be counted within the union's tally even though there is no genuine signing up of the employees to the union's cause. Employers have argued that membership consequent upon reduced or no fees may not be indicative of genuine support for collective recognition. Similarly it is suggested that recently joined members may not be indicative of genuine support. Unions do indeed advance a number of benefits to their members and membership, particularly in the context of reduced or free membership, and this may be equivocal evidence of support for collective bargaining.[1] In one case the employer successfully managed to argue that a union official lacked the authority to agree to a reduced membership fee with the consequence that the memberships of those recruited members were void, *MSF and Unipart Group of Companies Ltd* (TUR1/94/01) 7 February 2002. It is obviosuly important then for the union to be clear as to status of the members recruited in this way. The Government's review has invited submissions on the issue to consider whether there should be a difference in the way that the CAC treats membership checks where there has been free or reduced membership.

19.27   Finally on the issue of the 10 per cent membership test there is the question of whether this should be determined at the date the application is made or at the date at which the CAC panel considers whether the application is admissible. In *KFAT and Shoe Zone Ltd* (TUR1/150/02) the CAC panel extended the acceptance period where there was material to suggest that there was rising union membership. The first comparison by the case manager had not shown the necessary 10 per cent. A second check showed that membership had increased and the CAC panel appears to have accepted, by implication, that the date of its decision was the relevant date for considering the tests of admissibility. The CAC panel decided, however, that the application was not admissible because they were not satisfied that the second test was made out, which we will now consider.

19.28   The second question is whether a majority of the workforce would be likely to support recognition. The CAC will, in part, rely upon its industrial experience here and growing experience of ballots under the statutory scheme. Thus there is an assumption that members of the union would support recognition. A numerical majority of members of the union from the membership analysis would lead to the assumption that the second condition is satisfied. Lesser percentages have sufficed in some cases such as *MSF and Teachers Management Services Ltd* (TUR1/57/01) 30 April 2001 where the CAC accepted from its experience of industrial relations that behind the individuals who have joined the trade union will be workers who whilst supporting recognition prefer not to commit to union membership and others who support recognition but wish to become members of a trade union and pay their union subscriptions once, or if the union gains recognition. A density of 36 per cent of members of the union within the proposed bargaining unit was thus found to be sufficient to demonstrate a likelihood that a majority of workers would support recognition by the trade union to whom the 36 per cent belonged. It is right to note that this was in circumstances in which there was a high turnover of staff and in which union membership had varied between 30 and 50 per cent. Such high turnover is an increasing feature of industrial life and renders it more difficult for unions to organize. This is one of the reasons why unions are so keen to prevent a long drawn out process of the application for recognition. The union may itself rely upon other evidence in support of the application, and this would be particularly important where the membership levels satisfy the 10 per cent test but are not significantly higher and certainly not higher than 50 per cent. It may submit a petition conducted in the workplace, an informal ballot or signed statements, in the case of a small bargaining unit to support the contention that a majority would support recognition. Again the union may ask for the confidentiality of the workforce to be preserved by these materials (or at least the names and addresses contained within them) not being supplied to the employer.

The evidence relied upon needs to be current evidence of support and has to **19.29** be in support of collective bargaining; consequently it is important that the union accurately communicates what collective bargaining means when amassing such evidence of support. In *BALPA and Ryanair Ltd* (TUR1/70/01) 25 May 2001 the union relied upon the level of attendance at meetings, the level of membership of the union and correspondence from individual members in support of the assertion that there was majority support in favour of collective bargaining. The employer questioned whether the membership and attendance at meetings were necessarily indicative of support for collective bargaining as it believed that pilots joined the union for the benefits of membership of a professional organization rather than to see the union collectively bargain on their behalf. The CAC sought recruitment materials, newsletters and other materials from the union which might support their case that collective bargaining was a motivation for membership of the union. Having considered this evidence, the CAC panel concluded the union had established that it had the necessary percentage of members and that there was evidence on which to conclude that a majority of the workers may be likely to support collective recognition. Ultimately the application failed on a ballot.

A more direct method may be the submission of a petition circulated within **19.30** the bargaining unit. For example in *URTU and James Irlam & Sons Ltd*

(TUR1/74/01) 17 May 2001 in support of its position the union presented a petition containing 231 signatures. The case manager undertook an analysis of the membership list and the names on the petition. This analysis revealed that of the total of 334 names on both documents, a total of 89 people had either left the company or signed the petition twice. This left a total of 245 people who had indicated their support for the union either by being members of the union or by signing the petition which the CAC panel concluded established evidence of the likely majority in favour of recognition.

19.31   The wording of the petition needs to be clear so as to establish that it is indeed evidence of support for collective bargaining rather than general approval of the union. By way of example the petition submitted in *GMB and Video Duplicating Ltd* (TUR1/192/02) 9 August 2002 clearly defined the issue.

> We, the undersigned call upon the Management of Video Duplicating Company to recognize the GMB Trade Union and negotiate with them over our pay, working hours, health & safety and all other issues related to our contracts of employment

It is of note that the case manager's report on the petition submitted raised question marks about the veracity of some of the signatures to the petition. Because of the confidentiality agreed in respect of it the employer would be reliant upon the case manager to identify such issues about the petition. The CAC panel in considering the question of majority support assessed this on the basis of numbers on the petition excluding those which were questionable but still concluded that there was evidence upon which it could conclude that majority support was likely.

19.32   On the other hand in *UNIFI and Nottinghamshire Building Society* (TUR1/229/02) the CAC panel considered that a union petition which asked 'Please sign the petition to allow a free and independent ballot to be held' was ambiguous as to whether it was in support of union recognition and not merely in support of there being a ballot.

19.33   A variety of factors therefore may be considered for example in *TGWU and Linde Gas UK Limited* (TUR1/232/02) 24 April 2003 the CAC panel concluded that there had been stable union membership of approximately one third of the bargaining unit. A petition submitted by the union showed a total of 38.5 per cent of the workers supporting recognition. The CAC panel found the majority support test made out taking into account its industrial experience that there are those who favour recognition but who do not sign petitions or join the union. Further the union had not offered reduced subscriptions which the panel considered might have encouraged employees to join the union. The petition had also not been circulated in all of the geographically diverse sites within the bargaining unit and the panel again relied upon its industrial experience to conclude that had it been so it was reasonable to suppose that there would have been a level of support for recognition in the other sites. These factors will vary from case to case and CAC panel decisions are not binding on subsequent panels. Thus in *AEEU and Control Techniques Drives Ltd* (TUR1/109) membership of the union was 17.4 per cent and a petition in favour of recognition had been signed by 31.4 per cent of the workers. Here, whilst accepting the arguments of the union outlined above that membership levels may reflect wider support for recognition, the CAC panel concluded that in the absence of any evidence supporting increasing union membership the test was not made out.

The Government review has invited proposals for whether the CAC should give guidance as to submission of petitions.

19.34 As part of the conciliation process prior to the application being made ACAS may have by agreement between the parties conducted a membership check and/or a ballot of the proposed bargaining unit to determine the level of support. This material may be relied upon in support of the application if agreement could not be reached. It is of note that ACAS had conducted 70 ballots and 99 membership checks during the period June 1999 to May 2002. The Government's review has proposed that there should be a clear statutory basis for ACAS's conduct of the ballots and membership checks. This may serve to be a method of allaying some of the employer's concerns about the present system which relies heavily upon the case manager and the accuracy of the information supplied to him.

19.35 The employer additionally scrutinizes closely the information relied upon and may itself have conducted a poll in the workforce to assess the position. This is something which the union is likely to be aware of and the employer may be pressed to reveal the result, even if unfavourable to the employer. Thus in *TSSA and Rail Europe* (TUR1/154/02) 4 March 2002 the employer acknowledged in the course of the hearing before the CAC that its Human Resources Manager had conducted an informal ballot amongst the workers in the bargaining unit and that had indicated support for the collective recognition. There may be questions raised by both sides about the canvassing methods employed for such ballots. In *TGWU and Economic Skips* (TUR1/121/01) 16 October 2001 the employer had carried out a survey of the bargaining unit which it asserted showed, despite the level of union membership, that there was no support for collective recognition. The union questioned the process by which the company's survey had been conducted. The union stated that employees were invited one by one into the Managing Director's office, were provided with the questionnaire, required to complete it and hand it back. It was claimed that union members were intimidated by this process as union members had previously been dismissed. The union also claimed that during the process of completing the survey persons were advised that joining the union would result in lower pay. A copy of this letter was sent to the company for comment. The company submitted no further evidence on this matter. The union then conducted its own petition which showed a majority in favour of recognition. It was apparent that some members of the union had signed both the employer's survey and the union's petition. The CAC panel concluded that in the light of the employer's failure to answer the issues raised by the union the union's evidence would be preferred as establishing that a majority was indeed likely to be achieved by the union. It is interesting to note that a postal ballot was eventually conducted under the statutory scheme and the necessary majority for recognition was not present. In *GPMU v Sentinel Colour Print* (TUR 1/37/01) 28 February 2001 the employer opposed recognition on the grounds that less than half of the bargaining unit were union members and that some of those union members were not in favour of recognition in any event. The panel found that union members formed a majority of the workforce, but only barely. The employer attempted to rely on petitions, a survey and employees' letters to show that some union members would not be in favour of recognition. However the panel considered that the way in which the employer had made it known that they opposed recognition may have intimidated some employees and they found it suspicious that several of the employees' letters against recognition were in identical format. They applied the presumption that the workforce would be in favour of recognition because over half of them were union members and determined that the application was valid.

The three-year exclusion

19.36 The final condition on admissibility is that there is a time barrier, whether the union brought substantially the same admitted application in the last three years (para 39), or there has been a rejection of the union on a secret ballot either on recognition or de-recognition (paras 40 and 41). In these cases the application is also inadmissible. The relevant three-year period is calculated, in the case of a previous admitted application, from the date of acceptance by the CAC and in the case of the ballot from the date of the CAC's declaration that the union is not entitled to be recognized.

19.37 A critical aspect of the three-year rule is that exclusion operates where there has been an admitted application. Thus if the CAC has decided that the union's application is not admissible because, for example, it was not satisfied that the 10 per cent membership condition was satisfied, the union is not prohibited from making a new application by the three-year rule. The same is true if the union withdraws its application before the CAC determines whether it is admissible. If therefore the union considers in the light of the information submitted by the employer to the CAC that there is a danger that the application will be admitted but that on the proposed bargaining unit it will lose the ballot it may be well advised to withdraw the application and reconsider its position.

19.38 It should be noted that while the union can withdraw its application before it is accepted, once it has been accepted, it cannot be withdrawn after the CAC has made a declaration of recognition without a ballot (para 16(1)(a)) or has ordered that a secret ballot be conducted (para 16(1)(b)). Both before a decision on admissibility and after the parties may agree to give notice to the CAC to take no further steps on the application (para 17). That request is limited in time in that the notice to take no further steps must be given before the CAC has made a declaration of recognition without a ballot (para 17(3)(a)) or within the notification period, which is considered below, within which the CAC may be notified that the ballot should not be conducted (para 17(3)(b)).

19.39 The Government's review considered whether there should be any penalty on unions withdrawing before admission. It concluded that withdrawals were also consequent upon voluntary agreements and there should be no penalty on withdrawal as it may encourage the continuation of the application so as to avoid the penalty with a greater wastage of expenditure.

E. The Decision on Admissibility

19.40 Having considered the tests to be applied, which may in its discretion have included an oral hearing, the CAC panel decides if the application is admissible. If admissible the CAC will give formal notice of acceptance (para 15), and if not it is rejected (para 15). The statutory procedure normally lays down a clear timescale for each stage of the decisions on the statutory recognition procedure. One surprising area in which it lacks clarity is, however, on the question of when the tests for admissibility have to be determined. It could be at the date on which the application is submitted or it could be the date upon which the CAC panel makes its decision on admissibility. It may be highly relevant to know when the conditions apply, for example to consider whether the three-year exclusion period had expired. Equally with changing numbers of members the date for the determination of the 10 per cent membership test may be critical. There is further the possibility of the employer speedily seeking to negotiate a voluntary agreement with a friendly union to block the application before it is accepted. It may then be vital to determine the point at which the test is applied when the date of that voluntary agreement is known. This issue arose in the case of *USDAW and National Autoparts* (TUR1/28/00) 5 January 2001. USDAW made an application on 28 November 2000. The employer indicated that it was in discussions with GMB for the purposes of entering into a voluntary recognition agreement. On 13 December, the final day of the normal statutory period for its decision on the admissibility of USDAW's application, as the CAC panel was considering the case, it was notified by the employer that an agreement on recognition had been reached with the GMB. The signed agreement dated 13 December set out the right of the GMB to act as sole bargaining agency for collective issues concerning pay, hours and holidays, covering all employees in the company. The panel then extended the time limit for its decision on admissibility to 21 December to allow it to consider the effects of the changed circumstances and to enable the union to respond to this new development. They were thereby implicitly treating the date of its decision on admissibility as the relevant date and not the date the application was submitted at which time, on any view, there was no voluntary agreement in place. A decision in the end on this point was not necessary as on 21 December the GMB informed the CAC that it had terminated its agreement with the employer. The GMB had taken this decision after it became clear to them that 'USDAW appear to have recruited the majority of the production workers and drivers'. The CAC panel therefore proceeded to consider the other admissibility conditions.

It is thought that it is more consistent with the overall scheme of the legislation to take the crucial date as the date the application was submitted.

The Government review received submissions on the issue of whether there **19.41** ought to be a cut off point after which voluntary agreements could not be reached so as to block applications. The review however declined to recommend changing the procedures but decided to leave the unions to resolve the inter-union disputes on this point. The review did not find any significant evidence of disputes between unions not being resolved, as in the manner of the *Autoparts* case itself. From the unions' perspective, however, this does not resolve the difficulty of the recognition of the non-independent union by the employer to block the application by an independent union.

F. The Appropriate Bargaining Unit

If the CAC concluded that the application is admissible it gives notice to **19.42** the parties (para 15(5)). Unless the parties have by then agreed the proposed bargaining unit the CAC has then to consider whether the proposed bargaining unit is appropriate or some other bargaining unit is appropriate. Consistent with the underlying approach in the schedule, before it does so an attempt is made to try to help the parties to agree the bargaining unit. There is a period of 20 working days during which the CAC must try to help this occur, commencing on the day after that on which the CAC gave notice of acceptance of the application (para 18(2)). The CAC may again extend that period by notifying the parties with reasons for the extension (para 18(2)(b)). Two modifications are proposed to this part of the schedule as a consequence of the Government's review. The union may, with an un-cooperative employer be negotiating blind as to the workers who fall in the bargaining unit it has proposed. There is no obligation on the employer at present to provide this information. The Government's proposal is that there should indeed be such a requirement on the employer to disclose to the union the number of workers in the union's proposed bargaining unit, together with their grade and location at the commencement of this negotiating period. It is also proposed that the CAC should have the discretion to reduce the 20-working-day period in those cases where it is clear that there is no prospect that the negotiations will be fruitful.

19.43   At the end of that 20-working-day period, or such longer period as the CAC may have specified, the present position is that if the parties have not agreed the appropriate bargaining unit, the CAC must decide the *appropriate bargaining unit*. There is a 10-working-day period, subject again to extension by the CAC, for it to do this (para 19(2)).

19.44   The CAC in deciding that question must take into account (1) the need for the bargaining unit to be compatible with effective management (para 19(3)(a)) and (2) a list of matters in so far as they do not conflict with that need (para 19(3)(b)). These matters are namely, the views of the parties; existing (national and local) bargaining arrangements; the undesirability of fragmentation of bargaining arrangements in an undertaking; the 'character-istics' of the relevant workers or other employees; and the location of the workers (para 19(4)). The CAC's approach to this question was the subject of the only case on the schedule to have been argued in front of the Court of Appeal.

19.45   Reference has already been made to the facts of the important decision of *R (On the application of Kwik-Fit Ltd) v CAC* [2002] ICR 1212. It provides a valuable exercise in considering the issues which arise. It will be recalled that the union had proposed a bargaining unit based upon Kwik-Fit's two London divisions. The employer resisted that proposed bargaining unit. The union's case before the CAC was that the two London divisions had distinct employment terms from the remainder of the company, in particular a London weighting was paid and the two divisions had until recently operated a particular pattern of working hours. The union further contended that there was an identifiable management structure for the London divisions and additionally relied upon other examples of collective bargaining in the same industrial sector where bargaining had been de-centralized in this manner. It argued that this showed that this was not inconsistent with the effective management of a national organization. The employer's case focused instead upon the integrated and centralized nature of its operations and manage-ment. As to employment terms it stressed the homogeneity in the terms and conditions of the staff across the entire organization. The employer expressed further concern that allowing recognition at the divisional level would lead to multi-union recognition across the country leading to fragmentation of bargaining. The employer's submission was therefore that as an integrated, national company the only bargaining unit which was compatible with effective management would be one covering the whole of its operations.

The CAC panel approached the question of compatibility by asking itself whether the union's bargaining unit was *consistent or able to co-exist* with effective management. It concluded that it did not have to decide which bargaining unit was *most consistent* with effective management. The CAC panel concluded that '. . . we need to examine whether the union's proposed bargaining unit is found wanting and does not conflict with effective management.'

The panel decided that the union's proposed bargaining unit was compatible. Kwik-Fit sought judicial review of the CAC's decision. The thrust of the employer's application was that the CAC had erred in its approach as a matter of law and the bargaining units proposed respectively by employer and union should be treated equally in a consideration directed to determine the unit which was most consistent with effective management. That application was heard by Elias J. He held that the CAC's approach to consideration of the unit proposed by the union was correct in that it was not the duty of the CAC to find the *most* appropriate bargaining unit, since the focus was upon the unit proposed by the union. In doing so it was, however, obliged to consider the views of the employer. Those views may be expressed by advancing an alternative bargaining unit to illustrate the incompatibility with effective management of that proposed by the union or by raising proposed modifications to that proposed unit. The CAC's role was not then limited to a narrow one of a determination of whether the union's proposed unit was compatible with effective management independently of any potential modifications or other appropriate bargaining units and it could consider modifications and adjustment to the unit proposed by the union. He said:

> In my judgment in that determination it is perfectly proper for them to have, as one of their objectives, to seek to retain the essence or core of the union's proposed bargaining unit, even where they feel it should be modified. They must of course be satisfied that their chosen unit fairly accommodates the criteria in paragraph 19 and in particular is compatible with effective management. They are not constrained by an obligation to determine some concept of the most appropriate bargaining unit in the sense that it is the bargaining unit which best matches the specified criteria.

Elias J held on the facts of the particular case that the CAC had not properly directed itself to take into account the views of the employer, limiting itself only to a consideration of the union's proposed unit. The CAC appealed that decision to the Court of Appeal.

In the Court of Appeal Buxton LJ gave the leading judgment with which Latham LJ and Sir Denys Henry agreed. Buxton LJ allowed the appeal concluding that the CAC had not misdirected itself and that it had reached a decision which it was entitled to reach.

Buxton LJ's judgment was that the role of the CAC was a limited one, that it was to determine first whether the structure proposed by the union is appropriate for pay bargaining purposes and no more than that. Only then if it concludes that the unit is not compatible should it proceed to consider alternative bargaining units. The difficulty with that approach is that it limits the CAC's ability to determine as appropriate a different bargaining unit to that proposed by the employee. Thus in circumstances where, for example, the employer's views of the proposed bargaining unit suggest that some modification to the bargaining unit would lead to a bargaining unit which was more compatible with effective management, unless the CAC can conclude that the union's proposed unit is incompatible with effective management it cannot determine a bargaining unit which modifies or adapts that proposed bargaining unit.

19.46   That flexibility of thought has previously been evident in the approach taken by the CAC. In the period to 30 September 2003 the CAC had determined the bargaining unit in 68 cases. In 46 of these the union's proposed bargaining unit was accepted. In 10 cases the employer's proposed bargaining unit was accepted and in 12 cases the CAC adopted a modified form to that submitted by either of the parties. In the Government review submissions were made for the modification of this test and the review considered the law following the decision in the *Kwik-Fit* case. The unions wished to see the requirement of compatibility with effective management removed and some employers wanted the procedure to embrace a consideration of competing bargaining unit proposals in the manner advanced by the employer in the *Kwik-Fit* case. The Government review concluded that these changes would not be made but that the statute would be modified to make clear that the employer's views on the union proposal and any counter proposal would be considered in determining whether the union's proposal is compatible with the statutory criteria. Whether that will serve to correct the narrowness of approach which the *Kwik-Fit* decision leaves will have to await the proposed amendments when drafted.

We now turn to consider the specific matters which the CAC must consider. **19.47**

- The views of the parties

This is self-evident but it should be noted that the *Kwik-Fit* case requires full consideration to be given to the views of the employer (however expressed) on the union's proposed unit.

- Existing (national and local) bargaining arrangements

There may be existing bargaining arrangements, whether on a national or local level. The proposed recognition may be consistent with these structures or it may cut across them. A bargaining unit which cuts across such arrangements may not then be consistent with effective management of the organization as a whole.

- The desirability of avoiding small fragmented bargaining units within the undertaking

The proposed bargaining unit may itself create a small unit for recognition purposes which fragments these workers from a consistent bargaining unit with a wider workforce. Or conversely the proposed bargaining unit may leave a small group of workers who are not within the scope of the bargaining unit. An example of this is *Amicus, GMB and Alan Worswick* (TUR1/157/02) 28 April 2002. The union's proposed bargaining unit excluded six workers by comparison with that of the employer who wished them to be included in the bargaining unit. One of the factors influencing the CAC panel in its conclusion that the unit proposed by the union was not appropriate was that this small fragmented bargaining unit would be left. The CAC therefore determined its own bargaining unit, which was different from that of the employer, embracing five of the six workers within the new definition. The position of the sixth it considered to be different to that of the other five in that he performed a different job, as a cleaner.[2]

- The 'characteristics' of the relevant workers or other employees

In that consideration, including five of the six workers, the CAC in the *Alan Worswik* application were considering the characteristics of the workers in determining whether they fell properly within the bargaining unit proposed.

The characteristics of the sixth worker's job, as a cleaner, made him unsuitable to be included within the defined bargaining unit. Of importance here is the clarity of definition used by the union in the definition of the bargaining unit. For example in *TGWU and Linde Gas UK Ltd* (TUR1/232/2002) the union used generic industry terms such as 'testers' or 'drivers' in defining the bargaining unit. These did not fit with the definitions used by the employer in its job descriptions. This made it difficult for the CAC and the employer to understand which individuals fell within the proposed bargaining unit. Because the proposed bargaining unit was not easily definable, even applying the approach in the *Kwik-Fit* case, the panel concluded that the bargaining unit proposed by the union was not appropriate. The panel therefore proceeded to determine the unit which it considered appropriate. The panel considered the organizational charts submitted by the employer in support of the bargaining unit proposed by it and determined a bargaining unit which was different from both that proposed by the employer and the union.

• The location of the workers

This raises geographical issues of the location of the workers. The union's proposed bargaining unit may have identified workers in distinct sites, for example factories in different geographical locations. This may have implications for collective bargaining purposes. Market conditions in specific areas may dictate that pay is negotiated locally, and that would favour recognition at the local level. Structures may however mitigate against geographically local units. For example the management structure may be organized around national rather than regional structures and this was part of the employer's argument in the *Kwik-Fit* case. The employer will need to show that it does genuinely operate the company nationally on questions of terms and conditions. For example in *TGWU and Gala Casinos Ltd (t/a Maxims Casino Club)* (TUR1/119/01) 1 November 2001 the union's application had proposed a bargaining unit based upon casino staff at one specific casino. Terms and conditions of employment for all staff employed by the employer were fixed centrally. Although actual hours worked might vary locally and individuals might be employed to work different hours the standard hours did not vary. All staff had the same levels of holiday entitlement, varied only by seniority and job description. The same applied to centrally established rates of pay. No club manager had any authority to vary pay scales. If a local manager wished to recommend a variation for an individual employee that variation would have to be centrally approved. The employer operated three pension schemes dependent on seniority and level, but not on location and the bonus scheme applicable to Maxim's casino was common to all casinos. The employer further submitted that it had established Regional and Central Consultative Committees but that there was no machinery in existence which could provide for local negotiation on wages, hours and holidays. The business was a multi-site activity, but was centrally managed. The CAC concluded that the proposed bargaining unit would not be compatible with efficient management. In the view of the panel it would be virtually impossible for the employer to maintain its centralized structure for all other locations and types of employee whilst separately negotiating pay, hours and holidays for those employees within the proposed bargaining unit. Pressures would develop which would either force management to abandon its central system or to abandon meaningful bargaining within the unit. The CAC therefore determined a national bargaining unit was appropriate. It is of note that following this determination the application was withdrawn. Similarly in *ISTC and Hygena Ltd* (TUR 1/33/00) the union's proposed unit related to only one of the employer's six sites. The CAC panel accepted the employer's argument that as the same terms and conditions were applied across all of its sites and product and manufacture could be moved across the sites to meet market conditions effective management required all six sites to be within the bargaining unit.

The structure and organization of the employer then may pose particular difficulties for the union seeking to gain recognition and targeting that approach by focusing upon a specific site or geographical area. The difficulties can be seen in *GPMU and Getty Images Ltd* (TUR1/104/01) 31 October 2001. The union had proposed recognition for one particular site, but this represented 29 workers within a UK workforce of 500. Getty in fact was a multinational organization which had a global management structure. The CAC panel looked at the company's management structures and concluded that the only scope for discretion within the global structure was at national level. The principles for determining pay and conditions were decided at a global level with the detail set at national level to take account of economic variables and differences in national legal systems. That structure did not readily accommodate bargaining on a site basis. In the light of the numbers it also concluded that the union's proposed unit would create a small and fragmented bargaining unit. The CAC panel therefore concluded that the union's proposed bargaining unit was not appropriate and the appropriate unit was a national bargaining unit.

A further factor which is relevant is that there are members of another union within the bargaining unit which has been proposed. Thus the fact that there were members of the NUJ within the proposed bargaining unit of the BAJ in *BAJ and Mirror Group Newspapers Ltd* (TUR1/75/01) was something which was not fatal to the BAJ's application. The NUJ had been informed by the employer of the BAJ's application for recognition but had not responded. Further it is irrelevant that definition of the proposed bargaining unit includes a definition of workers where there are presently no workers within that definition, *GPMU and Eastern Counties Newspapers Ltd* (TUR1/51/01).

When the CAC panel has reached its conclusion on the question of the appropriate bargaining unit the CAC must give the parties notice of its decision. While the CAC does give reasons for its decision it is not under an obligation under the statute to do so.

G. Does the Application Remain Valid?

19.48 It is possible that the bargaining unit proposed by the union is not the bargaining unit determined by the CAC or that the parties have agreed an appropriate bargaining unit, after the admission of the application, which is different from that which was originally proposed. The CAC is concerned here with whether there has been a change in the substance of the bargaining unit. In these circumstances the CAC must once again consider the admissibility tests to decide if the application remains valid. Thus it must again consider each of the conditions previously identified to establish if they are met (para 20(1)). There is again a 10-working-day period for this determination subject to extension, with reasons, by the CAC (para 20(6)). A change in the bargaining unit may have presented a very different set of circumstances. Thus in *GPMU and Getty Images Ltd* (TUR1/104/01) the 10 per cent membership condition might have been established for the 29 employees at the single site but not for all 500 employee in the UK on the bargaining unit determined by the CAC. In *TGWU and Greene King Brewing and Brands* (TUR1/92/01) 10 May 2002 the CAC found the union's proposed unit of one particular distribution site was not appropriate, since there already existed a national agreement with the union covering other plants. The CAC concluded that the appropriate unit was one embracing those other plants. The effect of that decision was to bar the application because the determined bargaining unit now embraced workers for whom there was a collective bargaining agreement in place.

In determining the question of admissibility the CAC must again consider any evidence submitted by the parties (para 20(3)). **19.49**

If in the light of the changed circumstances the CAC concludes that that application is no longer valid it must give notice to the parties and take no further action under the schedule (para 20(4)). If however it concludes that it is still valid the CAC gives notice of this to the parties and that it is proceeding with the application (para 20(5)). **19.50**

H. The Problem of Different Union Applications

Previously we have considered the position of a joint application by two or more unions. It is however possible on the contrary for there to be competition between unions for recognition in respect of a group of workers, or at least over-lap in their proposed bargaining units. Paragraph 14 deals with this situation. **19.51**

The first situation arises in circumstances where the CAC has received more than one application for recognition from a union, and the proposed bargaining units include at least one worker who falls in each and the CAC has yet to accept any of the applications (para 14(1)). If this happens within the acceptance period, which is 10 working days starting with the last application which the CAC received, or such longer period as the CAC may specify with reasons to the parties, the CAC considers whether the 10 per cent test is met on each application. If, having considered the applications, the CAC concludes that either none of the applications meets the 10 per cent test or that more than one of them meets the test then it must accept none of the applications (para 14(7)). It follows that if it finds that only one meets the test only that one proceeds subject to meeting the other admissibility tests. The effect of the exclusion of all the applications is to make the unions go away and resolve a united position. No application has been accepted and so they are not barred from a new application. This can be seen in operation in the cases of *ISTC and Polypipe Buildings Products Ltd* (TUR1/197) and *Amicus and Polypipe Building Products Ltd* (TUR1/199). The bargaining units proposed on the applications submitted, within nine days of each other, **19.52** by the respective unions overlapped. Each application was valid so far as the 10 per cent membership test was concerned. The CAC panel therefore applied para 14(7) and declined to accept both the applications. Practically it is then for the unions to go away and agree either that only one will apply or that they should make a joint application. In the *Polypipe* case the unions agreed to make a joint application (*ISTC and Amicus v Polypipe Buildings Products Limited* (TUR1/278/03) 26 August 2003).

19.53 The second situation deals with the conflict arising later in the process. Here one application has been accepted and is proceeding. An application is made by another union in respect of a bargaining unit which has an overlap with the original application. Under para 38(2) the second application is not admissible while the first is still being processed (para 38(1)). The bargaining unit may of course change in either case during the process, whether by agreement or determination of the CAC. Consequently whilst there may have been no conflict at the beginning of the process a stage may be reached where there is an overlap. In this case because of the validity check which is applied under para 20, this problem should become apparent. It will do so in a manner potentially fatal to whichever of the applications has to have its validity considered again under para 20 or if they are each considered under para 20 the last to be so considered (para 38(1) and para 46(1)).

19.54 However if the first application has yet to have its bargaining unit agreed between the parties or determined by the CAC and the second application meets the 10 per cent test then the first is cancelled (para 51(2)). This was the fate of the application of ISTC in *ISTC v Faccenda Group* (TUR1/200/02) 22 October 2002. ISTC's application had been accepted but a subsequent application was made by the GMB which was consequently not admissible by reason of para 38. However as the ISTC application had yet to have its bargaining unit agreed or determined its application was cancelled.

Notes

[1] The argument was advanced by the employer in *ISTC v Mission Foods* (TUR1/256/03) 6 May 2003 where the union afforded a reduced membership fee for the members of the union at non-recognized workplaces. The employer argued that membership was equivocal evidence of support for statutory recognition as it asserted individuals may have joined for the other benefits of union membership. The CAC panel's view was that a major reason why workers joined a trade union

was to enjoy the advantages of collective bargaining. Unless then the employer submitted evidence to show that the members did not support statutory recognition the panel took membership as evidence of support for statutory recognition.

2   In *BECTU v BBC* (TUR1/274/03) 27 October 2003 the CAC panel concluded that the union's proposed bargaining unit would introduce collective bargaining for a small group of workers within the BBC's undertaking. This it concluded represented a fragmentation of bargaining within the undertaking. The unit proposed had in part been programme based, being in part based around workers engaged in a programme called 'River City', and the panel considered that recognizing it might encourage claims for the recognition of other programme-based bargaining units with further fragmentation of national bargaining arrangements. This the panel concluded was not consistent with effective management. It is further of note that having rejected the union's bargaining unit the panel found itself unable to impose its own unit. The employer had made no counter proposal and the panel had no evidence upon which to consider a more radical bargaining unit than that proposed by the union. The panel therefore decided that in these 'highly exceptional' circumstances it had no rational basis for applying the statutory criteria to decide an appropriate bargaining unit and it was not obliged by the legislation to devise one.

20

BALLOTING

A. Should a Ballot be Held?

If the application proceeds then the CAC must consider whether a ballot **20.01** should be held. The core question for the CAC to determine is whether a majority of workers in the bargaining unit support the union being recognized for collective bargaining.

The starting point is the membership of the union within the bargaining **20.02** unit. If the CAC is satisfied that more than half the workers in the bargaining unit are already members of the union then the CAC must, subject to the following, issue a declaration that the union is recognized as being entitled to conduct collective bargaining on behalf of the workers constituting the bargaining unit (para 22(2)). The question is determined on the evidence before the CAC, so that this will again be an analysis of comparison between memberships lists with lists of workers within the bargaining unit typically carried out by the CAC case manager.

Even majority membership within the bargaining unit however may not be **20.03** an absolute guarantee of automatic recognition. While effectively the presumption on majority membership is that there will be recognition, there are three conditions. If any of these are fulfilled the CAC must give notice to the parties that it nevertheless intends to hold a secret ballot of the workers in the bargaining unit asking whether they want the union to be recognized to conduct collective bargaining on their behalf (para 22(3)). Those conditions are (para 22(4)):

(1) The CAC is satisfied that a ballot should be held in the interests of good industrial relations.

(2) A significant number of the union members within the bargaining unit inform the CAC that they do not want the union (or unions) to conduct collective bargaining on their behalf.

(3) Membership evidence is produced which leads the CAC to conclude that there are doubts whether a significant number of the union members within the bargaining unit want the union (or unions) to conduct collective bargaining on their behalf.

20.04   Thus in *AEEU v Huntleigh Healthcare Ltd* (TUR1/19/00) the case manager's report revealed that 55 per cent of the bargaining unit were members of the union. There had, however, been a free membership period and 90 per cent of the union's membership had joined during that period. The CAC panel therefore concluded that this raised doubts as to why members had joined and whether a significant number of union members did indeed want the union to conduct collective bargaining on their behalf, or if they may have joined for other reasons taking advantage of the free membership. The CAC panel therefore ordered a ballot on the basis of condition (3). As considered above in *ISTC v Mission Foods* (TUR1/256/03) 6 May 2003 the CAC panel took a different approach. Even though there had been reduced membership fees in the absence of specific evidence from the employer that there was no support for collective bargaining, the panel accepted that the major reason why workers joined a trade union was to enjoy the advantages of collective bargaining and membership of itself was evidence of support for collective bargaining.

20.05   In *UNIFI and Turkiye Is Bankasi* (TUR1/90) 5 December 2001 the CAC had received 11 letters from employees within a bargaining unit of 16, 10 of whom were members of the union. Three of those 11 letters were received from union members. The letters stated that they opposed recognition and the CAC concluded that this constituted a significant number of employees with the bargaining unit so that condition (2) was satisfied and a ballot was ordered.

20.06   As an example of good industrial relations justifying a ballot, in *TGWU v Economic Skips Ltd* (TUR1/121/01) the CAC decided a ballot was in the interests of good industrial relations as there was before it conflicting evidence as to the wishes of the workforce. There was a sincerely held view on the part of the employer that the majority of the workers in the bargaining unit did not want recognition; and the employer expressed a willingness to co-operate fully with the union if a ballot demonstrated that the majority of the workers in the bargaining unit supported recognition. Another example was found in *GPMU and Red Letter Bradford Ltd* (TUR1/12/00) 24 January 2001. Whilst the CAC panel considered that there was likely to be a majority of workers in the bargaining unit supporting recognition it concluded that a ballot should be held. It did so for two reasons. First because there was uncertainty over the precise level of support for the union, three months had elapsed since the application had been made and differences of opinion had become apparent between the employer and union as to who actually worked in the bargaining unit. Secondly because relations between the employer and union had not been harmonious and it was felt by the CAC panel that a secret ballot would resolve uncertainty and clear the air.

20.07 The fact that it was anticipated by the employer that there would be a merger with another bank so that the bargaining unit would disappear was, however, not found to be a reason for ordering a ballot in the view of the CAC panel in *UNIFI and Bank Tejarat* (TUR1/144). The panel concluded that in the light of the evidence of the union membership there should be recognition without a ballot. If the merger took place then the employer could utilize those parts of the schedule which deal with changes in the bargaining unit which are considered below.

20.08 The above considerations all only arise on the basis that the CAC was satisfied that there was a majority of union members within the bargaining unit. If the CAC is not satisfied of this then it must order a ballot (para 23). There is no obligation on the CAC to give reasons for its decision whether or not to order a ballot, notwithstanding that there is a majority of workers in the bargaining unit who are members of the union (*Fullarton Computer Industries Ltd v CAC* [2001] IRLR 752, Court of Session). It does however conventionally give reasons, and these are subject to challenge only by judicial review where the inadequacy of the reasoning would not form the basis alone for a successful challenge of the decision.

B. The Form of the Ballot

20.09 If a ballot has been ordered then the parties have a notification period of 10 days. In this period the union, or the union and the employer, may notify the

CAC that they do not wish the ballot to take place (para 24). Thus the employer may not act without the union. This gives the union an opportunity to consider whether it is worth proceeding with the ballot if it believes that it is doomed to failure. If it goes ahead it cannot present another application for three years as we have already seen. It also provides an opportunity for the union and employer to reach a voluntary agreement which avoids the need for a ballot if the employer believes that the union will be successful in the ballot.

20.10 Assuming that this has not occurred the form which the ballot will take has to be decided by the CAC. There are three options: a workplace ballot, a postal ballot or a combination of the previous two. The normal method is for the CAC to decide between a workplace or postal ballot. The schedule specifically provides that the combination is only to be used when there are special circumstances. These can include factors arising from the location of the workers or the nature of their employment or other factors put to the CAC by the union or the employer (para 25(6)). There appears to have been a degree of fluidity about the establishment of special reasons before the CAC. For example relying upon its experience of ballots the CAC panel in *TGWU and NACAM UK Ltd* (TUR1/166/02) decided that a workplace ballot with postal voting for workers on long-term sick leave, maternity or annual leave would be the most appropriate. Such an approach has much to commend it pragmatically; indeed the Government's review has proposed that the Act should be amended to allow those away from work on the occasion of a workplace ballot to vote by post. The Government review has further indicated an intention to reserve a power to the Secretary of State to permit the CAC to allow electronic voting as one of the methods.

20.11 The primary considerations as to the form of ballot, whether it should be a workplace or postal ballot, are to be considered, taking into account (1) the likelihood of the ballot being affected by unfairness or malpractice of it were conducted at a workplace or workplaces; (2) costs and practicality; and (3) such other matters as the CAC considers appropriate (para 25(5)).

20.12 In *TGWU and King Asia Food Ltd* (TUR1/111/01) the CAC heard evidence that both parties had made allegations of intimidation and harassment and there did not appear to have been any improvement whatsoever in their relationship since the hearing to determine the bargaining unit. The CAC panel concluded in these circumstances that a postal ballot was less likely than a workplace or combination ballot to provoke further friction between the parties during the ballot. It should be noted that problems with the conduct of the first ballot in fact subsequently led to a new postal ballot being conducted and eventually a third ballot.

The workplace ballot must be a secret ballot and as we will see will be conducted by a qualified independent person (QIP). There are then safeguards against undue influence or intimidation. Thus in *BFAWU and Seabrook Potato Crisps Ltd* (TUR1/54) 3 September 2001 the CAC panel did not accept an employer's argument that a postal vote was inherently preferable as being more likely to prevent intimidation than a workplace ballot. In *Amicus and Black and Decker* (TUR1/215/02) 19 February 2003 the employer had undertaken a campaign against recognition with the apparent consequence that union membership had fallen after the application was accepted. The union had not had that opportunity to canvass and the CAC panel concluded that a postal ballot was appropriate set against that background of a continuous and persuasive communications process by the employer opposing recognition when the union had had no comparable opportunity to present its views. A postal ballot it considered would enable workers to have the opportunity to arrive at a decision away from an environment that may well be perceived by workers in the bargaining unit as hostile towards union recognition. It is interesting to note that the eventual ballot result was not in favour of recognition. **20.13**

The CAC's annual report for 2002/3 records that the panels had ordered 36 postal ballots, seven workplace ballots and 15 with a combination of both. The average participation was 75 per cent with workplace ballots recording a higher participation than postal ballots. **20.14**

The costs of ballot are split equally between the employer and the union, or if more than one union their half of the costs is divided between the unions (para 28(2)). The person appointed to conduct the ballot may send the demand to the parties for their share of the costs of the ballot. **20.15**

C. The Conduct of the Ballot

Once the method of conducting the ballot has been determined it is necessary for the CAC to appoint a qualified independent person (QIP) to conduct the ballot (para 25(2)). **20.16**

20.17 To be a QIP two conditions must be satisfied. First they must meet the requirements of the Recognition and Derecognition Ballots (Qualified Persons) Regulations 2000 SI 2000/1306 as amended by the Recognition and Derecognition Ballots (Qualified Persons) Order 2000 (Amendment) Order 2002 SI 2002/2268. These identify the qualifications necessary or specific organizations from which QIPs may be appointed. The individuals qualified are presently solicitors holding practising certificates or persons eligible for appointment as a company auditor under the Companies Act 1989, s 25. The organizations which are approved are: The Association of Electoral Administrators; Election.com Limited; Electoral Reform (Ballot Services) Limited; Involvement and Participation Association; Popularis Limited; and Twenty-First Century Press Limited.

20.18 Secondly there must be no reason for believing either that he will carry out any functions conferred on him in relation to the ballot otherwise than competently or that his independence in relation to the ballot might reasonably be called into question (para 25(7)).

20.19 Once appointed the QIP must conduct the ballot within 20 working days after they are appointed by the CAC, or such longer period as the CAC may decide (para 25(3)). The CAC has to inform the parties as soon as is reasonably practicable after the appointment of the QIP that a ballot is required, the name of the QIP, the period over which the ballot is to be conducted, the method by which the ballot is to be conducted and, if it is to be conducted at a workplace, the workplace or places involved (para 25(9)).

D. Access for the Ballot

20.20 As note above, the employer has previously in the application process had no obligation to allow the union access to the workplace. The position now changes. In particular the employer becomes subject to three important duties which he will fail to comply with at his peril.

20.21 The first duty is to co-operate generally, in connection with the ballot, with the union (or unions) and the person appointed to conduct the ballot; and the second and third duties are stated to be without prejudice the generality of this (para 26(2)).

20.22 The second duty is to give to the union (or unions) such access to the workers constituting the bargaining unit as is reasonable to enable the union (or unions) to inform the workers of the object of the ballot and to seek their support and their opinions on the issues involved (para 26(3)). This access takes place over the 20 working days.

The third duty is to do the following (so far as it is reasonable to expect the employer to do so)— **20.23**

(a) to give to the CAC, within the period of 10 working days starting with the day after that on which the employer is informed under paragraph 25(9), the names and home addresses of the workers constituting the bargaining unit;
(b) to give to the CAC, as soon as is reasonably practicable, the name and home address of any worker who joins the unit after the employer has complied with paragraph (a);
(c) to inform the CAC, as soon as is reasonably practicable, of any worker whose name has been given to the CAC under paragraph (a) or (b) but who ceases to be within the unit (para 26(4)).

The nuclear sanction behind these duties is that if the CAC is satisfied that the employer has failed to fulfil any of the three duties and the ballot has not been held it may order the employer: **20.24**

(1) to take such steps to remedy the failure as the CAC considers reasonable and specifies in the order, and
(2) to do so within such period as the CAC considers reasonable and specifies in the order.

If the employer then fails to comply with an order under para 27(1) and the ballot has not been held the CAC may proceed to issue a declaration that the union is recognized and the ballot is cancelled (para 27(2)). So far no declaration has been made but the threat of it is sufficient to bring a recalcitrant employer into line. **20.25**

The DTI has issued a Code of Practice on access during recognition and de-recognition ballots. This suggests that subject to exceptional circumstances the employer should allow the union to conduct one large scale meeting at the workplace, during working hours, of 30 minutes' duration, during each 10-working-day period of the access period. Further it suggests that where they would be appropriate having regard to all the circumstances, union 'surgeries' could be organized at the workplace during working hours at which each worker would have the opportunity, if they wish, to meet a union **20.26** representative for 15 minutes on an individual basis or in small groups of two or three. The circumstances would include whether there was a demand from the workforce for surgeries, whether the surgeries could be arranged off-site as effectively, whether the holding of surgeries would lead to an unacceptable increase in tension at the workplace. The Code of Practice also provides guidance about written communications with the workers.

20.27   In the 48 ballots which were conducted in the period to 31 December 2002 the CAC received formal complaints in only two cases. We have already seen something of the difficulties which were experienced in *TGWU and King Asia Food Ltd* (TUR1/111/01) 18 January 2001. Here it was necessary for the CAC to decide on disagreements between the parties as to the access arrangements. The union complained that the employer was placing restrictions upon access arrangements and refusing facilities for the union to hold on site surgeries. The CAC adjudicated between the parties and made an order under para 27(1), in doing so it cancelled a scheduled ballot, and met the costs of that ballot itself, rescheduling the ballot. The CAC's order provided for two 15-minute surgeries to be conducted by the union in a private room on site. Employees whose shifts did not fall within the period of the surgeries would be able to attend them with pay. The CAC additionally ordered that there could be two large scale meetings of 30 minutes during working time in the first 10 days of the access period and a further two meetings in the second period. There were additionally orders relating to the display of union material. The ballot was conducted again after the union's complaints about interference with the first postal ballot were upheld. Indeed eventually a third ballot was held. It is not entirely clear what the jurisdictional base for the exercise of the CAC's power in these circumstances was, the direct sanctions under the schedule relate to the position where the ballot has yet to be held. In *TGWU and Economic Skips Ltd* (TUR1/121/01) the CAC accepted the employer's complaints about the conduct of the ballot and purported to take into account the interests of good industrial relations and the CAC's general duty under Schedule A1, para 171 to promote fair and efficient practices and arrangements in the workplace to justify cancelling the ballot and ordering it to be re-run. The objective remains that the employer and the union should cooperate about the access arrangements, and for example in *BECTU v Sky Subscriber Services* (TUR1/222/02) the union and employer agreed to varied access arrangements and to an agreed letter of explanation to the workers within the bargaining unit as to the effect of a previous communication which appeared (according to the union) to threaten employee's jobs if they voted for recognition.

Even with such agreed arrangements difficulties can arise as to implementation. In *GMB v Video Duplicating Company Ltd* (TUR1/192/02) 5 March 2003 the CAC panel upheld a number of complaints by the union as to the employer's failure to discharge its duties in respect of what were agreed access arrangements. The CAC panel therefore made orders to require the employer to comply in respect of the agreed arrangements. The panel did, however, decline the union's application for it to review its previous decision that the ballot should take the form of a workplace ballot. The union had sought to argue that there had been pressure on the workers by reason of the employer's actions and that it would be appropriate to give the workers the opportunity to vote by post and increase participation. The CAC panel considered that there was nothing to suggest that there was greater participation with postal ballots and the presence of the QIP at the workplace ballot was protection against intimidation.

20.28

Whilst the union has access rights to workers at this stage it is of course only at the stage of the ballot commencing. In the review process it was recognized that the union should have a right of access at an earlier stage. The Government's proposal is to allow the union postal communication access through the medium of a third party, such as a QIP, from the date at which the union's application is accepted.

20.29

It is generally sensible for an employer not to be too heavy in its communication strategy since this may backfire against it. Many employers have developed sophisticated campaign messages during the access period, and this has been thought to have swung the vote. Several employers have used PR companies to assist them. A key question will be the timing of such messages; it is generally not advantageous to have too long a campaign.

20.30

21

THE CONSEQUENCES OF RECOGNITION

A. Declaration of Recognition or Non-recognition

The QIP will inform the CAC of the results of the ballot. If on considering **21.01** the ballot the union is supported by a majority of workers voting and at least 40 per cent of the workers constituting the bargaining unit then the CAC must issue a declaration that the union is recognized (para 29(3)). Thus if the bargaining unit compromises 100 workers even if 30 workers vote and all vote in favour recognition that will not be sufficient, since at least 40 of the workers in that example would have to be in favour for there to be the possibility of such a declaration. If that majority is not established then the declaration is that the union is not entitled to be recognized (para 29(4)) and the union may not reapply for three years.

As part of the review process the unions sought the removal of the 40 per **21.02** cent threshold which means in effect that a person not voting votes against recognition. They argue amongst other things that there is no analogous provision in Westminster elections and indeed if it were applied many MPs would not have been declared elected. The Government's review concluded that this did not, however, pose a substantial obstacle to recognition. There had been, to 31 December 2002, 48 ballots 17 of which had not led to recognition but only in one case had the union achieved a majority but failed to meet the 40 per cent requirement. There is thus no proposal for a change to this requirement.

21.03 It will be recalled that there is one situation where the application proceeds even though there is a recognition agreement in place for a non-independent union (para 44(4)). In order to deal with this situation in addition to the declaration of recognition for the union which has been successful in the ballot, the CAC has to resolve the position of the incumbent union. To do this the CAC issues a declaration that the bargaining arrangements of the incumbent are to cease to have effect (para 148).

B. Bargaining Procedures

21.04 Once recognized it is necessary for there to be a mechanism through which the union can bargain. This embraces fundamental issues such as who will meet to negotiate and how often will they meet. The ideal situation is that the parties themselves agree arrangements which are acceptable to both parties. If that is not possible then where there has been a statutory declaration of recognition the schedule provides a method for the determination of those bargaining procedures.

21.05 Following the declaration of recognition, a negotiation period commences. This period is one of 30 working days, although the parties may agree to extend it (para 30(4)). If no agreement is reached in this negotiation period then an application may be made, by either party, to the CAC for assistance (para 30(3)). If such an application is made the CAC must try to help the parties reach an agreement on a bargaining method during a period called the agreement period (paras 30, 31(2)). This is a period of 20 working days starting the day after that on which the CAC receives the application for assistance, although the CAC may, with the consent of the parties, extend that period (para 31(8)).

21.06 If during the agreement period the parties fail to agree a method then the CAC must specify a method by which they are to conduct collective bargaining. The parties have the ability jointly to apply to the CAC to stop the process at any point before it specifies the method to be used (para 31(7)).

In approaching the question of the method to be adopted there is a specified **21.07** default method which is contained in Trade Union Recognition (Method of Collective Bargaining) Order 2000. In deciding the method the CAC is required to take this into account but may depart from the method if it thinks it is appropriate to do so in the circumstances (para 168(2)). So by way of example in *UNIFI and Persia International Bank PLC* (TUR1/144/02) the CAC concluded that there were no circumstances to modify the specified method and determined that this was the method to be adopted.

Enforcement

There is an important distinction between a voluntarily agreed method and **21.08** one determined by the CAC. If the CAC determines the method then it has effect as if it were a legally binding contract between the parties (para 31(4)). If the parties agree a method then unless they have expressly agreed, in writing, that it is intended to be legally enforceable it will not have that effect (TULR(C)A, s 179). Further even if the CAC has specified the method, the parties are still free to agree in writing that the method specified by the CAC, in whole or in part, does not take effect as an enforceable contract (para 31(5)(a)). If, however, they agree in writing to vary or replace the method specified by the CAC then that agreement and consequently the modification will take effect as a legally enforceable contract.

As a legally enforceable contract either party could be the subject of an order **21.09** for specific performance to require them to perform the specified method, and the schedule provides that specific performance is to be the only remedy available (para 31(6)). It might then appear unattractive to a union to reach a voluntary agreement on the method to be adopted because that will lack the sanction of an order for specific performance. The provisions within the schedule for dealing with a breakdown in the method provide a solution to that problem and consequently there remains an attraction to agree a bargaining method which both parties can work with.

The method not carried out

Where there has been a declaration of recognition and the bargaining **21.10** method has been agreed between the parties but one or more of the parties is failing to carry out the method then the parties may apply to the CAC for assistance (para 32). In that event the process contained in para 31 applies which may lead to the CAC specifying a legally enforceable method. There is always then the threat of compulsion to bring the parties to the sense of agreeing a method and making it work. The question of compulsion under para 31 and para 32 arises once there has been a declaration of recognition. The underlying rationale of the schedule is to encourage the parties to reach a voluntary agreement without the need to proceed to a declaration by the CAC. It is important then to consider bargaining methods for those agreements.

C. Bargaining Methods for Voluntary Agreements

21.11   If a voluntary collective bargaining agreement, by which we mean a purely voluntary agreement, has been agreed between the parties then one would anticipate that they have themselves agreed a method of bargaining. If they were to fail to do so or if the method agreed breaks down then one would expect the agreement to be terminated and the union would initiate the statutory scheme by making a request for recognition. If the parties reached agreement after the statutory scheme had been initiated then there are specific provisions which apply contained within Part II of the Schedule. These forms of agreements are referred to as 'semi-voluntary' agreements.

D. Semi-voluntary Agreements

21.12   Para 52 provides the core definition of semi-voluntary agreements. This is an agreement for recognition which is made within a permitted period in consequence of a formal request for recognition. The agreement is one under which the union (or unions) is recognized as entitled to conduct collective bargaining on behalf of a group or group of workers employed by the employer. The permitted period begins with the request for recognition. It must follow that it must be a valid request for recognition. The permitted period may then end on occasion of the first of the following to occur:

- The union withdraws (or unions withdraw) the request for recognition.
- The union withdraws (or unions withdraw) any application under para 11 or 12 made in consequence of the request.

- The CAC gives notice of a decision under para 14(7) which precludes it from accepting such an application under para 11 or 12.
- The CAC gives notice under para 15(4)(*a*) or 20(4)(*a*) in relation to such an application under para 11 or 12 (*invalid application*).
- The parties give notice to the CAC under para 17(2) in relation to such an application under para 11 or 12 (*Notice from the parties for the CAC to cease consideration of the application*).
- The CAC issues a declaration under para 22(2) in consequence of such an application under para 11 or 12 (*A declaration of recognition*).
- The CAC is notified under para 24(2) in relation to such an application under para 11 or 12 (*notification that the parties do not wish to proceed with the ballot*).
- The last day of the notification period ends (the notification period being that defined by para 24(5) and arising from such an application under para 11 or 12) (*The notification period for holding a ballot*).
- The CAC is required under para 51(3) to cancel such an application under para 11 or 12 (*Cancelling an application where there is a competing application*).

Further the practical effect of para 52(4) and (5) is that the agreement will be a semi-voluntary agreement if reached in the period between the request for recognition and the end of the notification period.

It should be noted that there is a limitation on the scope of the recognition **21.13** in the case of a semi-voluntary agreement when considering the CAC's powers. The wider definition of collective bargaining under s 178 does not apply to the agreement reached, and the parties may have agreed on whatever issues they wish to agree to collective bargain upon (para 54). If however, as we will see below, it becomes necessary for the CAC to specify a bargaining method in respect of a semi-voluntary agreement it can only specify a method in relation to pay, hours and holiday (paras 63(2) and 53(4)).

Disputes

It is conceivable that there may be a dispute between the parties as to whether **21.14** a semi-voluntary agreement has been reached. In these circumstances, the CAC has the power to determine whether or not there is a semi-voluntary agreement (para 55). The CAC has the power to decide the question and issue a declaration as to whether it is an agreement for recognition. There is only one example of this power being exercised thus far, in *NUJ and Emap*

Healthcare and Emap Public Sector Management (TUR2/1/02). The union there had made a request for recognition on 17 December 2001. The parties entered into negotiation. It would appear that they agreed to extend the time period under para 10 to do so. Eventually a recognition agreement was signed on 21 August 2002. The CAC panel considered whether there had been a valid request and the agreement was reached within the permitted period; it concluded that it had been.

The regulation of semi-voluntary agreements

21.15 If an agreement is a semi-voluntary agreement then the employer is restricted from terminating the agreement for a period of three years commencing the day after the agreement was reached (para 56(1)). The union is not so restricted. After the three-year period expires the employer is free to terminate at will. These restrictions are, however, subject to the terms of the agreement itself (para 56(4)). The parties may therefore agree that it is terminable by either party in less than three years or specify a longer period. It will be seen that there may be changes of circumstance which could enable the employer to apply to the CAC within the three-year period.

A method of bargaining

21.16 If, despite having reached a semi-voluntary agreement for recognition, the parties are unable to agree a method of collective bargaining or the agreed method breaks down an application can be made to the CAC (paras 58 and 59). There are limitations upon the invocation of the CAC's power in these circumstances. First the recognition agreement has to be a semi-voluntary agreement. Secondly the small employer exemption applies at the date of the application to the CAC (para 60(3)). Had it always been a small employer there would never have been a valid request for recognition in the first place and so no semi-voluntary agreement could have come into being. If, however, the employer has reduced in size after an agreement has been reached, so that it falls within the small employer exemption, the agreement will continue to be a semi-voluntary agreement but the parties cannot seek the assistance of the CAC to determine the method of collective bargaining. The third limitation (para 60(4)) will have the same effect if the union has lost its certificate of independence as this is a requirement of a valid request. If a valid application is made to the CAC then and the CAC has determined that it is a valid application and accepted it (para 62(5)), it operates a procedure that mirrors that in the case of the specification of a bargaining method following a statutory declaration of recognition (para 62). The CAC decides if the application is admissible. If it does so there is an agreement period, again 10 working days subject to extension, during which the CAC must try to help the parties reach an agreement on a method by which they will conduct collective bargaining. If at the end of that period the parties have not reached agreement the CAC must specify the method by which the parties are to conduct collective bargaining.

22

CHANGES AFFECTING THE
BARGAINING UNIT

A. Introduction

The considerations in previous chapters have focused upon the recognition   **22.01**
by statutory declaration of a bargaining unit which has either been agreed
between the parties or has been determined by the CAC. Circumstances can
of course change since sites may close, employers may change, workers may
be re-organized with the consequence that the bargaining unit for which
collective bargaining has been recognized may no longer fit the changed
circumstances. Part III of the Schedule thus deals with changes affecting the
bargaining unit. On the point of changing employers it is appropriate to
consider the impact of the Transfer of Undertakings (Protection of
Employment) Regulations 1981 (TUPE).

The application of TUPE

It is beyond the scope of this work to consider the circumstances in which   **22.02**
the regulations generally will apply (see *Transfer of Undertakings*, ed Bowers,

Jeffreys, Napier & Younson, Sweet & Maxwell). If the bargaining unit formed part of an undertaking which was transferred then consequential upon the application of TUPE the worker's employer will change and all rights and obligations in respect of the transferor employer automatically transfer to the transferee (reg 5(1)). There are then two provisions under TUPE which have relevance to the issue under discussion:

6 Effect of relevant transfer on collective agreements
Where at the time of a relevant transfer there exists a collective agreement made by or on behalf of the transferor with a trade union recognized by the transferor in respect of any employee whose contract of employment is preserved by Regulation 5(1) above, then—
  (a) without prejudice to section 18 of the 1974 Act or Article 63 of the 1976 Order (collective agreements presumed to be unenforceable in specified circumstances) that agreement, in its application in relation to the employee, shall, after the transfer, have effect as if made by or on behalf of the transferee with that trade union, and accordingly anything done under or in connection with it, in its application as aforesaid, by or in relation to the transferor before the transfer, shall, after the transfer, be deemed to have been done by or in relation to the transferee; and
  (b) any order made in respect of that agreement, in its application in relation to the employee, shall, after the transfer, have effect as if the transferee were a party to the agreement.

9 Effect of relevant transfer of trade union recognition
  (1) This regulation applies where after a relevant transfer the undertaking or part of the undertaking transferred maintains an identity distinct from the remainder of the transferee's undertaking.
  (2) Where before such a transfer an independent trade union is recognized to any extent by the transferor in respect of employees of any description who in consequence of the transfer became employees of the transferee, then, after the transfer—
  (a) the union shall be deemed to have been recognized by the transferee to the same extent in respect of employees of that description so employed; and
  (b) any agreement for recognition may be varied or rescinded accordingly.

22.03 It would appear to follow that if there is a voluntary or semi-voluntary recognition agreement and there is a transfer and the undertaking transferred, or part of it, retains an identity distinct from the remainder of the new employer's business, the union is deemed to be recognized by the new employer. An example of the concept of the retaining of identity would be the transfer of a particular manufacturing site which the new employer continued to operate but by contrast a technical support team which transferred with the worker being integrated into the new employer's own technical support team would lose its identity. Assuming that reg 9 applied there remains a difficulty with reg 9(2)(b). Is the effect of that sub sub regulation that the recognition agreement may be rescinded pursuant to the regulation? It appears to have that effect. There is no difficulty with a purely voluntary agreement since it could, short of having been expressed to be legally binding, be terminated without effect. In the case of a semi-voluntary agreement under the schedule however the Act dictates that it cannot be terminated by the employer before its third anniversary. A possible construction is that reg 9 is permissive only in so far as the new employer is able to bring the recognition agreement validly to an end. So far there is no authority on the point.

A separate problem is the effect of a statutory declaration. Strictly that would **22.04** appear to involve no agreement at all. Regulation 9 could arguably embrace that situation as the effect of the declaration is that the union is recognized. There would be no agreement for recognition and so the issue under reg 9(2)(b) would not apply. The issue would then be one of deciding whether there had been a change in the bargaining unit. This issue is considered under Part III of the Schedule.

B. The Scope of Part III

Part III of the Schedule is concerned with changes in the bargaining unit. In **22.05** the previous chapter we considered the position of semi-voluntary recognition agreements. In common with voluntary agreements they fall outside the scope of this Part. This Part only applies where there has been a declaration of recognition (para 64(1)). That may not present a particular problem for a union in circumstances where there has been a change in circumstances as it is free to terminate both a voluntary and semi-voluntary agreement at will, unless it has agreed otherwise. The employer which finds itself facing changed circumstances during the currency of a semi-voluntary agreement does not have the same freedom of action. It could conceivably be contended that the circumstances have changed so significantly that the semi-voluntary agreement has been frustrated but that requires a major change in the structure of the unit.

22.06 For Part III to apply there must then be a statutory declaration of recognition. Further bargaining arrangements must be in place, either as a consequence of an agreement between the parties or as specified by the CAC. In the first application under this Part the employer's application was rejected because no bargaining arrangements were in place: *Bank Tejarat and Unfi* (TUR3/1/00).

22.07 Part III may be considered in two sets of circumstances: first where either party believes that the unit is longer appropriate; secondly where the employer believes that the unit has ceased to exist.

The bargaining unit is no longer appropriate

22.08 If either the union or the employer believes that the original bargaining unit is no longer an appropriate bargaining unit then it may apply to the CAC for a decision as to what the appropriate bargaining unit is (para 66(2)). In order for such an application to the CAC to be admissible the CAC must first decide that the original bargaining unit is no longer appropriate by reason of any of the following matters (para 67(1)):

(1) a change in the organization or structure of the business carried on by the employer;
(2) a change in the activities pursued by the employer in the course of the business carried on by him;
(3) a substantial change in the number of workers employed in the original unit (para 67(2)).

22.09 There is a 10-day working period, unless extended by the CAC on notice to the parties with reasons (para 68(6)) during which the CAC must decide if any of these circumstances has arisen. If the CAC decides that none of those situations has arisen then the application is not admissible and no further steps are taken (para 68(4)). If it does find that any of theses circumstances has occurred it must give notice of acceptance to the parties. This can be seen operating in practice in *GMB v Ardengate Ltd* (TUR3/3/03) 17 October 2003. The employer made an application under para 67(1). The CAC panel concluded that the workers within the original bargaining unit had transferred to a new corporate entity following a reorganization in which it was amalgamated with what had been a separate trading company with a consequent new management structure. The new entity additionally changed the nature of the business activities undertaken from that undertaken by the original business unit. The conclusion of the panel was that on the balance of probabilities the original unit was no longer appropriate by reason of the matters specified in para 67(2)(a) and (b). The CAC panel therefore accepted the employer's application.

The first period

Following notice of acceptance of the application, a first period of 10 work- **22.10** ing days, or such longer period as the parties may agree and notify to the CAC, commences (para 69(4)). In this period the parties will seek to agree a new bargaining unit. If such an agreement is reached the parties inform the CAC that they have agreed a bargaining unit, or units, which is different from the original (para 69(1)). The parties may have agreed a variation which cuts across existing recognition agreements with other unions. The CAC must then consider whether the new bargaining unit proposed by the parties includes any workers who fall within an 'outside bargaining unit'. An outside bargaining unit is defined to be a unit:

(1) which is not the original unit;
(2) for which a union is (or unions are) recognized as entitled to conduct collective bargaining on its behalf;
(3) the union (or at least one of the unions) is not a party referred to in para 64, these are the unions under the original statutory declaration.

If any of the workers do fall within the outside bargaining unit then the CAC **22.11** takes no further steps under this part of the schedule (para 69(2)). Thus if union A is recognized in respect of a bargaining unit where there is a change of circumstances and a new bargaining unit is agreed between the parties but a worker under that definition is actually the subject of a different collective bargaining agreement with union B then no further steps are taken under Part III. This is of course consistent with the original approach to an admissible application in respect of recognition for a bargaining unit.

If however an agreement is reached between the parties which does not cut **22.12** across an outside bargaining unit the CAC must issue a declaration that the union, or unions, are recognized to conduct collective bargaining in respect of the new unit, or units (para 69(3)). The method of collective bargaining for the old unit will apply to the new unit or units with any modifications which the CAC considers necessary to take account of the change, which the CAC will then specify in the declaration (para 69(3)). There may be workers who were within the original bargaining unit who are not within the scope of the definition of the new bargaining unit. The CAC will then make a declaration that the collective bargaining arrangements have ceased to apply in respect of those workers (para 73(2)).

The second period

22.13   If the parties have been unable to reach an agreement within the first period as to the new bargaining unit then the CAC must proceed to a determination during a second period. The second period is a period of 10 working days, unless extended by the CAC on notice to the parties with reasons (para 70(7)). In this period the CAC must decide whether the original bargaining unit continues to be the appropriate bargaining unit and if not it decides what other bargaining unit or units are appropriate (para 70(2)). In deciding whether the original unit continues to be appropriate it must take into account the following:

(1)   a change in the organization or structure of the business carried on by the employer;

(2)   a change in the activities pursued by the employer in the course of the business carried on by him;

(3)   a substantial change in the number of workers employed in the original unit (para 70(3)).

These are the same questions as were determined on the admissibility of the application but there remains the prospect that circumstances may have changed following the end of the first period.

22.14   The CAC in deciding what other bargaining unit or units are appropriate considers the need for the unit to be consistent with effective management and does so taking into account the same matters as were taken into account in the determination of the original bargaining unit (para 70(4) and (5)). There is an important question of construction here in that the wording which caused the Court of Appeal in the *Kwik-Fit* case [2002] ICR 1212, in obiter dicta to conclude that the primary focus was upon the union's proposed unit is not present here. It would seem that it is open to the CAC to decide the bargaining unit which is most consistent with effective management. This may mean that it concludes that two or more bargaining units are appropriate. In such a case it must ensure that the definitions are such that no worker falls within more than one of the new units (para 70(6)). If the conclusion of the CAC is that the original unit remains appropriate then no further steps are taken under the Part (para 71).

As a consequence of the CAC's definition of the new bargaining unit or units **22.15** there may be workers who cease to be within the scope of the new bargaining unit or units. How the position of these residual workers is resolved is considered further below after we consider the second basis for a change in the bargaining unit.

The employer's belief that the bargaining unit has ceased to exist

The change of circumstances may give rise to a position where the bargaining unit has ceased to exist. For example this may arise if the union was recognized in respect of a specific site or part of a business which has closed. If in these circumstances the employer believes that the bargaining unit has ceased to exist and wishes the bargaining arrangements to cease to have effect (para 74(1)) it must give the union (or each union) a notice under para 74(2), and give a copy of the notice to the CAC. **22.16**

Para 74(2) sets out certain requirements for a valid notice. It must: **22.17**

(1) identify the unit and the bargaining arrangements,
(2) state the date on which the notice is given,
(3) state that the unit has ceased to exist, and
(4) state that the bargaining arrangements are to cease to have effect on a date which is specified in the notice and which falls after the end of the period of 35 working days starting with the day after that on which the notice is given.

The CAC, within a period of 10 working days, unless extended by the **22.18** CAC on notice to the parties with reasons (para 76(5)) must determine whether the employer's notice complies with these requirements. The CAC decision in *Bank Tejarat and Unfi* (TUR3/1/00) is an example of the CAC deciding this question. Here it was determined that the notice was invalid because it did not specify the bargaining arrangements because there were none. In such circumstance the CAC decides that it does not comply and gives notice to this effect with the consequence that the notice is treated as if it had not been given (para 74(4)). If the notice is found to be valid the bargaining arrangements will cease to have effect on the date specified in the notice unless the union has made an application to the CAC under para

75. In *GMB v Ardengate Ltd* (TUR3/3/03) 17 October 2003 the employer had additionally served notice under para 74 on the union. The CAC had accepted that this was a valid notice and had given notice to the union that the bargaining arrangements would cease to have effect in 10 working days if the union did not make an application under para 75. The union made an application under para 75.

C. The Union's Application

22.19 Where a valid notice has been given and the CAC has decided that it was valid then the union (or unions) may within 10 working days after it is given notice of the CAC's decision, apply to the CAC for the determination of the following questions:

(1) whether the original unit has ceased to exist; and if not
(2) whether the original unit is no longer appropriate by reason of
   (a) a change in the organization or structure of the business carried on by the employer; or
   (b) a change in the activities pursued by the employer in the course of the business carried on by him; or
   (c) a substantial change in the number of workers employed in the original unit.

22.20 If the union makes such an application, the CAC must first decide if the application is admissible. There is a period of 10 working days, unless extended by the CAC on notice to the parties with reasons, to decide this (para 76(6)). If the application is valid, and apart from the time period the only requirements appear to be the use of a specified application form with supporting documents if any (para 92), the CAC gives notice to the parties. The CAC then has a period of 10 working days, unless extended by the CAC on notice to the parties with reasons (para 77(5)) to decide the questions, that is the decision period. The CAC will give the employer and the unions an opportunity to put their views on the questions but it must decide the questions before the end of the decision period (para 77(1)).

22.21 If the CAC's conclusion is that the bargaining unit has not ceased to exist and that the original bargaining unit is no longer appropriate by reason of the specified matters it notifies the parties of this decision and the employer's original notice is treated as if it had not been given (para 77(3)).

If however the CAC's decision is that the original bargaining unit has ceased **22.22** to exist it gives notice to the parties to this effect and the bargaining arrangements cease to have effect on the termination date (para 77(2)). That is the later of either the date in the employer's notice or the day after the last day of the decision period (para 77(6)). As we have seen in *GMB v Ardengate Ltd* (TUR/3/03) 17 October 2003 the union made an application under para 75. The CAC panel concluded that the original bargaining unit had not ceased to exist. It did, however, conclude that it was no longer appropriate by reason of the matters specified in para 75(3)(a) and (b); its structure organization and activities had changed. In parallel with this, as set out above, it had decided this on the employer's application under para 67. By both routes then the parties had to proceed to try to agree a new bargaining unit or have the CAC specify it.

The third possibility is that bargaining unit has not ceased to exist but the **22.23** original bargaining unit is no longer appropriate by reason of any of the matters specified in para 75(4). In these circumstances the CAC gives notice of its decision to the parties (para 77(4)). It is then necessary for a new bargaining unit to be agreed or defined.

Paragraphs 78–81 therefore provide a procedure which is the same as that **22.24** under paras 68–73 as considered above where the bargaining unit has ceased to be appropriate thus providing either for the parties to agree or for the CAC to specify a new bargaining unit.

D. The Consequence of the CAC's Deciding upon a New Bargaining Unit

In either of the above procedures it may have been necessary for the CAC to **22.25** determine a new bargaining unit. There are then consequential issues for that new unit, for example should the old union still actually be recognized for it. Paragraphs 82–89 then apply to resolve these questions. It should be noted that these paragraphs only apply where the CAC has determined the new bargaining unit, so that if the parties have agreed the bargaining unit then they must resolve these issues between themselves (para 82). It may be that the CAC has actually decided that more than one new unit is appropriate in which case the procedure in those paragraphs is followed for each new unit (para 82(3)).

22.26 The paragraphs again provide for the concept of the outside bargaining unit to be considered and whether the new units cut across such outside bargaining unit. The definition of an outside bargaining unit is slightly different, and indeed there are two forms. These are a statutorily recognized outside bargaining unit and a voluntary outside bargaining unit. The statutory outside bargaining unit is a bargaining unit which fulfils three conditions, namely:

(1) it is not the original unit;

(2) a union is (or unions are) recognized as entitled to conduct collective bargaining on its behalf by virtue of a declaration of the CAC; and

(3) the union (or at least one of the unions) is not a party referred to in para 64.

22.27 If the new bargaining unit determined by the CAC contains, in the opinion of the CAC, at least one worker falling within a statutory outside bargaining unit then the CAC must make declarations in respect of the workers in the new unit. Those declarations are that the old bargaining arrangements cease to apply as do the bargaining arrangements under the outside bargaining unit so far as they apply to the workers in the new unit (para 83(2)). This extends to the bargaining arrangements in the statutory outside bargaining unit in so far as they apply to the overlapped workers. This has the effect of de-recognizing all unions for the workers within the new bargaining unit together with the bargaining arrangements in respect of them. The CAC gives 65 working days' notice of this termination although the CAC may give a shorter period of notice if to maintain the relevant bargaining arrangements would be impracticable or contrary to the interests of good industrial relations. The notice starts the day after the date on which the declaration is issued (para 83(8)). This could be where the conflict of recognition is causing industrial unrest between the unions and or the employer.

22.28 There is then the concept of a voluntary outside bargaining unit. This is defined as follows:

(1) it is not the original unit;

(2) a union is (or unions are) recognized as entitled to conduct collective bargaining on its behalf;

(3) the union (or at least one of the unions) is not a party referred to in para 64, these are the unions under the original statutory declaration.

If in the opinion of the CAC at least one worker falls within a voluntary **22.29** outside bargaining unit, but none of the workers falls within a statutory outside bargaining unit (para 84(1)) a slightly different approach is taken in that the voluntary outside bargaining arrangements are not affected even in respect of the overlapping workers. This is consistent with the objective of achieving and supporting voluntary arrangements. This is achieved by the declarations which the CAC must make in this case. Those declarations are that the old bargaining arrangements, being only those relating to the original bargaining unit, cease to apply, to the workers in the new unit excluding those in the voluntary outside unit who continue to be subject to the bargaining arrangements for that unit. The CAC gives 65 working days' notice of this termination although the CAC may give shorter period of notice if to maintain the relevant bargaining arrangements would be impracticable or contrary to the interests of good industrial relations, the notice starts the day after the date on which the declaration is issued (para 84(5)).

In circumstances where the CAC has formed the opinion that no workers in **22.30** the new bargaining unit fall in either a statutory outside bargaining unit or a voluntary outside bargaining unit the CAC has to consider the support for the union in the new bargaining unit. The CAC has to decide whether the difference between the original unit and the new unit is such that the support of the union within the new unit needs to be assessed (para 85(1)). If the conclusion is that the union does not need to be assessed the CAC issues a declaration that the union is recognized for collective bargaining purposes for the workers in the new unit and the previous bargaining method takes effect with such modifications as the CAC considers are necessary to take account of the change of bargaining unit (para 85(2)).

If however the CAC decides that the union's support needs to be assessed the **22.31** CAC has to decide the following questions:

(1) whether members of the union (or unions) constitute at least 10 per cent of the workers constituting the new unit; and
(2) whether a majority of the workers constituting the new unit would be likely to favour recognition of the union (or unions) as entitled to conduct collective bargaining on behalf of the new unit (para 86(2)).

If the CAC decides one or both of these questions in the negative then it **22.32** issues a declaration that the bargaining arrangements in respect of the new unit are to cease (para 86(3)). If however the CAC decides both questions in the affirmative and it is satisfied that a majority of the workers in the new bargaining unit are members of the union then it issues a declaration that the union is recognized to conduct collective bargaining in respect of the new bargaining unit (para 87). This, it will be appreciated, mirrors the original procedure for the recognition of the union. In doing so it also provides that if the CAC decides that any of the qualifying conditions are present it must give the parties notice that it intends to hold a secret ballot. Those qualifying conditions are:

(1) the CAC is satisfied that a ballot should be held in the interests of good industrial relations;

(2) a significant number of the union members within the new unit inform the CAC that they do not want the union (or unions) to conduct collective bargaining on their behalf;

(3) membership evidence is produced which leads the CAC to conclude that there are doubts whether a significant number of the union members within the new unit want the union (or unions) to conduct collective bargaining on their behalf.

In respect of the evidence for condition (3), the following points must be noted:

(1) it is evidence about the circumstances in which union members became members; and

(2) it is evidence about the length of time for which union members have been members, in a case where the CAC is satisfied that such evidence should be taken into account.

22.33 If the CAC decides that both conditions at para 86(2) are satisfied but it is not satisfied that a majority of the workers in the new bargaining unit are members of the union the CAC again gives notice of its intention to hold a secret ballot (para 88(2)). As with the recognition process there is a notification period of 10 days during which the union may notify the CAC that it does not wish the ballot to be conducted (para 89). This has the consequence that the bargaining arrangements for the members of the new unit cease to have effect (para 89(2)). If there is no notification by the ballot the CAC conducts the ballot adopting the same procedure as that considered above for recognition under Part 1 of the schedule, para 89(5). The result of the ballot determines whether the CAC makes a declaration that the union is recognized in respect of the new unit (para 89(6)), or that the existing bargaining arrangements cease (para 89(7)).

E. Residual Workers

If the CAC has determined a new bargaining unit, either as a consequence of **22.34**
either party applying on the basis that the bargaining unit is no longer appropriate or the employer's application that the bargaining unit no longer exists,
workers may have fallen outside the scope of the new unit.

In principle these workers are the subject of declarations that the original
bargaining arrangements cease to apply.

There is then the particular situation of the workers who are within the defi- **22.35**
nition of the new bargaining unit but fall within the scope of statutory
outside bargaining unit. The CAC will have made declarations as we have
seen in respect of these workers (para 83). It must now consider each statutory outside bargaining unit where this situation has arisen (para 91(2)).
These are then referred to as a 'parent unit'.

The CAC then considers each such parent unit and identifies those workers **22.36**
within it who are not in the new bargaining unit it has defined. These are, in
other words, those workers who are not in the overlapping group. This group
is called the residual unit (para 91(3)). The CAC now issues a declaration
that the union which was recognized for the statutory outside bargaining
unit is now recognized for the residual unit (para 91(4)). Its original declaration falls away and any method of collective bargaining that applied still
applies but with any necessary modification rendered necessary by the
change which the CAC specifies in the declaration (para 91(7)). There is an
exception to the process so that no declaration shall be issued in relation to a
residual unit if the CAC has received an application in relation to the parent
unit under paragraph 66 (original unit no longer appropriate) or paragraph
75 (employer believes original unit has ceased to exist) (para 91 (5)).

Example

So, for example, suppose in the case of company A, union B was statutorily **22.37**
recognized in respect of a bargaining unit consisting of particular grades of
clerical staff. Company A undergoes a process of internal reorganization so
that the original grading of clerical staff has changed. Company A gives
notice to union B that the bargaining unit has ceased to exist. Union B's position is that the unit has not ceased to exist but considers that the re-organi-
zation renders the present unit no longer appropriate. Consequent upon the

union's application to the CAC (para 75) the CAC panel concludes that the unit has not ceased to exist but decides that it is no longer appropriate. The parties are unable to agree a new bargaining unit and the CAC decides the new appropriate bargaining unit (para 79). However the new appropriate bargaining unit determined by the CAC now includes workers at a site in respect of which union C has been statutorily recognized for all the workers. Some of the workers in the new appropriate bargaining unit for union B therefore fall within the statutory outside bargaining unit of union C. The CAC panel therefore must issue a declaration that the relevant bargaining arrangements for union B for its original unit cease to have effect as do those for union C in respect of the overlapping workers (para 83).

22.38 Considering then the application of para 91, these overlapping workers are residual workers in respect of whom the unit recognized for union C was their parent unit. The workers in the parent unit, excluding those overlapping workers, are termed the residual unit. The CAC now issues a declaration that union C is recognized as entitled to conduct collective bargaining on behalf of the residual unit (para 91(4)).

23

DE-RECOGNITION

A. Introduction

Part IV of the Schedule deals with de-recognition of a union. As recognition **23.01** may block an application by another union the procedures regulating de-recognition represent the only way in which a 'sitting' tenant union may be removed, unless there has been a change or cessation in the bargaining unit. A separate part, Part VI, deals with de-recognition where the sitting union is not independent. Here we are only concerned with recognized independent unions and the de-recognition procedures only apply where the recognition is consequent upon a declaration of the CAC that the union is recognized (para 92). Thus the procedures do not apply to voluntary or semi-voluntary agreements. As we will see there are three separate procedures but all of them may only be invoked after a period of three years has elapsed since the CAC's declaration (para 97). We will consider each of the grounds for de-recognition in turn.

B. Small Employer Exemption

23.02 Over the duration of the recognition period even though there may have been no changes in the circumstances of the bargaining unit meriting an application the employer may have reduced in size. If the employer has, with any associated employers, an average of fewer than 21 workers in any 13-week period ending after the third anniversary of the recognition declaration (para 99) and the employer wishes the bargaining arrangements to cease to have effect the employer must serve notice on the union and give a copy of the notice to the CAC (para 99(2)).

The notice must meet certain conditions:

- It must identify the bargaining arrangements.
- It must specify the period of 13 weeks in question.
- It must state the date on which the notice is given.
- It must be given within the period of five working days starting with the day after the last day of the specified period of 13 weeks.
- It must state that the employer, taken with any associated employer or employers, employed an average of fewer than 21 workers in the specified period of 13 weeks.
- It must state that the bargaining arrangements are to cease to have effect on a date which is specified in the notice and which falls after the end of the period of 35 working days starting with the day after that on which the notice is given.

The same averaging calculations, provisions about work outside Great Britain and the provisions in relation to seafarers apply to this application as they did to the original request for recognition (para 99(4) to (7)).

23.03 Having received the application the CAC has to decide whether it is valid. There is a period of 10 working days for the CAC to do this, or such longer period as the CAC may notify to the parties with reasons (para 100(5)). If the CAC decides that the notice is not valid then it notifies the parties of its decision and the notice is treated as of no effect (para 100(2)).

23.04 If the CAC decides that the notice is valid it gives the parties notice to that effect. The bargaining arrangements will cease to have effect on the date specified in the notice unless the union makes an application under para 101. The union has a period of 10 working days starting with the day on which the notice is given by the CAC to make an application to the CAC for the determination of one of two questions (para 101(b)), these being:

(1) whether the period of 13 weeks specified under para 99(3)(*b*) ends on or after the relevant date, that being the third anniversary of the declaration; and

(2) whether the statement made under para 99(3)(*e*) that the employer together with any associated employer or employers, employed an average of fewer than 21 workers is correct.

The union's application is subject to requirements of service to make it **23.05** admissible. There are some additional bars which make the application inadmissible. Paragraph 101 provides:

(4) An application is not admissible if—
  (*a*) a relevant application was made within the period of 3 years prior to the date of the application,
  (*b*) the relevant application and the application relate to the same bargaining unit, and
  (*c*) the CAC accepted the relevant application.
(5) A relevant application is an application made to the CAC—
  (*a*) by the union (or the unions) under this paragraph,
  (*b*) by the employer under paragraph 106, 107 (*these relate to an employers request to the CAC for a secret ballot to decide if bargaining arrangements should be ended where the employer has requested the termination of arrangements*) or 128, (*an employees request to the CAC for a secret ballot in circumstances where it is said the de-recognition is automatic*) or
  (*c*) by a worker (or workers) under paragraph 112 (*a workers application to end the arrangement*)

The basis upon which each of the applications which are relevant for this bar **23.06** to operate, these being under paras 106, 107, 112 and 128, is considered below. For present purposes it is necessary to know that if any of those applications are accepted by the CAC then in relation to the same bargaining unit the union is blocked from making an application for the determination of the questions relating to the size of the small employer for three years from the date of the application. Even more restrictively the union is blocked if the union had previously made an application for these questions to be decided in the previous three years. If for example the employer had served a notice that the number of workers was under 21 and the union made an application under para 101(1) and the CAC decides that the employer has 21 or more workers then in the next three years the employer is free to serve another notice, under para 99(2) and while the CAC must decide if it is a valid notice the union is unable to challenge the notice. Whilst one can see a desire to avoid extensive litigation between the parties it is difficult to understand why the union should be so blocked. The union is however not without options as it could immediately serve a new request for recognition and then an application and no doubt the issue of the size of the employer would be properly determined with the union being heard. This appears to be a very cumbersome way of getting to that position.

23.07   Once the CAC receives an application from the union it gives notice to the parties and has to decide whether the application is admissible (para 102). The period for deciding whether the application is admissible is 10 working days, or such longer period as the CAC may notify to the parties with reasons (para 102(6)). The CAC must consider evidence which the parties submit to it on this issue (para 102(3)). If the CAC decides that the application is admissible then it gives the parties the opportunity to put their views on the question of the 13-week period and the size of the employer and the CAC decides the question within 10 working days, or such longer period as the CAC may notify to the parties with reasons (para 103(4)). If the CAC decides the questions in the employer's favour the bargaining arrangements cease to have effect on the later of the dates specified in the employer's notice or the last day after the period during which the CAC makes the decision (para 103(2)).

23.08   If the CAC decides either of the questions in the union's favour the employer's notice is treated as being of no effect (para 103(3)).

C. Employer's Request to End Arrangements

23.09   Once the third anniversary of the declaration of recognition has passed any employer may make a request to the union for the bargaining arrangements to be ended (para 104). It will be noted that this is a mirror of the recognition process.

That request must:

(1) be in writing;
(2) be received by the union (or each of the unions);
(3) identify the bargaining arrangements; and
(4) state that it is made under this schedule (para 104(2)).

There is then a first period of 10 days starting with the day after the union **23.10** receives the request or the last union receives the request (para 104(6)). In that first period the union may consider the position. If it is agreed to end the bargaining arrangements in that period no further steps are taken under the schedule (para 104(1)).

If in that period, the union informs the employer that the union does not accept the request but is willing to negotiate, or the unions inform the employer that the unions do not accept the request but are willing to negotiate, then a second period of 20 working days, or such longer period as the parties agree, commences after the end of the first period. This is the period in which the parties may negotiate the position (para 105(7)). The parties can ask ACAS to assist in conducting the negotiations (para 105(5)).

If the union fails to respond to the original request or in the first period it **23.11** informs the employer that it does not accept the request (para 106(1)), the employer may apply to the CAC for a secret ballot to decide whether bargaining arrangements should be ended (para 106(2)).

In the same way as a union is blocked on a request for recognition the **23.12** employer may be blocked from asking for a de-recognition ballot if the union proposes that ACAS be requested to assist and the employer rejects the request or fails to respond within 10 working days (para 107(3)).

There are requirements about the service of the application and the CAC **23.13** must decide whether the employer's application is admissible (para 111). There are specific conditions which may render the application inadmissible.

The employer's application is subject to requirements of service to make it **23.14** admissible and there are some additional bars which make the application inadmissible. Para 108 provides:

> The employer's application, under para 106 or 107 is not admissible if
> (*a*) a relevant application was made within the period of 3 years prior to the date of the application,
> (*b*) the relevant application and the application relate to the same bargaining unit, and
> (*c*) the CAC accepted the relevant application, para 109
> A relevant application for these purposes is an application made to the CAC—
> (*a*) by the union (or the unions) under this paragraph 101 (*the union's application for determination of the questions under small employer procedure*),

(*b*) by the employer under paragraph 106, 107 (*these relate to an employer's request to the CAC for a secret ballot to decide if bargaining arrangements should be ended where the employer has requested the termination of arrange-ments*) or 128, (*an employee's request to the CAC for a secret ballot in circum-stances where it is said the de-recognition is automatic*) or

(*c*) by a worker (or workers) under paragraph 112 (*a worker's application to end the arrangement*)

23.15   The effect is then to create a three-year period free from applications. There is a further condition for a valid application in that it is not admissible unless the CAC decides that:

(1) at least 10 per cent of the workers constituting the bargaining unit favour an end of the bargaining arrangements, and
(2) a majority of the workers constituting the bargaining unit would be likely to favour an end of the bargaining arrangements.

23.16   Again this is the reverse of the recognition process. There is an acceptance period of 10 working days, or such longer period as the CAC may notify to the parties with reasons (para 111(6)), during which the CAC must decide if the application is admissible. All the same practicalities as to the submission of evidence on this question should apply. If the CAC decides that the appli-cation is not admissible then it gives notice to the parties and no further steps are taken. If it decides that the application is valid then it also give notice to the parties (para 111(5)). The CAC then proceeds with the de-recognition ballot procedure which is considered below.

D. The Workers' Application to End the Arrangement

23.17   If there is a sitting union with the benefit of statutory recognition this would block an application by a new union even if it has succeeded in recruiting a majority of workers. An application may be made by a worker or workers within the bargaining unit however. Again this can only be made later than the third anniversary of the declaration of recognition (para 112).

23.18   The application is made to the CAC and served on the employer (para 112(2) and (3)).

23.19   Again there is a bar on the application being admissible in certain circum-stances. The application will be inadmissible if:

(1) a relevant application was made within the period of three years prior to the date of the application under para 112;
(2) the relevant application and the application under para 112 relate to the same bargaining unit; and
(3) the CAC accepted the relevant application.

A relevant application being determined for these purposes as an application made:

(*a*) by the union (or the unions) under this para 101 (*the union's application for determination of the questions under small employer procedure*);
(*b*) by the employer under paras 106, 107 (*these relate to an employer's request to the CAC for a secret ballot to decide if bargaining arrangements should be ended where the employer has requested the termination of arrangements*) or 128, (*an employee's request to the CAC for a secret ballot in circumstances where it is said the de-recognition is automatic*); or
(*c*) by a worker (or workers) under para 112 (*a workers' application to end the arrangement*).

An application under para 112 is not admissible unless the CAC decides that— **23.20**

(1) at least 10 per cent of the workers constituting the bargaining unit favour an end of the bargaining arrangements; and
(2) a majority of the workers constituting the bargaining unit would be likely to favour an end of the bargaining arrangements.

There is an acceptance period of 10 working days, or such longer period as the CAC may notify to the parties with reasons (para 115(6)) during which the CAC must decide if the application is admissible. Here the CAC must consider evidence submitted by the worker, the union or the employer. In this context there is then a tripartite aspect to the process. **23.21**

If the application is not valid then the CAC gives notice to this effect (para 115(4)), then no further steps are taken under the schedule. **23.22**

If the application is admissible, then a negotiation period commences of 20 working days or such longer period as the CAC may decide with the consent of the worker, the employer and the union. The CAC has to help the parties to either agree to the end of the bargaining arrangements or to the withdrawal of the application by the worker (para 116(1)). If the application was **23.23** admissible and no agreement is reached and the application is withdrawn then the de-recognition ballot procedure is applied by the CAC (para 117(2)).

E. The De-recognition Ballot

23.24 The de-recognition ballot procedure may either have arisen because of the employer's request to end the bargaining arrangements or on a workers' application. The process of the ballot is set out at paras 117–120. This is the mirror of the recognition ballot process. The important differences are:

(1) There is no provision equivalent to the notification period in which the parties may tell the CAC that they do not want the ballot to be held.

(2) A majority of the workers voting and at least 40 per cent of workers constituting the bargaining unit must vote for the ending of the bargaining arrangements (para 121(3)).

(3) The sanction for the employer failing to comply with the duties imposed upon it in ballot and the failure then to comply with the CAC's order that it should do so also have to be varied. It becomes the dismissal of the employer's application for the bargaining arrangements to end (para 119(2)). A different sanction has to be provided in the case of it being a workers' application under para 112 which is being determined. Here the order which the CAC has made against the employer can be recorded in the county court and enforced as if a county court order (para 119(3)). Thus the sanction becomes proceedings for contempt of court.

F. De-recognition where the Original Recognition was Automatic

23.25 This part of the schedule deals with de-recognition where a declaration of statutory recognition was made:

- without a secret ballot in circumstances where the CAC was satisfied that a majority of members of the bargaining unit were members of the union (para 22(2)) and the parties have agreed the collective bargaining method under para 30 or 31 (para 122(1)); or

- without a secret ballot in circumstances where the CAC was satisfied that a majority of members of the bargaining unit were members of the union (para 22(2)) and the CAC specified the method by which they were to collectively bargain under para 31(3); or
- without a secret ballot in circumstances where the CAC was satisfied that a majority of members of the bargaining unit were members of the union following the determination of a new bargaining unit (para 87(2)).

The schedule then provides procedures for the employer to request the end **23.26** of the bargaining arrangements, after that is the third anniversary of the CAC's declaration of recognition (para 125).

The process for the request mirrors that for an employer's request considered **23.27** above. The process is set out at paras 127–133 and mirrors the form of an employer's request for de-recognition save that the basis for the request is that fewer than half the workers constituting the bargaining unit are members of the union. Again if it is not found to be inadmissible or withdrawn a secret ballot of the workers within the bargaining unit will be conducted.

G. De-recognition of the Non-Independent Union

There can have been no statutory declaration of recognition here as we are **23.28** concerned with unions which have no certificate of independence. The part therefore applies if:

- an employer and a union (or unions) have agreed that the union is (or unions are) recognized as entitled to conduct collective bargaining on behalf of a group or groups of workers; and
- the union does not have (or none of the unions has) a certificate under TULR(C)A, s 6 that it is independent.

Applications to end such recognition are made by a worker or workers in the **23.29** bargaining unit. Thus an independent union which is blocked from an application by the employer having recognized a non-independent union cannot make a direct assault on that non-independent union's recognition. It needs therefore a worker or workers to initiate an application under para 137 to have the bargaining arrangements ended. The process of the application takes the same form as a worker's request above save that the conditions of admissibility are different. The application is admissible if the CAC decides that:

(1) at least 10 per cent of the workers constituting the bargaining unit favour an end of the bargaining arrangements; and

(2) a majority of the workers constituting the bargaining unit would be likely to favour an end of the bargaining arrangements.

23.30 Further the application will not be admissible if:

(1) the union (or any of the unions) has made an application to the Certification Officer under s 6 for a certificate that it is independent; and

(2) the Certification Officer has not come to a decision on the application (or each of the applications) (para 140).

23.31 Once again there is an acceptance and a negotiation period. The period may be extended if during the negotiation periods it becomes clear that the union had made an application for a certificate of independence to the Certification Officer (para 143), and the Certification Officer has yet to come to a decision. If the decision is to grant the certificate then the CAC declares this and the effect is as if the application had not been made by the worker (para 144(2)). If the decision is that the union was not independent then the procedure continues.

23.32 One consequence of the wording is that the union's application to the Certification Officer only has this effect if it was made before their application to the CAC under para 137. The union cannot then make an application for a certificate of independence as a reaction to the workers' application.

23.33 If a valid application is made and it is not withdrawn or an agreement is not reached to end the bargaining arrangements then matters will progress to a re-recognition ballot (para 147).

H. Loss of Independence

23.34 Part VII deals with loss by a union of its certificate of independence. The Part applies in cases where there has been a statutory declaration of recognition (para 149(1)) or the following conditions are met:

(1) the parties have agreed that a union is (or unions are) recognized as entitled to conduct collective bargaining on behalf of a bargaining unit;

(2) the CAC has specified to the parties under para 63(2) the method by which they are to conduct collective bargaining; and

(3) the parties have not agreed in writing to replace the method or that para 63(3) shall not apply.

If the certificate of the union is withdrawn by the Certification Officer, or if **23.35** the recognized unions are more than one then the certificates are withdrawn for each of the unions (para 152(2)) and the effect is that the statutory recognition and bargaining arrangements are withdrawn. The unions are still recognized for collective bargaining purposes but on the basis that they are treated as if their recognition had been agreed (para 152(4)). As voluntary arrangements they may be terminated by the employer and they are not the subject of enforcement by specific performance.

The unions may challenge the withdrawal of their certification and may have **23.36** appealed the decision of the Certification Officer. In this case para 153 provides for bargaining arrangements to be reinstated if the appeal against the decision of the Certification Officer is successful.

I. Appeal

As noted above there is no right of appeal against the decision of the CAC. **23.37** The only route open to a party is to seek judicial review of the CAC's decision. This does raise the question of the CAC's own recognition that it has made an error. There is no express provision in the nature of an Employment Tribunal's power to review its decisions. This was recognized by the CAC in *TGWU and Gala Casinos Ltd (t/a Maxims Casino Club)* (TUR1/119/01). In this case the original application had referred to the employer as Maxims Casino Club. The application was admitted but before the bargaining unit was determined the employer said that it had been incorrectly named and asked for the application to be declared invalid. The CAC's decision was however that it had no power to withdraw or vary its decisions. The decision to accept the application remained a valid decision of the CAC unless and until it was overruled on judicial review. Where there has been procedural slip and material was not taken into account in its original decision a differently constituted CAC panel seems to have been able to find itself able to review its decision (*ISTC and Eminox Ltd* (TUR1/152/02)).

24

VICTIMIZATION

The schedule provides protection for workers from victimization consequent **24.01** upon the exercise of their rights under the schedule. That protection is provided by para 156(1) which provides that a worker has the right not to be subjected to any detriment by any act, or any deliberate failure to act, by his employer if the act or failure takes place on the grounds set out in para 156(2). The grounds specified in para 156(2) are:

- The worker acted with a view to obtaining or preventing recognition of a union (or unions) by the employer under this schedule.
- The worker indicated that he supported or did not support recognition of a union (or unions) by the employer under this schedule.
- The worker acted with a view to securing or preventing the ending under this schedule of bargaining arrangements.
- The worker indicated that he supported or did not support the ending under this schedule of bargaining arrangements.
- The worker influenced or sought to influence the way in which votes were to be cast by other workers in a ballot arranged under this schedule.
- The worker influenced or sought to influence other workers to vote or to abstain from voting in such a ballot.
- The worker voted in such a ballot.
- The worker proposed to do, failed to do, or proposed to decline to do, any of the things referred to above.

If however the employee has acted unreasonably this does not fall within **24.02** specified grounds (para 156(3)). The concepts within this definition of 'detriment', 'act', 'deliberate failure to act' and 'on the grounds' are familiar from other forms of worker and employee protection. It can be anticipated that they will be interpreted in a parallel way. The test of unreasonable action on the part of the worker is not however defined and this appears to be left to the Tribunal's discretion on the facts. The protection is based upon individual rights, so that there is no form of remedy for the union collectively.

24.03 This remedy is not intended to embrace a detriment which consists of dismissal within the meaning of the Employment Rights Act 1996. For this exclusion to apply the worker would have to be an employee. The protection for such a dismissal is provided by the Employment Rights Act 1996 and we will consider this below.

24.04 If a worker who has a complaint that they have suffered a detriment contrary to para 156(1) then the remedy lies by application to an Employment Tribunal (para 156(5)), the paragraph specifically provides that this is the only remedy available to the worker (para 156(6)).

24.05 The schedule adopts time limits for the bringing of that complaint which import the jurisdictional principles which will be familiar from unfair dismissal and discrimination claims. The worker must present their complaint to the Employment Tribunal before the end of a period of three months starting with the date of the act or failure to which the complaint relates, or if that act or failure is part of a series of similar acts or failures (or both), the last of them (para 157(1)(a)). The tribunal may, under para 157(1)(b), additionally consider an application within such further period as it considers reasonable if it is satisfied that it was not reasonably practicable for the complaint to be presented before the end of the period under para 157(1)(a). In interpreting those time provisions where an act extends over a period of time, the reference to the date of the act is a reference to the last day of that period (para 157(2)(a)). Further a failure to act is treated as being done when it is decided upon (para 158(2)(b)). In determining when that decision is made, in the absence of evidence establishing the contrary, the employer is taken to have decided on a failure to act when it does an act inconsistent with the doing of the failed act or, if it has not done such an inconsistent act, when the period expires when it might reasonably have been expected to do the failed act if it were to be done (para 157(3)).

24.06 If a complaint is presented the evidential burden is upon the employer to show the ground upon which it acted or failed to act (para 158). If the Tribunal concludes that the ground was one of the those specified in para 156(2) it makes a declaration to this effect and makes an award of compensation to the worker. That compensation, as in unfair dismissal, is that which the tribunal considers to be just and equitable in all the circumstances having regard to the infringement complained of and to any loss sustained by the worker which is attributable to the act or failure to act (para 159(3)). The worker is subject to the duty to mitigate the loss (para 159(4)). The compensation may be reduced to reflect the extent to which the worker caused or contributed to the act or failure complained of, if the tribunal considers it just and equitable to make such a reduction (para 159(5)).

There is no limitation on the total amount of that compensation save that if **24.07** the detriment complained of is the termination of the worker's contract, but that was not a contract of employment, limitations are indeed imposed (para 160). The limitation is that the total compensation must not exceed the total of the basic award, which a tribunal could award had the worker been working under a contract of employment under the Employment Rights Act 1996, s 119, and the maximum limit on a compensatory award for unfair dismissal imposed by s 124 (1) of that Act (para 160). Thus a worker, who is not an employee, can recover no more compensation for the detriment of the termination of their contract than they could were they to have been an employee who had been unfairly dismissed.

The worker who is an employee and suffers a detriment which amounts to a **24.08** dismissal for the purposes of the Employment Rights Act 1996 must look to that Act alone for redress. Paragraph 161 provides that for the purposes of the protection against unfair dismissal afforded by the Employment Rights Act 1996, Part X the dismissal will be regarded as unfair if the dismissal was made for a reason specified in para 161(2) or if there was more than one reason that was the main reason was such a reason (para 161(1)). The reasons specified under para 161(2) are the same, save that they define the individual as an employee rather than a worker, as those set out above under para 156(2). There is no qualifying period of employment for the right not to be unfairly dismissed for these reasons to be acquired (para 164).

Paragraph 162 makes specific provision for redundancy situations. Here the **24.09** employer may have sought to advance redundancy as the reason for an employee's dismissal. If however it is shown that the circumstances constituting the redundancy applied equally to one or more other employees in the same undertaking who held positions similar to that held by the dismissed employee, but who have not been dismissed, and the reason (or if there is more than one reason the principal reason) why the dismissed worker was selected for dismissal was one of the prohibited reasons then that too will be an automatically unfair dismissal (para 162).

24.10   In the case of an employee who is found to have been dismissed in circum-stances where it to be regarded as being unfair for these reasons their compensation will be determined with the normal principles applicable to any unfair dismissal.

INDEX

399